∞

Life of Christ

Fr. Giuseppe Ricciotti

Life of Christ

Popular Edition

Translated by
Alba I. Zizzamia, D. in L.

Abridged and edited by
Aloysius Croft

SOPHIA INSTITUTE PRESS
Manchester, New Hampshire

Nihil obstat: John A. Schulien, S.T.D., Censor librorum
Imprimatur: Moyes E. Kiley, Archiepiscopus Milwauchiensis
February 6, 1952

Sophia Institute Press
Box 5284, Manchester, NH 03108
1-800-888-9344

www.SophiaInstitute.com

Sophia Institute Press® is a registered trademark of Sophia Institute.

paperback ISBN 978-1-64413-756-7

ebook ISBN 978-1-64413-757-4

Library of Congress Control Number: 2022937955

First printing

Contents

Critical Introduction

The Life of Christ

Translator's Note

The present translation has been edited and all quotations, including those from Hebrew, Greek, and other texts, have been checked by the Rev. Patrick W. Skehan, professor of Semitic languages, Catholic University of America, Washington, DC, and it has been read for accuracy of the rendering from the Italian by the Right Reverend Monsignor Francesco Lardone, director of ecclesiastical studies of the same university, to both of whom the translator is deeply grateful.

— Alba I. Zizzamia
Trinity College
Washington, DC
October 4, 1946

Acknowledgments

Many of the New Testament quotations in this book are taken from *The New Testament of Our Lord and Savior Jesus Christ: A Revision of the Challoner-Rheims Version*, by license of the Confraternity of Christian Doctrine, owner of the copyright.

The texts of Matthew 9:36; Mark 7:9–13; and Luke 2:46–50 are from *The New Testament*, by Rev. F. A. Spencer, O.P., by permission of the Macmillan Company, publishers.

∞

Life of Christ

∞

Introduction

Jesus is the greatest paradox in history. He appears in a region of minor importance in the Roman Empire, in a nation that its conquerors describe as "a contemptible collection of slaves" (Tacitus). Not once in His life does He emerge from among this people, not once does He evince any desire to know the world of the learned, the politicians, and the warriors who control the civil society of His day. In His own region, He spends at least nine-tenths of His life in a humble little village, proverbial for its worthlessness. There He is simply a carpenter. For thirty years no one knows who He is except for two or three people who are as silent as He.

Suddenly, when He is past thirty, He emerges into public life and begins a new activity. He has no human means of any kind at His disposal, no weapons, no money, no academic knowledge, no political support. He spends almost all His time among poor folk, fishermen and peasants; with particular solicitude He seeks out publicans, harlots, and others rejected by good society. Among these He works miracles in great number and variety. He joins to Himself a little group of fishermen who follow Him constantly as His particular disciples. His activity lasts less than three years.

He preaches a doctrine that is neither philosophical nor political, but religious and moral exclusively. It seems to be composed of everything that all the various philosophies have rejected, of all that the entire world has cast as far from it as it could. What is evil for the world is for Jesus a good; what the world deems good, for Jesus is an evil. Poverty, humility, submission, the silent sufferance of insult and injury, withdrawing oneself to give way to others — these are the greatest of evils in the world and the greatest goods to Jesus. Conversely, wealth, honors, dominion over others, and all the other many things that spell happiness for the world represent a total loss for Jesus, or at least a serious danger.

The world, in fact, sees only the visible and the tangible; Jesus declares that He sees the unseen. The world fixes its gaze on nothing but the earth, and it sees it from below. Jesus fixes His gaze on Heaven especially, and He contemplates the earth from Heaven. For Jesus, the earth takes its meaning only from Heaven. The present life has value only as preparation for a future life; it is a toilsome and impermanent dwelling, but it has value as a runway, from which to take off for the flight toward a permanent joy-filled home. The tenants of the impermanent dwelling who place their hopes in it alone, and refuse to leave it, comprise the kingdom of the world. Those who remain in it only through obedience, but aspire constantly to their permanent home, constitute the Kingdom of God.

Between the two kingdoms there is, and will be, relentless warfare, which will go on until one or the other is utterly defeated. The respective strengths of both kingdoms derive from love, but for different objects. The subjects of the kingdom of the world love only themselves or what is useful or pleasing to themselves. The subjects of the Kingdom of God love God, first of all, and then the whole hierarchy of beings down to those who are useless and who do evil, and for these they have a particular love, and they seek to do good to those who do evil or do not know how to do good. For them, to give is to acquire, and therefore they know no hatred, which is the peak of avarice. Of this Kingdom of God, the strength of which is the love of God and of men, Jesus is the founder.

The Kingdom of God is the kingdom foretold by the ancient prophets of Israel, who predicted that its founder would be the Messiah promised the chosen people. In preaching His antiworld doctrine Jesus is conscious of His identity as the Messiah, but He does not declare Himself in the beginning in order that the crowds, throbbing with politico-messianic hopes, may not interpret His doctrine as a political proclamation and acclaim Him as a national leader.

His personal mission is directed solely to the chosen people, the depositary of God's ancient promises; when those promises have been fulfilled, however, the effects of His mission will pour over all the peoples of the earth.

To this end, He institutes a permanent society, the Church.

But the majority of the chosen people do not accept His preaching, and those most hostile to Him are precisely the leaders of that people — the chief priests from the Temple and the Pharisees from the synagogues. These leaders are convinced of His miraculous power, and they would not take issue with Him on many points of His teaching. But they do not forgive His outspoken denunciation of the hypocrisy of the ruling classes and His unflinching condemnation of the empty formalism that is withering their religious life. After having unwillingly tolerated Him for a time, they arrest Him through treachery, condemn Him in the tribunal of their nation on religious charges, and have Him condemned a second time in the tribunal of the representative of Rome on political charges.

Jesus dies on the Cross.

After three days, those who have condemned Him are convinced that He has risen. His disciples, at first unconvinced, yield later to the evidence of their senses, for they see Him and touch Him with their hands a number of times, and speak with Him just as they did before His death.

∽

But the paradox of Jesus continues, unchanged, even after His death. Just as in His first life He was the antithesis of the world, so the institution that He founded continues in the most incredible manner to be a negation of the world.

He left no echo of Himself in the upper circles of the society of His time. In the whole Roman Empire the historians ignore Him, the learned are unaware of His teachings, the civil authorities have at the most noted His death in their records. The very leaders of His nation, satisfied at His disappearance from the scene, are more than ready to forget Him altogether. His institution seems to have been reduced to the agony of His own tortured body on the Cross. The world gloats over its agony, just as the chief priests stood gloating at the foot of His Cross.

And instead, this institution shuddering in agony suddenly rises up again to gather into its arms the entire world. There are three centuries of persecution and slaughter, three centuries that seem to prolong the agony of the Cross and reecho the three days in the sepulcher, but after the third century civil society becomes officially the disciple of Jesus.

The kingdom of the world is not overthrown, however, and the war goes on in different forms but with the same obdurate tenacity as before. Jesus, or His institution, becomes increasingly the "sign of contradiction" in the history of human civilization. His paradoxical and burdensome doctrine has been accepted by infinite numbers of men and practiced with intense love, even to the supreme sacrifice. Infinite numbers of others reject it and hate it rabidly. It might be said that the efforts of the most civilized portion of humanity have all been concentrated on this "sign of contradiction," either to exalt it or to trample it underfoot.

Certain it is that Jesus is today more alive than ever among men. All have need of Him, either to love Him or to curse Him, but they cannot do without Him. Many men in the past have been loved intensely — Socrates by his disciples, Julius Caesar by his legionaries, Napoleon by his soldiers. But today these men belong irrevocably to the past; not a heart beats at their memory. And when their ideals are opposed (for they are still being advocated), no one thinks of cursing Socrates or Julius Caesar or Napoleon, because their personalities no longer have any influence; they are bygones. But not Jesus; Jesus is still loved, and He is still cursed; men still renounce their possessions and even their lives both for love of Him and out of hatred for Him.

No living being is as alive as Jesus.

∞

He is the "sign of contradiction" in His historical reality also. That the celebrated historians of the official world of His time are unaware of His existence is not surprising, for these historians, dazzled by the splendor of the Rome of Augustus, lacked the sharpness of vision — and even the documents — to discover an obscure barbarian from among a "contemptible collection of slaves." But this does not mean that the figure of Jesus is historically less documented and less certain than that of Augustus and others of his famous contemporaries. Certainly we today desire to know much more about Him than we do; but if the things we know are too few for our desire, in compensation the writers who have recorded them enjoy a prime authority. Of these four writers, two are eyewitnesses who were at Jesus' side night and day for almost all His public life. The other two knew and abundantly questioned similar witnesses. All four narratives are told with precious simplicity and lack of ornament and with a dispassionateness before the facts that rises far above their sympathies. No doubt the four Gospels are propaganda; their authors wrote them to acquaint the world with Jesus and spread belief in Him. But for that very reason they had to take the way of objectivity and truth, because thousands of witnesses were ready to contradict them had these narratives been prejudiced or fabricated.

But here, as in everything else, the "sign of contradiction" is contradicted again. It is said that the Jesus presented by the four historians cannot be true because He is supernatural. The portrait painted by the four evangelists must be reduced to natural, rational proportions, and the miraculous trimmed away. This is the program of rationalist criticism. Many are the theories of the critics, and contradictory of one another; on one point only do they agree perfectly, and that is that the Gospel narratives are not historical and therefore that the Jesus of tradition is false.

Now all this is no more than one episode in the centuries-long conflict between Jesus and the world. We said that the conflict will not end until one has completely defeated the other; that is why the world defeats Jesus in the historical field by erasing as much as it can of His figure and personality.

But what has happened in the past? What will happen in the future?

∞

The Gospels tell us that the Jesus whom the Pharisees sealed in His tomb rose again. History tells us that the Jesus afterward killed a thousand times has always come back more alive than ever before. And the conflict around the "sign of contradiction" will continue, as long as there are men upon the earth.

∞

Critical Introduction

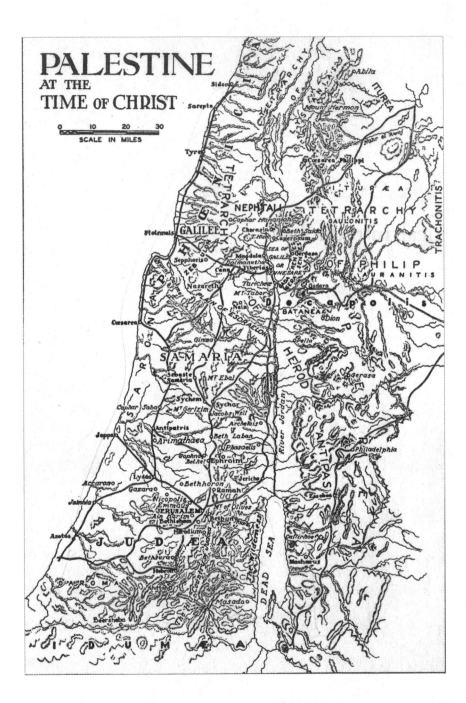

Chapter 1

∞

The Place and the Time

The region where Jesus lived is that strip of Mediterranean coast that joins southern Syria to Egypt. Throughout the centuries this region has had various names and different boundaries. Today it is called *Palestine*.

Palestine is flanked by the Mediterranean on the west and the Syro-Arabian desert on the east. On the north and south her boundaries are not so well-defined, although in the north a clear enough division is marked by the Lebanon mountain range. This descends parallel to the Mediterranean and is bordered on the interior by the Anti-Lebanon range, from which Mount Hermon rises like a vanguard. The pass between Hermon and Lebanon may be considered the northern boundary of Palestine. The southern boundary is represented in general by Idumaea and the desert regions that extend directly below Beersheba and the Dead Sea. These are the two boundaries, northern and southern, frequently referred to in the Old Testament phrase, "from Dan to Beersheba," to denote that part of Palestine inhabited by the Hebrews. Its length, from the southern slopes of Mount Lebanon to Beersheba, measures 153 miles; its width, from the Mediterranean to the River Jordan, varies from a minimum of 23 miles in the north to a maximum of about 93 miles below the Red Sea. The total area of Palestine is 9,700 square miles, that is, slightly larger than that of the state of Vermont (9,616 square miles).

The entire region is divided into two parts by the deep depression through which flows the River Jordan. It stretches south from Mount Taurus between Lebanon and the Anti-Lebanon range, keeps sinking deeper as it advances through Palestine, reaches its lowest level in the Dead Sea, and, continuing east of the peninsula of Sinai, finally joins the Red Sea.

Through the length of this unusual trench runs the only important river in Palestine, the Jordan, which rises on Mount Hermon and flows on into the Dead Sea, where it ends.

The Jordan a little above the Dead Sea

About 25 miles from the confluence of its various sources the Jordan forms Lake Huleh, which is from 9 to 15 feet deep and almost 4 miles wide. From Huleh the river makes a swift descent of about 10 miles to form Lake Tiberias, called Gennesaret in ancient times. The latter, almost oval in shape, is about 7.5 miles across at its widest point and 13 miles long. From Lake Tiberias the Jordan proceeds about 68 miles to the Dead Sea. At first the average width of the river is about 80 feet, its depth from 6 to 9 feet, and its banks are covered with wild and luxuriant vegetation. But about 6 miles from the Dead Sea, the vegetation grows scantier, the water becomes brackish, and the stream wider and more shallow.

The Mediterranean coast, from the southern slopes of Lebanon to the promontory of Mount Carmel, has a width of from 1.5 to approximately 4 miles, and east of it rise the highlands of the interior. The lower part of the coast, from Carmel to below Gaza, is uniform and straight, its southern expanse attaining a width of 12.5 miles. Covered with the sands of the Nile, this shore was for the ancients a coast without ports since it has no harbors except the very inferior one at Jaffa. Only Herod the Great's tenacity and wealth enabled him to build the excellent harbor at Caesarea that today is a heap of ruins. The shore from Carmel to Jaffa was the plain of Sharon, celebrated in the Bible for its loveliness. The stretch of coast south of Jaffa was, properly speaking, Philistia, the country of the *Pelishtim* (Philistines). This name was later extended to all of *Palestine*.

The region west of the Jordan is divided into two parts by the valley of Esdraelon, which, from north of Carmel, proceeds diagonally toward the southeast. The territory to the north of this valley is Galilee, which is mountainous in the north and a little less so to the south. Below the valley of Esdraelon extend first Samaria and then Judea; both are hilly, falling off on the eastern side through stretches of desert land.

In Jesus' time, while Judea with its capital at Jerusalem formed the true citadel of Judaism, Samaria, to the north, presented an acute contrast. The Samaritans were descendants of foreign settlers imported into that region by

Hill of Samaria

Typical bit of the Holy Land: bare hills and flat-topped houses

the Assyrians toward the end of the eighth century BC, and they gradually fused with the Israelite peasants left there. Their religion was at first substantially idolatrous; it was later purified of gross idolatries, and by the end of the fourth century BC the Samaritans had their own temple on Mount Garizim. For them, naturally, the center of Yahweh's legitimate worship was Garizim, as opposed to the Jewish temple in Jerusalem, and they considered that they alone held the deposit of patriarchal religious faith. This caused constant and rabid hostilities between Jews and Samaritans, nourished by the fact that travel between Galilee to the north and Judea to the south had to cross Samaria.

The Transjordan region, generally hilly and in ancient times well irrigated and rich in forest lands, was never occupied completely by the Hebrews. Before the advent of the Greek colonies, there had been numerous Aramaic settlements there, especially in the northern part; then Hellenic colonies firmly established the Greek element, represented for the most part, at the time of Jesus, by what was called the Decapolis — the *ten cities*.

This was a group of Hellenistic or Hellenized cities, perhaps united in a kind of federation. Their number varied in different periods but was approximately ten, hence the conventional name of the group.

Palestine is a subtropical region and has, practically speaking, only two seasons: the winter, or rainy, season from November to April; and the dry, or

Jerusalem from the northeast

The Tyropean valley, between Mount Moriah and Mount Zion

summer, season from May to October. Rains in summer are extremely rare, while the average fall of winter rains almost everywhere exceeds twenty-three inches. Although the temperature varies somewhat with the region, snowfalls are rare and light and occur for the most part in January; frost at night is also rare.

Chronology of the Life of Christ

The sequence of the events in Christ's life is completely buried in a mist of uncertainties, not only as to the events themselves but as to their relation to contemporary history as well. We cannot be absolutely sure of the day or year of His birth or when He began His public life or how long it lasted or the day or year of His death.

Some medieval mystic would perhaps have discovered a mysterious providence in this, especially since the only time the official Christian world tried to penetrate that mist of uncertainty it made a serious error, as if in punishment for its boldness. When the Scythian monk of the sixth century, Dionysius the Little, set the date of Jesus' birth in the year of 754 of Rome, he fixed it at least four years too late, and the modern Christian world, which still follows his reckoning, perpetuates his error.

Actually, our uncertainties are due not to mystical causes but to lowly historical reasons that are simple enough. As we shall see in Chapter VII, all we know of Christ's life was handed down to us in the catechesis of the

Bethlehem of Juda, birthplace of Jesus

early Church from which the four canonical Gospels derive. But it was never the intention of any of these to present a "life" of Jesus in the modern sense of the term. It is possible that the evangelists had the same concept of biography as we have but paid no attention to the chronological outline, simply because their intention was not to write biography. As a matter of fact, the two evangelists whose narratives came closest to being biographies are Luke and John, the two who are also most generous with chronological information, the former in regard to contemporary history, the latter for the sequence of events in themselves. These two evangelists furnish the only available dates for a modern biography of Jesus.

The Birth of Jesus

One certain factor in determining the date of Jesus' birth is that He was born before the death of Herod the Great — that is, before the end of March or the beginning of April in 750 AUC[1] or 4 BC. But how long before the death of Herod was Jesus born? Various considerations help us to narrow the field of possibilities.

One is Herod's order to put to death all the children born in Bethlehem "from two years old and under" (Matt. 2:16), for this supposes that the infant Jesus was within those limits. Hence, we may argue that Jesus was born much less than two years earlier, because it is reasonable to assume that Herod would allow a generous margin in order to be certain of his victim. This two-year period, however, does not date back from the death of Herod but from the visit of the Magi who furnished him with the basis for his reckoning. On the other hand, when the Magi came, they found Herod still in Jerusalem, whereas we know that the old king, seriously ill, moved to the warmer climate of Jericho before he died. We may surmise that this transfer of residence took place when the first cold of the winter of 749 AUC set in, or four months before Herod's death.

This gives us the following sequence: the birth of Jesus; the arrival of the Magi in Jerusalem; the decree to slaughter all babies two years old and under; Herod's departure for Jericho; the death of Herod. To determine the time relation between the two extremes — the birth of Jesus and Herod's death — we must reckon with the two years in Herod's decree, remembering that they represent much more time than was necessary for his purpose, and then we must consider the four months we have just indicated. There is, besides, the

---

[1] AUC (*Ab Urbe Condita*) — From the Founding of the City of Rome. The Romans dated all events from the founding of their city.

interval between the arrival of the Magi and Herod's departure for Jericho. About this we know nothing. And third, there is also the interval between the birth of Jesus and the visit of the Magi, and here we know only that it could not have been less than the forty days of the purification, for Joseph would certainly not have presented the child in Jerusalem and exposed Him to such serious peril if His death had already been decreed there. On the other hand, this interval may be considerably longer than forty days.

In conclusion, reckoning backward from the date of Herod's death, we may conclude that the margin of time allowed in the two years decreed by Herod balances the four months and the two intervals we have just mentioned with a little extra period of time left over. Hence, Jesus was born a little less than two years before the death of Herod — that is, at the beginning of the year 748 of Rome or 6 BC.

Many scholars have gone hunting for other evidence in astronomy — that is, they have tried to identify the Magi's star with some extraordinary meteor. These attempts have nothing to recommend them but their good will, for they have mistaken the road. It is enough to consider the details of the Gospel account to perceive that the appearance of the star is recorded as utterly miraculous and therefore cannot be made to obey the laws of natural meteors.

The numerous attempts to determine even the season in which Jesus was born have likewise been futile. The fact that on the night of Jesus' birth there were shepherds outside Bethlehem watching their flocks in the open does not prove that it was a warm season, perhaps spring, as some have reasoned. We know that in southern Palestine especially, where Bethlehem is located, flocks were left out even through the winter nights without any discomfort.

Length of Jesus' Public Life

How much time elapsed between Christ's baptism, which for all practical purposes may be considered the beginning of His public activity, and His death? In other words, how long did Jesus go about preaching?

In tracking down this question, John is our best and only guide. Now, his Gospel mentions three separate Paschs: the first at the beginning of Jesus' public life right after the marriage in Cana; the second at about the middle of His public life; the third on the occasion of His death. Besides these, John mentions other Hebrew feasts: after the second Pasch he speaks of the feast of Tabernacles and the Dedication of the Temple, which must have fallen between the second and third Paschs. Hence, if we confine ourselves to this data, we must conclude that the public life of Jesus lasted the two years included between the first and third Paschs plus the few months that elapsed between His baptism and the first Pasch mentioned.

We can get no help in this regard from the Synoptics, yet an occasional vague reference in them does indirectly confirm the sequence indicated by John. In the parable of the sterile fig tree, which Jesus relates toward the end of His public life, He says: "Behold for three years I come seeking fruit … and I find none" (Luke 13:7). This may be an allusion to the length of time Jesus has been preaching during which He has, metaphorically speaking, looked in vain for fruit on a sterile tree. If we suppose that the number three here is to be taken literally, then we have a confirmation that this is the third year of Jesus' public life as we learn from John.

It is also indirectly confirmed in Mark 6:39, which says that on the occasion of the multiplication of the loaves and fishes, the multitude sat down upon the "green grass." Hence it was spring in Palestine, perhaps March, just before the Pasch; and that is just what John says explicitly, mentioning in connection with the same episode the second Pasch in the course of Jesus' public life.

The Date of the Death of Jesus

All four Gospels explicitly set the death of Jesus on a Friday during the Pasch. From John we learn that this is the third Pasch in Jesus' public life.

Now, the month Nisan, in which the Pasch was celebrated, began with the new moon, like the other months in the Hebrew calendar; and the Pasch, celebrated on the fourteenth day of Nisan, coincided with the full moon. Here the field is wide open for astronomical research to determine what year of the Christian era best fulfills the conditions.

The first condition is historical. If Jesus began His public life approximately between October 1, AD 27, and August 18, AD 29, and continued it for two years and some months, then His death could not have occurred before the year 29. On the other hand, Jesus could not have been put to death later than His thirty-seventh year. He began His public life when He was about, perhaps a little over, thirty, and it lasted about two years and a half. Hence, even if we take the outside figure in reckoning with that "about thirty," Jesus could not have been more than thirty-seven at the end of His public life ($34 + 2\frac{1}{2} = 36\frac{1}{2}$ or roundly 37). In any case, the object of our particular scrutiny will be the years between AD 28 to 34, which must include that in which Jesus died.

The second condition is based on an apparent disagreement, which we will consider when we discuss the Passion, between the Synoptics and John with regard to the *date* of Jesus' death; according to the former it would seem to have occurred on the fifteenth Nisan; according to John on the fourteenth. Hence, any astronomical calculations must consider both these dates.

The last condition is that the day in question must be a Friday.

If we accept the reckonings of the most authoritative modern astronomers, we arrive at the following:

AD 28: The fourteenth Nisan fell on Tuesday, March 30, or Wednesday, April 28, or Thursday, April 29; the fifteenth Nisan fell on Wednesday, March 31, or Thursday, April 29, or Friday, April 30.

AD 30: The fourteenth Nisan fell on Friday, April 7, or on Saturday, May 6; the fifteenth Nisan fell on Saturday, April 8, or on Sunday, May 7.

AD 33: The fourteenth Nisan fell on Friday, April 3, or on Sunday, May 3; the fifteenth Nisan fell on Saturday, April 4, or on Monday, May 4.

AD 34: The fourteenth Nisan fell on Wednesday, March 24, or on Thursday, April 22; the fifteenth Nisan fell on Thursday, March 25, or on Friday, April 23.

The year 28, though it contains a possible Friday, April 30 (fifteenth Nisan), is to be discarded because it is earlier than the historical conditions we have noted seem to warrant.

The only year that satisfies all the astronomical requirements and in addition dovetails with the other chronological data we have gathered up to this point is the year AD 30. If Jesus was born about two years before the death of Herod, then He was truly "about thirty" at the beginning of His public life, being, according to this count, thirty-two or thirty-three and, after two and a half years of public preaching, thirty-four and a half or thirty-five and a half years old. Finally, His death occurred on a Friday.

This is clear enough, but in all honesty we must admit it is not certain. And the lack of certainty is due to the astronomical calculations involved rather than to the historical data and arguments. The calculations quoted above are probably most accurate since they were arrived at by celebrated scientists of our day; the difficulty lies in the fact that we cannot say the same for the calculations on which the Jews at the time of Jesus based their calendar.

In reality it seems certain that in those days the Jews did not yet possess a fixed calendar but established their principal dates according to their own direct observation of the various astronomical phenomena; these dates were chiefly the first day of the year and of the month. In addition, a day was intercalated, on the same basis, after certain months and a month after every third year in order to make the lunar year correspond more or less with the solar year.

The principal phenomenon considered was naturally the new moon. The whole matter was simplest and easiest when the new moon could be seen from Jerusalem itself. Then the priests assigned to that office had signal fires lit on the nearby Mount of Olives to announce to the surrounding countryside and thence to the outlying districts that the new month would begin on the following day. But often the new moon was not visible in Jerusalem because of climatic or astronomical conditions, and then they had to wait for messengers from various districts to arrive and announce to the authorities in the capital that they had seen the new moon. The carrying of this message was considered urgent enough to dispense even from the Sabbath rest so that it might be sped immediately to Jerusalem. If no messenger arrived, the day spent waiting was reckoned with the previous month as an additional day and the new month began the next day.

It was still more difficult to fix the first day of the year, which, according to the religious calendar of the Jews, had to coincide with the first day of the month Nisan. In fact, it was necessary to add a thirteenth month every third year as we have noted, and this was done on the basis of the crops, which had to reach a certain stage of development. The first barley of the new harvest had to be ripe by the Pasch (fourteenth Nisan) because on one day during the feast (sixteenth Nisan) a sheaf of it was offered in the Temple as the sacrifice of the firstfruits.

With so much leeway in the data and so much uncertainty in any possible calculations, it is no wonder at all that scholars, even in these last decades, fix the dates for the life of Jesus with the greatest diversity.

Finally, it will be noted that these findings have been obtained by examining only the data contained in the four Gospels and comparing it with secular documents but that no attention has been paid to Church tradition in this regard. In fact, there is no such "tradition" in the true sense; there are only the individual opinions of various early writers, and these are often impossible and sometimes contradictory; not rarely they are completely unfounded and only infrequently do they seem to echo earlier and reliable information.

In them the birth of Jesus is very often assigned to some year later than 4 BC (the death of Herod), which is plainly absurd. The length of Jesus' life varies. His public life is usually extended from one to three years (sometimes there are variations in the same writer), but it is also suggested that it was even longer. The date of His death is scattered all the way from AD 21 to 58.

We may give some attention, however, to an opinion that places the death of Jesus in the consulship of L. Rubellius Geminus and F. Fufius Geminus, the year 782 of Rome and AD 29. This report, which we find already in Tertullian and perhaps even in Hippolytus, is later echoed by many other documents, which put the death of Jesus under the "two Gemini." But this report is not without discrepancies either, and above all we find so many other ancient writers who either ignore it or explicitly contradict it that for all practical purposes it has almost no value.

The following outline is offered by way of summary. The historical basis for it is contained in the preceding paragraphs, which, however, clearly point out that we cannot accept the whole outline with complete certainty (except negatively, insofar as the dates excluded are concerned); it has the merit of probability only and this, too, varies with each of the dates.

Chronological Table of the Life of Jesus

- *Birth of Jesus:* Toward the end of the year 748 AUC, 6 BC. Beginning of the ministry of John the Baptist: toward the beginning of AD 28 (or October–December of 27).
- *Baptism of Jesus and Beginning of Public Life:* Shortly after preceding date; Jesus is thirty-two or thirty-three years old.
- *First Pasch in the Public Life of Jesus:* March–April in the year 28; Jesus is thirty-two and a half or thirty-three and a half years old.
- *Second Pasch:* March–April in 29; Jesus is thirty-three and a half or thirty-four and a half years old.
- *Third Pasch and Death of Jesus:* April 7, in 30, the fourteenth day of Nisan; age of Jesus, thirty-four and a half or thirty-five and a half years.

Chapter 2

∞

Herod the Great and His Successors

Jesus, who was killed on the charge that He had proclaimed Himself king of the Jews, was born under a king of the Jews who was by birth neither a king nor a Jew.

Herod the Great, whose subject Jesus was, was not of Jewish blood. His mother, Kypros, was an Arab, his father, Antipater, an Idumaean, and neither of them was of royal lineage. The little that did seem Jewish about him was a veneer that had been applied to his ancestors by violence.

The very name of Herod (meaning "descendant of heroes") shows how little of the Jewish spirit his father had absorbed when he gave his circumcised son a name out of Greek mythology. And the son, in truth, realized in more ways than one the omen his father invoked for him in the name. Herod was truly of heroic proportions in activity and tenacity, in sumptuous magnificence, and especially in cruelty. But these "heroics" were rooted deep in a boundless ambition, in a real frenzy for power, which was the motive behind all his actions.

Though he came up from nothing and encountered enormous obstacles, he succeeded in building himself a throne at Jerusalem; in fact, he set it up on the ruins of another throne, the one the Maccabees, the heroes of Jewish religion and nationalism, had built for their descendants. This Jewish throne, already tottering from the intrigues of the Idumaean Antipater, was pulled down once and for all by the craftiness and energy of his son, Herod. And the latter owed his triumph to the moral and material support of Rome.

Herod was always loyal to Rome, because even in the East she was the strongest power; and among Rome's representatives he was always the devoted partisan of the strongest. His politics were not concerned with abstract ideologies but with his own practical advantage. At first he took sides with Caesar, but without being a Caesarist, so much so that when the dictator was killed, he immediately sided with his murderer Cassius, but without being a republican. From Cassius he went over to the latter's enemy, Antony, and when he, too, was defeated, cast his lot with Antony's rival Octavian. But Herod never abandoned Octavian, because the latter became the all-powerful Augustus — that is, the undisputed representative of all-powerful Rome.

At Rome, in the autumn of 40 BC, Herod was proclaimed king, at least in name, by grace of Antony and Octavian. His first official act after that proclamation was to ascend the Capitoline Hill between Antony and Octavian to offer the sacrifice of thanksgiving to Jupiter Capitolinus according to Roman usage. This act shows the true piety of the Idumaean king of the Jews and is almost a foreshadowing of his subsequent policy toward religion. For him, personally, one god was as good as another. Deeply skeptical, he considered religion at most a social phenomenon that politics must take into consideration.

And, astute politician that he was, he almost never offended the religious sensibilities of the Jews; in fact, he acquired great merit in their eyes because he completely rebuilt the Temple of Jerusalem and made it one of the most famous edifices in the Roman Empire. This undertaking, however, was motivated either by a desire to allay the resentment that his subjects felt toward him or by that passion for sumptuous constructions then characteristic of those in power throughout the empire. Certain it is that any true feeling of Jewish piety was utterly foreign to his enterprise.

Nor did he show any greater respect for the most revered persons in the Jewish religious system: he elected high priests at will, and he threw them out of office with the same dispatch that he lopped the heads off the influential Sanhedrists, Pharisees, and doctors of the Law whenever those heads gave evidence of thinking differently from the despotic monarch.

Herod never entered into purely religious questions; but he followed them attentively from without, either because of their possible effects in the political field or sometimes because of a vague feeling of superstition. Thus, with the condescension typical of the skeptic who yields to social conventions, he did not refuse to observe such prescriptions of a religious nature as were not too burdensome to him.

But despite these and other seeming expressions of Jewish piety, Herod's court was a pagan court, far surpassing many other Oriental courts in corruption and obscene frivolities. Its magnificence was maintained by the treasures of David's tomb in Jerusalem, among other things, and this Herod himself secretly entered by night in order to direct the plundering, so slight was the veneration he felt for the venerable founder of the kingdom of Jerusalem.

The Jewish people, for the most part under the influence of the traditionalist Pharisees, could in no way relish a sovereign who was by birth an Idumaean and in practice a pagan. In addition, he had a heavy hand in the matter of taxes. Herod knew very well that his subjects hated him and that they rejoiced whenever misfortune befell the royal household. But for this lack of affection from his subjects he substituted the consciousness of his own power, and he answered every show of popular resentment by sharpening his sword.

And here we see Herod's true character, both as a man and as a ruler. His madness for power, which was, as we have said, the incentive behind all his actions, was wonderfully nourished by his unspeakable cruelty, in which he particularly realized the "heroism" announced in his name. Without the least exaggeration it can be said that Herod is one of the bloodiest men in all history, as we may well conclude from the following incomplete assortment of his exploits.

In 37 BC, as soon as he had succeeded in conquering Jerusalem with the help of Roman legions, Herod put to death forty-five adherents of his rival, the Hasmonean[2] Antigonus, and many members of the Sanhedrin.

In 35 BC, his brother-in-law Aristobulus was drowned by his order in a pool in Jericho.

In 34 BC, he had Joseph killed, who was both his uncle and his brother-in-law.

In 29 BC, he committed his most tragic crime — he killed the Hasmonean Mariamne, his wife, with whom he was hopelessly in love, simply on the strength of calumnies contrived in court against her.

A few months later he also killed his mother-in-law, Alexandra, the dead Mariamne's mother.

Around 25 BC, his brother-in-law Kostobar was killed by Herod's order, and so were several members of the Hasmonean party.

His beloved Mariamne had given Herod several children, who were his favorites because of his memory of their mother. Two of them, Alexander and Aristobulus, he sent to be educated in Rome where they were accorded a kindly welcome in the court of Augustus. But when they returned to Jerusalem, Herod killed them, too, although Augustus did everything he could to save them.

Along with Alexander and Aristobulus, Herod had the mob kill three hundred officials accused of siding with the two young men.

---

[2] The Hasmoneans were the descendants of the Maccabees, who traced their ancestry back to a certain Hashmon.

In 4 BC, only five days before his death, he had another son killed, Antipater, his firstborn, whom he had designated heir to the throne. He was so pleased with Antipater's death that although his physical condition was hopeless, he seemed to rally and improve.

As the end drew near, he decided to close his life with an act that was a worthy summary of it. He foresaw that his death would occasion the liveliest jubilation among his subjects, but he wanted to be escorted to his tomb with a profusion of tears. For that reason perhaps, he summoned many illustrious Jews from all parts of his kingdom to Jericho, where he lay ill, and when they arrived he had them confined, charging his servants to slaughter them immediately after his death. Thus, the desired tears were guaranteed for his funeral, at least from the families of the murdered men.

Besides, only a short time before in nearby Bethlehem, the same Herod had ordered the slaughter of a number of infants under two years of age in whom he saw a menace to his throne. This fact, also perfectly consistent with the man's character, is recounted only by St. Matthew, while Herod's biographer, Flavius Josephus, makes no mention of it. His silence, however, is easily explained: even if the biographer had found (which is not at all certain) some data concerning the massacre at Bethlehem, would he be likely to tarry over a heap of obscure victims, children of poor shepherd folk, when the whole long life of his subject was strewn with higher mounds of much more illustrious victims? Actually, the accounts of St. Matthew and Flavius Josephus supplement each other insofar as the several incidents are concerned, while they agree perfectly in the picture they present of Herod's character.

After an illness lasting several months and attended by the crudest suffering, Herod the Great died in Jericho at about seventy years of age, thirty-seven years after he had been proclaimed king in Rome. It was the year 750 from the founding of the city of Rome and 4 BC. The exact date is uncertain, but it was at the end of March or the beginning of April. His remains were transferred with solemn pomp to Herodium, the modern Jebel Fureidis ("Mount of Paradise"), a hill on which Herod had built his tomb some time previously.

From the top of this hill, scarcely four miles distant to the northwest, could be seen the town of Bethlehem where Jesus had been born, two years before.

After Herod's death, the last of his three wills remained to be carried out. This provided for succession as follows: Archelaus, son of Herod and the Samaritan Malthace, was named heir to the throne with direct dominion over Judea, Samaria, and Idumaea; Antipas, Herod's other son by Malthace, was named tetrarch of Galilee and Perea; lastly, Philip, son of Herod and Cleopatra of Jerusalem, was named tetrarch of the northern regions, Trachonitis, Gaulinitis, Batanea, Auranitis (and Ituraea).

The will, however, had first to be approved by Augustus. In addition, various persons were opposed to it, among them Antipas, who in the preceding will had been named not tetrarch but actual heir to the throne. Also opposed to it were many prominent Jews who were tired of the vexations inflicted by the dead Herod and foresaw worse to come at the hands of his kinsmen; hence they preferred to come under the direct rule of Rome.

First Archelaus and soon afterward his brother and rival, Antipas, set out for Rome, each to plead his own cause. Each of them, but Archelaus especially, hoped to win the necessary investiture from Augustus and return with the actual power of king. But the Jews were not idle either. When the several uprisings that broke out in Jerusalem had been quelled by Roman troops, they sent to Rome a delegation of fifty members to ask that the Herodian monarchy be suppressed so that they might live in peace and in accordance with traditional Jewish customs under Rome's protection.

Faced with this choice of contenders, the shrewd Augustus came to a decision that seemed contrary to Rome's direct advantage while it aimed at reconciling the claims of the rival princes. He rejected the request of the Jewish delegates for annexation to the empire. On Archelaus he conferred the government of the territories assigned to him by his father without, however, granting him the title of king. For the moment he appointed him tetrarch only, allowing him to hope that he would later be proclaimed king if he rendered a good account of himself. To the other two heirs, Antipas and Philip, Augustus granted the respective territories assigned to them in the will along with the title of tetrarch. All this took place in the year of Herod's death, 4 BC.

Subsequent events proved Augustus's decision wise. Archelaus stood the test only a short time. His cruel and tyrannical government did not earn him the expected title of king but complete loss of power. In AD 6 a new delegation, this time of Jews and Samaritans both, went to Rome to lay before the emperor their charges against the tetrarch. Augustus summoned the accused before him to plead his case, but not satisfied with his answers, he exiled Archelaus to Vienne in Gaul and annexed his territories to the empire.

The tetrarch Antipas, or Herod Antipas, lasted longer (until AD 40), but only to meet in the end the same fate as Archelaus. He had probably been educated in Rome, and of all Herod's sons he best reflected his father's character so far as his domineering manner and love of display were concerned. Yet he had neither his father's industriousness nor his creative energy. Like his father, he, too, flattered the emperor by dedicating to him or to members of his family the various constructions he erected in his own territories.

The one who really dug Antipas's grave was a woman, the famous Herodias. Shortly before AD 28, Antipas went to Rome, where he was the guest of his half brother Herod Philip. This Herod Philip, living as a private citizen in Rome, was married to Herodias, who was also his niece. She was a most ambitious woman and could not resign herself to the retired life she was obliged to lead with her husband, Herod Philip. The arrival of the visitor Antipas confirmed an earlier plan of theirs, for this highly prominent man, who enjoyed the confidence of Tiberius, had already shown a decided tenderness for the lady. To be sure, there were several serious impediments to a definite union between them. But his passion and her ambition swept away all obstacles, and they agreed that as soon as he returned to his own territories he would repudiate his wife, who was the daughter of Aretas, king of the Nabateans. Then Herodias would abandon her old husband to fly to the new, who would be waiting for her on his throne with open arms. But Antipas's lawful wife got wind of the arrangements, and to avoid the humiliation of being repudiated, she managed to have her husband send her to the sumptuous fortress of Machaerus, situated on the border between his territories and her father's. From there she fled to her father. With one obstacle thus out of the way, Herodias came to Antipas from Rome, dragging after her the daughter she had had by her first husband, a certain Salome, who was only a little girl but who had learned in Rome to dance quite well.

From then on King Aretas thought of nothing but revenging the outrage offered his daughter, while Antipas's subjects did nothing but grumble against this shameless violation of their national and religious laws. But the grumbling was secret only, for no one dared to brave the arrogance of the ruler and the jealous rage of his adulterous and incestuous concubine. Only one person had the courage to do so and that was St. John the Baptist, whose authority among the people was very great and whom even Antipas regarded with a certain superstitious reverence. John was imprisoned in the Machaerus.

John remained in prison about ten months. This prolonged stay could not have been very agreeable to Herodias, who would have preferred to be rid immediately of her austere and unyielding censor.

Antipas, however, was not disposed to stain his hands with John's blood, either because of the awe he felt for him or because of his fear that the populace might rise against him at the news that the man they so venerated had been killed in this unjust and cowardly manner. But Herodias kept watching for the opportunity to accomplish her desire, and finally it came. Her little dancing daughter obtained for her the head of the prisoner, and when the adulterous mother was able to seize that head in her hands and finger it, she considered herself revenged and triumphant.

Instead, this was the beginning of her downfall, for King Aretas was also watching his opportunity for revenge. In AD 36 a boundary dispute between the two monarchs led to war, and Antipas was thoroughly defeated. Then the arrogant tetrarch humbly begged the distant Tiberius to help him, and the emperor ordered Vitellius, the Roman legate in Syria, to proceed against Aretas. But Vitellius, who had his own grudges against Antipas, set out on the expedition only half-heartedly and sought every excuse he could to drag it out. Fortune favored him, for when he arrived in Jerusalem with his army, he was met with the news that Tiberius had died (March 16, AD 37). Naturally that meant the end of his expedition, and Antipas's defeat went unavenged.

The final downfall of the tetrarch came two years later and was directly caused by Herodias. The feverish woman went mad with envy when in AD 38 her brother, Herod Agrippa I, appeared in Palestine. Until a few months before he had been a debt-ridden adventurer; but after the election of his friend Gaius Caligula, he had acquired an astonishing fortune in Rome. Caligula had also made him a king, granting him the territories that bounded Antipas's lands on the north. When she saw him risen to such heights, Herodias could not but compare him with her Antipas, who after so many years still had the lowly rank of simple tetrarch. Undoubtedly, to win such fortune as Agrippa had, it was necessary to present oneself in the capital of the empire and there busy oneself personally for one's own interests. Once convinced of this, the frantic woman persuaded the reluctant Antipas to go to Rome.

But Agrippa, suspicious of the travelers, sent one of his freedmen after them with letters that, it seems, calumniated Antipas. When he unexpectedly found himself facing a charge of treason instead of the hoped-for proclamation of his kingship, Antipas could give no clear account of himself. Caligula, therefore, judged him guilty, exiled him to Lyons in Gaul, and assigned his territories to his accuser Agrippa. Herodias, whose ambition had caused the catastrophe, voluntarily followed the deposed tetrarch into exile.

This happened between AD 39 and 40.

The third of Herod the Great's immediate heirs, the tetrarch Philip, does not figure directly in the story of Jesus. He governed his territories until his death, in AD 34, and he seems to have been a mild and even-tempered prince. But at one time he, too, must have suffered a slight softening of the brain, for in his old age he married the dancer Salome, daughter of Herodias, who was his grandniece and at least thirty years his junior.

He completely rebuilt Paneas, near the headwaters of the Jordan, and named it Caesarea in honor of Augustus; but it was commonly called Caesarea Philippi (Philip's Caesarea) to distinguish it from the Caesarea on the seacoast that had been built by Herod the Great. On the northern shore of Lake Gennesaret, a little east of where the Jordan enters it, Philip completely rebuilt the town of Bethsaida also and named it Julia in honor of Augustus's daughter.

Chapter 3

∞

The Roman Procurators

Pontius Pilate

When the tetrarch Archelaus was deposed and exiled, Augustus annexed Judea, Samaria, and Idumaea to the empire. Now that a convenient opportunity had presented itself, he satisfied the desire of the Jewish delegation that had gone especially to Rome ten years before to ask him to annex Palestine.

When a region entered under the direct jurisdiction of Rome, it was either made into a province or incorporated into one of the already existing provinces. The frontier provinces, which were less secure and heavily garrisoned, Augustus kept himself, and those in the interior, which were quiet and had only small garrisons, he left to the senate. There were, then, *senatorial* provinces and *imperial* provinces. The former were governed by proconsuls appointed usually for one year. Augustus acted as general proconsul for all the imperial provinces, but he governed them through his legates, whom he appointed himself. To some provinces, however, that required particularly delicate handling (like Egypt), Augustus sent not a *legate* but a *prefect*. To regions recently annexed or presenting special difficulties, he sent a *procurator*.

Archelaus's territories were annexed to Syria, which lay to the north and was an imperial province. It was not a complete annexation, however; a procurator was sent into the new territories as their immediate governor, but his office was superintended by the legate to Syria, who could intervene in the procurator's territories in more important matters.

The Roman procurator of Judea usually lived in Caesarea-by-the-Sea, the sumptuous city recently built by Herod the Great and the only one having a harbor. The procurator often went to Jerusalem, especially for the feasts (e.g., the Pasch), since that city was a better center for surveillance. The palaces of Herod at Caesarea and Jerusalem respectively served as *praetoria*, as the procurator's residence was called, but in Jerusalem he also used the strong

Ruins in the harbor of Caesarea; columns are of Herodian constructions

and comfortable Antonia Fortress north of the Temple for conducting public business. The military garrison of Jerusalem was quartered in the Antonia.

The procurator was the military commander of the region, but he did not have any Roman legions under him; these were composed of Roman citizens and were stationed in the province of Syria. His soldiers were auxiliaries recruited from among the Samaritans, Syrians, and Greeks, since the Jews enjoyed the privilege of exemption from military service. Five "cohorts" of infantry and one "wing" of cavalry, it seems, composed the garrison of Judea, a force of a little over three thousand men. One cohort was always stationed in Jerusalem.

As head of the government, the procurator had charge of levying taxes and collecting the various revenues. The collection was farmed out to rich contractors — the publicans — who paid the procurator a fixed sum that they then set out to recover by collecting appropriate taxes. The agents subordinate to these general tax-farmers were the *exactores* or *portitores*.

It is not necessary to mention how much the people hated all of them, publicans and *exactores* alike, or how much oppression and extortion resulted from the system, especially if the tax-farmers subleased their contracts as they often did. The whole weight of this complicated trafficking ultimately bore upon the taxpayer.

As administrator of justice, the procurator had his own tribunal, in which he exercised the power to pronounce the death sentence. For ordinary cases,

Site of Fortress Antonia

however, the local tribunals of the nation continued to function in Judea. First among them was that of the Sanhedrin in Jerusalem about which we shall have more to say in the following chapter.

Under the procurators, the old national order of Judaism was substantially preserved. The real head of the nation remained the high priest. Actually, his election and removal from office depended on the procurator and the legate to Syria. After Judea's annexation to the empire, the procurator stood at the high priest's elbow to superintend his politics and represent the imperial exchequer.

In religious matters, the Roman authorities, true to their tradition, never deviated from the canon of respect not only toward the institutions of the nation but often toward its prejudices and eccentricities as well. The Romans even tried at times to take part in the traditional customs in order to show their sympathy as well as respect for them.

Many were the privileges Rome granted the Jews or allowed them to keep. Out of respect for the Sabbath rest, they were exempt from military service and could not be called into court on that day. Out of respect for the Jewish Law, which forbade images of living beings, the Roman soldiers entering the garrison in Jerusalem had orders not to take with them the ensigns bearing the image of the emperor. For the same reason, Roman money coined in Judea did not bear the emperor's image but simply his name together with symbols acceptable to Judaism. Gold and silver coins bearing the objectionable image were to be found in Judea, it is true, but they had been issued elsewhere. The worship of the emperor was not imposed on Judea either, although in the other provinces of the empire it was a fundamental rule of government.

Judea under the Roman procurators was in no way worse off than Judea governed by Herod the Great or even by some of his predecessors. Naturally much depended on the particular good sense and integrity of the individual procurators.

Of the first procurators of Judea we know little or nothing that has any direct bearing on the story of Jesus. The first was Coponius, who came into office in AD 6 — that is, as soon as Archelaus was deposed. Upon his arrival, he and the legate to Syria, Sulpicius Quirinius, had the census taken in the territory, for Rome considered a regular census of persons and property the necessary basis of future administration.

The first procurator appointed by Tiberius was Valerius Gratus (AD 15–26). From the beginning he apparently had trouble finding a high priest who would cooperate with him, since he immediately deposed the one he found in office, that is, Ananus (Annas), and in four years provided him with four successors, with the last of whom, Joseph, called Qayapha (Caiphas), he did apparently get along. Valerius Gratus was succeeded by Pontius Pilate in AD 26.

The historians Philo and Flavius Josephus and the Gospels all mention Pilate, and the very least all three sources tell us is that he was a cantankerous and stubborn man, violent, extortionate, and tyrannical in government. Some of these accusations may be exaggerated, but in any case, it is certain that Pilate was not a successful procurator. He not only hated the Jewish people, but he felt a compelling need to show them his hatred. But the emperor of Rome stood in his way, and so did the legate to Syria, who superintended everything and made his reports to Rome, and so Pontius Pilate had to restrain himself in the expression of his ill will.

It was probably in the beginning of his procuratorship that Pilate ordered the soldiers who were going to garrison Jerusalem to carry into the city for the first time the standards bearing the emperor's image. He shrewdly commanded them to do this by night, however, in order not to provoke resistance and to present the city with the accomplished fact. The next day many Jews rushed to Caesarea, completely dismayed by so great a profanation, and for five days and nights they besought the procurator to remove the ensigns from the Holy City.

Pilate refused. In fact, on the sixth day, annoyed by their insistence, he had his troops surround them at the public audience and threatened to kill them if they did not go home immediately. But here those magnificent traditionalists conquered the cynical Roman. When they saw they were surrounded by soldiers, they threw themselves to the ground, bared their necks, and declared they were ready to be slain rather than renounce their principles. Pilate, who had not expected this turn of affairs, gave in and had the ensigns removed.

Later there was the question of the aqueduct. To furnish Jerusalem with an adequate water supply, since it needed it greatly, especially for the Temple, Pilate decided to build an aqueduct that would carry water from the great reservoirs situated southeast of Bethlehem (the modern "Solomon's Pools"), and he appropriated several funds of the Temple treasury to finance the undertaking. This use of consecrated money provoked riots and demonstrations. Pilate then scattered among the rioters many of his own soldiers disguised as Jews, and at a given moment they whipped out the clubs hidden on their persons and belabored the mob, leaving many dead and injured in the street.

In the end, Pilate fell victim to his own method of governing. In AD 35 a false prophet, who had acquired a great reputation in Samaria, promised to show his followers the sacred vessels of Moses' time, which were believed to be hidden in Mount Garizim near Samaria. But on the appointed day, Pilate

Nabulus, in Samaria, in Mount Garizim in the background

ordered his soldiers to occupy the summit of the mount. When a numerous multitude had gathered anyway, the soldiers attacked them. Many Samaritans were killed and many more taken prisoner, and the most prominent of these Pilate put to death. The Samaritan community formally accused him of this insane massacre before Vitellius, who was legate to Syria. Because the Samaritans were noted for their loyalty to Rome, he accepted their charge, deposed Pilate without further ado, and sent him to Rome to answer for his actions before the emperor. It was the end of the year AD 36.

When Pilate arrived in Rome, Tiberius had died (March 16, AD 37). Just what end finally overtook the man who condemned Jesus to death, history does not know. Folklore and legend have undertaken to fill the gap, however, attributing to him marvelous adventures in this world and the next, and consigning him sometimes to the bottom of Hell and sometimes to Paradise as an actual saint.

Chapter 4

∞

The Temple, the Priesthood, and the Great Sanhedrin

The Temple frequented by Jesus was that built by Herod the Great. Hence, it was actually the third Temple. The first, built by Solomon, had been destroyed by Nabuchodonosor when he captured Jerusalem in 586 BC. The second, rebuilt after the Babylonian exile, was dedicated in 515 BC and remained in use until after the time of Herod, who completely demolished it to build the third.

The "sanctuary" of Herod's Temple was exactly like that of Solomon's except that it was higher, but the outer structures surrounding it were much more extensive. The ancient Temple had risen on the city's eastern hill, the top of which was now almost doubled in area by constructions erected up its slopes. On the site thus obtained were built three porticoes or courts, which rose on successively higher planes, proceeding inward. The first or outside portico was open to everyone and was therefore called the Court of the Gentiles since pagans might frequent it; but at a certain point within there was a stone balustrade with Greek and Latin inscriptions reminding them that they were forbidden to proceed farther under pain of death. Beyond this balustrade and up a short flight of steps was the "inner court," surrounded by very thick walls and divided into two parts; the outer section was called the Women's Court because the Israelite women might enter that far within the Temple; the inner division was called the Court of Israel, and this only the men could enter. Another flight of steps led to the Court of Priests, in which stood the altar of sacrifice under the open sky, and finally, at the top of still another stairway, rose the true "sanctuary."

The "sanctuary" had a vestibule and was divided into two chambers. The first, called the Holy Place, contained the golden altar for incense, the table for the showbread, and the seven-branched candlestick of gold. The second was called the Holy of Holies because it was considered the dwelling place of the God of Israel and therefore the most holy place on all the earth. There,

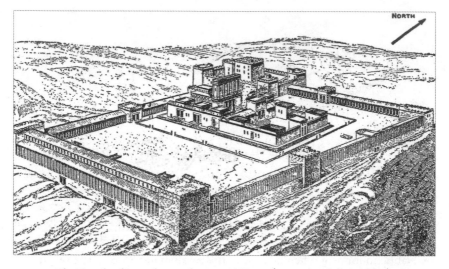

The Temple of Jerusalem at the time of Christ (restoration by De Vogué)

in Solomon's Temple, had been kept the Ark of the Covenant, but since this had been destroyed, the "Holy of Holies" in the new Temple remained a mysteriously dark and empty room.

The Court of the Gentiles was enclosed on the east and south by two famous porticoes. The one on the east, overlooking the Cedron, was commonly called Solomon's Porch. The southern colonnade, commonly called the Royal Porch, extended from the valley of the Cedron on the east to the Tyropoeon Valley on the west. This was a truly remarkable construction, worthy to stand beside the most famous porticoes of Athens and Rome, but it was completely Greek in style and had nothing Hebrew about it. It was composed of 162 huge columns with most exquisite Corinthian capitals, arranged in four rows to form a triple nave.

The Court of the Gentiles was the great meeting place for all who lived in Jerusalem or were passing through the city. Pagans went there to transact business just as they would have gone to the forum in their own cities. The Jews frequented it to hear the famous doctors of the Law teaching there or disputing some question among themselves; and finally everyone was drawn to it by the thousand and one curiosities typical of so crowded a place and the news of all kinds that could be gathered there.

During the Hebrew feasts especially, the Court of the Gentiles became a public marketplace. To the pilgrims from Palestine or abroad, the hawkers installed under the porticoes or in the great open square sold oxen, sheep, and everything else necessary for the temple sacrifices, while the money changers behind their improvised counters were ready to exchange the various types of Palestinian coinage for the foreign money of the faithful returned from elsewhere. Only after passing through this inferno of stench and noise did one reach the place of expiation, where only the Israelite might enter and cleanse himself of his sins before God, in silence and in prayer.

At the northwest corner of the Temple and joined to it rose the Antonia Fortress, which had also been completely rebuilt by Herod on the site of a former tower. Flavius Josephus concludes his minute description of it with this important information: "But on the corner where it joined to the two porticoes of the Temple, it had passages down to them both, through which the guard ... went several ways among the cloisters with their arms, on the Jewish festivals, in order to watch the people, that they might not attempt any innovations; for the Temple was a fortress that guarded the city, as was the tower of Antonia a guard to the Temple; and in the tower were the guards for all three ⌊places: city, Temple, and Antonia⌋."

For these practical reasons as well as for its nearness to the Temple, the Roman procurator — as we have already mentioned — often used the Antonia to conduct public business, especially when he had to deal with large groups of people. The royal palace of Herod, more aristocratic and further away from the Temple, was not so well suited for such circumstances.

The Priesthood

The Levitical priesthood, with the high priest at its head, presided over the Temple. The high priest was also head of the Jewish nation; in him were joined the supreme religious and civil authority. This was in theory; in practice, especially at the time of Jesus, the actual power of the high priest was not that great.

At that time the high priests were almost always chosen from among certain particularly influential sacerdotal families that formed a privileged and aristocratic group within the sacerdotal class. The high priest was chosen for life and in ancient times it had been the exception when he was deposed, but from the time of Herod the Great, the exception became the rule and a high priest rarely died in office. From the beginning of the reign of Herod the Great to the death of Jesus, about sixty-five years, there were approximately fifteen high priests, several of whom held office only a year or less. The former high priests, with the other members of their privileged families, formed the group to which the Gospels and Flavius Josephus refer as "the chief priests."

General view of the site of Solomon's Temple

Once elected, the high priest was the chief minister of public worship and head of all the services in the Temple. He had to celebrate personally only the ceremony of the Day of Atonement, but he sometimes officiated on other solemn feast days also, such as the Pasch.

With regard to civil matters, the high priest functioned principally as head of the Sanhedrin, the presidency of which was automatically his. But here especially his actual power dwindled under Herod the Great, who pointed out with his sword the road the head of the Sanhedrin was to follow. The Roman procurators were less brutal about it, but they watched his actions and reviewed his most important decisions to remind him, among other things, that the miter of the priest was no royal crown. In fact, even the high priest's vestments were kept in the Antonia, to be taken out only on the principal feast days and immediately returned to the fortress. But in AD 36, after Pontius Pilate was deposed, the Romans renounced this practice, which was hateful to the religious sensibilities of the Jews.

The fact that they were always Sadducees was another reason why the moral prestige, if not actually the official authority, of the high priests was at a very low ebb at the time of Jesus. Not only was this aristocratic faction cordially disliked by the people, but its doctrinal tendencies were opposed by the democratic Pharisees and therefore by the scribes, the majority of whom were also Pharisees. Now, the high priest should have sat on the chair of Moses as supreme moderator and interpreter of the theocratic Law, but in reality "the Scribes and the Pharisees have sitten on the chair of Moses" (Matt. 23:2); in other words, they set up another chair in opposition to that of the high priest, turning the multitude from him and leaving him only his self-interested Sadducees.

The high priests who figure directly in the story of Jesus are two, Annas and Caiphas.

Josephus pictures Annas as a "most happy man" for two reasons: he himself had been high priest for a very long time, and then he had been succeeded in office by five of his sons. Josephus might have mentioned that his son-in-law Joseph, called Caiphas, also succeeded him, which brings out even more clearly the monopoly of the high priesthood exercised by the influential families mentioned before. Annas still had very great authority even after he was removed from office, for he secretly or openly controlled the pontificates of his five sons and his son-in-law.

Annas's son-in-law Joseph, called Caiphas, was appointed in AD 18 by Valerius Gratus, the procurator who had deposed his father-in-law, and he remained in office until AD 36. He was high priest, therefore, when Jesus was condemned, although on that occasion Annas wielded the actual authority.

In the Temple, under the supreme jurisdiction of the high priest, officiated the descendants of the tribe of Levi, who were still divided into the two ancient classes of priests and simple Levites. The priests performed the ordinary liturgical functions, both those of the official public ceremonial and those required by the individual piety of the faithful. The simple Levites helped the priests in preparing for and carrying out the ritual, and they had general responsibility for the menial duties in the Temple.

The Levites who were not priests, therefore, formed the lower clergy, and outside of the Temple they had no particular importance in the social and cultural life of the nation.

The priests were divided into twenty-four classes or groups, which served each a week in turn in the Temple. Each group was headed by a priest for whom it was named, and his assistants were assigned by lot to their particular duties. Most of the priests lived in Jerusalem or in the immediate neighborhood, but some resided in rather distant towns, to which they returned after their week of service in Jerusalem. This was true also of the ordinary Levites.

The priest's duties pertained to the ritual. The necessary requirements for a sacrificial animal, the precise amount of a given libation, the rites involved in preparing and making certain sacrifices, the precepts to be observed in specific functions, and in general all the written or traditional rules governing the liturgy — all this constituted the knowledge of which he was so proud. He was the one who, with scrupulous care and accuracy, slaughtered the animals, sprinkled the blood, and burned the incense prescribed by God Himself. These were the duties of the priest's office, and he was more deserving than any other member of society because with these offerings of blood and incense he placated God and secured His protection for the community. The prophets had indeed stressed in their preaching the part that the spirit must play in the observance of the ritual, but actually it entered very little into the functions of the priesthood as it was exercised "professionally" by the Hebrew priests.

Among the lower clergy, especially the Levites, and also among the priests from less prominent and less urbanized families, there must have been many deeply religious spirits who secretly meditated on the ancient benefits God had bestowed on Israel and anxiously awaited the fulfillment of His promises. The good, sound Levite element was, as always, the least conspicuous, the least likely to be spoken of in the ordinary events of social life. The people's gaze was drawn to those showy and arrogant priests who held sway in the Temple and shared the administration of public affairs with the Roman procurator, with whom they had a clear enough understanding. In the eyes of the people, these bosses of finance and politics — if not of religion — were the real priesthood, the virtual descendants of Levi and Eli. It was therefore natural that the common people should have no love for them.

The Great Sanhedrin

We have spoken several times of the Sanhedrin.

At the time of Jesus, this was the greatest institution in Judaism next to the high priesthood. It was the supreme national-religious body.

The great Sanhedrin came into being about two hundred years before Christ as a limited form of self-government conceded to the Jews by foreign kings. Under Jewish rulers — the Maccabees and their successors — the great Sanhedrin enjoyed very little real power, and later the tyrannical Herod left it the mere shadow of authority.

On the other hand, the Sanhedrin acquired a great deal of power under the Roman procurators. The Romans applied in Palestine their constant principle of permitting subjected peoples complete freedom in religious matters and a restricted autonomy in civil affairs, and they found it convenient to entrust the administration of this twofold liberty to the great Sanhedrin in Jerusalem. Then, too, this body was composed largely of the aristocracy, which in the provinces was much more acceptable to the Romans than the innovators who represented the common people.

The great Sanhedrin consisted of seventy-one members, including its president, the high priest. The members were divided into three groups.

The first, that of the "chief priests," comprised both those who had already held that office and the most important members of the families from which the high priests were chosen.

The second was composed of the "ancients," that is, citizens who because of wealth, or for some other reason, exerted a conspicuous influence on public life and could therefore make an effective contribution to the administration of civil affairs. Members of these two groups were for the most part Sadducees.

The third group was that of the scribes, or doctors of the Law, composed for the most part of laymen and Pharisees but numbering also some priests and Sadducees among its members.

Under the Roman procurators, the decisions of the Sanhedrin carried executive weight, and the Jewish or Roman police could be called upon to enforce them. Rome had limited its executive power only in the matter of the death sentence, which the Sanhedrin could pronounce but could not execute without express confirmation of the Roman magistrate. In any case, to avoid capital punishment as much as possible was a solemn legal principle, which seems to have been faithfully followed, and evidently the death sentence was extremely rare.

The Sanhedrin was convoked by the high priest and held its meetings in the "chamber of hewn stone," situated at the southwest corner of the inner court that only Israelites might enter. In special emergencies the Sanhedrin could be called to meet even in the house of its president, the high priest. There were no meetings on the Sabbath or on feast days.

Besides the Sanhedrin of Jerusalem, there existed minor Sanhedrins in the different Jewish communities in Palestine and abroad. Every well-organized community must have had one. Its members were the most prominent Jews of the locality and its president the ruler of the synagogue.

Chapter 5

∞

Sadducees, Pharisees, Scribes, and Other Jewish Groups

The Sadducees and the Pharisees

At the time of Jesus, the Sadducees and the Pharisees constituted the two principal factions of the Jewish people. They represented two currents of thought or tendencies that, though completely opposed to each other, were both based on sacred principles of the Jewish nation. If we examine them together, the very contrast between them will help to define them more precisely.

It is generally believed that the Pharisees were the conservatives and the Sadducees the liberals, more given to innovations. This may have been true in practice, but from the juridical-religious point of view the designation should be reversed, for the Sadducees claimed that *they* had preserved the true moral heritage of Judaism, and they rejected as innovations the particular tenets of the Pharisees.

In reality, the two currents stemmed from the different attitudes the various classes in the nation assumed toward the Greek culture when it began to conflict with Judaism, that is, from the time of the Maccabees (167 BC) on.

The revolt of the Maccabees, directed against the Hellenizing policy of the Seleucid kings, was supported particularly by people of the lower classes, heartily averse to all foreign institutions, who called themselves the Hasidim (in Hebrew, "pious"). On the other hand, within the nation there were a number of other Jews, dazzled by the splendor of this foreign culture, who viewed Hellenism with a favorable eye, and these belonged principally to the wealthy and the sacerdotal classes. When the national-religious insurrection triumphed, the aristocrats within the Jewish nation who favored Hellenism disappeared or kept silent. Shortly afterward, however, when the national dynasty of the Hasmoneans, descendants of the Maccabees, had been established, the two currents emerged once more although their relative positions had somewhat changed; that is, the very Hasmonean sovereigns who owed their throne to the lower-class Hasidim began to oppose them and to draw for support on the sacerdotal and aristocratic classes instead.

The reason for the change is clear. The Greek world was pressing in so closely on the reconstituted Jewish state that the governing Hasmoneans could not avoid all political relations with it, nor could they prevent its pagan culture from seeping into their own territories. To the Hasidim these dealings with and infiltrations of Greek culture seemed political defeat and above all religious apostasy; hence, they were gradually alienated from the Hasmoneans they once had favored and became their enemies.

Once they joined the opposition, they called themselves "the Separated," in Hebrew *Perushim*, in Aramaic *Perishayya*, whence *Pharisees*. Their adversaries, the majority of whom were of sacerdotal rank, called themselves *Sadducees* from the name of *Sadoq*, the ancient founder of an illustrious sacerdotal family.

But from whom or what did the Pharisees consider themselves "separated"? They kept aloof from all that was not Jewish and that, for that very reason, was also irreligious and impure, since for Judaism, religion and legal purity were, practically speaking, inseparable concepts. But here arose their conflict with the Sadducees, which turned out to be a doctrinal one as well — namely, what was the true fundamental norm of Judaism? What was the supreme and absolute law that was to govern the chosen nation?

The Sadducees answered that it was the Torah, that is, the "written Law" that Moses had given to the nation. The Pharisees, on the other hand, replied that the Torah was only a part of their national-religious constitution; there existed in addition the more extensive "oral Law," composed of the innumerable precepts of "tradition."

An immense amount of material went to form this oral Law. Besides narrative and other elements, it included an elaborate system of precepts that covered the most varied activities of civil and religious life, from complicated rules for the liturgical sacrifices to precepts for washing dishes before meals, from the detailed procedure of the public courts to the question whether or not it was lawful to eat fruit that had dropped from a tree on the Sabbath.

This whole unwieldy mass of traditional beliefs and customs almost never had any true connection with the written Torah; but the Pharisees frequently discovered some connection by subjecting the text of the Torah to arbitrary interpretation, or they appealed to their own cherished principle that God on Sinai had given Moses not only the written Law, containing 613 precepts, but also the oral Law, which was much more extensive and no less binding.

As a matter of fact, this oral Law was the more binding. With the passing of time, as the doctors of the Law, or scribes, gradually worked the vast subject matter of tradition into a system, it came to assume a practical importance greater than that of the written Torah.

Once having established this principle, it is clear that the Pharisees could make as many laws as they pleased, drawing all their decisions from their oral Law. But it was precisely this principle that the Sadducees rejected. They recognized no law but the written Law, the Torah, and refused to accept the oral Law and the "tradition" of the Pharisees. They, the Sadducees, were the faithful guardians of the simple Hebrew spirit, the true "conservatives," and therefore they opposed the arbitrary sophisms of these modernist Pharisees.

The Sadducees' answer was unquestionably clever, especially since with their seeming conservatism they avoided the heavy burdens imposed by the Pharisees while at the same time the door was left open for an understanding with Hellenism and Greco-Roman culture. Hence the governing classes, which were obliged to maintain relations with the non-Jewish world. The Pharisees, on the other hand, drew their support from the people, who were hostile to everything foreign and deeply attached to those traditional customs from which the Pharisees derived their oral Law. Hence the paradox: the Sadducees were conservative about the Law but laxist in practice, while the Pharisees seemed innovators so far as the written Torah was concerned but their innovations were meant to be a safeguard and protection of the old.

The results of the principal difference between Sadducees and Pharisees are evident in their teachings on life after death. The former accepted only the written Law, and since they did not find in it any clear doctrine concerning the resurrection and the afterlife, they rejected both these tenets. The Pharisees, on the other hand, drew from "tradition" the doctrines that the Sadducees rejected. And since the study of the Law, especially of the oral Law, was the most binding obligation and the noblest pursuit for every Jew, they dedicated themselves to it completely. In fact, the Law was the armory from which every norm for public and private, religious and civil life was to be drawn. Hence, they, the custodians of this armory, were more important than the priesthood and royalty.

It would be untrue and unjust to say that the whole elaboration of the Law accomplished by the Pharisees was false, but it certainly contained much that was trivial. There were some truly precious pearls, the heritage of the spiritual teaching of the prophets, to be found in that sea of useless and pedantic commentary; but the disparity was far too great between the breadth of the sea and the scarcity of the pearls, between the top-heavy legal machinery and its slender spiritual framework. The useful was drowned in too much that was useless.

Even with respect to the actual conduct of the Pharisees it is impossible to give any judgment that would be valid for all of them. We find Jesus on friendly terms with Pharisees like Simon, Nicodemus, Joseph of Arimathea. On the other hand, the sternest invectives Jesus uttered are directed against the Pharisees and not the Sadducees, just as among the former he found the most tenacious opposition to his mission.

The Pharisees came from various social classes and to some extent even from the lower clergy, but they were closely united by their great aim, which was to observe legal purity and keep "separate" from all that was impure. Whether rich or poor, they were obliged to be most strict in observing to the last detail the three principal sets of precepts — that is, those concerning the Sabbath rest, the rules for legal purity, and the laws governing public worship (tithes, etc.). Anyone with sufficient education to discuss legal questions was a "scholar," while one who did not was an ordinary citizen called *hedjot*.

The Pharisees called all the other Jews "people of the land," which was a term of disparagement; but even more disparaging was the practical attitude they maintained toward these fellow countrymen.

On this point, too, both Christian and Jewish sources agree. In the Gospel of St. John (7:49), the Pharisees exclaim, "But this multitude, that knoweth not the Law are accursed!" The word *multitude* here means the non-Pharisees or "people of the land," "rustics" who are "ignorant of the Law" and completely "accursed." Even a wealthy Jew or a member of the high priesthood could be in the Pharisees' eyes a "rustic," one of the "people of the land." The standard of judgment was the practice and knowledge of the Law according to Pharisaic principles, and membership in the chosen class of the "separated."

Only rarely did non-Pharisees answer this class pride with scorn or hostility. The common people, especially in the cities, and the women among them particularly, were wholeheartedly on the side of the Pharisees and cherished a boundless respect for them. It was possible to say that the Pharisees "have so much power over the multitude, that even if they say something which is contrary to the king or to the high priest they are immediately believed." Such popular support was the true strength of these aristocrats of dogma.

The Scribes

There remains to be considered the exact concept in the word *scribe* and its relation to *Pharisee*. The Gospels frequently pair the two, and rightly so in view of the actual conditions of the time. But in theory not all scribes were Pharisees, as in practice not every Pharisee was a scribe because he might not have the necessary education — that is, he might not be a "scholar."

Scribe denoted par excellence the man of the Law, whether priest or layman, Pharisee or Sadducee. But at the time of Jesus only very few scribes were priests and Sadducees; the great majority were laymen of Pharisaic beliefs. That is why the Gospels couple them.

As early as the Babylonian exile, some among them completely dedicated their lives and work to the Law, the one good they still possessed, in order to preserve it with all care, transmit it with complete accuracy, and examine and apply it with scrupulous study. Such a man was par excellence "the man of the book" not only because he was its most diligent copyist but especially because he was a teacher in the broadest sense. He was, therefore, one skilled in the Law, and the title of honor, *Rab, Rabbi* ("great," "my great one") was reserved for him.

The authority of the scribes was very great as early as 200 BC, but it became even greater as time went on until it constituted a real throne of glory rising opposite the throne of the priesthood. In fact, at the time of Jesus, while the priesthood had kept its liturgical duties and its rank in the hierarchy of Jewish theocracy, it had lost all influence so far as the spiritual formation of the multitude was concerned. The true "spiritual father" of the people, their catechist and moral guide, was no longer the priest but the scribe. As the priests took less and less interest in the Law, the laity supplemented them in the spiritual direction of Judaism. As the priesthood gradually became identified with the Sadducees, the lay doctor of the Law became increasingly Pharisaic. Thus, at length the sphere of the priesthood was restricted to the Temple liturgy and political intrigue while the scribe sat as teacher in the schools of the Law, preached as the representative of Moses in the synagogues, and moved as a model of holiness through the streets and homes of the reverent multitude.

The Zealots and Herodians

The Zealots came most probably from the Pharisees. Substantially they were Pharisees. Flavius Josephus states that the Zealots "are in agreement with the opinion of the Pharisees, except that they have a most ardent love of liberty and admit no head or lord but God alone." Evident in their attitude was a fidelity to the national-theocratic principle, which was fundamental in Pharisaic teaching. The difference lay in the fact that most Pharisees did not apply this principle to political matters, while the Zealots did so with complete rigor, carrying it out to its ultimate consequences. Hence, they were called "Zealots," those who were "zealous" in fulfilling the national-religious law.

It was actually a political incident that produced the Zealots. When in AD 6 Sulpicius Quirinius began the census of Judea, but lately annexed to the Roman Empire, the people saw in the measure a proof that the chosen nation of Yahweh was being sacrilegiously subjected to the domination of impure foreigners. Nevertheless, the greater part of them submitted to it, being persuaded to do so even by some of the outstanding priests. The majority of the Pharisees also complied. But Judas of Gamala, called the Galilean, offered resistance. The rebellion was put down by the Romans.

The Zealots did not yield after this first defeat, however. Though they scattered and hid from the Roman authorities, they kept alive the spirit of opposition to the yoke of the foreigner, which later burst into flame in the final rebellion of the Jews. Meanwhile the difference between them and the ordinary Pharisees became more and more pronounced, for the latter maintained a passive and compliant attitude toward the Roman authorities.

Among the disciples of Jesus, the apostle Simon is called "Zealous" (Luke 6:15; Acts 1:13) and also the "Cananean" (Matt. 10:4; Mark 3:18). This second name is Aramaic, meaning "zealous," a Zealot.

The "Herodians," also mentioned in the Gospels (Mark 3:6; 12:13; Matt. 22:16), did not represent any true or distinct political party and much less any religious group or current of thought. Rather they must have been Jews who openly supported the Herodian dynasty in general, and its most authoritative representative, the tetrarch Herod Antipas, in particular. They were not, properly speaking, members of his court, however. They could not have been very numerous, nor could they have had much prestige among the people.

Chapter 6

∞

Jewish Beliefs and Practices

Of all the prescriptions of the Jewish religion, the two most important at the time of Jesus concerned the rite of circumcision and the observance of the Sabbath.

Circumcision was the distinguishing mark of membership in the chosen nation of Yahweh, the certificate of spiritual descent from Abraham and of the right to share in the benefits of the covenant he had made with God. The child was circumcised on the eighth day after birth. Any Jew could perform the operation, but it was done preferably by the father and usually at home. On this occasion the infant was officially given his name.

If strictly applied, the Sabbath precept would have meant abstaining from any form of manual effort whatever, hence even from defending one's life when threatened by armed force (as some Jews did during the persecution of Antiochus Epiphanes), and also from all that might be necessary to satisfy the needs of the body. But obviously the requirements of daily living were not compatible with such rigorous observance of the precept, hence the numerous rabbinic rules that tried to preserve it as much as possible in theory without being entirely impractical.

The Jewish Sabbath, according to the Hebrew calendar, began at sunset of our Friday and lasted until sunset of the following day. Friday afternoon was called the "vigil of the Sabbath" or "parasceve," that is, "preparation." This second term was due to the fact that everything necessary for the inactive Sabbath was prepared on that afternoon, including food, since lighting a fire was one of the prohibited actions.

Claims of a superior nature might break in upon the strictness of the Sabbath rest, but even here the minute reasoning of the rabbis continues unabated. Thus, it was lawful to prepare the sacrifice of the Pasch, but everything not strictly necessary to its preparation was to be omitted; the priest on duty in the Temple could perform the manual tasks required by the prescribed ritual, but if he cut his finger, he could treat it only within the Temple itself.

Except for this stifling legislation, the Jewish Sabbath was a day of spirituality and joy. The Talmud itself prescribed that the best foods were to be reserved for this day, though prepared on the vigil, and it was a day, too, for festive garments and ornaments. A good part of it was spent at religious services in the synagogue or at home, or in devotional reading.

While circumcision concerned the Jew only once in his lifetime and the Sabbath only once a week, a complicated array of laws, from which he was never free, followed him into every action at every hour of his night and day. These were the precepts concerning purity and impurity.

For the Jew, the moral stain of sin implied a kind of physical stain also, just as physical contact with certain objects that were the result of sin, or in some way reflected it, impaired the spiritual integrity and produced a kind of moral stain. Cases of this kind were innumerable and furnished even more inexhaustible material for rabbinic legislation than did the Sabbath rest.

When we remember that such legislation extended from the matter of washing the hands to the various types of pure and impure foods and a thousand other daily acts, we have some idea of the rigor with which rabbinic casuistry hemmed in all social life on the basis of a religious principle. For the pious Israelite, this mass of legislation was a bed of thorns that constantly tore his anxious conscience without affording him any of the consolation of real devotion. This was true of the great majority who did not go beyond sheer formalism. But there were chosen souls who, searching more deeply, did attain a spirituality like that which must have inspired the observance of legal purity already defined in the Old Testament.

Besides the weekly Sabbath, there were annual feasts to be observed, principal among them the Pasch, Pentecost, and the feast of Tabernacles. These were called "feasts of pilgrimage" because for them every male Israelite who had reached a certain age was obliged to go to the Temple of Jerusalem.

The Pasch was celebrated in the month called Nisan, which corresponded roughly to the period of March fifteenth to April fifteenth of our calendar. The feast began on the evening of the fourteenth day of Nisan and was followed immediately by the "feast of the Azymes," celebrated on the seven succeeding days (the fifteenth to the twenty-first Nisan); hence these eight days were called either the Pasch or the Azymes. From the tenth or eleventh hour of the fourteenth Nisan, the last crumb of leavened bread disappeared from every Jewish house, since on the rest of that day and the seven days following, the use of unleavened bread was absolutely obligatory. On the afternoon of the fourteenth, the Paschal victim, a lamb, was sacrificed in the inner court of the Temple by the head of the family or group making the offering. The blood of the victims was gathered up and given to the priests, who sprinkled it at the altar of holocausts. Immediately after the sacrificial ceremony and still within the Temple court, the animal was skinned, certain of its entrails were removed, and then it was brought back to the family or group to which it belonged.

On that afternoon, the courts of the Temple resembled a slaughterhouse. In fact, the multitude of Jews who flocked to the Temple from Palestine and elsewhere was enormous, and since the Temple court could not accommodate at one time all those who had come to offer their lambs, they were arranged in three relays. The first entered at about two in the afternoon, and between groups the entrance gates were closed. In all, as many as two hundred thousand lambs might be slaughtered. A flock that large, even of lambs, was enough to produce a veritable lake of blood and redden all the walls and pavements of the Temple.

The lamb was then brought home and roasted the same evening for the Paschal feast, which began after sunset and regularly lasted until midnight or longer. There were to be no less than ten and not more than twenty persons at each festive board, and they reclined on divans arranged in a circle about the table. The ritual wine was passed at least four times during the meal; other wine could be taken before the third serving of the ritual wine but not between the third and fourth. We cannot be certain whether or not all the guests drank from one large goblet or whether each had his own. Perhaps both methods were permissible.

The meal began with the pouring of the first cup of ritual wine and the recitation of a prayer that invoked a blessing first upon the feast day and then upon the wine. Unleavened bread was served and wild herbs, along with a special sauce in which they were to be dipped. Then came the roast lamb. The second cup of ritual wine followed, after which the head of the family, usually in response to a conventional question from the son of the house, explained the meaning of the feast and recalled the benefits bestowed by Yahweh upon His chosen nation and its deliverance from Egypt. Next came the recitation of the first part of the Hallel, a hymn composed of the Hebrew Psalms 112–117, and then the blessing with which the real banquet began, after, of course, the customary washing of the hands. This part of the meal was not governed by any particular ceremonies, and the foods served were various. The third cup of ritual wine followed and then a prayer of thanksgiving. The second part of the Hallel was recited, and finally the fourth cup was passed.

This, at least in general, was the manner in which the Pharisees, and therefore also the great number of people who followed them, celebrated the Pasch at the time of Jesus.

The feast following that of the Pasch was called the feast of the (seven) Weeks or Pentecost. The second term is Greek ("fiftieth" day) and like the first denotes the length of time between Pentecost and the Pasch. The feast itself lasted only one day, on which loaves of bread made from the newly harvested wheat were offered in the Temple along with other special sacrifices.

About six months after the Pasch came the feast of the Tabernacles, which fell at the end of September or the beginning of October and lasted eight days. It was a gay and popular feast, and since it recalled the sojourn in the desert and at the same time celebrated the end of the vintage and the harvest, the people built little booths of green branches like tabernacles in the squares and on the terraces, hence the name of the feast. In addition, they went to the Temple bearing a bunch of palm, myrtle, and willow in the right hand and a citrus fruit in the left. On the night of the first day, the Temple was magnificently illuminated, and in the morning of the first seven days, the priest poured upon the altar a little water that had been brought, in procession, from the spring of Siloe.

Modern girl of Bethlehem

The tenth day of the same month, Tishri, was the Day of Atonement or Yom Kippur, a day of rest and strict fast, on which the high priest officiated in person. On this one day in the year, he entered the "Holy of Holies," and he performed the symbolic ceremony of the scapegoat.

There were two other feasts of a popular character. That of the Dedication took place on the twenty-fifth Kislev (at the end of December) and lasted eight days. It celebrated the reconsecration of the Temple by Judas Maccabeus in 164 BC and was called also the "feast of light" because the Temple was brilliantly illuminated for the occasion. The feast of Purim ("lots"), on the fourteenth and fifteenth Adar (February–March) commemorated the liberation of the Jews by lot at the time of Esther.

Fast was obligatory for all Jews on the Day of Atonement only, but there was other public and private fasting as well. Many fasted voluntarily on the anniversary of past disasters, such as the destruction of Jerusalem by Nabuchodonosor in 586 BC, and the Sanhedrin could prescribe public fasting during calamities, such as epidemics, droughts, and the like. There was also a great deal of fasting prompted by individual piety; the Pharisees especially were much concerned with fasting on Mondays and Thursdays.

At the time of Jesus, the fundamental principles of the early Jewish religion had been for the most part preserved, but often modified and occasionally transformed. Let us examine briefly some of the concepts that have the most direct bearing on the story of Jesus.

There was in His time a more highly developed belief in the world of spirits than in earlier times. This was occasioned by contact, during and after the exile, with the Persians, whose religion included a considerable angelology. The Jewish belief in spirits, however, always conceives all spirits as being subordinate to the one God and does not extend to them the worship proper only to the Divinity.

There were innumerable spirits, and they were divided into two classes, good and evil. The former are the special ministers of God and the friends of man; the latter are subject to divine power but are hostile to it and are the enemies of man. Though spiritual, neither are completely immaterial; they are possessed of an ethereal, fluid substance that is luminous or opaque depending on the good or evil qualities of the individual spirit.

The Jews were uncertain regarding the origin of the evil spirits; some believed them to be the spirits of the "giants" begotten of angels who allowed themselves to be seduced by the daughters of men (cf. Gen. 6:1ff.), but there is more evidence of the other belief that they were former angels fallen from their state of glory. Their leader is a being at first commonly called the

Modern Ashkinazi Jew of Jerusalem

Palestinian woman grinding wheat, using the same method as in the time of Christ

satan, that is, "the accuser" "the adversary," always with the definite article. Later, however, the title became a proper name, and the article was dropped, *Satan*; other more recent titles for him are Belial (Belair), Beelzebul (Beelzebub), Asmodeus, Mastema, and a few others of various origins.

The evil spirits wander about in the lowest strata of air or live in deserted places, in tombs and other impure spots, and sometimes even in houses occupied by men. Often they take up their abode in a man's body and possess him. They occasion or foster all physical and moral ills, causing sickness, accidents, madness, scandal, discord, and war. They tempt the just, guide the impious, promote idolatry, teach magic, and, in short, systematically oppose the law of the God of Israel.

No less highly developed than this angelology at the time of Jesus were the ideas of the Jews regarding the next world. The fundamental ones in early times were the following: The dwelling place of the dead was called Sheol, imagined as an immense cavern in the subterranean regions of the world. There the shades of the departed wandered through a land "that is dark and covered with the mist of death, a land of misery and darkness" (Job 10:21–22), though elsewhere they are spoken of as being still subject to human emotions and apt to communicate with the living if properly conjured up. No one who has descended into Sheol can ever return. The earliest documents do not furnish any clear or unequivocal evidences of belief in reward or punishment for the inhabitants of the land of the dead as a consequence of their earthly behavior.

These vague and uncertain concepts persisted for a long time even after the Babylonian exile. But during the exile there had been planted the germs of a new leaven that was gradually to change the state of the question and require a solution better suited to the new times.

Ezekiel had asserted the moral principle of individual retribution in contrast to the belief in collective-national retribution that had governed early Hebraism, and this new principle was bound to influence the question of the next world. Throughout the entire book of Job, an unknown and lonely individual of lofty intellect had struggled with the problem of the relations between moral goodness and earthly happiness; but his conclusion was more negative than positive, for since he found that there is not always an infallible correlation between them, he took refuge in an act of faith in the supreme justice of God. But men began more and more to wonder whether the present life, so clouded by injustice, was not to be followed by another on which justice would shine in full splendor. In other words, would they not one day emerge from Sheol in a resurrection that would see all the wrongs of this world righted?

At the time of Jesus, belief in the resurrection was widespread among the Jews of Palestine with the sole exception of the Sadducees. Details, however, varied; for example, it seems that many denied the wicked would rise again, believing instead that they would be annihilated.

Palestinian Judaism taught that two great events were to precede this resurrection in the life beyond, namely, the advent of the Messiah and the drama of the end of the world. Very often these two happenings were linked together.

In the two centuries preceding and the one following the birth of Jesus, the great Elect (Hebrew, *Mashiah*; Greek, *Christos*, "anointed"), who the ancient prophets had promised would liberate and glorify Israel, was awaited with the most anxious longing, and his coming was associated with the actual conditions in which the nation found itself. This Messiah was to inaugurate an age of happiness in Israel that would be the just reward for the long humiliation it had suffered until then. Yahweh, by delivering His chosen nation through the Messiah and causing it to triumph over its enemies would bring about His own triumph. Israel's reign over all the pagan nations would be also the reign of the one true God over all the sons of men, the Kingdom of God on earth. Hence, all looked toward that great one to come and speculated on the time of his coming, on the manner in which he would accomplish his mission, on his exploits among the pagan nations, and like questions.

At the time of Jesus, all agree that the Messiah will be a descendant of David, as ancient tradition has stated. He is often called the "Son of Man," as in Daniel 7:13. Four great kingdoms have successively risen and fallen in the past, but the fifth, the kingdom of the Messiah, will endure for eternity. Though, in the past, four rulers in the form of four great beasts have risen from the sea and though a horn on the fourth beast (Antiochus IV Epiphanes) has crushed the saints of the Most High, all these forces hostile to God will be destroyed by one "like the Son of man," who in Heaven receives all power from the "Ancient of days" and then descends upon earth to establish triumphantly his everlasting kingdom, in which the saints of the Most High will reign supreme and receive homage from all kings (Dan. 7).

Needless to say, both during and after the time of Jesus numerous imposters took advantage of the general feverish messianic hope and paraded before the eager populace as envoys of God. Their attempts naturally ended either in tragedy beneath the Roman sword or in farce midst the jeers of their compatriots. But the multitude had such great faith in them that even in the year 70 after Christ, when Jerusalem had been invaded by the Romans and the Temple was already in flames, these false messianic prophets still found disciples ready to believe in the imminent miraculous intervention of God.

Chapter 7

∞

The Sources

The numerous writings of antiquity that speak of Jesus fall naturally into two groups: Christian and non-Christian. This classification is important, for it enables us to judge the impartiality of the respective testimonies; but we must also apply the criterion of time, for a testimony is usually more authoritative the nearer it is to the facts attested. For practical purposes, however, it is easier for us here to follow the first grouping, because the attempt to fix the time of the various writings involves many highly controversial questions. Naturally we must keep these latter in mind also.

Non-Christian Sources

The Jews, countrymen and contemporaries of Jesus, should furnish us with the earliest data concerning Him, but unfortunately this is not the case. Jewish sources, while not altogether silent on the subject, are almost as sparing of information as the pagan sources.

Official Judaism

After the destruction of the Jewish state in AD 70, that is, about forty years after the death of Jesus, the spiritual life of Palestinian Judaism was represented exclusively by the Pharisees. True to their principles, they devoted themselves to collecting and preserving the oral "tradition," which, with the Bible, now formed the only spiritual heritage of Judaism. In the Jewish writings produced by these Pharisees up to the fifth or sixth century, we find that Jesus and His work are known, but often the reference to Him is veiled and indirect, without mention of His name.

The stories told of Jesus in the official writings indicate the Jewish attitude toward Him during the first centuries of the Christian era; but it would be neither scientific nor dignified to discuss their reliability as documentary material for the biography of Jesus. In general, they might be termed "burlesque and obscene legend."

Flavius Josephus

Josephus, a priest of Jerusalem, was born AD 37–38. In the Jewish revolt against Rome in 66, he was at the head of the first rebel troops to engage the Roman forces in Galilee. After several defeats, he surrendered to the enemy commander, the future emperor Vespasian, whose faithful servant he later became.

Between 75 and 79, Josephus published *The Wars of the Jews*, in which he recounted the events preceding the insurrection and the whole course of the war. This work is most useful in the study of the historical background of Jesus' times, and though it is marred by various mistakes, we have nothing that can take its place. Between 93 and 94, Josephus published his *Antiquities of the Jews*, in which he relates the history of the Hebrew nation from its beginnings up to the outbreak of the war against Rome. A little after 95, he published the *Contra Apionem*, a defense of Judaism, and after 100 he published the *Life* (his own), which is an apologia for his politics.

In these writings, though he has a great deal to say of Jewish or Roman personages named in the Gospels, he mentions Jesus or the Christians only three times. Once he speaks with great respect of John the Baptist and his death. Again he mentions with equal respect the violent death of James, "the brother of Jesus, called the Christ." About the authenticity of these two passages there are no reasonable doubts despite the hesitancy of a few modern scholars in their regard.

This is not the case with the third passage, a literal translation of which follows:

> Now about this time there was a certain Jesus, a wise man, if indeed he must be called a man. He was in fact the worker of extraordinary things, the teacher of men who accept the truth with pleasure. And he drew to himself many of the Jews and many Greeks also. This man was the Christ. And when Pilate, because the principal men among us denounced him, had punished him on the cross, those who had loved him from the beginning did not cease. In fact, he appeared to them on the third day alive once more, the divine prophets having already spoken these and thousands of other wonderful things concerning him. And even today the tribe of those who from him are called Christians has grown no less. (*Antiquities of the Jews*, XVIII, 63–64)

This passage was not questioned until the sixteenth century. The first doubts cast upon it were based entirely on internal evidence — that is, it did not seem that a Jew and a Pharisee like Josephus would do Jesus so much honor. The conclusion, therefore, was that the passage had been inserted by some unknown Christian hand. The question has been debated down to our own times, and there are champions and adversaries of the authenticity of the passage in every camp.

To me it seems the passage as it exists today could have been interpolated by a Christian hand, although its substance is certainly genuine; nevertheless, it is equally possible and even more likely that it is genuine and written just as we have it today by the pen of Josephus.

Roman and Other Writers

In the second decade of the second century, three Roman authors speak of Christ and of the Christians.

Pliny the Younger's famous letter to Emperor Trajan, written about 112, testifies to the fact that in Bithynia, governed by Pliny, there were many Christians, who were "accustomed to gather before daybreak and sing hymns to Christ as if he were a God."

The *Annales* of Tacitus are to be dated a little earlier than 117. Speaking of Nero and the fire in Rome in 64, he says that this emperor, to dissipate the rumors that he himself had ordered the fire to be started, "presented as the guilty ones and visited with the most refined punishments those whom the populace, hating them for their crimes, called *Crestiani*. The author of this denomination, Christ, in the reign of Tiberius, had been condemned to death by Pontius Pilate; but, though checked for the moment, the deadly superstition broke out afresh, not only throughout Judea, where this evil originated, but also throughout the Urbs [Rome], where all outrageous and shameful things gather from every region and are exalted" (*Annul.,* XV, 44). This pagan testimony from distant Rome confirms certain information about Jesus that was circulating in Palestine in the preceding century.

Some years later, about 120, Suetonius confirms the fact that under Nero "the Christians, a race of men given to a new and evil superstition, were subjected to torture"; but when he speaks of the preceding reign of Claudius, he offers some new data, for he states that this emperor "expelled from Rome the Jews, who, at the instigation of Crestus, rioted frequently." There is no reasonable doubt that the epithet *Crestus* used by Suetonius is the Greek term *christos*, a translation of the Hebrew *messiah*, especially since even later we find the Christians called *crestiani*. We may therefore conclude that about twenty years after the death of Jesus, the Jews living in Rome were given to noisy quarrels regarding the character of "Christ," or Messiah, attributed to Jesus. Suetonius, who writes seventy years after the events have taken place and who knows very little about Christianity, thinks that this *Crestus* was present in Rome and personally provoked the riots.

Then we have a letter of Emperor Hadrian, written about 125 to the proconsul of Asia, Minusius Fundanus; it sets forth rules for the trials of Christians. Another letter addressed about 133 to the consul Servianus, in which incidental mention is made of Christ and the Christians, is also attributed to Hadrian.

Note, however, that these Roman writers never mention the name *Jesus* but only that of *Christ* (Chrestus).

There is nothing more to be gleaned from non-Roman writers of the first two centuries.

We have a letter in Syriac of a Semite, Mara bar Serapion, addressed to his son Serapion and containing a reference to Jesus. With honor and respect he mentions along with Socrates and Pythagoras a "wise king" of the Jews who was put to death by His own nation, which because of that was punished by God with exile and the destruction of its capital. It is clear, therefore, that the letter was written after the events in Palestine in 70, but it is impossible to fix a precise date for it. It might well belong to the late second century.

Christian Sources

Documents Not Contained in the New Testament

There are many Christian writings of the first centuries that concern Jesus but are not included in the New Testament. Some of them resemble in form the various parts of the New Testament. There are, for example, gospels, acts, epistles, apocalypses, comprising the so-called apocryphal books. Others take the form of ecclesiastical writings, such as constitutions, canons, and so forth, and these are the so-called *pseudepigrapha*.

Lastly, these writings sometimes consist of little sayings or deeds contributed to Jesus that are not included in the New Testament but that are found by themselves or in the works of the early Fathers or in some manuscript of the New Testament or even in recently discovered fragments of ancient papyri; these tiny excerpts are called *Agrapha* or *Logia*.

In general, the apocryphal gospels were born of the desire to justify some particular doctrine on the basis of the life and teachings of Jesus, or else to embellish with further details the information about Him in the canonical Gospels. In the first instance, we have the writings that are heretical in origin or at least controversial, and these are the more numerous; in the second, we have the popular tales with their fondness for the miraculous and wonderful. Often the two are interwoven, and it is impossible today to fix a precise line of division between them.

This abundant and fanciful embroidery of the Gospel narrative began as early as the second century, and it continued to flourish until the Middle Ages. But only a small portion has come down to us. Many other works are mentioned by early Christian writers, but the works themselves have been lost and we know very little about them.

The brief writings called Agrapha or Logia form a class apart and should perhaps be judged separately. The Agrapha, that is, the "unwritten," are short sayings attributed to Jesus that have been handed down through channels other than the Sacred Scriptures or apart from the four canonical Gospels. The Logia, "sayings," are also short maxims attributed to Jesus, and all of them belong to the class of Agrapha. The term *Logia* is commonly applied today to those sayings that scholars have been discovering in Egypt for the past forty years in fragments of ancient papyri. The Agrapha, on the other hand, are attested in various ancient documents over and above the apocryphal literature — for instance, in the works of one or another Father of the Church, or in some isolated manuscript of the New Testament.

Since St. Paul himself quotes as the word of Jesus a maxim not contained in the Gospels, "It is a more blessed thing to give than to receive" (Acts 20:35), it is not impossible that other remarks should have been preserved orally for a long time in the early Church and then written down sometime during the first centuries of Christianity. In fact, quotations of this kind are to be found in early Fathers widely separated in time and locality. Thus, in the first century, St. Clement of Rome attributes to Jesus the saying: "As you shall do, so shall it be done to you; as you shall give, so shall it be given you; as you shall judge, so shall you be judged; as you shall be kind, so shall you be treated with kindness" (1 Cor. 13); in the third century, the Alexandrian Origen ascribes to him the aphorism: "He who is near to me, is near to the fire; he who is far from me, is far from the kingdom" (*in Jer.*, XX, 3). And the quotations, which also contain occasionally some little detail regarding the life of Jesus, might be multiplied to include other times and places as well.

What are we to think of these Agrapha in the early Christian writers? It is impossible to give a blanket opinion of them; they must be considered singly. In general, however, though some of the Agrapha may be authentic, it is extremely difficult to give concrete proof of it for any one of them.

There has been an abundant harvest of Logia during the past forty years, and they are sometimes quite long. When the first of them began to come to light, several scholars considered them remnants of ancient collections antedating the canonical Gospels, for which they were the source. But today, when we have so much more material and are better able to judge it, the almost unanimous opinion is exactly the opposite, namely, that these Logia are later than the canonical Gospels and come from them as well as other sources.

New Testament Documents apart from the Gospels

When we consider the New Testament writings other than the Gospels, our horizon grows wider, but even here we can discover no additional information except for a certain few isolated doctrinal precepts. These writings do contain strictly biographical material about Jesus, but it merely confirms few, albeit important, facts already set forth in the Gospels. This confirmation, however, is most precious, especially if its source is earlier than our canonical Gospels and is independent of them. Such is the case with the works of St. Paul.

The epistles of St. Paul begin to appear about twenty years after the death of Jesus and continue for the next fifteen, occupying approximately the period between 51 and 66, during which our Synoptic Gospels were either being published or prepared. These epistles, therefore, are documents written independently of the Synoptic Gospels, and for the most part they antedate them. Besides, these epistles were composed entirely in view of the circumstances of the time of writing; that is, St. Paul writes to his various addressees for reasons connected with his apostolate. Never in any way does he attempt to give even a partial account of the life of Jesus, because he is speaking to Christians who are already acquainted with it. Only incidentally does he record an act or saying of Jesus where this will serve to strengthen his argument. Yet if we collect all these scanty bits of information, we find we have a not-too-meager sheaf. In fact, a miniature life of Christ could be gleaned from the information in the Letters to the Romans, Corinthians, Galatians, and Hebrews alone.

A few other kernels of information may be culled from the other writings of the New Testament, especially from the Acts of the Apostles, whose author, however, is St. Luke, a Synoptic evangelist.

The Gospels

The word *evangel* (gospel) originally meant the recompense given a messenger bringing good news, or even the good tidings themselves. Christianity used this term from the first to designate the most precious "good tidings" of all, those announced by Jesus at the beginning of His ministry, when He "came into Galilee, preaching the good tidings of the kingdom of God" (Mark 1:14–15). These "good tidings" were essentially this: "The kingdom of God is at hand."

But this announcement underwent a development in which the content of the "good tidings" was translated into reality through the teachings, the life, and the redemptive death of Jesus. Consequently, the whole sum total of facts representing the salvation prepared by Jesus for all mankind was later termed "good tidings," in the sense of a message of salvation already effected and completed.

For several years after the death of Jesus the "good tidings" were spread exclusively by word of mouth. This method, after all, was that used by Jesus Himself, who preached only, without leaving anything written down. The Christians called this method *catechesis*, that is, "reechoing," because the teacher made his words "reecho" in the presence of his disciples. Hence the disciple who had completed his course of instruction was the "catechized," that is, one to whom the good tidings had been "reechoed."

But the spread of the "good tidings" was so wide and so rapid that it became impossible, practically, to entrust it entirely to oral tradition for any length of time. It became necessary very soon for the spoken word to be supplemented by the written. We know, in fact, that as early as the sixth decade of the first century, writings containing the "good tidings" were already in circulation and that they were "many" (Luke 1:4). This new aid in the diffusion of Christianity was like a second highway opened parallel to the first, and from then on the "good tidings" advanced along both roads. But even when the oral "good tidings" changed their mode of transmission to become written Gospel, both remained in substance a "catechesis."

It is, therefore, important to note that the written Gospel never pretended to eliminate or even adequately substitute for the oral Gospel, because, apart from other considerations, the latter was far richer and contained much more material than that set in writing. In this regard we have the valuable testimony of Papias of Hierapolis, who, writing about 120, asserted that he had sought what the apostles and others of Jesus' immediate disciples had taught by word of mouth and for this reason: "I deemed indeed that the things contained in the books would not profit me as much as those [communicated] by a living and abiding voice" (in Eusebius, *Hist. eccl.*, III, 39, 4).

What was the first and principal subject of Christian catechesis, whether written or oral? If the Christian faith was founded on the person of Jesus, then the first step on the road to this faith was to learn the facts concerning Him, and we have explicit testimony that Christian instruction began with the "things that are of Jesus" (Acts 18:25; cf. 28:31); and we are occasionally given brief summaries of catechesis, which do contain just such facts (Acts 1:22; 2:22ff.; 10:37ff.). Actually, a Christian would not have been a Christian if he did not know what the Christ, Jesus, had done, what doctrines He had taught, what permanent rites He had established, what proofs had demonstrated the genuineness of His mission — in short, if he did not possess at least a summary knowledge of Jesus' life.

Now among the preachers of the "good tidings" was a special group who apparently were entrusted in a particular way with transmitting the narrative and the testimony regarding the things of Jesus; hence, these preachers naturally came to be called the "bringers of the good tidings," or the "evangelists" (Eph. 4:11; 2 Tim. 4:5; Acts 21:8).

Thus, we reach the storehouse from which the "many" writers took their materials who, as we have noted, recounted the things of Jesus as early as the sixth decade of the first century and whose work was done at the same time as, or even before, the composition of the canonical Gospels. This great common storehouse is called "catechesis"; and unquestionably there was in substance only one Christian catechesis, though it might be presented differently by each of the various preachers of the "good tidings."

On the other hand, the early Church did not take an interest in all the "many" writings that appeared during the first century but concerned herself with only four of them. On these four alone the Church bestowed official character as history; in them she recognized the inspiration of God and therefore included them in the list of Holy Scriptures called the canon. They are the four canonical Gospels, the four "Good Tidings" of the New Testament. But the Church never lost sight of the one single origin of her four Gospels. Though the writings were four, their source was one, and *that was the catechesis*.

This attitude of the early Church with regard to the common source of the four Gospels is witnessed by the titles under which they have come down to us. In both Greek and Latin the titles read "according to Matthew," "according to Mark," "according to Luke," "according to John." This was inspired by the idea that the *Gospel* in reality was only one, that derived from the catechesis, though it was presented in four ways, that *according to Matthew*, that *according to Mark*, and so forth.

The foregoing observations are extremely important for understanding what the Christians considered the true foundation of the historical authority of the Gospels. That foundation was the authority of the Church, the one fourfold Gospel being the genuine and direct product of her catechesis. The separate authors of the four presentations of the Gospel had authority insofar as they represented the Church, under whose authority they were sheltered. But by believing those four authors, the Christian really believed in the one Church, while if, through them, he had not been able to arrive at the Church, he would not have believed in their Gospel.

In conclusion, the historical process by which the Gospels came into being was the following: the oral "good tidings" were older and more extensive than the written; both were products of the Church, by whose authority they were fostered. This means that the written Gospel presupposes the Church and is based on it.

We find, however, all these elements gathered into our first three Gospels, called the Synoptics, just as we find that the Synoptics in their turn follow one general pattern, which is as follows: the ministry of John the Baptist and the baptism of Jesus; Jesus' ministry in Galilee; His ministry in Judea; the Passion, death, and Resurrection. In Matthew and Luke this outline is introduced by a more or less full account of the infancy, which forms a kind of preamble to the usual pattern while the real body of the story begins with the ministry of John the Baptist.

We do not know who the authors of the lost writings were. Some may have been actual disciples of Jesus, and therefore eyewitnesses of the events narrated. However, a comparison of Luke 1:1 with 1:2 seems to indicate that authors and witnesses were not one and the same, but that the former depended for their information on the latter and were not — at least the majority of them — themselves eyewitnesses of the events.

As for the authors of the canonical Gospels and the type of catechesis on which each bases his writing, we have only to seek out the testimony of tradition, proceeding from the period of preparation to that of the actual composition of the four Gospels.

Matthew

A constant tradition, dating back to the beginning of the second century, attributes the first Gospel to the apostle Matthew, also named Levi, a former publican. All Christian antiquity, in a great number of testimonies, attributed to St. Matthew our first canonical Gospel and no other writing.

When the former publican Matthew set to this work, he was certainly long accustomed to writing, for he had had to do much of it in the past to keep the accounts of his tax collector's bench. The other apostles (except perhaps for the two well-to-do sons of Zebedee), on the other hand, though not illiterate, must have been much more familiar with oars and nets than with parchment and quill, especially just after the death of Jesus when they began their mission. All had been eyewitnesses to the works of Jesus, but Matthew's familiarity with writing gave him a technical advantage over the others, and this must have led them to assign him the task of writing down their oral catechesis.

When St. Matthew began his work, it is possible, though not proved, that some other writings containing the sayings or works of Jesus were already in circulation. Any such compositions, however, would certainly have been nothing more than brief sketches written on the initiative of some private individual and therefore lacking any official character. On the other hand, the assignment given Matthew was to meet the need, created by the ever-widening spread of the Gospel, for an ample and official written reproduction of the oral catechesis of the apostles. The catechesis to be written down could be none other than that already endorsed by Church practice, the general plan of which had been sketched by him who held the preeminent position among the official preachers of the good tidings. It was, therefore, the type of catechesis mapped out by Peter, without excluding elements contributed by other apostolic sources. In conclusion then, Matthew's writing, while it followed the outline of St. Peter's catechesis, summed up the thought of the whole apostolic college.

A document like Matthew's, composed by an eyewitness of the events, vouched for and contributed to by other eyewitnesses, set within the general outline of an official plan of instruction, and fuller in extent than any other writing on the same plan, was bound to acquire a singular importance. In fact, we find that the Gospel of Matthew, just as it was first in order of time, was also the most used from the very earliest times.

Yet from the beginning the language in which it was written furnished a serious obstacle to the wide use and diffusion of St. Matthew's work. This original Semitic language, whether Hebrew or Aramaic, was not understood by non-Jewish Christians or even by the numerous convert Jews of other lands who knew no language but Greek.

But the obstacle was overcome by the various readers and catechists, and "each one then interpreted them as he was able." Some catechists must have made extemporaneous oral translations of the passages they happened to need in their ministry. Others probably made written translations also of certain parts, or more rarely of the whole work. However, the good will characterizing this activity was not always accompanied by adequate knowledge, especially of the language of the original, or even of that into which the translation was being made.

But the Church, which had fostered by her authority the catechesis written in a Semitic dialect by St. Matthew, must at a certain point have extended her care also to the translations of that text lest she be taken to recommend translations that did not deserve the honor. We do not know precisely what happened, but the results are clear and eloquent. The oral and extemporaneous translations must have grown constantly fewer as there were gradually fewer catechists able to understand the original Semitic text. The written translations, partial or complete, were used privately but not officially, and so they were bound sooner or later to be lost. Only one translation was not lost and has come down to us, and that because it was officially adopted by the Church as a substitute for the too-difficult Semitic text of the original, namely, the Greek text of our canonical Matthew. Who made the translation we do not know.

In the Greek, Matthew's Gospel had an immeasurably wider field of influence and could reach out to a non-Jewish audience as well. On the other hand, there must have been in the Semitic text (as we see by comparing it with the other two Synoptics) certain phrases apt to be misunderstood by these new readers. Hence, the translator, in order better to adapt the work to the new field of instruction, forestalled these possibilities of error by softening certain expressions without altering their fundamental meaning.[3] It also seems probable that he shifted some of the passages, grouping them differently from the original text in an arrangement more like that of Mark and Luke, because it seemed to him more practical for catechetical reasons.

But the fact that the Church adopted his translation and that the earliest ecclesiastical writers used it as a canonical text shows that his rendering of the original Semitic manuscript was "substantially identical." The severity that the Church later displayed toward the apocrypha, which also took refuge, though falsely, behind glorious names and which sometimes were actually free variations of canonical books, is a guarantee for the Greek translation of Matthew.

The fact that the translation of Matthew is not slavishly literal underlines a most important principle for the interpretation of the Gospel narratives in general. That is, the evangelists themselves are free from any slavish literalness

---

[3] For instance, Mark 6:5 says that Jesus "could not do any miracles there, only that he cured a few that were sick"; in Matthew 13:58, this is softened somewhat to read, "And he wrought not many miracles there, because of their unbelief."

in their accounts; for they differ in their terms even when recording texts that originally had one specific wording or pronouncements of especially important doctrinal significance. For example, the inscription Pilate caused to be affixed to the Cross of Jesus was undoubtedly worded in one specific way; yet this one text is reported with the following variations: "Jesus of Nazareth, the King of the Jews" (John 19:19); "This is Jesus, the King of the Jews" (Matt. 27:37); "This is the King of the Jews" (Luke 23:38); "The King of the Jews" (Mark 15:26). Still more important is the example of the passages concerning the Eucharist, which Jesus instituted only once and in very precise terms. Yet even here the difference in the actual phrases in which it is recorded in the three Synoptics and in St. Paul (1 Cor. 11:23–26) are self-evident.

All this goes to prove that early Christian catechesis and the canonical evangelists, who drew upon it, were anxious to give a faithful presentation not so much of the phrase itself as of the substance; they sought to adhere strictly not to the letter but to the essential meaning. And the Greek translator of Matthew imitates their freedom in the choice of vocabulary.

It is clear from his treatment that St. Matthew is addressing Christians of Jewish origin. Undoubtedly his aim is historical, that is, to record the teachings and the works of Jesus; but he does so in what seems to him the most effective manner for readers who already believe in Moses. In the Gospel of Matthew more than in any of the others, Jesus appears as the Messiah promised in the Old Testament. That is why the evangelist takes special care to bring many episodes to a close with the reminder that "all this came to pass that there might be fulfilled what was spoken . . ." with reference to some passage in the Old Testament.

Jesus' teaching also is presented with special attention to its relation both to the Old Testament and to the prevailing Pharisaic doctrines and attitudes. The new teaching does not abolish the Old Testament but perfects and completes it. Only Matthew records Jesus' assertions that He came not to destroy the Law and the prophets but to fulfill them (Matt. 5:17–18). As for the Pharisees, Jesus' teaching is the perfect opposite of their doctrine. Not only is the threat, "Woe to you, Scribes and Pharisees, hypocrites," repeated fully seven times in one chapter, but throughout this Gospel the abyss between the two is emphasized more than in the other Synoptics.

Similarly, Matthew alone points out that Jesus' ministry was directly addressed only to the Jewish nation just as the preparatory ministry of the apostles was directed to Israel only. Even the term *Gentiles* applied to the pagans still reflects in Matthew's words the scorn that Judaism had for non-Jews and that considered *Gentile* practically synonymous with the abhorred term *publican*. These expressions either are softened or disappear altogether in the later Synoptics, which are addressed particularly to Christians of pagan origin.

Beneath this Jewish crust, however, the Gospel of Matthew is strictly universal. It is more than any other the "Gospel of the Church." The word *Church* is used by Matthew alone among the evangelists. And this institution established by Jesus is not reserved to the Jews but open to all the nations. In fact, the pagan Gentiles shall, practically speaking, supplant the Israelites in the possession of the Kingdom of God (21:43).

Since Matthew is writing for readers brought up in Judaism, and since he has besides a definite aim in their regard, he uses literary devices common in the rabbinic schools, the practical purpose of which was to afford a useful memory aid. Just as he divides the "sayings" of Jesus into five main groups, he also arranges individual maxims or facts in groups of five, seven, or ten.

Frequent also is his use of "parallelism," a characteristic of Hebrew poetry, and especially of "antithetic parallelism"; that is, a given statement is followed by the negation of its contrary by way of confirmation. The entire Sermon on the Mount (chaps. 5–7) — that is, the first of the five groups of "sayings" — is actually a chain of such devices.

Mark

The second Gospel is attributed to St. Mark. The Acts speak several times of a "John who was surnamed Mark" whose mother, named Mary, had a house in Jerusalem. Other passages speak of "John" (Acts 13:5, 13) and of "Mark" (Acts 15:39; Col. 4:10; Phil. 1.24; 1 Pet. 5:13). It is undoubtedly the same person in all the three instances since it was common for the Jews at that time to add a Greco-Roman name to their own Jewish one. It is certain, too, that Christian antiquity attributed the second Gospel to this John Mark.

The house of Mark's mother in Jerusalem was a meeting place for the Christians of the city, and there Simon Peter took refuge when he was miraculously freed from prison in AD 44. Mark was the cousin of the distinguished Barnabas, who, with Paul, took him to Antioch. But during Paul's first missionary voyage, Mark left the two at Perge in Pamphilia, and returned to Jerusalem, thus arousing Paul's displeasure. This did not alienate Mark's affections, for some ten years later, about 61–62, Mark was once more with him in Rome. Between 63 and 64, Mark was in Rome with Peter, for the latter sends from "Babylon" (Rome) greetings from his "son" Mark (1 Pet. 5:13). In 66, Mark was in Asia Minor, for Paul, writing to Timothy in Ephesus, urged him: "Take Mark, and bring him with thee, for he is useful to me for the ministry" (2 Tim. 4:11).

In this New Testament data, Mark's contacts with Paul are more numerous and important than those with Peter. But tradition emphasizes more his relations with Peter, showing that it does not derive from the information given in the New Testament. In reality, since Peter calls Mark his "son," it is probable that he baptized him; and it is also probable that Peter cherished a particular affection for Mark's family since he fled directly to his house upon his miraculous escape from prison. The New Testament says nothing about Mark's sharing in Peter's apostolate, but this fact is strongly attested by later tradition, especially with regard to the composition of an evangelical work.

The oldest and most authoritative documentation is furnished by Papias, who writes:

> This also did the Presbyter say: Mark, having become the interpreter of Peter, wrote exactly, but not with order what he remembered of the things spoken or performed by the Lord. He, in fact, did not hear the Lord nor was he among his immediate disciples, but later ... he was among the followers of Peter. The latter gave instruction as was necessary but not ... with the aim of arranging in a particular order the sayings of the Lord; hence Mark is not guilty of any defect in writing certain things just as he remembered them. To one thing only did he pay especial attention, namely, to omit none of the things which he heard and not to report any of them falsely. (Eusebius, *Hist. eccl.,* II, 39, 15)

In what sense did Mark become the "interpreter" of Peter? The word in itself can mean either interpreter of the words (a translator) or interpreter of the thought (a kind of secretary). Both meanings are acceptable and in fact have been accepted. After all, it is possible that both apply in that Peter — who in the first years of his apostolate outside Palestine must have known little Greek and less Latin — could have used Mark first as an interpreter in the modern sense of the term and later as a secretary.

According to Papias, therefore, Mark's writing is an "exact" rendering of Peter's oral catechesis: that is why it lacks "order," for Peter gave his instructions to suit the occasion, "as was necessary" for a particular group of listeners, without trying to "set in order," systematically or completely, the things "spoken and performed" by Jesus. All this information is confirmed in our Gospel of Mark. Mark does resemble a collection of biographical anecdotes, which would be the "certain things" the author remembered according to Papias, and it does not have the full account of the discourses that we find in Matthew.

About 200, Clement of Alexandria adds important details regarding the place and circumstances in which this Gospel was written. Speaking of St. Peter's apostolate in Rome, Eusebius says: "The minds of Peter's listeners were illumined by such a flame of devotion that they ... insisted that Mark, whose Gospel is now in circulation and who was a follower of Peter, leave also in writing a record of the instruction given them by word of mouth."

As for the time of composition of Mark's Gospel, the almost uniform testimony of antiquity is that he was the second evangelist in point of time and therefore preceded Luke. From the evidence, we can say that sometime between 55 and 62 Mark wrote down his memoirs of St. Peter.

This Gospel is the shortest of the four and only one-tenth of its content is peculiar to it alone, the other nine-tenths being included in the other two Synoptics. The narrative, brief as it is, deals with many miracles of Jesus, a few parables, and a very few discourses. All except four of the miracles recounted in the other two Synoptics are found in Mark's Gospel, but he includes others that they do not mention. On the other hand, his writing does not contain any discourses of fundamental importance, like the Sermon on the Mount, just as he has none of the earnest solicitude of Matthew about showing that the ancient messianic prophecies found their fulfillment in Jesus.

Mark's description of events is vivid and straightforward, and he includes unexpected details often lacking in the other two Synoptics; yet his Greek is poor, his sentences plain and even crude, his style elementary and uniform. We seem to be reading the letter of an intelligent rustic describing the wonderful events he has witnessed. The narrative of such a writer will be the more vivid and direct the more he has been impressed and the more simple and limited are the literary mechanics at his disposal.

These observations fit perfectly the picture delivered to us by tradition.

While Peter needed Mark as an "interpreter," the latter on his part must have had a bare working knowledge of foreign languages. In the course of his instructions, Peter had told his story in the simple but effective manner of the eyewitness, and his interpreter set it in writing with whatever skill he possessed.

Besides, the majority of Peter's listeners in Rome were from a pagan background, knowing little or nothing about Hebrew doctrines and traditions; and it is for this reason that in Mark Jesus is presented not so much as the Messiah awaited by the Hebrews but as the Son of God, the wonder-working Lord of nature, the conqueror of the infernal powers. On the other hand, doctrinal questions of particular interest to the Jews, such as the observance of the Law and so forth, are here omitted.

It is probable that we feel the presence of Peter's Roman audience in the episode of Simon the Cyrenean who helped Jesus to carry His Cross. The other two Synoptics also recount the incident, but only Mark adds that Simon was "the father of Alexander and Rufus" (15:21). Why this identification if the two sons are not named again in any of the Gospels? The end of Paul's Letter to the Romans seems to offer some explanation, for the apostle sends his greetings to "Rufus, elect in the Lord and his mother and mine" (Rom. 16:13), who are obviously in Rome. It is clear that this Rufus was outstanding among the Christians of Rome, and so was his mother if Paul venerates her so much that he calls her his own mother. The mention of Rufus in Mark is equally unexplainable unless it refers to a very well-known person, and therefore it is natural to suppose that the two are one and the same individual, especially since the name *Rufus* must have been rare in Jerusalem, the city from which this man came.

And finally, the treatment of Peter in Mark is peculiar to this Gospel. While some episodes contain a few details concerning him, such as the cure of his mother-in-law, there is no passage whatever in praise of him, and in fact those episodes that do him most honor, such as his walking on the waters, even the conferring of the primacy upon him — all included in the other Synoptics — are omitted. This confirms the tradition that concerns us here, for St. Peter in all probability would not dwell in his preaching on incidents that redounded to his own glory, and his "interpreter" has reflected his modesty in this Gospel.

Luke

The third Gospel is attributed to Luke, the name being perhaps an abbreviation of Lucanus.

In the first generation of Christianity, Luke appears as the satellite to the splendor of Paul, who calls him "the most dear physician" (Col. 4:14). Originally from Antioch, Luke was a Greek by birth and education and became a Christian well before the year 50, although we are sure he was not among the immediate disciples of Jesus and had never seen him. Shortly after 50, he is at Paul's side through the latter's second missionary journey, probably in the capacity of physician also, because of Paul's recent illness. From that time on, Luke was Paul's shadow in almost all the latter's travels except for what was probably a long separation after their sojourn in Philippi. He joined Paul again in Philippi during the apostle's third missionary voyage, about 57, and finished the journey with him, going as far as Jerusalem. During Paul's two-year imprisonment in Caesarea, Luke, it seems, could not stay near him; but he accompanied him in his journey to Rome, sharing with him the adventures of the crossing. During the apostle's first imprisonment in Rome, Luke stayed near; later, faithful unto death, he attended him during his second Roman imprisonment, earning from him the moving tribute: "Only Luke is with me" (2 Tim. 4:11).

Writing to the Corinthians in 57 or 58, St. Paul mentions, without naming, a "brother, whose praise is in the gospel through all the churches" (2 Cor. 8:18). St. Jerome and other early writers believe that this unnamed "brother" is none other than St. Luke.

Luke is credited both with the third Gospel and also the Acts of the Apostles, which deals largely with Paul's adventures and contains long passages in which the narrator speaks in the first person plural, indicating that he was present at the events he is recording. Not only do all the early writers agree in attributing these works to St. Luke — and his case is strengthened by the fact that the prologues of both (cf. Luke 1:1–4 with Acts 1:1–2) indicate they are from the same pen — but so do most of the modern authorities.

The Greek, the physician, the disciple of Paul are all reflected clearly in Luke's Gospel. The Greek man of letters is apparent from the opening lines of his first work; unlike the other books of the New Testament but in conformity with Greek usage, they contain an elaborate introduction.

Luke's language is certainly not classical Greek, but his vocabulary is rich and often literary, his sentences polished and dignified. There are traces of Semitic influence in construction and even in the choice of words, however, especially in the first two chapters, which recount the infancy of Jesus, which would indicate that for these the author depended more on Jewish sources.

We cannot prove merely from his writing that the author of the third Gospel was a physician. But several little touches in his work serve to confirm the tradition that called him one. Modern research has brought out the many technical terms in Luke that are to be found also in the writings of a number of Greek physicians. True, such expressions may be found also in nonmedical writers who occasionally affect a certain medical knowledge, but Luke could have no reason for introducing such terminology into episodes already narrated in the other Synoptics except the fact that he himself was a physician.

We can also detect the "clinical eye," so to speak, in certain of Luke's descriptions, especially when we compare them with the parallel passages in Mark: the symptoms are given particular attention in the episodes of Peter's mother-in-law, the Gadarene demoniac, the woman with the issue of blood, the demoniac boy, the woman bent double. And it is only Luke who tells us of the bloody sweat Jesus suffered in Gethsemane.

Lastly, Luke more than any of the other evangelists delights in portraying Jesus as the supreme healer, of both bodies and souls. He is the only one who has Jesus' fellow townsmen call Him "physician" by way of challenge, and shortly afterward, as if in answer to that challenge, he relates that "virtue [power] went forth from him and healed all" (6:19). Then from the spiritual point of view Luke pictures Jesus as the compassionate healer of ailing humanity, the tender comforter of the afflicted, gentle, and meek, pardoning those who have gone most astray. Hence Dante describes St. Luke, without naming him, most appropriately as the "chronicler of the meekness of Christ."

The disciple of Paul is no less evident in Luke's writings. About a hundred words common to these two authors are not found in any of the other New Testament writers. We also, not rarely, find phrases that are typical of them. But this kinship appears especially in content, which emphasizes the great principles stressed in Paul's catechesis, such as the universality of the salvation wrought by Jesus, His "goodness and kindness" (Titus 3:4), the value of humility and poverty, the power of prayer, the joyousness of spirit characteristic of the faithful, and the like. Not that he expresses these thoughts in Paul's very words, for Luke was not for him the "interpreter" Mark had been for Peter; rather, they are the beacons that guide his course.

When did Luke write his Gospel? Certainly after the other two Synoptics, according to the almost constant tradition of antiquity, which places it third in the series of Gospels; hence it follows Mark, which is no later than 61. On the other hand, Luke wrote his Gospel before the Acts of the Apostles, the introduction of which refers to it explicitly. In all probability, according to the prevailing opinion among modern scholars, the Acts were written before Paul's release from his first imprisonment in Rome and therefore before the great persecution under Nero in 64 — that is, all considered, in 62 or 63. St. Luke's Gospel, then, preceded the Acts, if only by a short time.

Luke addresses his Gospel to a definite person, Theophilus, to whom he later addresses the Acts as well. This Theophilus is called by a term that may have been equivalent to our "excellency" and possibly indicates the man's station; but we know nothing else about him. In any case, Luke is looking beyond to a multitude of other readers.

The brief prologue to Theophilus, in which St. Luke sets forth the circumstances, scope, and method of his work, is of supreme historical value; it might be called the most important document we have regarding the date of composition of the Synoptic Gospels. Hence we quote it here in its entirety (Luke 1:1–4): "Forasmuch as many have taken in hand to set forth in order a narrative of the things which have been accomplished among us, according as they have delivered them unto us who from the beginning were eyewitnesses and ministers of the word, it seemed good to me also, having diligently attained to [followed up] all things from the beginning [or even "for a long time"] to write to thee in order, most excellent Theophilus, that thou mayest know the verity of those words in which thou hast been instructed."

The "many" prior to Luke cannot be taken to mean only two, namely, the Gospels of Matthew and Mark, which are known to us. The term *many* may on the whole suggest about ten writings, in which, of course, the two we know may be included. But even amid this plenty, Luke thinks a new work will be useful. He has not witnessed these things himself, but the long and diligent searches he has made in the one mine of information, namely, the reports of the "eyewitnesses" and "ministers of the word," lead him to hope that this new work will serve to deepen for others the "certainty" of the catechetical "discourses."

Luke is the only evangelist who links his narrative with the principal events in contemporary history, to set the Christian picture against the background of all humanity, thus showing that he is a historian of wide vision who perceives that Christianity has initiated a new era in the story of mankind.

As for the chronological sequence, Luke follows Mark, so much so that the latter brief Gospel seems to have served as his general outline; in fact, about three-fifths of the material in Mark is included in Luke. Yet, though he follows Mark's pattern, Luke omits some things, transposes others, and above all makes copious additions. About one-half the contents of Luke are peculiar to this Gospel and are not included in the other two Synoptics. The additions include seven miracles and about twenty parables together with the account of the birth and infancy of Jesus, which is not identical with Matthew's.

Evidently this fresh information is the fruit of the "diligent" studies Luke refers to in his prologue. But where did he find it?

The same prologue points to tradition as one source, though without being specific. It is not difficult, however, to glimpse among the "eyewitnesses" and "ministers of the word" first the revered teacher Paul, and then other well-known persons whom Luke may have met in Antioch, Asia Minor, Macedonia, Jerusalem, Caesarea, and Rome. It is no hazardous guess to presume that his reliable informants included the apostle Peter and possibly James, as well as the "evangelist" Philip with whom he lived in Caesarea.

The specific mention of certain women is significant. "Certain women" had followed Jesus, "who had been cured of evil spirits and infirmities: Mary, who is called the Magdalene, from whom seven devils had gone out, and Joanna, the wife of Chuza, Herod's steward, and Susanna, and many others, who used to provide for them out of their means" (Luke 8:2–3; cf. 24:10). Neither Joanna nor Susanna are mentioned by the other evangelists although they were well-to-do women of high social position. Perhaps Luke's mention of them is a tactful allusion to one source of his information.

No less delicate but much more precise is his reference to another woman of incomparable dignity and importance, the Mother of Jesus herself. The only eyewitness and source of information for many of the things this Gospel tells us about the conception, birth, and infancy of Jesus could have been no one but Mary, Jesus' own mother. Twice in the course of his narrative — within a short space and in practically the same words — Luke draws our attention to the fact that "Mary kept all these words, pondering them in her heart" (2:19) and, shortly afterward, that "his mother kept all these words in her heart" (2:51). This repetition of thought and expression is eloquent in its deliberate reticence. Whether or not Luke knew Mary personally we do not know; but even if he had never spoken with her, he could still have obtained the very precise information she was able to furnish from the apostle John, in whose home she lived after the death of her son. A late tradition, not recorded before the sixth century, makes Luke the painter of Mary's portrait, and still later legends are full of many more such portraits. But in reality the portrait of the Mother of Jesus was painted by the pen and not by the brush of St. Luke. It shines forth from his description of Jesus' infancy, spent beneath His Mother's thoughtful gaze, and it was from this description that Christian painters later took their favorite themes.

Luke is writing not only for Theophilus, but also for other Christians who are of more or less the same spiritual mold — converts for the most part from paganism. Hence, he includes certain explanations that would have been unnecessary for Jewish readers, such as the fact that the Jewish feast of the Azymes is called the Pasch; and he omits other things that a convert from paganism might misunderstand, like the precept Jesus gave the apostles not

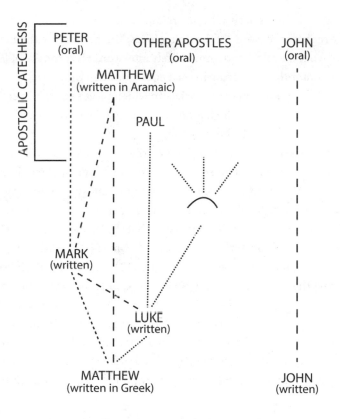

The relationship among the four Gospels

to go in the direction of the Gentiles. Again he softens certain expressions that might have seemed somewhat harsh to Gentile ears; for instance, instead of "Do not even the Gentiles do that?" (Matt. 5:47), he has "For even sinners do that" (Luke 6:33). The same tactfulness prompts him to add special little particulars complimentary to the Gentiles, like the cordial welcome John the Baptist gives the soldiers, the centurion's generosity toward the Jews, and even the charity and gratitude to be found among the abhorred Samaritans.

In addition, Luke's writing aims especially to spread the "good tidings" of kindness and mercy, picturing Jesus not only as the Savior of all men without distinction but as the friend, in a special way, of the most sinful, the most lowly, and the disinherited of the earth. Luke is the only one who records the parable of the Prodigal Son, a literary miracle of psychological insight. Only in Luke does the shepherd place on his shoulders the lost sheep he has just found and, on his arrival home, rejoice over it with his friends. No one but Luke records the words of the dying Jesus, "Father forgive them, for they know not what they do!" and immediately afterward His promise of Paradise to the repentant thief suffering his last agony beside Him.

The perfect opposition to the society in which Luke's readers lived is in the very nature of his Gospel, which exalts woman, praises poverty, and eulogizes the joyousness of a simple, humble life.

The spirit of serene joyousness that breathes through Luke's Gospel seems the natural consequence of his special love for purity and poverty. St. Paul had already urged the faithful to "rejoice in the Lord always; again I say, rejoice" (Phil. 4:4), repeating the commendation elsewhere in identical or equivalent words. The reason for this joyousness was that the "kingdom of God is ... justice, and peace, and joy in the Holy Spirit" (Rom. 14:17), and that the "fruit of the Spirit is charity, joy, peace ..." (Gal. 5:22). In this the disciple follows his teacher; the first two chapters of his Gospel contain the four metrical compositions (*Magnificat*; *Benedictus*; *Gloria in altissimis*; *Nunc dimittis*) that are unique expressions of this spiritual joy and are not in the other Gospels. Finally the work is brought to a close with the statement that the apostles, after watching Jesus ascend into Heaven, "returned to Jerusalem with great joy. And they were continually in the Temple, praising and blessing God" (24:52–53).

John

The three Synoptic Gospels contain no direct identification of their authors. On the other hand, at the end of the fourth Gospel, the only non-Synoptic, we do find such identification, however veiled: "This is the disciple who bears witness concerning these things, and who has written these things" (John 21:24), the "this" referring to a "disciple whom Jesus loved," mentioned four verses earlier.

If this statement, which brings the whole work to a close, is not exactly an autograph, it may be considered a kind of cryptic signature.

In a moment we shall see how the characteristics of the fourth Gospel correspond to those of John the apostle. First let us listen to what early tradition says of him.

John stood at the foot of the Cross with Mary, the Mother of Jesus, and "from that hour, the disciple took her to his own [house]" (John 19:27). After Pentecost, John appears with Peter in Jerusalem and then in Samaria. When Paul goes to Jerusalem in 49 to attend the council of the apostles, he finds John there. After this, we do not find the guardian of Jesus' Mother in Palestine again; probably he left by the year 57, for when Paul returns to Jerusalem, he makes no mention of him. Later tradition points to John in Asia Minor, in Ephesus, toward the end of the first century. During the persecution of Jews and Christians inaugurated by Domitian (81–96), John was exiled to the island of Patmos where he wrote the book of Revelation. After Domitian's death, he returned to Ephesus. Here he died a natural death at a very advanced age, perhaps in the seventh year of Trajan's rule, or AD 104.

The author of the fourth Gospel shows more accurate knowledge of the geography of Palestine than the writers of the Synoptics, and he presents many surprising little details that could have been omitted without affecting the narrative in any way. If he did not omit them, it is because he was very sure of himself. There are at least ten localities in Palestine specified in the fourth Gospel exclusively; not one of these designations has been proved untrue, and several have been shown to be exact beyond our expectation. We may take two as examples.

In John 1:28, there is mention of a "Bethany beyond the Jordan," otherwise unknown; on the other hand, in 11:18 we learn that Bethany is only 15 stadia, or about 3,060 yards, from Jerusalem, while the distance from Jerusalem to the Jordan is about 25 miles. But there were two Bethanys (just as there were two Bethlehems). The Bethany on the Jordan was near a ferry crossing over the river. Ancient installations have recently been discovered on the site.

In 19:13 we are told that Pilate, in the course of the trial, "brought Jesus outside, and sat down on the judgment-seat, at the place called Lithostrotos,

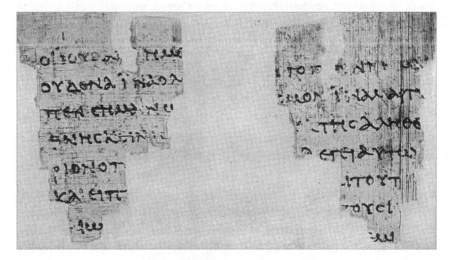

Papyrus containing John 18:31 ... 38

but in Hebrew, Gabbatha." Excavations made a few years ago have furnished us with definite information on this place with the double name.

We find the same accuracy in the timing of John's narrative, as if to prove the axiom that the two eyes of true history are geography and chronology.

When we compare the time sequence of events given us in the Synoptics with that in the fourth Gospel, we have the impression that John goes out of his way to specify whatever is indefinite in them. From the Synoptics alone, Christ's public life could be condensed into one year or less. John, however, expressly mentions three different Paschs and thereby extends it to at least two years and some months.

John's Gospel is full of passages that reveal a thoroughly direct and personal knowledge of his facts on the part of the narrator. He is well acquainted with what the Synoptics have written, but he deliberately travels a different road. Without pretending to exhaust his subject, he does aim to supply in part what the Synoptics have omitted. By actual count, they do not include 92 percent of the content of his Gospel. Sometimes, of course, the two accounts are necessarily parallel because of the subject, but even in these instances John stands out as the eyewitness who is anxious to specify and complete the narrative. This is most evident in the account of the Passion.

That John travels a different road from the Synoptics is apparent from the whole content of his Gospel. The Synoptics emphasize Jesus' ministry in Galilee; John, the ministry in Judea and Jerusalem. John relates only seven miracles, but five of these are not included in the Synoptics. He gives more space to the doctrinal discussions of Jesus, especially His debates with the Jewish leaders, than to His actions. In these discourses, as in the rest of this Gospel, characteristic concepts frequently appear that are rare or omitted altogether in the Synoptics — for example, the symbolic terms *Light, Darkness, Water, World, Flesh,* or the abstract terms of *Life, Death, Truth, Justice, Sin.*

But though John does not follow the Synoptic tradition, he never loses sight of it. Even his silence is an indirect use of the Synoptic tradition in that he takes for granted that his readers are familiar with it.

It is apparent from his style and method of exposition that the author of the fourth Gospel was of Jewish origin. He uses not only Semitic expressions like "rejoiceth with joy," "son of perdition," and so forth, but also Semitic words that he regularly translates for the benefit of his readers, like "Rabbi" and "Rabboni," "Messiah," "Cephas," "Siloe." His periods are quite elementary and bare in outline with none of the Greek fondness for subordinate clauses or complicated arrangement. On the other hand, his style shows a tendency toward parallel ideas so characteristic of Hebrew poetry. For example:

> No servant is greater than his master,
>> nor is one who is sent greater than he who
>> sent him....
> He who receives anyone I send, receives me;
>> and he who receives me, receives him who sent me.
>
> (13:16, 20)

It is true he was a fisherman, but the Gospels seem to suggest that his father Zebedee was a well-to-do owner of boats and therefore could have given his son some formal education. However this may be, it was in perfect harmony with Palestinian custom to pursue knowledge and practice a trade at the same time.

If the ardent John, a true "son of thunder" (Mark 3:17), began while still very young to follow first John the Baptist and then Jesus, he might well have lost this last teacher when he was little more than twenty years old. Then, true to the custom of the region, he concentrated on the study of the new Law of perfection and love that had been proclaimed by his last teacher and the memory of which persisted bright and clear in his spirit.

John's catechesis, fully worked out in his mind before it was ever written down, must have existed also in oral form for several decades. As the disciple meditated on his memories of the Master, he passed them on to the faithful committed to his care, first in Palestine, then in Syria and Asia Minor.

In these later fields of action, John, now advanced in years and wearing increasing authority because of the gradual disappearance of the other apostles, met a new kind of obstacle. The opposition was no longer coming from the old groups of Judaizing Christians that had so molested Paul, but from the various Gnostic[4] currents in large part pre-Christian, which toward the end of the first century were beginning to seep into the channel of Christianity. It was necessary to stem these currents, and John kept drawing fresh and

---

[4] Gnosticism was a very complex system of religious doctrines and practices, which tended to reduce revelation to a mere philosophy. Among other things it taught that Christ was not truly God, and that He took only an apparent body. The teaching of the Gnostics is *Gnosis*, that is, knowledge. Gnosticism was one of the gravest threats to the new Christian teaching.

increasingly appropriate material from the treasures of his memory to make his catechesis particularly effective against this new threat.

At a certain point, the disciples of the aged apostle affectionately compel him to put in writing the essential part of his catechesis. John dictates it, but at the end of the whole writing there is affixed as a seal a declaration of authenticity made both by the one who had conceded and those who had requested the writing: "This is the disciple who bears witness concerning these things, and who has written these things; and we know that his witness is true" (21:24).

This prehistory explains the special nature of John's writing, which has been called the "spiritual" Gospel par excellence. In every possible way he emphasizes the transcendence and divinity of Jesus the Christ because this is his principal aim in the fight against pagan Gnosis.

But this same thesis is already to be found in the Synoptics, though less fully developed or barely sketched — especially in Mark. Of the innumerable things he could have said about Jesus, John selected certain particulars that had not been told before but that it was most opportune to tell at that time; he did not invent them and he connected them with other common and widespread information. There emerged a Jesus more resplendent with divine light, but that was due to John's choice of material, just as the Jesus of the Synoptics is a more human figure equally as a result of the choice of material in the Synoptics. Each biographer has portrayed his subject from the particular angle of his contemplation, and each has given us a whole, if not a complete, picture; but none of them has pretended to reproduce all the many individual features of Christ's personality.

If the discourses and dialogues of Jesus in the fourth Gospel are extraordinarily sublime, they are not therefore any less historical than those in the Synoptics. It would be unhistorical to suppose that Jesus spoke in the same manner on every occasion whether He was addressing the mountaineers of Galilee with whom we usually find Him speaking in the Synoptics, or arguing with the subtle casuists of Jerusalem with whom John has Him speaking for the most part. Even with His disciples, Jesus must have taken a different tone at different times; we might expect His words to be more simple at first when they had just begun to follow Him and more difficult later, until He lifted them to heights never reached before in His farewell discourse at the Last Supper. Then, too, among the disciples themselves He must have had His more intimate friends for whom He reserved certain confidences; and the most intimate among these, as we know, was John, who is therefore the most important witness of all even from a purely historical point of view.

Now, this extraordinary witness begins his writing with the assertion that Jesus is the divine Logos — the Word — become man. Even here he shows his sound historical sense though his approach is theological: the Logos, who is with God from all eternity, became a man a few years ago and "we saw his glory — glory as of the only begotten of the Father" (1:14). Never, however, does our trustworthy witness with his scrupulous historical honesty, state that Jesus calls Himself the Logos; it is John who gives Him that name in the prologue to his Gospel, in the epistle that might well be called its companion piece, and in the book of Revelation. In the whole New Testament, the word *Logos* occurs only in these three parts. We may conclude from this that the term was not used in the catechesis that came from Peter and from Paul; but it must have been usual in the catechesis of John, for he uses it in the first verses of his writing with no explanation whatever, taking for granted that his readers know what he means. The term itself was a familiar one in Greek philosophy. But John's concept of the Logos is exclusively his own, with no true parallel in previous concepts. As for the word itself, John seems to have used it to express his concept because it was suited to his thought and already familiar in the Greco-Roman world that he wished to approach, in order to conquer it for the Logos Jesus.

It is said that whenever a tempest overtook Columbus in the course of his voyages, he would stand in the prow of his ship and there recite over the storm-tossed sea the beginning of the Gospel of John: "In the beginning was the Word, and the Word was with God, and the Word was God.... All things were made through him." Above the tumultuous elements of creation resounded the eulogy of the Logos who had created them; it was the explorer of the world commenting in his own fashion on the explorer of God.

∞

The Life of Christ

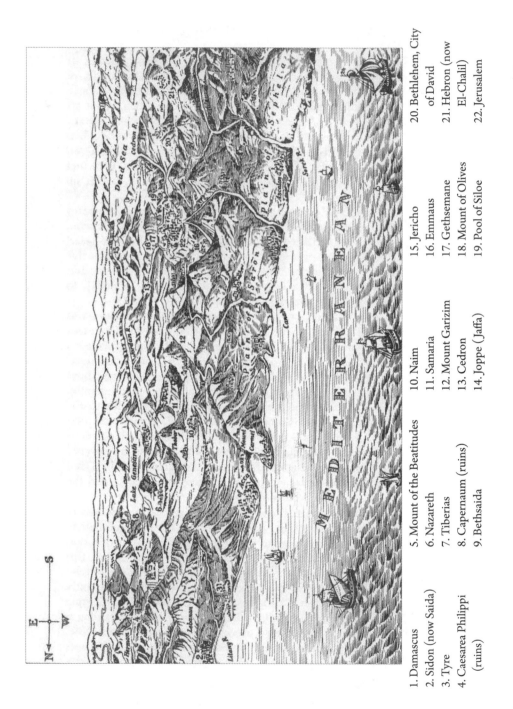

1. Damascus
2. Sidon (now Saida)
3. Tyre
4. Caesarea Philippi (ruins)

5. Mount of the Beatitudes
6. Nazareth
7. Tiberias
8. Capernaum (ruins)
9. Bethsaida

10. Naim
11. Samaria
12. Mount Garizim
13. Cedron
14. Joppe (Jaffa)

15. Jericho
16. Emmaus
17. Gethsemane
18. Mount of Olives
19. Pool of Siloe

20. Bethlehem, City of David
21. Hebron (now El-Chalil)
22. Jerusalem

Chapter 8

∞

Jesus' Life before His Public Ministry

The Whole World Being at Peace

In the years immediately preceding the Christian Era, the Roman Empire, or rather the whole then-known world, was at peace. The year 8 BC marks the beginning of a peace that is not disturbed until after the birth of Christ, when insurrections of Germans, Dalmatians, and Pannonians culminate in the defeat of Quintilius Varus in the Teutoburg forest (AD 9). In Rome, the Temple of Janus, which had been closed only twice in all the history of Rome before Augustus and twice by him, was now closed again in 8 BC, "the whole world being at peace," as the Church proclaims every year on the anniversary of Jesus' birth.

Augustus, the author of this Roman peace, had reached the peak of his glory. And in this period the master of the world was given honors hitherto unknown in the empire; temples and cities were dedicated to him, and he was proclaimed to be of divine, not human, origin. He was the "new Jove," "Jove, the Savior," the "star rising over the world."

Among all his titles, however, we do not find that Augustus was ever called the "prince of peace," as he may well have deserved. But seven centuries earlier, a Hebrew prophet did use this very expression, bestowing it on the future Messiah as a final and definitive title:

> For a child is born to us, and a son is given to us . . .
> and his name shall be called . . .
> the Prince of Peace. (Isa. 9:6)

It is true that in Hebrew the expression "prince of peace" has a much broader meaning than the same term in Latin. The Hebrew for the word for *peace* indicates "well-being," perfect "happiness." But along with "happiness," the future Messiah, whom the prophet foresaw as a "prince," could not fail to give his kingdom peace in the sense of freedom from war as well, for where there is war there is not only no peace but much less is there happiness.

The Tidings Brought to Zachary

It was the year 747 of Rome (7 BC) "in the days of Herod, king of Judea" (Luke 1:5). There was at that time a priest of the Temple of Jerusalem, named Zachary. He was wedded to Elizabeth, who was of a sacerdotal family, and they lived in the "hill country" of Judea. The town in which they made their home is not named for us, but tradition identifies it with the modern Ain-Karem (St. John in the Mountains), about four miles southwest of Jerusalem. The couple was advanced in years and had never been granted that most joyful blessing of a Hebrew household, children. Conscious that their whole lives had been dedicated to the great commandments of their religion, they wondered why God had denied them this consolation.

The time came for the class to which Zachary belonged to take its turn of service in the Temple. When the lots were drawn for the various daily functions, the privilege of offering incense on the altar of incense fell to Zachary. This offering was made twice daily, at the morning and the evening sacrifice. The altar of incense was in the "holy place," which only the priests might enter, while the faithful remained outside and watched from a distance as the priest came and went in the "sanctuary." When Zachary had entered the holy place, there appeared to him an angel of the Lord, standing at the right of the altar of incense. And Zachary was troubled and fearful. "But the angel

Ain-Karem today

said to him: Do not be afraid, Zachary, for thy petition has been heard, and thy wife Elizabeth shall bear thee a son, and thou shalt call his name John" (Luke 1:10–13). For the Hebrews more than any other people, the name was an *omen*, an augury; in this case, John meant "Yahweh (God of Israel) has shown mercy." The angel, in fact, continued to assure Zachary that in the birth of this son, he, the father, and many others would rejoice. The child would be great before God and he would not drink wine or any strong drink; he would be filled with the Holy Spirit even in his mother's womb, and he would summon many Israelites back to their God. More than that, he would be a precursor, who with the spirit and power of Elias would go before the Lord to prepare Him a fitting welcome from a people well-disposed.

The angel's announcement transcended all possible human expectations. According to the Holy Scriptures, certain prophets or other personages had been filled with the Holy Spirit on special occasions, but only of Jeremias do we read that in his mother's womb he had already been marked by God for a sublime mission. In ancient times the prophet Malachias had foretold that a precursor would appear before the Messiah, and all believed that this was to be the prophet Elias, who had gone to Heaven in a fiery chariot. But Elias could not be reborn as the son of Zachary nor could he infuse his spirit and power into another.

For these reasons, Zachary's first frightened awe was followed by a diffident suspension of judgment. "And Zachary said to the angel: How shall I know this [to be true]? For I am an old man, and my wife is advanced in years. And the angel answered and said to him: I am Gabriel, who stand in the presence of God, and I have been sent to speak to thee and to bring thee this good news. And behold thou shalt be dumb and unable to speak until the day when these things come to pass, because thou hast not believed my words, which will be fulfilled in their proper time" (Luke 1:18–20). The punishment, if it was really such, was an additional proof of the extraordinary promise.

Meanwhile the people were waiting for the priest to come out in order to chant the hymn that accompanied the sacrifice to be offered on the altar of holocausts, and they wondered at his delay. Finally, Zachary appeared on the threshold, but he did not pronounce the customary benediction over the people, nor could he "speak to them, and they realized that he had seen a vision in the temple. And he kept making signs to them, and remained dumb" (Luke 1:22).

When his week of service in the Temple was ended, Zachary, still mute, returned to his home. Shortly afterward, "Elizabeth his wife conceived, and secluded herself five months, saying: Thus has the Lord dealt with me in the days when he deigned to take away my reproach among men" (Luke 1:24–25).

The evangelist Luke, who is fond of coupling his episodes, immediately follows this incident with another that is very similar but at the same time marks a great advance in the fulfillment of the divine plan. The announcement and conception of the precursor is followed by the announcement and conception of the Messiah Himself.

The Annunciation

The scene of the second episode is laid far from Jerusalem, in Galilee in the north of Palestine. There, about eighty-eight miles from Jerusalem by the modern highway, lay Nazareth. Today it is a charming little city of about ten thousand inhabitants, but in Jesus' time it must have been anything but charming and nothing more than a negligible little village. The Gospels, which alone mention the village, record also the disparagement with which a man from that neighborhood was regarded: "Can anything good come out of Nazareth?" (John 1:46).

Nevertheless, there must have been a human settlement there from very ancient times. Recent archaeological probings have brought to light numerous caves opened in the side of the hill. The cruder of these served as storehouses for provisions, while the more comfortable ones, to the front of which some simple kind of construction had been added, served also as dwelling places. Since every human settlement in ancient Palestine seems to have been near

The white-walled houses of Nazareth

Nazareth today

some source of water, Nazareth, too, had its well. This is today called the Virgin's Fountain, and the apocrypha have woven many a fancy about it, but in Jesus' time it was perhaps the only reason why the thirsty caravans ever visited the village.

Now, in one of those dwellings in Nazareth lived a "virgin betrothed to a man named Joseph, of the house of David, and the virgin's name was Mary" (Luke 1:27). Mary, too, belonged to the house of David. The descendants of

The Virgin's Fountain

David had for centuries been living in obscurity, and not even during the national resurgence under the Maccabees did any of them distinguish themselves. Their simple life as ordinary private citizens had favored their leaving their place of origin, many of them going to settle in various parts of Palestine but without forgetting the ties that bound them to the family home.

The name *Mary*, in Hebrew *Miryam*, was common in Jesus' day, but we find it only once in the Old Testament, as the name of Moses' sister. Its meaning is completely uncertain notwithstanding the more than sixty interpretations that have been suggested for it. It would seem, too, that in Jesus' time the original Hebrew pronunciation had been modified to *Maryam* and that the word had acquired a new meaning.

The canonical Gospels tell us nothing of Mary's family and the apocrypha tell us too much. A "sister" of hers is mentioned only incidentally (John 19:25). We are told that Elizabeth was Mary's "kinswoman," but we do not know the degree of this relationship, which must have been through marriage because Elizabeth belonged to the tribe of Levi, while Mary, being of the family of David, belonged to the tribe of Juda. Perhaps Elizabeth's father was of Levite descent while her mother was from the house of David.

Now, six months after Elizabeth had conceived (Luke 1:26), the same angel Gabriel who had announced that event was sent by God to Mary in Nazareth, and when he "had come [in] to her, he said: Hail, full of grace, the Lord is with thee.... She was troubled at his word and kept pondering what manner of greeting this might be" (Luke 1:28–29). Similar to Zachary's is the bewilderment of the one beholding the sudden apparition; but in this case the perplexity is produced by the majestic words uttered. This was the troubled bewilderment of a humble spirit conscious of its own "lowliness." But Mary was not frightened, because even in the presence of the vision she "kept pondering in herself."

"And the angel said to her: Do not be afraid, Mary, for thou hast found grace with God. And behold thou shalt conceive in thy womb, and shalt bring forth a son; and thou shalt call his name Jesus. He shall be great, and shall be called the Son of the most High, and the Lord God will give him the throne of David his father, and he shall be king over the house of Jacob forever; and of his kingdom there shall be no end" (Luke 1:30–33). The angel's salutation had prepared the way somewhat for this message, profoundly solemn though it was. She who is "full of grace" and has the "Lord with her" finds the explanation of these privileges in the rest of the angel's message, which refers explicitly to the Messiah and uses the messianic expressions of the Old

Testament. The very name to be given the child is foretold, just as the name of Zachary's son had been. *Jesus*, Hebrew *Jeshuᵃ'*, means *Yahweh has saved*; hence the child's mission will be to bring salvation from Yahweh. In short, the angel has announced to Mary that she is to be the mother of the Messiah.

She does not question the message, nor does she ask for any definite sign. She begins instead to reflect on the humblest way in which her motherhood might be accomplished, and that was the natural way, by which all men, including Zachary's son, have been conceived. But she has one objection against this, and she presents it in the form of a question: "And Mary said to the angel: How shall this be done, because I know not man?" This is the usual Hebrew euphemism for the cause of natural conception. To appreciate Mary's question here, we must remember what Luke has just told us concerning her, that she was "a virgin betrothed to a man named Joseph."

Among the Hebrews, legal marriage took place, after certain preliminary arrangements, in two successive ceremonies, the betrothal and the wedding itself. The betrothal was not, as it is today, simply a promise to marry, but a perfectly legal marriage contract. Hence a betrothed woman was already a wife; her betrothed husband could send her a bill of divorce, and if he died, she was considered his widow. If she was unfaithful, she was punished as an adulteress. After this betrothal-marriage, the couple continued to live each with his respective family for a period. This was usually a year if the bride was a virgin and a month if she was a widow; and it was spent in preparing the new home and its furnishings.

The wedding took place after the aforementioned lapse of time and consisted of the bride's solemn reception into her husband's home. Then the legal formalities were over, and they lived together publicly as man and wife.

Generally, a girl was betrothed when she was twelve or thirteen years of age, and sometimes a little earlier. Hence, at the time of her marriage she would be thirteen or fourteen. That was probably Mary's age when the angel appeared to her. A man was betrothed between the ages of eighteen and twenty-four, and this was probably Joseph's age.

In conclusion, then, we know from Luke that Mary was a betrothed virgin; from Matthew (1:18) we learn besides that Mary was with child before she went to live with Joseph, that is, before the wedding. Now, in the light of this information, what do Mary's words to the angel mean: "How shall this be done, because I know not man?"

Considered in themselves, they can have only one of two meanings: either they refer to the well-known natural law by which every child must have a father, or they denote the intention not to submit to this law and therefore a renunciation of motherhood. However we examine them, it is impossible to discover a third meaning in them.

Now, when spoken by Mary, a betrothed girl, the words in question cannot have the first of these two meanings, because they would make no sense. To one who thus expressed herself, it would have been but natural to reply, "What has not happened until today may duly happen tomorrow." Hence, we must accept the second meaning, in which the verb "I know not" expresses an intention for the future. All languages, in fact, have some expression in which the present is used with future meaning, especially when it refers to a continued action or state in the future (e.g., I am not getting married).

Mary's difficulty, then, is expressed in her "I know not," an avowed intention for the future that justified her question, "How shall this be done?" Christian tradition, which has unanimously interpreted Mary's words in this manner, has, it is true, chosen the simplest and easiest way, but also the only reasonable one.

However, if Mary intended to remain a virgin, why had she consented to be betrothed according to the Jewish Law?

On this point we can find an explanation in the Jewish customs of the day. Ancient Hebraism looked with no favor on the unmarried state, and the chief concern of the family was to have as many children as possible. For the Hebrews, an unmarried woman was like a person without a head, "because the husband is head of the wife." This is still the attitude of the modern Arabs.

Hence, yielding to custom, Mary had been betrothed. But her intention to remain virgin, which she so confidently calls to the angel's attention, shows us the attitude of her spouse, Joseph, who would never have been accepted as such had he not agreed to respect Mary's intentions.

The angel refers to Mary's secret intention in his reply: "The Holy Spirit shall come upon thee, and the power of the Most High shall overshadow thee. And therefore also [He that is born shall be] holy . . . shall be called the Son of God." Mary's question is answered and her vow is safe. The power of God will descend directly upon her, and just as in ancient times in the desert the glory of Yahweh hung like a cloud over the Hebrew tabernacle, overshadowing it, so will He overshadow the living tabernacle that is the Virgin Mary, and the son who shall be born of her shall have no Father but God. Her son shall realize in perfect manner the title *Son of God*, which was true only figuratively of other personages in the Old Testament who had borne it. The Messiah could be called "Son" only by God, who gave Him His divine nature from eternity, and by His virgin Mother, from whom He took His human nature.

Now the angel's message has been fully and clearly presented. Mary has asked for an explanation; and she has received it. And this episode continues to unfold like that of Zachary. Just as he had received a definite sign, which he requested, so Mary is given a sign that she has not requested. Hence the angel continues: "And behold Elizabeth, thy kinswoman, also has conceived a son in her old age, for nothing shall be impossible with God."

Mary makes no reply to the sign she has not asked for; she simply answers: "Behold the handmaid of the Lord; be it done unto me according to thy word." The maiden in the little house in Nazareth, though chosen to be the Mother of the Messiah, is nevertheless fully aware of her "lowliness," and so she calls herself not God's minister nor His collaborator, but His "slave"; only then does she accept the invitation delivered by the angel.

And then the "Word was made flesh" (John 1:14): the Messiah was numbered among the children of men.

Seven centuries earlier, the prophet Isaias had prophesied an extraordinary *sign* from God in these words: "Behold a virgin shall conceive, and bear a son, and his name shall be called Emmanuel [God-with-us]." Matthew, who, as we have seen, is careful to point out how the messianic prophecies have been fulfilled, here quotes this one of Isaias as being verified by Jesus and His Mother (Matt. 1:22–23).

The Birth of John the Baptist

Immediately after the two parallel episodes, Luke gives us the meeting of the two heroines. Mary, to whom the news of Elizabeth's pregnancy had been given as a sign, set out to visit her kinswoman to rejoice with her; besides, the angel's words clearly indicated that special ties would exist between the two children soon to be born as they already did between their mothers. The trip from Nazareth to the "hill country" of Judea was not a short one. If we suppose that the town of Zachary was really Ain-Karem, it was about a four days' trip by caravan. But immediately after the Annunciation, Mary went "with haste," entered into the house of Zachary, and greeted Elizabeth.

At the meeting, the two mothers were given special divine illuminations. The angel had told Zachary his son would be filled with the Holy Spirit even from his mother's womb; Elizabeth, in her turn, had wrapped herself in a silence equal to Zachary's muteness, and she perhaps thought that no one

The desert country of Judea

knew of her pregnancy, just as she was certainly unaware of Mary's. But Mary's arrival shed a sudden light on everything.

> And it came to pass, that when Elizabeth heard the salutation of Mary, the infant leaped in her womb. And Elizabeth was filled with the Holy Ghost, and she cried out with a loud voice, and said: Blessed art thou among women, and blessed is the fruit of thy womb! And whence is this to me, that the mother of my Lord should come to me? For behold as soon as the voice of thy salutation sounded in my ears, the infant in my womb leaped for joy. And blessed [is she] who has believed [that] those things shall be accomplished that were spoken to [her] by the Lord. (Luke 1:39–45)

Before their encounter much of what had happened was clear to the two women, but much more was still veiled in mysterious shadow. Now their meeting was like a sudden dawn that throws into bold relief the whole landscape of God's plans.

The people of the Orient are easily given to improvising songs or poetry on occasions of great joy. In ancient times, Mary the sister of Moses, Deborah the prophetess, and Anna the mother of Samuel had on solemn occasions improvised canticles that were preserved in the Holy Scriptures and were certainly known to Mary. And in that hour of exultation, Mary, too, sang out her heart in poetry. Inspired by the Holy Scriptures and especially by the canticle of Anna, she recited her *Magnificat*:

> My soul doth magnify the Lord,
> and my spirit hath exulted
> in God my Savior,
> because he hath regarded the lowliness of
>   his handmaid;
>
> For lo, from henceforth, all generations
> shall call me blessed;
> because he who is mighty hath done great
>   things to me;
>   and holy is his name.
>
> And his mercy is from generation unto generations,
> to them that fear him.
> He hath shown might in his arm;
> he hath scattered the proud in the conceit
>   of their heart.
>
> He hath put down the mighty from their thrones,
> and hath exalted the lowly;
> he hath filled the hungry with good things;
> and the rich he hath sent empty away.
>
> He hath succored Israel his servant,
> being mindful of his mercy,
> as he spoke to our fathers,
> to Abraham and his seed forever. (Luke 1:46–55)

Insistent here is the contrast between lowliness and greatness, between humble poverty exalted and pride abased, between hunger that is satisfied and the fullness that still hungers. Mary sees in herself only the lowliness of the handmaid, but she is aware also that the powerful arm of God has raised up her littleness, accomplished great things in her, and she foresees that all generations shall call her blessed.

Could a more "unlikely" prophecy than this be imagined? It was about the year 6 BC, and an unknown little girl no more than fifteen years old, living in a tiny village, was confidently proclaiming that all generations would call her blessed!

Mary remained with Elizabeth for three months until it came time for her kinswoman to be delivered, and then she returned to Nazareth. We cannot be certain whether she was still at Zachary's house when John was born.

And when her time was come, Elizabeth gave birth to a son, and the news of the event brought her kinsfolk and neighbors to congratulate her. On the eighth day after his birth, the newborn infant was to be circumcised and receive his name, but here disagreement arose. Usually, the grandfather's name was bestowed on the firstborn in order to continue the family tradition and at the same time to avoid confusion between son and father. But in this extraordinary instance, when the father was dumb and as old as a grandfather besides, it seemed permissible to give the child his father's name. All, in fact, insisted that he be called Zachary, but his mother insisted that he be called John, and she well knew why this must be.

Her friends, however, could not understand her strange choice, especially since no one of Zachary's family had been called John. Only the father's decision could prevail over the mother's, and so the busybodies turned to him. But he was dumb, and perhaps deaf too, and they conveyed their difficulty to him with gestures. Then Zachary asked for a waxed tablet, such as was used for brief messages, and wrote on it: "John is his name." The matter was settled, and all were left wondering.

And "immediately" after the name was settled upon (Luke 1:64), Zachary recovered his speech and began to talk, blessing God. And he "was filled with the Holy Spirit and prophesied saying: Blessed be the Lord God of Israel ..." This is the canticle *Benedictus* (Luke 1:68–79), used so much in Christian liturgy; it exalts the fulfillment of the promises made by God to Israel and sees in the newborn child the precursor of this fulfillment, for he is to go "before the face of the Lord to prepare his ways."

The advent of the Savior, then, was imminent, for His herald had already appeared. The fact that the powerful of the time, within and outside of Israel, knew nothing of one or the other did not matter. God was not seeking the aid of the powerful to accomplish His plan of salvation. One thing only had God accepted from the potentates of the time — the peace that was reigning then throughout the world under the authority of Rome.

Before leaving the story of the newborn John to continue that of Mary, Luke anticipates a bit to tell us that "the child grew, and was strengthened in spirit; and was in the deserts until the day of his manifestation to Israel" (Luke 1:80). These deserts, where John probably went as a young man, were in all likelihood the regions southwest of Jerusalem known as the *desert of Judea.*

Joseph, the Spouse of Mary

Up to this point our informant has been Luke. Now we must listen to Matthew, too, who tells the story of Jesus' conception much more briefly but with one or two new details. In Matthew's narrative, Joseph, whom Luke barely mentions, also figures in the foreground. Now, just as we are justified in believing that Luke's principal informant was Mary herself, either directly or through John, so we may suppose that Matthew had informants from Galilee who had been associated with Joseph, as, for example, James, the "brother" of Jesus.

Matthew tells us that Mary is the spouse of Joseph and before they come together she is found with child. Joseph has not been forewarned of the supernatural conception and only later does he become aware of it — probably not until after Mary's return from her visit to Elizabeth in the fourth or fifth month of her pregnancy. When she returned to Nazareth, her physical condition was evident. "Whereupon Joseph her husband being a just man, and not willing publicly to expose her, was minded to put her away privately." Joseph, a legitimate "husband," could "have put Mary away" by giving her a bill of divorce, which would have exposed her to public reproach. To avoid this, he considers "putting her away privately," and he decides to do this "being a just man." This last phrase is the most important in the whole sentence and the true key to the explanation.

In a case of that kind, an upright Jew who was convinced of his wife's guilt would have given her a bill of divorce with no further ado, considering this not only his right but perhaps also his duty. Joseph, on the other hand, *because* he is a "just man," does not do this; therefore, he was convinced of Mary's innocence and consequently decided it was unjust to expose her to public dishonor.

On the other hand, how could Joseph explain Mary's condition? Did he think that, blameless herself, she had suffered violence during those months of absence? Mary's continued and deliberate silence — which would have been natural for a reserved maiden — might well favor a suspicion of that kind. Or did Joseph come closer to the truth and catch some glimmering of the supernatural, of the divine, in what had happened? We do not know, because Matthew says nothing about it; but from Joseph's decision to break his bond with Mary without injuring her reputation, we conclude that he acted both as one convinced of her innocence and as a "just man."

Joseph's perplexity was not allowed to last very long. "But while he thought on these things, behold, an angel of the Lord appeared to him in a dream, saying: Do not be afraid, Joseph, son of David, to take to thee Mary thy wife, for that which is begotten in her is of the Holy Spirit. And she shall bring forth a son, and thou shalt call his name Jesus; for he shall save his people from their sins" (Matt. 1:20–21). The name *Jesus* that the child was to receive had already been communicated to his mother; here the reason for the name is explained, for he "shall save" and so forth.

After the angel's warning, Joseph took Mary into his home. The usual wedding ceremonies were probably celebrated. Friends and relatives, no doubt, attended the modest little feast but certainly remained ignorant of the profound mystery hidden within the new family.

And Joseph, of the tribe of Juda and the house of David, a carpenter by trade, became the legal head of that little family.

The Birth of Jesus

The fact that Joseph and his family belonged to the house of David, originally of Bethlehem, soon had its legal consequences in the census ordered by Rome and carried out under Quirinius or Cyrinus as the name is Anglicized.

Oriental attachment to the place of family origin was and still is very strong. Among the Hebrews, a tribe was divided into great "families," and the families were subdivided into "paternal" houses, which in turn gave rise to new families that swarmed from the original hive to settle elsewhere. But wherever they went, the new family groups preserved the memory both of the family and its place of origin. They could tell you, for instance, that the tenth or the twentieth ancestor of the family was So-and-So, son of So-and-So, who had lived in such-and-such a village.

This attachment to the cradle of one's ancestry provided the basis for the census among the Jews. Hence, when the census was decreed, Joseph was obliged to present himself in Bethlehem "because he was of the *house* and *family* of David" (Luke 2:4), which came originally from Bethlehem.

Bethlehem is today a town of about seventy-five hundred inhabitants, situated approximately six miles south of Jerusalem and twenty-five hundred feet above sea level. Its name was originally *Beth-Lahamu*, "house of the god *Lahamu*," a Babylonian deity worshiped also by the Canaanites of that locality. When the Hebrews succeeded the Canaanites, the name came to be taken in the Hebrew sense, *bethlehem*, "house of bread." The house of Ephrata settled there, and from then on the place was also called Ephrata. Then, in the line descending from Isai (Jesse), David was born.

At the time of Jesus, Bethlehem was a humble little village. In the eighth century BC, the prophet Micheas had called it "little" among the many clans of

General view of Bethlehem

the tribe of Juda. The village and its surrounding country must have housed no more than one thousand inhabitants, most of them shepherds or poor peasants. It was, however, on the caravan road from Jerusalem to Egypt, and a stopover, or rather caravansary was built there by Chamaam, who was perhaps the son of one of David's friends, and it was therefore called the "hospice of Chamaam."

It is ninety-five miles by the modern highway from Nazareth to Bethlehem, and in Jesus' days the distance may have been somewhat less. Hence it was a three or four days' journey by caravan. It is not certain whether Joseph alone was obliged to appear personally in Bethlehem or whether Mary was also included in the decree. In either case, the fact is that Joseph went there "with Mary, his [betrothed] who was with child" (Luke 2:5). These last words may be a delicate reference to at least one of the reasons why Mary went too — that is, the fact that her time of delivery was near and she could not be left alone. But another reason — besides the possibility that she was included in the order — may have been that the two were thinking of moving permanently to Bethlehem. Since the angel had announced that God was to give the child the throne of David his father, what was more natural than to think of returning to the country of David to await the fulfillment of the mysterious plans of God? Several centuries before, the prophet Micheas had pointed to "little" Bethlehem as the place from which he would come who was to rule over Israel.

The journey must have been very tiring for Mary. The roads of the region were so poor the caravans of camels and donkeys could barely manage them. At that particular time, with all the confused traffic occasioned by the census, they must have been more crowded than usual and that much more uncomfortable. Our travelers may have had at best a donkey to carry their provisions and other necessary baggage — one of the same tribe of donkeys that can still be seen in Palestine today trudging ahead of a line of camels or following a group of foot travelers. The three or four stopovers required in the journey were perhaps spent in the homes of friends or more probably in the public inns, where, with the other travelers, they slept on the ground among the camels and donkeys.

In Bethlehem, conditions were even worse. The village was spilling over with people crowded into all the available lodgings and the caravansary. Luke calls it the inn, but it would be a mistake to think of it as even remotely resembling the most modest hostelry in any modern town. The caravansary of those days was a moderate-sized space enclosed by a rather high wall and having only one entrance. Along one or more sides of this wall ran a colonnade, which might be partitioned off at one point to form a large room with one or two smaller ones beside it. This was the whole "inn"; the animals were bedded down in the middle of the enclosure under the open sky, and the travelers took shelter in the portico or in the large chamber if there was room; otherwise they settled down with the animals. The smaller rooms, if any, were reserved for those who could pay for such luxury. And there, in the midst of that confused jumble of men and animals, some haggled and bargained while others prayed to God, some sang while others slept; a man might be born and another might die, all amidst that filth and stench with which the encampments of traveling Bedouins in Palestine reek even today.

Luke tells us that when Mary and Joseph arrived in Bethlehem, "there was no room for them in the inn" (2:7). This phrase is more studied than it seems at first. If Luke had meant merely that not another person could fit into the caravansary, it would have been enough to say "there was no room"; instead he adds "for them," which is an implicit reference to the fact that Mary was soon to give birth to her son. This may seem a subtlety, but it is not. In Bethlehem, Joseph undoubtedly had acquaintances or even relatives from whom he might have requested hospitality; though the village was crowded, some little corner could always be found for two such simple people. But naturally, at such times, even the poor little private houses, consisting usually of only one room on the ground floor, were as crowded as the inns and just as public, so far as the occupants were concerned; there was no privacy or reserve of any sort. Hence it is easy to understand why Luke specifies that there was no "room *for them*"; since her time was near, Mary was seeking privacy most of all.

"And it came to pass while they were there, that the days for her to be delivered were fulfilled. And she brought forth her first-born son, and wrapped him in swaddling clothes, and laid him in a manger" (Luke 2:6–7). Mention is made only of the "manger," but given the customs of the time, this clearly enough denotes a stable, which in those days meant a grotto or small cave cut in the side of one of the little hills near the village. The stable that Mary and Joseph found may have been already partially occupied by animals; it may have been dark and filthy, but it was somewhat removed from the village and therefore quiet and private, and that was enough for the expectant Mother.

Hence, when the two arrived in Bethlehem and saw the crowds of people, they made the best of the hospitality offered by the lonely cave in the hillside. There they decided to stay until they completed the formalities of the registration and the child was born, an event Mary expected at any moment. Joseph probably prepared some little corner in the place that seemed more comfortable and not quite so dirty. He perhaps made a bed of clean straw, took from the knapsack their provisions and other necessities, and arranged them on the manger attached to the wall, and there they were, completely settled.

In short, poverty and purity were the reasons why Jesus was born in a stable: the poverty of His legal father who did not have enough money to secure a private room among so many competitors, and the purity of His Mother who wished to surround His birth with reverent privacy.

When Jesus was born, Mary "wrapped him in swaddling clothes and laid him in a manger." In these words our physician-evangelist, with his usual delicacy, is telling us that the birth took place without the assistance of other persons. The Mother herself takes care of the newborn infant, wraps Him up and lays Him in the manger. Not even Joseph is mentioned here. It is only the later apocryphal narratives that become concerned about a midwife and make Joseph go about in search of one; in Luke's narrative there was no place for her. It was not for nothing that the expectant Mother had sought so anxiously a quiet and secluded place.

Thus Mary "brought forth her first-born son,"[5] whom the angel had heralded as heir to the "throne of David his father." But the future kingdom of

---

[5] The expression is typically Hebrew: "firstborn son" is the Hebrew *bekor,* a term of special legal significance because the firstborn was to be presented

the newborn babe — at least in these first manifestations — foreshadowed something very different from the other kingdoms of His day; for the royal audience chamber of this princely heir was a stable, His throne a manger, His canopy the cobwebs hanging from the roof, the clouds of incense the warm reek of the dung, and His courtiers two homeless human beings.

The kingdom of this prince, however, displayed even from its beginning certain characteristics that were completely new and unknown in the kingdoms of the time. Of the three persons composing that stable court, one represented virginity, one poverty, and all three humility and innocence. Just seven miles to the north glittered the court of Herod the Great, in which virginity was a completely unfamiliar word, poverty was abhorred, and humility and innocence took the form of attempts on one's father's life, the murder of sons, adultery, incest, and sodomy. The true contrast between the two lay not in the dung in the one and the gold in the other but in their moral characteristics.

In any case, the homage of courtiers was due the newborn descendant of David, courtiers whose social position was not too different from that of David, the shepherd, or the two permanent attendants to His manger throne. Besides, since the angel had said that the babe was to be called the "Son of the Most High," there was also due Him the homage of the courtiers of the Most High.

---

to the Temple, and Luke employs this word almost as if to prepare us for the presentation of Jesus in the Temple, which he alone of the four evangelists narrates. But the use of the term here has furnished the pretext for attributing to Luke the implied information that Mary later had other children, otherwise the word "firstborn" would not make sense. As early as the fourth century, St. Jerome answered this in his reply to Helvidius, the first exponent of this argument, pointing out that "Every only-begotten is a first born, though not every first born is an only son. First-born does not mean him after whom came others, but him before whom no child is born"; but in vain, and Lucian's argument continued to be repeated: "If he is the first he is not the only child; and if he is the only child he is not the first." It was natural that the Protestant Reformation should adopt Luke's words as a battle cry against the Catholic veneration for Mary.

In the year 5 BC, that is, a few months after the birth of Mary's "firstborn," a Jewish bride died in childbirth in Egypt. In her epitaph she is made to say among other things, "Destiny has led me to the end of my life in the birth-pangs for my first-born son." Contrary to the reasoning of Helvidius and his followers, the death of this young mother proves that her firstborn was also her only child, as in the case of Mary.

Now, Bethlehem was and still is on the edge of a plain, or rather an uncultivated tract that is good only for pasturing flocks. The few sheep owned by the inhabitants of the village were gathered at night into the surrounding caves and stables, but the large flocks remained always out on the heath night and day, summer and winter with shepherds to guard them. Shepherds like these had the very worst reputation among the scribes and Pharisees, for since they led a nomadic life on the plains where water was not abundant, they were dirty, smelly, ignorant of all the prescriptions regarding the washing of hands, the choice of foods, and so forth. They were, besides, reputed to be thieves.

But though excluded from the law courts of the Pharisees, these lowly shepherds enter the royal court of the newborn Son of David by invitation of the celestial courtiers of the Most High.

> And there were shepherds in the same district living in the fields and keeping watch over their flocks by night. And behold an angel of the Lord stood by them, and the glory of God shone round about them and they feared exceedingly. And the angel said to them: Do not be afraid, for behold, I bring you good tidings of great joy, which shall be to all the people. For there has been born to you today in the town of David a Savior, who is Christ the Lord. And this shall be a sign unto you: you will find the infant wrapped in swaddling clothes and lying in a manger. And suddenly there was with the angel a multitude of the heavenly host, praising God and saying:
>
> > Glory to God in the highest
> > and peace on earth among men of good will![6]
> >
> > (Luke 2:8–14)

---

[6] This "good will" is the divine good will toward men. Other early manuscripts have "good will" in the nominative; that would make a division into three verses, as follows:

> Glory to God in the highest
> and peace on earth:
> good will to men!

But a division of the thought in three verses is irregular, while two give us a perfect parallel (glory-peace; in the highest-earth; God-men); besides, the conjunction *and* would be more appropriate at the beginning of the third verse than the second, or would be necessary at the beginning of both.

Shepherds' field near Bethlehem

This episode follows immediately after the account of the Nativity, and it is undoubtedly the narrator's intention to show that only a few hours elapsed between the two. Hence, Jesus was born at night, and the vision of the shepherds also occurred at night.

After due praise had been offered to God in the highest heavens, one thing only was announced to the shepherds: "Peace on earth."

Now there was peace at that time, but it was a transitory peace, and its few years' duration were as so many seconds on the great timepiece of human existence. The *Savior*, that is *Christ* (Messiah) *the Lord*, took advantage of those few seconds to be born among men, and the first thing He did was to have His celestial courtiers proclaim *peace*. But His was a peace of new coinage, dependent upon an entirely new condition. The peace of those brief years depended upon the Roman Empire; it was a Roman peace, maintained with twenty-five legions.

The new peace of *Christ the Lord* was subject to the *good will* of God: those who become worthy of that good will and on whom it is bestowed will enjoy the new peace. They are the *peacemakers*, and they will be proclaimed blessed because their title is *children of God*.

The shepherds understood from the angel's appearance and his words that the Messiah had been born. They were rough, unlearned men, it is true, who knew nothing of the vast doctrine of the Pharisees; but as simple Israelites they did know of the Messiah promised by the prophets, and they had probably talked of Him often during their long night watches. Now the angel had given them a *sign* by which to recognize Him: they would find a child wrapped in swaddling clothes and lying in a manger. Perhaps the messenger had even pointed in the direction of the cave where they were to find Him. Hence these shepherds were still on familiar ground. They also took refuge in those caves against the rains or the cold. More than one of them, perhaps, had sheltered his wife in one while she gave birth to her baby and had laid his own newborn child in a manger. And now they heard that the Messiah Himself shared their humble circumstances. They went therefore "with haste" says Luke (2:16). They would, perhaps, have been slow to set out for the court of Herod had the Messiah been born there. Reaching the cave, they found Mary and Joseph and the infant. And they wondered. And being lordly in spirit, however poor of purse, they asked for nothing and went back to their sheep. But now they felt a great need of glorifying and praising God and of telling others what had happened.

Before bringing this episode to a close, the careful Luke points out that "Mary kept all of these words [meaning "events"], pondering them in her heart." This is another delicate reference to the source of his information.

The Purification

The Holy Family probably did not stay long in the cave, perhaps only a few days. As the census progressed, people left for home and there was more room in the houses of the village. One of them was taken by Joseph for his little family, and that was the "house" the Magi entered a few weeks later (Matt. 2:11). In this house perhaps the infant was circumcised, as the Law prescribed, eight days after His birth, receiving the name of Jesus, which had been spoken by the angel both to Mary and to Joseph.

Despite the fact that the child was the "Son of the Most High," Joseph and Mary fulfilled all the legal obligations toward Him. And they also fulfilled the prescriptions binding on themselves. According to the Hebrew Law, a woman after childbirth was considered unclean and must keep to herself for forty days, if her child was a boy, eighty if a girl. Then she was to present herself in the Temple for purification and make an offering, which, for the poor, was fixed at a pair of doves or pigeons. If the child was her first and a male, then according to the Law, he belonged to Yahweh like the firstlings of the flocks and the firstfruits of the field. Hence his parents were to buy him back by paying five shekels to the Temple. The child need not be brought to the Temple to present him to God, but the young mother usually did so to invoke upon him the blessings of Heaven.

These customs were observed in Jesus' case. After forty days Mary went up to the Temple to be purified, offering the prescribed gift of the poor, and she took Jesus with her to present Him to God and pay the five shekels. Though the two pigeons or doves cost very little, the five shekels represented a sizable sum for those as poor as Mary and Joseph. In fact, an artisan would barely have earned five silver shekels, about four gold dollars, in a whole two weeks of labor, and Joseph probably had had little or no opportunity to work during their time in Bethlehem. However, the meager savings that probably accompanied them from Nazareth no doubt took care of this expense, which they had surely foreseen.

There certainly was nothing about that group of three entering the Temple of Jerusalem to attract the attention of the people idling in its porticoes, listening to the discussions of the teachers or trading in the "Court of the Gentiles." So many young mothers came every day that there was no reason why our three should receive special notice. But on that particular day there was one there in the court who was able to see what the others did not: "And behold, there was in Jerusalem a man named Simeon, and this man was just and devout, looking for the consolation of Israel; and the Holy Spirit was in him. And it had been revealed to him by the Holy Spirit, that he should not see death, before he had seen the Christ of the Lord" (Luke 2:25–26).

Of this Simeon we are told only that he was "just and devout," and all we can gather from his words is that he was advanced in years. There is nothing to indicate that he was a priest, much less the high priest as one of the apocrypha would have it. He was an ordinary layman who kept apart from political activities and lived in the fear of God, busied with his pious works as the shepherds of Bethlehem were busy with their sheep, and like them he was "waiting for the consolation of Israel," the Messiah. And just as the shepherds were informed by the angel, Simeon was forewarned by the Holy Spirit that his expectation was to be fulfilled. Thus, on that day he "came by inspiration of the Spirit into the Temple. And when His parents brought in the child Jesus, to do for Him according to the custom of the law, he also received Him into his arms, and blessed God, saying:

> Now thou dost dismiss thy servant, O Lord
> — according to thy word — in peace!
> Because my eyes have seen thy salvation,
> which thou hast prepared before the face of all peoples:

> A light of revelation to the Gentiles,
>   and a glory for thy people Israel.
>
>   (Luke 2:27–32)

Now the aged man desired no more; now he could set out on the journey from which no traveler returns. Yet even "his [the child's] father and mother were marveling" (Luke 2:33) at his words, whereupon the contemplative turned to them. But as Mary alone had the precious prerogative of a real parent, it was to her that Simeon addressed himself: "Behold this child is destined for the fall and for the rise of many in Israel, and for a sign which shall be contradicted. And thy own soul a sword shall pierce, that the thoughts of many hearts may be revealed" (2:34–35).

Is it perhaps that in the salvation wrought by that child, the Mother is to be so united with her Son that it will be impossible to strike Him without wounding her at the same time?

Luke, who is fond of twin episodes, gives us next the incident of Anna.

He calls her a "prophetess," and there have been others in ancient Israel. This Anna was truly a woman of God. Left a widow after seven years of marriage, she had spent her life in the Temple courts in fasting and prayer, and she was now eighty-four years old. She, too, "coming up at that very hour ... began to give praise to the Lord, and spoke of him [the infant Jesus] to all who were awaiting the redemption of Jerusalem" (2:38).

The Magi

Besides the heavenly ministers, Luke has pictured for us around the newborn Messiah only very humble courtiers, the shepherds and the two old people in the city. Matthew mentions none of these but presents instead personages who are not only eminent but in addition — and this is rather unexpected in the most Israelite of the four evangelists — they are not Israelites and therefore are numbered among the abhorred Gentiles. If Luke had given us this new episode, we should have said that he did so to show the fulfillment of Simeon's prophecy regarding the "revelation of the Gentiles"; but since it is Matthew there is nothing to do but accept the facts.

> Now when Jesus was born ... there came Magi from the East to Jerusalem, saying: "Where is the newly born king of the Jews? For we have seen his star in the East and have come to worship him." But when King Herod heard this, he was troubled, and so was all Jerusalem with him. And gathering together all the chief priests and Scribes of the people,

he inquired of them where the Christ was to be born. And they said to him: "In Bethlehem of Judea; for so it is written by the prophet: 'And thou Bethlehem, of the land of Juda, art by no means least among the princes of Juda; for from thee shall come forth a leader who shall rule my people Israel.'" (Matt. 2:1–6)

The unexpected strangers were *magi*, and they came from the East. This is our only specific information concerning them, and it is vague enough. The vaguest term of all is the *East*, which, geographically speaking, indicated all the regions beyond the Jordan, where we find first the vast Syro-Arabian desert, then Mesopotamia (Babylonia), and finally far-distant Persia. Now, it is precisely to Persia rather than to either of the two nearer regions that the word *magi* takes us, a word that is Persian in origin and intimately associated with Zoroaster (Zarathustra) and his teaching.[7]

The *magi* originally were the disciples of Zoroaster. As a class they seem very powerful in most ancient times and remained powerful in the Persian Empire down to the eighth century after Christ. They probably studied the movements of the stars as all learned people did in those days and regions, but they certainly were not astrologers and sorcerers.

The Magi who had come to Jerusalem had seen a star in the East, understood that it was the star of the "king of the Jews," and consequently journeyed from the East to adore Him.

As for the star, I have already stated my opinion that Matthew intended to present it as miraculous and that it is therefore not to be identified with any meteor or comet. Shortly afterward he will tell us that when the Magi left Jerusalem, the star went before them like a torch to show them the way. But given the miraculous nature of the star, how can we explain the fact that the Magi recognized it as the star of the "king of the Jews"? What did they, in far-off Persia, know of a king of the Jews awaited in Palestine as the Savior?

The fact that the Magi recognize the star is, in Matthew's narrative, associated with the very nature of the star itself; that is, the miraculous phenomenon is miraculously recognized as the sign of the newborn king. Thanks to recent studies we know much more today than formerly about

[7] Zoroaster, a Persian religious leader, lived about seven hundred years before Christ. His religious teaching was marked by unusual spirituality and moral insight and marked an advance among non-Jewish people toward pure morality and belief in one God.

the Magi's cultural background and possible knowledge of the messianic expectations of the Jews. We know that in accordance with a native tradition, the Persians were awaiting a kind of savior and that they knew of a similar expectation in Palestine.

Matthew does not tell us how many Magi came; popular tradition set the number anywhere from two to twelve but favored the number three, undoubtedly because of the three gifts they offered. Around the ninth century it even names them, Caspar, Melchior, and Balthasar.

These strangers are completely unaware of the political conditions in Jerusalem, for as soon as they enter the city they begin to ask: "Where is he that is born of the Jews?" There was no king of the Jews but Herod, and it was enough to know the very least about his character to be sure that any possible competitor would no sooner be discovered than his days if not his hours would be numbered. Hence, in the very interests of the child they sought, that question was as dangerous as it was naïve.

The aged tyrant, who on the mere suspicion of conspiracy had murdered two of his sons and was about to murder a third, could not fail to be upset at the inquiry. But he saw immediately that if it did conceal a threat, it was a far different one from any of the others he had taken care of. At the bottom of all this was some religious superstition, very likely that old daydream about the Messiah-King for whom his subjects were waiting but whom he was not expecting in the least. In any case, it would be well to take precautions. He would get definite information first, then play his hand craftily as usual.

Since this was obviously a religious question, Herod consulted not the whole Sanhedrin but the two groups in it who were most skilled in such matters, that is, the "chief priests and Scribes of the people," and he set before them the abstract question "where the Christ [the Messiah] was to be born."

His consultants answered that the Messiah was to be born in Bethlehem, and they quoted as proof a passage of Micheas: "And thou, Bethlehem Ephrata, though thou art little among the thousands[8] of Juda, out of thee shall come forth for me (one who shall be) ruler in Israel, and his goings forth [his origin] are from of old, from ancient days. Therefore shall he [God] deliver them [to the power of the enemy] till the time wherein she that is to give birth has borne." The reply of the scribes as recorded by Matthew is not a complete or exact quotation of the prophet's words, but the meaning is the same. Bethlehem

---

[8] A thousand was the numerical basis for divisions of the population in ancient times.

is named as the birthplace of the Messiah. Hence this designation was the traditional Jewish one in those days.

The answer must have puzzled Herod. Bethlehem was an ordinary little place, and his agents there had noticed nothing suspicious. Nevertheless, the star, the unknown Magi, and especially that title of "king of the Jews" all combined to excite his curiosity and to disturb his peace. To satisfy the one and restore the other, there was nothing to do but use the Magi in such a way as not to arouse their suspicions or anyone else's.

That was what Herod did. He sent for the Magi "secretly" (Matt. 2:7), for he wished neither to appear too gullible in attaching much importance to persons who were perhaps a little unbalanced nor to forego his precautionary measures. Having questioned them on the time and the manner in which the star had appeared, he let them go on to Bethlehem; as soon as they found the newborn child, they were to let Herod know so that he, too, might go to adore him.

After their audience, the Magi "went their way. And behold, the star that they had seen in the East went before them, until it came and stood over the place where the child was. And when they saw the star they rejoiced exceedingly. And entering the house, they found the child with Mary his mother, and falling down they worshipped him. And opening their treasures they offered him gifts of gold, frankincense, and myrrh. And being warned in a dream not to return to Herod they went back to their own country by another way" (Matt. 2:9–12). We have only the skeleton of the story, with no details of time or place. But we may gather that the Magi spent at least one night in Bethlehem since they were warned "in a dream." We learn, too, that Joseph's family had left the cave and were living in a house.

Since they were going to do homage to a "king," the Magi had brought the offerings required by Oriental etiquette. The palace of Herod in Jerusalem shone with gold, and clouds of fragrant resin and incense rose from the censers along its halls and porticoes. In keeping, then, with the ceremonial of the courts, the Magi offered gold, incense, and the fragrant resin that all Semitic peoples called *mor*, whence our word *myrrh*. Herod himself was lavish with gifts to other kings, especially those more powerful than himself. The Magi could not be as munificent as Herod, but in compensation they had the joy of seeing their gifts accepted and of realizing besides that they were very timely. While all three were an acknowledgment of the royal dignity of the infant, the gold particularly was a boon to the strained finances of that little court that owned nothing, not even the roof above it.

Having offered their homage, the travelers departed after a while for their own country, though not by way of Jerusalem and Jericho, but perhaps by that other road that skirted the Herodian fortress of Masada and ran along the edge of the western shore of the Dead Sea. And nothing more was ever heard of them.

The Slaughter of the Innocents

Herod, meanwhile, was waiting for the Magi to return. But as the days passed and they failed to appear, he must have suspected that his plan had not been quite cunning enough. When his suspicions became certainties, he became himself again and, in one of those terrible rages that generally preceded his orders for slaughter, he made a typically Herodian decision. He commanded that all male children under two years of age in Bethlehem and its surroundings be killed. He based the age limit on what the Magi had told him concerning the apparition of the star, allowing a generous margin in order to be sure that the child would not escape him.

But the child did escape, for though He did not have Herod's secret police at His service, He had about Him the heavenly courtiers who had attended Him on the night of His birth. Before Herod's assassins could arrive, an angel appeared in a dream to Joseph and said to him: "Arise, and take the child and his mother, and flee into Egypt, and remain there until I tell thee; for Herod will seek the child to destroy him" (Matt. 2:13). Joseph set out that very night on the road that led away from Jerusalem toward Egypt.

While the three fugitives, with perhaps the usual little donkey, stopped at Hebron or Beersheba to make some provisions before braving the desert, Herod's order was being carried out in Bethlehem. The male children, two years old and under, were all murdered.

What probably was the number of victims? A likely bit of information tells us that Bethlehem and its territories numbered slightly more than one thousand inhabitants, and we may conclude from this that there were about thirty babies born there every year. In two years, there would be sixty. But since the sexes are about equally represented and Herod had no reason to destroy the girl babies, only one-half of the newly born would have fallen victim to his cruelty, namely, the thirty male children. Even this number is too large, however, because infant mortality in the Orient is very high and a goodly number of babies never reach the age of two. Hence, we may set our figure between twenty and twenty-five.

This inhuman slaughter unquestionably has historical value; it is perfectly in keeping with Herod's character. But if Augustus had been informed of it, the news would not have created much stir in Rome.

A few months after the massacre in Bethlehem, the monster who ordered it, now long since reduced to a mass of rotting flesh, sank to his death. The true finesse of history, however, is to be seen not so much in his death as in his burial. He was entombed on the Herodium, from whose summit could be seen the site of the cave in which his feared rival had been born and the place where the slaughtered babies had been buried. Today from the top of the Herodium you will see nothing but ruins and desolation. Only in the direction of Bethlehem are there any signs of life.

The Sojourn in Egypt

Meanwhile, the three fugitives of Bethlehem had entered the desert. Keeping step with their little donkey, anxiously trying to follow the less beaten trails, looking behind every now and then to see if they were being followed by the soldiery, they drew farther away from human intercourse and remained isolated for at least a week, which is the probable length of their journey.

In order to make time, they must have taken the comfortable road, which passed through Hebron and Beersheba; but at a certain point they probably turned right to find the old caravan route, which skirted the Mediterranean and joined Palestine to Egypt. At Beersheba began the barren wasteland, but the ground was still solid underfoot. Farther down, however, nearer the delta of the Nile, begins the real desert, the "sea of sand," where there is never a bush or a blade of grass or a stone.

According to the apocrypha, the crossing of this region was a triumphal procession for the fugitives, for the wild beasts ran to crouch meekly at the

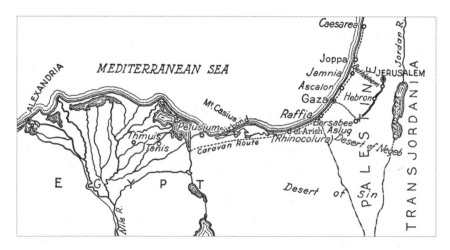

The old caravan route between Palestine and Egypt; probable route of the flight

A desert scene

feet of Jesus and date palms lowered their branches that He might gather their fruit. In reality, the journey must have been difficult and exhausting, especially because of the lack of water.

In 55 BC the same journey was made by the Roman officers of Gabinius, who knew more than a little about difficult traveling yet feared that crossing more than the war that was awaiting them in Egypt (Plutarch, *Antony*, 3).

Our three travelers had to drag themselves over the shifting sands in the exhausting heat by day, spend their nights on the ground, and sustain themselves with the little food and water they were able to carry with them. And their journey lasted a good week. A modern European or American can form a clear picture of such a journey only if he has spent sleepless nights in the open in the desolate wastes of Idumaea (the Negeb of the Bible) and by day has watched some small band of travelers toil by through the sandy mist overhanging the desert, their donkey laden with provisions or bearing a woman with a child at her breast, the little company proceeding in thoughtful silence to disappear across the solitude. Anyone who has had such an experience has seen more than just a bit of local color; he has witnessed historical evidences of the journey of the three refugees from Bethlehem.

At Rhinocolura, Herod's threat ceased, for that marked the boundary between his kingdom and Roman Egypt. From there to Pelusium the journey was less worried if no less difficult. At Pelusium, the usual entrance into

Egypt, there were other human beings and various conveniences, and the gold brought by the Magi must have rendered excellent service.

Matthew tells us nothing of the place nor the length of time of the sojourn in Egypt (though the apocrypha and later legends, as usual, tell us a great deal); nevertheless, we can be reasonably sure the stay was brief. If Jesus was born at the end of the year 748 of Rome, the flight into Egypt could have taken place only a few months later, that is, after the forty days of Mary's purification and the arrival of the Magi. Since this interval may represent several weeks or several months, the flight is usually assigned to spring or summer of the year 749.

The fugitives had been in Egypt a few months when news came of Herod's death, which occurred in March or April of the year 750. And then once more the angel appeared in a dream to Joseph and commanded him to return with the child and its Mother "into the land of Israel" (Matt. 2:20). And the refugees went back to their own country.

Nazareth

When they reached Palestine, Joseph learned that Herod's son Archelaus was governing Judea and therefore Jerusalem and Bethlehem. Since the new ruler's reputation was an evil one, he decided not to return to their former dwelling and thus renounced the intention — if indeed it had been an intention — to settle in Bethlehem. In his perplexity, he was given another revelation in a dream, and as a result he returned to Nazareth, ruled not by Archelaus but by Antipas. Matthew closes the incident by stating that they settled in Nazareth "that there might be fulfilled what was spoken through the prophets: He shall be called a Nazarene" (2:23).

When Joseph returned to Nazareth, toward the middle of the year 750 of Rome, the child Jesus was about two years old. From this time until the beginning of His public ministry there runs a period of more than thirty years in which He lived a hidden life. Of all this long time we know nothing except for two bits of information, both preserved by Luke, the historian whose source is the recollections of Jesus' Mother.

In the first place, the physician-evangelist states that when the three settled in Nazareth "the child grew, and became strong, full of wisdom; and the grace of God was upon him" (Luke 2:40); and shortly afterward, as if to point out that this continued, he repeats that at the age of twelve Jesus was advancing "in wisdom and age, and grace with God and men" (2:52).

Hence Jesus developed not only outwardly in the sight of men, but inwardly before God. As He grew in body and His sensitive and intellective

General view of Nazareth

faculties developed, so did He grow in experiential knowledge; He developed gradually through childhood, boyhood, young manhood, and maturity both physically and intellectually.

The other item Luke gives us concerning these years is that on one occasion Jesus was lost and found again in Jerusalem.

The parents of Jesus — so Luke (2:41) calls them simply — went up to Jerusalem every year for the Pasch, as every good Israelite did on this most important of the "feasts of the pilgrimage." Mary, being a woman, was not obliged by law to go and neither was Jesus before His thirteenth year. Yet many women accompanied their husbands, and the more devout fathers used to take their children with them even before their thirteenth year. Certainly Jesus was taken there even as a small child, but this episode occurred when He was twelve.

From more distant places like Nazareth, pilgrims made the journey with relatives or friends, forming little caravans that traveled and spent the nights together at the stopovers along the route. There must have been three or four such night stops between Nazareth and Jerusalem, the distance being about seventy-five miles (eighty-eight by the modern road). They reached the Holy City a day or two before the feast and stayed there through the Pasch or for the whole octave. That year, when it came time for the departure, Jesus remained behind in Jerusalem without His parents' noticing it. Though He was not with them, the two had no reason to suspect that He had stayed in the city.

The Oriental caravan is governed by a discipline all its own, with nothing strict about it. Everyone obeys the schedule for departure and arrival, but otherwise they are perfectly free. Along the road the party may break up into any number of groups journeying a certain distance apart, and the travelers may shift from one group to another as they wish. Only in the evening do they all meet again as they reach the stopover for the night. Any boy of twelve, who among the Jews was almost "on his own," shared this easy discipline with his elders and probably enjoyed it much more than they, while he knew very well how to conduct himself. Thus, during the first day's journey, Jesus' parents thought He was with some other party in the caravan, but when they arrived at the first stopping place and looked for Him among the various groups coming in, they realized He was missing.

In great distress, they turned back to Jerusalem, and the next day was spent partly in the return journey and partly in their first inquiries through the city, all of which proved fruitless, so that they were obliged to continue the search until the third day. Then

> they discovered him in the temple, sitting among the doctors of the Law, listening to them and asking them questions; and all his hearers were amazed at his understanding and his answers. And when they saw him they [his parents] were struck with astonishment, and his mother said to him: "My Child, why hast thou treated us so? Indeed thy father and I have been searching for thee in great distress!" "Why did you search for me?" he asked them. "Did you not know that I must be in my father's house?"[9] Now they did not comprehend what he said to them. (Luke 2:46–50)

At the end of the same century, Flavius Josephus wrote that when he was fourteen years old, he was already famous in Jerusalem for his knowledge of the Law and that the chief priests and other prominent people used to consult him on difficult questions. Many other passages in his works betray him as something of a boaster and a humbug, hence we have every right not to believe what he writes here. But there may be a kernel of truth in the incident insomuch as, being of lively intelligence, he may casually have engaged now and then in a kind of discussion with some doctors of the Law who had come

---

[9] This seems to be the meaning of the Greek text; it is the interpretation favored by the early Fathers, especially the Greeks. The English renderings are divided on this point and the Douay has "about my Father's business." — Trans.

to his house for other reasons. In fact, the rabbis accepted into their schools little boys of six; and naturally they paid more attention to those who seemed more intelligent and engaged in discussion with them as equals.

But the scene described by Luke is entirely different from that in Josephus. Jesus is in the Temple, in one of the courts where the doctors habitually gathered for discussions. He does not dictate opinions but conforms to the regular procedure of the rabbis, which consisted of listening, asking questions, and proceeding with order so that the solution of the problem would result from the combined contribution of all taking part in the discussion. But the contribution of this unknown boy was so extraordinary both for the appropriateness of His questions and the keenness of His observations that the first to be astonished at Him were the subtle jurists of Jerusalem.

And Mary and Joseph, who probably heard some of the discussion as they waited for it to end, were astonished too. Yet their amazement was different from that of the doctors; it was the wonder of those who know many things but who have not yet foreseen all their consequences and especially have never before seen those consequences in action. Mary's grieved exclamation was natural for a mother. Her son answers her as the Son more of a heavenly Father than of an earthly mother. If He has for the moment abandoned His human family, it is for the one reason that could have prompted Him to do so, that is, the fact that He was in the spiritual house of His heavenly Father. Jesus' answer is a summary of all His future mission.

Luke, who is writing after the event, can interpret Jesus' answer in this way, that is, not as referring to the material Temple of Jerusalem as the words might first suggest. But being a precise historian, he adds immediately that Jesus' parents "did not comprehend what he said to them." They did not understand, although they knew so many things about Jesus, for the same reason that they were so amazed when they found Him among the doctors. They had not foreseen all the consequences of the things they knew. And who could have confessed this bewilderment at Jesus' answer if not Mary herself.

That is why Luke repeats here again his precious reference: "And his mother kept all these words in her heart" (2:51). It is still another discreet and respectful allusion to his source.

We know nothing else of those thirty years that Jesus spent in Nazareth. Returning there after the episode in the Temple, He was "subject to them," to Mary and Joseph.

Big things had been happening around the world in those thirty years. In Rome, the temple of Janus was reopened, for the period of world peace was ended. In Judea, Archelaus left for exile and Roman procurators took his place. Augustus, at the age of seventy-six, ceased to be the master of this world and became a god in the next by decree of the senate. In Nazareth, meanwhile, it was as though Jesus did not exist. Similar outwardly to all those of His own age, He danced on His Mother's knee, then helped her child-fashion, then assisted Joseph in the shop, later began to read and write, recited the customary prayers, attended the synagogue. As a young man He probably took an interest in the fields and the vineyards, in the work Joseph was doing, in questions concerning the Jewish Law, in the Pharisees and Sadducees, in political events in Palestine and abroad. To all appearances, His days were spent quite simply in this wise.

His daily language was Aramaic, spoken with the accent peculiar to the Galileans, which betrayed them the minute they began to talk. But since His country was a border territory in which there was continual contact with the surrounding Greek populations, a certain knowledge of Greek was almost necessary. Hence it is probable that He used Greek sometimes and even more probable that He used Hebrew.

Jesus also had relatives. As His Mother had a "sister" (John 19:25), so He had "brothers" and "sisters" who are mentioned more than once by the evangelists (and also by Paul, 1 Cor. 9:5). Four of these "brothers" are known to us by name — James, Joseph, Simon, and Jude (Matt. 13:55; Mark 6:3). His "sisters" are not named, but there must have been several because mention is made of "all" of them (Matt. 13:56). The mention of such a numerous troop of relatives is in complete harmony with the customs of the Orient, where the ties of kinship are traced out and cherished in their most distant ramifications. Hence those who are closest are designated by the term *brothers* and *sisters*, though they may be only cousins of various degree. In the Hebrew Bible the nouns meaning "brother" and "sister" often denote persons far removed in kinship, especially since in ancient Hebrew there is no precise term for cousin exclusively. The "brothers" and "sisters" of Jesus, therefore, were His cousins.

Now, not all these many relatives looked on Jesus with favor. In the middle of His public life we find that "not even his brethren believed in him" (John 7:5). Nor is it reasonable to suppose that this antipathy began with Jesus' public life. It was rather the open manifestation of an old feeling toward Him that had brooded in the hearts of His kinsmen even during His life in Nazareth. Jesus Himself gives us the reason for this, though in general terms: "A prophet is not without honor except in his own country, and among his own kindred, and in his own house" (Mark 6:4). In any case, besides these resentful kinsmen there were others most faithful to Him, who undoubtedly surrounded Him with their kindness even while He was still an obscure boy. First among them all were Mary and Joseph, then "James the brother of the Lord" (Gal. 1:19), that is, James the Less, then others (Acts 1:14), some of whom perhaps had shed with time their earlier resentment.

After the account of Jesus' childhood, we find no further mention of Joseph, nor do we catch any glimpse of him during the public life. Everything points to the supposition that Jesus' legal father died during the hidden years of his son's life. If he had survived those years as Mary did, some mention of him would surely have been preserved in the ancient catechesis and therefore in the Gospels that derive from it. Officially nothing remained of him except the title of his fatherhood, which he bequeathed with his trade to his putative son: "Is not this the carpenter's son?" (Matt. 13:55); "Is not this the carpenter, the son of Mary ...?" (Mark 6:3).

Chapter 9

⟨∞⟩

From the Beginning of the Public
Ministry to the First Pasch

John the Baptist; the Baptism of Jesus

Up to this point, Luke's narrative has been divided between John the Baptist and Jesus. The evangelist has left them both boys, saying of each that he was growing in strength and wisdom.

At the end of these thirty hidden years, John appears in public to be followed soon afterward by Jesus. John has been announced as the precursor or herald, and such he is to be much more in his public life than in his unnoticed birth.

During his long sojourn in the desert, John had lived an austere, solitary life. Since, when he appears in public, we find him "clothed in camel's hair, with a leathern girdle about his loins, and eating locusts and wild honey" (Mark 1:6), we may suppose this was his way of life during the years of solitude. After all, both his dress and his food were usual with those who thus lived a hermit's life. Even today the Bedouins of Palestine weave their cloaks of camel's hair and for want of something better eat locusts, which they sometimes dry and store.

In the fifteenth year of the reign of Tiberius, "the word of the Lord came to John, the son of Zachary, in the desert" (Luke 3:2). His mission to prepare the way for the coming Messiah is about to begin, and he inaugurates it by proclaiming: "Repent, for the kingdom of heaven is at hand!" (Matt. 3:2). From this general announcement, he comes down to particulars. Of all those who come to him he demands two rites — a physical ablution and open confession of their sins. Noticing many Pharisees and Sadducees among those flocking out to him, he greets them with the words: "Brood of vipers! Who has shown you how to flee from the wrath to come? Bring forth therefore fruit befitting repentance, and do not think to say within yourselves: We have Abraham for our Father. For I say to you that God is able out of these stones to raise up children to Abraham. For even now the axe is laid to the root of the trees. Every tree therefore that is not bringing forth good fruit is to be cut down and cast into the fire" (Matt. 3:7–10).

Of the many messianic preachers both before and after John, all without exception declared that the sons of Abraham were the first people of the earth, and to assure a real political supremacy for them, they all had recourse to arms. But it absolutely never occurred to any of them to improve his followers morally.

John traveled in the opposite direction. He declared that sons of Abraham could rise up from the stones; he promised no kingdoms or supremacy; he appealed to no armed force; he ignored political matters; he worked no miracles; he was poor and naked; but one moral admonition contained all his preaching: the Kingdom of God is close at hand, hence change your way of thinking!

In fact, the very first word of his proclamation, "Repent!" meant just this: "Change your way of thinking!" The Greek word means "change your mind"; in Hebrew it means to "return" from a false road in order to set out on the right one. In both languages the idea is the same, a complete change in the heart of man.

Now, deep, sincere feeling naturally seeks expression, and an external act may be evidence of an inner spiritual one. So John required those "changing their way of thinking" to confess their sins as sign of the change, and to undergo a physical ablution as its proof and symbol.

In other ancient religions, public acknowledgment of sins and some form of bodily washing were included in special rites for the reason that the first answers a natural impulse of the human spirit when it becomes conscious of wrongdoing, and the second is the easiest and most spontaneous symbol of spiritual cleanliness.

Judaism practiced both rites on various occasions. John's originality lay in the fact that he required these rites as preparation for the Kingdom of God, which he now proclaimed as near at hand.

Hence this kingdom concerned the spirit above all else just as these rites did, completely unlike those heralded by all other messianic preachers. The kingdom heralded by John was altogether new. If his teaching was not completely original, that was because it was directly related to the ancient teaching of Israel's authentic prophets. They, too, had insisted on works of justice much more than on the ceremonies of the liturgy, on the circumcision of the heart more than that of the flesh; they, too, traveled the road of the spirit more than that of ritual formalism. And it was precisely this road of the spirit, too often forsaken by Judaism of his own day, which John entered anew. The old standard-bearers of Israel, the prophets, had long since vanished. Now John rose up as the last and final prophet. Later, in fact, Jesus is to say: "Until John came, there were the Law and the Prophets; since then the kingdom of God is being preached" (Luke 16:16).

Many flocked from Judea and Jerusalem to hear John preach. His immediate and permanent disciples led the same austere life, but with the others who came to him he was very understanding and forgiving. He commanded neither publicans nor soldiers to forsake their professions; he merely ordered the former not to be extortionate and the latter not to commit violence. This gentle attitude did not please the Pharisees and Sadducees, who had run out with the crowd to hear him and had elicited the far-from-gentle invective quoted above, and later the scribes and Pharisees especially took their revenge by questioning or openly denying the legitimacy of his mission. Despite these difficulties, however, the current started by John became very powerful.

John lingered for the most part along the banks of the Jordan, at that part of the river most accessible to those coming from Jerusalem, that is, a little above its entrance into the Dead Sea. It was a convenient place to perform the ablution ceremonies in the river. He did go elsewhere on occasion, however, probably when the heavy rains left the riverbank slippery with mud or the current dangerous.

The Jordan — a possible site of Our Lord's baptism

Meanwhile, the crowds thronging to hear him were growing, and among them the question had begun to circulate as to whether he was not the Messiah; the profound moral difference between him and other preachers of the messianic kingdom had impressed everyone. But John abruptly quashed this tentative hope with a clear, precise statement. He was not the great One who was to come; he immersed — Greek, "baptized" — only with water, but after him would come One more powerful than he who would baptize with the Holy Spirit and with fire. The One to come shall also winnow: with fan in hand He will clean His threshing floor, gathering the wheat into His barn and throwing the chaff into the fire.

To the scribes and Pharisees these words had a revolutionary ring. The threshing floor was evidently the chosen nation of Israel; but who were the wheat and who the chaff? If the good grain meant the disciples of the rabbis who observed the "traditions," and the chaff all others, then they agreed perfectly with John. But this singular preacher gave little guarantee that his opinion was at all like theirs if only because he showed such kindness to publicans and soldiers.

Enough; there was nothing to do but await the great One to come announced by John and meanwhile keep careful watch over this precursor of His.

One day, along with the crowd came Jesus. He was coming from Nazareth, no doubt with other countrymen of His because John's fame must have spread even to Galilee. He was lost among the penitents, one among many. No one knew Him, not even John, His kinsman. Referring later to this day, John gave testimony of Jesus: "And I did not know him. But he who sent me to baptize with water said to me: He upon whom thou wilt see the Spirit descending, and abiding upon him, he it is who baptizes with the Holy Spirit" (John 1:33).

That John does not know Jesus is not surprising if we remember his life. As a boy he had left his father's house to live in the desert. Meanwhile, his parents, both of them old when he was born, must have died; but both, and especially his mother, must have been with him in spirit even in the desert. After all, why had he withdrawn into the desert if not because of the extraordinary things his parents, and his mother especially, had told him of his birth? He was a man of faith and lived entirely by his faith.

Perhaps this was also the reason why he had not tried to know in person the mysterious son of Mary who had been born six months after him. He knew Him spiritually, and for the rest, his faith told him that God in His own time would have him know Him personally. But he had a kind of premonition. When he caught sight of Jesus in the crowd preparing to be baptized, the voice of the Spirit made him surmise in that one among many the Messiah and his kinsman, even though he had not yet seen the predetermined sign. When Jesus had overcome John's reluctance, he baptized Him, and his suspicion became certainty. For there appeared the sign by which Jesus was to be recognized. Apparently a penitent but confessing no sin, He had gone into the water, and as He emerged, the heavens opened and the Spirit descended in the form of a dove and remained on Him, and from above was heard a voice saying: "Thou art my beloved Son, in thee I am well pleased" (Mark 1:11).

The Desert and the Temptation

In fulfilling the rite of His precursor, Jesus associated Himself with John's ministry and at the same time began His own. But for every great undertaking there is a proximate as well as a remote preparation, and Jesus obeyed this common norm also, prefacing His public life with a period of preparation.

This lasted forty days. It is related that Jesus, after His baptism, was "led by the Spirit into the desert to be tempted by the devil, and when he had fasted forty days and forty nights, afterwards he was hungry" (Matt. 4:1–2). This is not to be interpreted as the ordinary Jewish fast. The Jews fasted until sunset but ate in the evening, whereas Jesus' fast is uninterrupted for forty days and forty nights, exactly like that of Moses and Elias.

It is clear that this fact is recorded as absolutely supernatural. Besides, early Christian catechesis could have learned of it from none other than Jesus Himself. There was no witness to those forty days; "he was with the beasts," as Mark says (1:13), summing up this period in a few words while the other two Synoptics treat it more fully.

According to a tradition that goes back perhaps to the fourth century, the place where Jesus spent this fast is the mountain the Arabs today call the mount "of the forty days." The mountain rises about sixteen hundred feet above the Jordan Valley, walling it in completely toward the west above Jericho. Hence, if Jesus was baptized in the Jordan in the vicinity of Jericho — as is probable — He would have had to walk only a few miles to reach the place of His retreat.

The extraordinary circumstances, even from the physical point of view, in which those forty days were spent we seem to glimpse in the words of the two evangelists, who tell us that Jesus was hungry "afterwards" (Matt. 4:2), or when "they [the forty days] were ended" (Luke 4:2). Are we, then, to suppose that He did not feel any hunger before? Did He perhaps spend those forty days in an ecstasy so deep and so transcendent that the ordinary life of the body was almost suspended? These are questions that the historian cannot answer.

Southern corner of the Temple area (the pinnacle of the Temple)

When, after forty days, Jesus did feel hunger, He was confronted by the tempter, to whom Mark refers only as "satan" and Luke as the "devil," while Matthew uses both terms. Mark does not list the separate temptations, nor, for that matter, does he mention Jesus' hunger. The other two Synoptics record three separate temptations but in different order. That in Matthew seems to be preferable.

"And the tempter ... said to him: 'If thou art the Son of God, command that these stones become loaves of bread!' But he answered and said: 'It is written, "Not by bread alone does man live, but by every word that comes forth from the mouth of God"'" (Matt. 4:3–4). The tempter had challenged Jesus to use the miraculous power that was His as Son of God in order to obtain something that was obtainable by nonmiraculous means. Jesus answered that the bread that man needs may be obtained not only through the usual natural means but also through a special disposition of Divine Providence, as in the case of the manna, without the use of miraculous powers at the mere prompting of others. The tempter's purpose had been to discover whether Jesus was and knew Himself to be the Son of God, and He had failed. The solicitude for physical sustenance to which he subordinated miraculous power, Jesus subordinated instead to God's providence.

The second temptation, like the third, is in a completely superhuman realm: "Then the devil took him [with him] into the holy city and set him on the pinnacle of the temple and said to him: 'If thou be the Son of God, throw thyself down; for it is written, "He will give his angels charge concerning thee, and upon their hands they shall bear thee up lest thou dash thy foot against a stone." ' Jesus said to him: 'It is written further, "Thou shalt not tempt the Lord thy God" ' " (Matt. 4:5–7). The devil therefore invites Jesus to prove that He is the Messiah. If He is the Son of God, what more splendid demonstration of it than to cast Himself into space there before the people crowding the Temple courts, for the angels will rush to bear up the falling Messiah and set Him on the ground as gently as the leaf falls cradled in the breeze.

The devil quotes Scripture this time — that is, Psalm 90 [91]:11–12 — just as Jesus had done in the previous temptation. But as St. Jerome observes, he shows himself to be a poor interpreter, for the psalm promises divine protection to those who are devout and observe God's law, not to one who arrogantly challenges God. And Jesus' second quotation, from Deuteronomy 6:16, corrects the devil's distorted interpretation of the Scriptures.

"Again the devil took him to a very high mountain, and showed him all the kingdoms of the world, and the glory of them. And he said to him: 'All these things will I give thee if thou wilt fall down [at my feet] and worship me!' Then Jesus said to him: 'Begone, Satan! For it is written, "The Lord thy God shalt thou worship and him only shalt thou serve" ' " (Matt. 4:8–10). Luke adds a few details to this account, namely, that the vision of the kingdoms took place "in a moment of time" or, as we should say, "in the twinkling of an eye," and

The Mountain of Temptation

that the devil, in pointing out their power and glory, declared, "For to me they have been delivered, and to whomever I will give them."

In this last statement the father of lies was perhaps lying a little less than usual. But even so, the exaggerated boastfulness of his claim is self-evident, for the Sacred Scriptures repeatedly declared that all the kingdoms of the earth belonged not to the devil but to Yahweh, God of Israel, together with His Messiah. It is noteworthy, however, that the third temptation (which Luke places second) does not begin with the challenge, "If thou be the Son of God," as the first two did. Had the devil perhaps been convinced of the contrary, or did he think such a formula of doubt unnecessary in this last, most violent attack?

We know nothing about this, just as we do not know the "very high mountain" on which the vision of the kingdoms took place, and which Luke does not even mention. No one familiar with Palestine can consider it Tabor or Nebo as some commentators have in the past, for these are modest little peaks and not even all of Palestine can be seen from their summits. But even from Mont Blanc or some other higher mountain, the natural view would never have included "all the kingdoms of the world." It was, therefore, a vision, and while it did occur on the top of the unnamed mountain, it was brought about by preternatural means.

All three temptations bear a marked relationship to the messianic mission of Jesus, against which they are directed. The first tries to sidetrack Him to a convenient and comfortable messianism; the second to a messianism entrusted to empty wonder-working exhibitions; the third to a messianism spending itself in political glory. Just as Jesus has now overcome the three temptations, so in His subsequent activity will He continue to contradict the principles on which they were based.

After the third temptation, Matthew adds that the devil, as if in obedience to Jesus' command to be gone, actually left Him, and "behold angels came and ministered to him" (Matt. 4:11). Luke does not mention the angels but offers a detail regarding the devil's departure. He "departed from him for a time" (Luke 4:13). There is no danger of mistaking the "time." It is the coming Passion of Jesus.

The Decline of John and the Rise of Jesus

Meanwhile, John the Baptist continued his ministry, and the potentates of Jerusalem continued to watch him with increasing vigilance.

Who, after all, was this independent hermit, neither Pharisee nor Sadducee, neither Zealot nor Romanophile, neither Essene nor Herodian, who administered a baptism not included in the Jewish ceremonial and preached a "change of mind" not contemplated in the casuistry of the scribes? Undoubtedly the man exercised a moral influence of the first order and multitudes were trooping out to him from Jerusalem and Judea as well as from distant Galilee. Hence, those in Jerusalem who held the reins of Judaism could no longer let him go unbridled. He was either with them or against them. Let him declare once and for all who he was and what he wanted!

To get this information they had recourse, naturally, to a committee, which, since the matter concerned everyone more or less, was made up of priests and Levites (for the most part Sadducees) and of representative Pharisees. The committee appeared at Bethany beyond the Jordan where John was preaching at the time, not to accuse but to investigate. Its members represented the most important and right-thinking Jews, who had the right to know the truth, hence they asked John: "Who art thou?" (John 1:19).

The question of the worthies from Jerusalem had a definite purpose. The throngs that followed the Baptist kept asking with increasing insistence whether or not he was the Messiah, and the committee wanted to find out what John himself thought about it.

But John "confessed, and did not deny, and he confessed: 'I am not the Christ [Messiah]'" (John 1:20). And they replied: "Are you then Elias whom all await as the precursor of the Messiah? Are you the prophet, equal to Moses, who is to appear in the messianic age?" To these questions John answered: "No." "But who are you, insisted the delegates, for we have to bring some answer back to Jerusalem!" And John said, "I am the voice of one crying in the wilderness. 'Make straight the way of the Lord,' as said Isaias the prophet" (Isa. 40:3).

This answer did not satisfy the commission, especially the Pharisees. So they replied. If you are not the Christ nor Elias nor a prophet, then why do you baptize? And then John repeated what he had already said to the multitude: he was baptizing with water, but in their midst stood one whom they did not know, who would come after him, whose sandal strap he was not worthy to loose.

The day after this encounter, Jesus, having ended His fast, came once more to John near the river. John caught sight of Him and pointing Him out to his disciples, he exclaimed: "Behold the Lamb of God, who takes away the sin of the world! This is he of whom I said: After me there comes one who has been set above me, because he was before me"; and after alluding to the miraculous apparition at the time of Jesus' baptism, he concluded: "And I have seen and have borne witness that this is the Son of God" (John 1:29–34).

The metaphor "Lamb of God," which John uses here, suggested to his hearers the real lambs sacrificed every day in the Temple and especially during the celebration of the Pasch. Some listeners better versed in the Scriptures may have recalled that Isaias had described the future Messiah as a sheep led to the slaughter for the evil deeds of others. The connection between the two concepts of Son of God and sacrificial lamb probably escaped most of John's listeners, but to him it must have been very important for he repeated it on the following day.

The next day (this specific information is given us by the careful evangelist John, 1:35), while John was speaking with two of his disciples, he again saw Jesus nearby, and pointing to Him he again exclaimed: "Behold the Lamb of God!" The two disciples, struck by the phrase and by its repetition, left John and began to follow Jesus, who was moving away. Jesus turned around and saw them, and asked them: "What is it you seek?" And they answered, "Rabbi … where dwellest thou?" And Jesus said to them, "Come and see." And they accompanied Him to where He was staying. Since the crowd that came to hear John was so great, this was probably one of the huts used by those guarding the crops, which are still in use in the valley about Jericho. It was about four in the afternoon. John's two disciples were so overcome by the power of the unknown Rabbi that they stayed with Him the rest of that day and undoubtedly through the night as well.

The two of them had come down from Galilee. One was Andrew, the brother of Simon Peter; the other is not named, but in this particular narrative, that is enough to indicate that it was the evangelist John, the witness who was able to recount all these things so precisely as to the day and the hour. It was the youth, not yet twenty, destined to become the "disciple whom Jesus loved."

After that first stay with Jesus, the enthusiastic Andrew had to share his joy with his brother Simon. When he found him, he said to him: "Do you know? We have found the Messiah!" And so Peter went back with him to Jesus. Jesus looked at him and then said: "You are Simon, the son of John; but you shall be called Cephas."

In Aramaic *kepha* means "rock," but it does not seem to have been used as a proper name either in the Old Testament or at the time of Jesus. Simon probably had no idea what that announcement signified, or he may have thought that the unknown Rabbi was following some train of thought of His own.

Galilee

On the day after that, as we are told by the evangelist who witnessed these things, Jesus returned to Galilee. The spiritual link between His mission and that of the precursor had been forged and now there was nothing more to keep him in Judea.

Jesus' first return to Galilee is not recorded in the Synoptics, which mention only the second, after the precursor had been imprisoned. As usual, John supplies what they have omitted. He does not describe the journey but goes on to speak of what happened after Jesus' arrival in Galilee. Hence that is where the following events took place.

With Jesus must have gone the three disciples who had left John the Baptist, namely, the brothers Andrew and Simon Peter, and John. They were all from the town of Bethsaida, on the border of Galilee, which seems to have been the first stop on the return trip. Upon their arrival, the three could not have failed, in their excitement, to tell their relatives and friends all that they knew of Jesus, pointing Him out enthusiastically to their townsmen. Among them, Jesus met a certain Philip, and He said to him: "Follow me!" And Philip, no doubt already fired with enthusiasm by the accounts of his three fellow townsmen, obeyed with alacrity.

In fact, he began to tell others of the wonderful Rabbi, but he met a cold reception. Having come upon his friend Nathanael, he confided to him with joy: "Do you know? We have found him of whom Moses and the prophets speak! It is Jesus, son of Joseph of Nazareth!" Nathanael must have been a man of great poise and tranquility. He was besides from Cana, near Nazareth, and so he was well acquainted with the country of the Rabbi whose praises were being sung so vigorously. When he heard that he came from that pitiful little cluster of huts, he answered disparagingly: "Can anything good come out of Nazareth?"

This answer in no way chilled Philip's ardor, and he presented his proof: "Come and see!" And Nathanael came and saw and was conquered.

As soon as Jesus spied the skeptical Nathanael approaching, He exclaimed: "Behold a true Israelite, in whom there is no guile!" Undoubtedly he merited the praise; proof of this lies in his very misgivings upon hearing that the Messiah had been found. With so many dreamers and charlatans claiming to find the Messiah in themselves or others, a sincere Israelite had every right to be suspicious. Hence he asked: "Whence knowest thou me? Jesus answered and said to him: Before Philip called thee, when thou wast under the fig tree, I saw thee!" (John 1:48).

It was an old custom in Palestine to have a thick-leaved fig tree near one's little house and to enjoy an occasional hour of peace and quiet in its shade. Hence, when Jesus said He had seen Nathanael in that shady retreat, He was not announcing an extraordinary discovery from a physical point of view. But there must have been something spiritually extraordinary about it to occasion

Nathanael's surprise; that is, the thoughts he was pondering within himself in that place must have been somehow related to this very meeting. Was he thinking of the true Messiah, having heard the rumors about the Jesus who had arrived in his town? Was he asking God in his heart for a "sign"? We can give no definite answer, but it is clear that Nathanael found the words addressed to him perfectly true. Jesus had truly *seen* him, not in the shade of the fig tree but within His innermost thoughts.

The guileless Israelite was stunned; an impetus of ardor invaded his calm self-possession: "Rabbi, thou art the Son of God! Thou art King of Israel!" Nathanael agreed now with Philip and recognized Jesus as the Messiah. He was a warmhearted man, perhaps a little too warmhearted. Jesus, in fact, answered: "Because I said to thee that I saw thee under the fig tree, thou dost believe. Greater things than these shalt thou see." Then turning also to Philip and perhaps to others present, he continued: "Amen, amen, I say to you, you shall see heaven opened and the angels of God ascending and descending on the Son of Man!"

Nathanael is mentioned only in John and not in the Synoptics. On the other hand, they list among the apostles a certain Bartholomew, whom John never mentions. It is probable that the same person had both names, as was common enough in those times, especially since in the lists of the apostles Bartholomew is usually named with Philip, the friend of Nathanael.

The Wedding Feast at Cana

John tells us that on the "third day" after the interview with Nathanael "there was a marriage in Cana of Galilee, and the mother of Jesus was there; and Jesus also was invited, and his disciples to the marriage" (John 2:1–2). Since, as we have noted, Nathanael was from Cana, it is possible that it was he who invited Jesus and his disciples — Andrew, Peter, John, and Philip — to the wedding, which may have been that of some relative or friend of his. It seems clear from John's words, however, that the "mother of Jesus was there" even before her son arrived, and that would lead us to suppose that there was also some bond between Mary and one of the wedded couple. As relative or friend, she had probably gone there a day or two in advance to help with the preparations, particularly the bride's, which were many. There is no likelihood whatever in certain later fancies that would make the groom Nathanael himself, or the evangelist John, or others.

The event at Cana was the Jewish ceremony of the wedding, not the betrothal. The feast that accompanied it was certainly the most solemn occasion in the whole life of folk in the lower or even the middle classes, and it could last for several days.

When the bride emerged from the industrious ministrations of her relatives and friends, she was decked in gay and elegant finery. She wore a crown on her head, her face was made up, and her eyes were bright with collyrium. Her hair and nails were tinted, and she was laden with necklaces, bracelets, and other jewels, most of which were counterfeit or borrowed. The groom, also wearing a crown and surrounded by the "friends of the groom," went in the evening to lead his bride from her home to his. She was waiting for him surrounded by her friends, who carried lamps and cheered the groom when he arrived. All went in procession to the groom's house, the whole town joining in with lamps, music, singing, dancing, and all the noise of merriment. The feast was held in the home of the groom, and there were songs and speeches filled with good wishes and sometimes not entirely free from suggestive allusions, especially when the dinner was well along and the guests were somewhat tipsy.

In fact, the wine was unstinted and the drinking hearty, it being so rare an occasion for people who all year long led a spare, drudging existence. It was special wine they drank, which had been set aside a long time before just for this feast. After all, one reads in the Scriptures that wine gladdens the heart of man, and those good people were going to obey the Scriptures at least in the gladness of the wedding feast.

Jesus chose to take part in such a celebration, so gay and friendly, so human even in its weaknesses. Perhaps when Jesus was still a little boy in Nazareth, His Mother had told Him now and then that she, too, had had a bit of a wedding feast when she had come to Joseph's house to live. A new family had been founded then, which Jesus honored and sanctified with thirty years of filial obedience. Now that He is about to leave that family, it is as though He looks back with something of regret and stays to honor and sanctify the moral principle that is the foundation of all families. This is why Jesus, who was born of a virgin and died a virgin, participated in a wedding at the very beginning of His public ministry.

In Cana, Jesus met His Mother after a separation of about two months. This had been perhaps His first long absence from home; and since Joseph was dead, the shop had been idle and Mary without companionship. In that first lonely separation she must have thought more than ever of her son's birth and the mission that had been predicted for Him, surmising perhaps that this was now about to begin. And as she pondered these things, she probably had to parry the questions of the inquisitive women of the town or of relatives, who would want to know why Jesus had left her alone, and when He would come back. Now at Cana she saw Him again, already wearing the title of *Rabbi*, acclaimed as a teacher and surrounded by enthusiastic disciples. But Rabbi or no, Mary, true to motherhood the world over, still treated Him as her son, just as she had treated the twelve-year-old boy discussing important questions in the Temple.

As a good mother and housewife, she was probably helping with other women to see that everything went as it should. But toward the end of the dinner, either because the host had miscalculated, or because unexpected guests had arrived, the wine, the most important thing of all, began to run short. The good housewives serving it were in great consternation; it was a disgrace for the family whose feast it was. The guests would not spare their protests or their jibes, and the festivities would come to an abrupt and inglorious end.

Mary immediately noticed the situation and foresaw the embarrassment of her hosts. The presence of her Rabbi son had much more meaning for her than

Street scene in Cana of Galilee

for any of the others, and she associated it now with what she had guessed of Him through the lonely time in Nazareth. Was His hour perhaps not come?

Governed by these thoughts, Mary, amidst the general distress that could barely be concealed, said softly to Jesus: "They have no wine. And Jesus answered: Woman, what is that to me and to thee? My hour is not yet come" (John 2:3–4).

Jesus spoke these words in Aramaic, and they must be interpreted according to their meaning in that language. In the first place *woman* was a title of respect, something like the English "(mi) lady." A son ordinarily called the woman who had borne him "mother," but in special circumstances he might show her greater reverence by calling her "woman." Jesus calls His Mother "woman" once again as He hangs from the Cross (John 19:26).

More characteristic is the other expression, "what [is that] to me and to thee?" The significance of this phrase depends more on the circumstances in which it is spoken, on the tone of voice, the gestures, and so forth, than on the literal meaning of the words in themselves. All languages have idioms, in which the words are a mere pretext for expression and cannot be translated literally into any other language. In our case, we might achieve a close enough paraphrase of the Hebrew expression with something like this: "What [reason is there] for me and for thee [to discuss this]?" which might be rendered in English: "Why do you discuss this with me?" In short, it was an elliptic phrase that asked why two parties should have become involved in a discussion, an action, or whatnot.

With this answer Jesus declined Mary's invitation and gave as His reason the fact that His hour was not yet come. Hence, in those four simple words "they have no wine" (if, in fact, that was all Mary said), there was a hidden request to perform a miracle. Jesus was aware of this, but He refused. The time had not come to prove with miracles the authenticity of His mission, for that of His precursor John was not yet ended.

But the conversation between Mary and Jesus was not over. In fact, its most important words were never spoken except in an exchange of glances. Just as in the Temple after His first refusal, Jesus obeyed His Mother immediately and left the house of His heavenly Father, so after this refusal, too, He proceeded to grant her request. In the mute dialogue that followed the spoken one, Mary was assured of her son's consent. So without wasting any time she turned to the servants and said: "Do whatever He tells you!"

In the court of the house there were six jars containing water for purification of the hands and various utensils as prescribed by Jewish Law; hence the jars must have been of stone, for according to the rabbis, this did not contract impurities as terra-cotta did. And they were large jars, each containing two or three times the normal Jewish "measure," which was about ten gallons; hence all together they held about 150 gallons. Since the dinner was long and the guests many, most of the water had been used and the jars were about empty.

Then Jesus told the servants to refill the jars to the brim. Off they ran to the nearby well or cistern, and after a few trips the jars were full again. There was no more to be done; and He "said to them: Draw out now, and carry to the chief steward of the feast. And they carried it" (John 2:8). It had all happened in a few minutes, even before the chief steward had had time to note the women's consternation or realize that there was no more wine. Mary's gentle tact had kept the domestic calamity from being noticed.

When the chief steward of the feast found a different wine set before him and tasted it as was his duty, he was so astonished that he forgot all formality and spoke out with peasant bluntness. Going up to the groom, he "said to him: 'Every man at first sets forth the good wine, and when they have drunk freely, then that which is poorer, but thou hast kept the good wine until now!'" (John 2:10).

With this "first" (as John emphasizes) of the miraculous "signs" wrought by Jesus, He "manifested his glory, and his disciples believed in him." What was the effect of that miracle on the guests at the feast? When their heads cleared and they had forgotten the taste of that mysterious wine, did they ever think of the moral significance of what had taken place?

After the wedding feast, Jesus went to Capernaum, "he and his mother, and his brethren, and his disciples; and they remained there not many days" (John 2:12).

This stay in Capernaum was short because Jesus had decided to go up to Jerusalem for the coming Pasch, but from then on Capernaum served as His usual dwelling place in Galilee, becoming His adopted home in place of Nazareth. He had already detached Himself from His family, and to the institution of the family He had paid the homage of His first miracle. Now He also detached Himself from His village and moved to a place more convenient for the mission about to begin.

Capernaum was on the northwest shore of Lake Tiberias, not far from where the Jordan flows into it. It was about nine miles north of the city of Tiberias and about twenty-five miles east of Nazareth, near the border between the territory of Herod Antipas and that of Philip. Hence it had a customhouse and there was constant travel through the town. On the lake there was a little harbor suitable for fishing boats. The religious life of the inhabitants must have been intense and was probably not disturbed very much by the Greek influences entrenched a short distance above them. Like Jesus, His first disciples from neighboring Bethsaida, like Peter and Andrew, also came in time to settle in Capernaum. As for Simon Peter, it is probable that he already had some relatives there. If, like a good son-in-law, he has his mother-in-law living there with him, it is not too hardy to suppose that his wife came originally from Capernaum. Later, Capernaum came to be designated as Jesus' "own city" (Matt. 9:1), although the same document shortly afterward still calls Nazareth "his own country" (Matt. 13:54).

Modern fishermen near Bethsaida

Chapter 10

∞

From the First to the Second Pasch

The Traders in the Temple

A few months had passed since Jesus' baptism. Now the Pasch of the new year was approaching. Jesus had decided to make the pilgrimage for this Pasch, so He set out from Capernaum for Jerusalem.

When He reached the Temple, He saw before Him the usual scene that took place there especially during the great feasts. The outer court of the Temple had become a stable reeking with dung, and it echoed with the bellowing of oxen, the bleat of sheep, the cooing of doves, and the cries of the traders and money changers installed within its porticoes. In that court it was possible to hear only faintly the hymns rising within the inner Temple and to glimpse but dimly the glow of the distant holy lamps. There were no other visible signs of religion in that vast enclosure. To be sure, Jesus had witnessed similar scenes on previous pilgrimages to Jerusalem, but then His public life had not begun. Now His mission was under way, and in proof of it He must act as "one having authority" (Matt. 7:29; Mark 1:22).

Having made a kind of whip of cords, He began to strike at men and beasts and overturned the tables of the money changers while their little heaps of coins went scattering across the pavements; out He drove them all, clearing the sacred enclosure: "Get out of here! Do not make the house of my Father a place of business" (John 2:16). "Is it not written: 'My house shall be called a house of prayer for all nations'? But you have made it a den of thieves" (Mark 11:17).

Theoretically no one could take exception to His action, as the Pharisees themselves were well aware. But in actual practice, they might yet ask why Jesus had taken it upon Himself to perform such an act of authority instead of urging the officials in charge of the Temple to do so. Who had given Him the authority to do it? Indeed, to put it more explicitly, how was it that this man, just up from Galilee, assumed, as His first actions seemed to indicate, an attitude of complete independence toward the established authorities very like John's?

Hence certain Jews, undoubtedly of importance, approached Him and said: "What sign dost thou show us, seeing that thou dost these things?" In answer Jesus said to them: "Destroy this Temple, and in three days I will raise it up!" The Jews therefore said: "Forty-six years has this Temple been in building and wilt thou raise it up in three days?" This answer indicates that His questioners did not understand to what He was referring, and undoubtedly neither did the evangelist who witnessed and recorded the incident. The Jews had asked for a "sign," that is, a miracle. Since His mission was challenged, Jesus offered a real proof of it, but this proof was to be understood only many months later; at the moment it did not satisfy the malevolent curiosity of His questioners.

Although Jesus does not satisfy the malicious request for a "sign," nevertheless during that first Paschal sojourn in Jerusalem, "many believed in his name, seeing the signs that he was working" (John 2:23). But this was not so much faith from the heart as faith of the intellect, and Jesus wanted the former much more than the latter. That was one reason why He "did not trust himself to them, in that he knew all men" (John 2:24), while He had trusted Himself to the rough but generous disciples from Galilee. Even the faith of the intellect, however, is a preparation for, and invitation to, faith of the heart, and it is at this point precisely that St. John presents to us an interview between one who already believed with his mind and Jesus who lifted him into quite another sphere. We seem to be watching a baby chick borne above the clouds in an eagle's grasp, and it is a favorite scene with the "spiritual" evangelist, who gives us others like it.

Nicodemus

There was at that time in Jerusalem an outstanding Pharisee and "teacher" of the Law, an honest, upright man. But he was a member of the Sanhedrin, and his social position evidently required that he be very cautious about what he did in public. He was called Nicodemus. When he saw the "signs" wrought by Jesus, he was deeply shaken; perhaps he had been one of the few Pharisees who recognized the mission of the precursor John and accepted his baptism. On the other hand, his position and still more his Pharisaic training and mentality warned him to be careful with regard to the unknown wonder-worker. In this mental conflict he managed to find a middle course, and he went to visit Jesus by night.

The conversation was a long one, lasting perhaps throughout the night, but the "spiritual" evangelist records only its salient points, those best suited to the purpose of his Gospel. Nicodemus began the discussion, and coming straight to what had shaken him to the soul, he said to Jesus: "Rabbi, we know that thou hast come a teacher from God, for no one can work these signs that thou workest unless God be with him."

This man recognized that Jesus' mission was not a human one but something much higher, in fact, divine. Jesus' answer refers to the implication in Nicodemus's words: "Amen, amen, I say to thee, unless a man be born [from above][10] he cannot see the kingdom of God." Nicodemus was too intelligent to take these words literally. But he could not quite grasp their precise spiritual significance, and so to elicit an explanation he pretended to be very dense: "How can a man be born when he is old? Can he perhaps enter a second time into his mother's womb and be born again?"

This feigned stupidity is shrewder than it seems. Nicodemus is setting himself up as judge of the teaching that Jesus is about to explain to him, but Jesus' answer reduces him to an unlearned apprentice. One cannot "see the kingdom of God" unless he has already entered into it, and his entrance into it is not accomplished by human means: "Amen, amen, I say to thee, unless a man be born again of water and the Spirit, he cannot enter into the kingdom of God. That which is born of the flesh is flesh; and that which is born of the Spirit, is spirit."

In Hebrew the word for *spirit* also meant "puff" or "gust" (of wind). Jesus plays on the double meaning of the word to add a concrete example: "Do not wonder that I said to thee: You must be born from above. The wind [also] blows where it will, and thou hearest its sound but dost not know where it comes from or where it goes. So is everyone who is born of the Spirit." Though intangible and invisible, the wind is a reality in the physical world. Thus, in the spiritual world, the influence of the Divine Spirit cannot be regulated by human reasoning nor is its essence scrutable, but it manifests itself in its effects. The Spirit causes us to be born to a new invisible life in a manner reminiscent of the way the first visible life of the universe burst from brute matter at the breath of God hovering over the waters.

The reference to John's baptism is clear, and perhaps the conversation that followed revealed that Nicodemus had received it. In any case, the new

[10] The expression "from above" in Greek can also mean "again," as we have it in our Douay and Confraternity versions; but here it is preferable to take it in the first meaning, which it seems to have as John himself uses it in 3:31; 19:11, 23.

life that Jesus here says is bestowed by the Holy Spirit and by water is not the effect of John's rite, a baptism of water only and a mere symbol; it is the effect of the rite that is the fulfillment of that symbol, administered with water and the Holy Spirit. The latter is the baptism of Jesus, and the precursor himself gave testimony of it.

The comparison between the action of the Spirit and that of the wind takes Nicodemus into a world in which the Pharisee is lost and bewildered. Hence he no longer pretends to be slow of wit, but he is not yet ready to admit he is the unlearned pupil. So with all sincerity but some diffidence he exclaims: "How can these things be?"

Jesus' reply is a reflection on Nicodemus's position: How is this? "Thou art a teacher in Israel and dost not know these things?" What, then, do you teach, if you do not teach the action of the Spirit on the soul? After this beginning, Jesus' discourse must have proceeded at some length, not without interruptions and replies from Nicodemus. The evangelist omits the words of the Pharisee and presents only a selection from all that Jesus spoke that night (John 3:11–21). But it is not forcing the context to deduce from that selection some of Nicodemus's answers and remarks (as in the reference to the serpent in the desert) or even a metaphor or two that springs from the lamplit setting in which the conversation took place (for example, the reference to light and darkness).

What must have been Nicodemus's state of mind as he listened to Jesus? Unless Jesus clarified His pronouncements with explanations the evangelist has omitted, Nicodemus could not understand them very well. As in His conversation with the Jews after driving the traders from the Temple, however, Jesus was not speaking for Nicodemus only. Though the Pharisee went to Him by night, we are not told that he found Jesus completely alone. In a dim corner of the room it is possible to glimpse a wide-eyed youth who breathlessly follows the whole interview and stamps every word of it in his memory. It is the beloved disciple, who when he is very old will tell the story of that conversation.

Despite his talk with Jesus, Nicodemus did not become a true disciple of His, almost in proof of the words he heard that night, that the breath of God breathes where it will. Yet he was always kindly disposed toward Jesus even after the Crucifixion. He dares to spend a word in Jesus' favor in the Sanhedrin, and he spends much more in money for the spices to prepare His body for burial. Jesus' nocturnal visitor was not generous of soul, but he was generous of purse; he was not a Peter, but neither was he a Judas.

The Twilight of John's Ministry

After Nicodemus's visit, Jesus remained for some time in Judea, but seems to have moved away from the treacherous capital somewhat to the north. The open country afforded Him and whoever wished to come to Him more freedom of action away from the suspicious vigilance of the ancients and the Pharisees. The place where He stayed was well supplied with water, for we unexpectedly find that Jesus' disciples are themselves baptizing like John.

Was this the baptism of water and the Holy Spirit spoken of to Nicodemus? Almost certainly it was not. The fourth Gospel, in fact, points out explicitly that Jesus was not administering this baptism in person but that His disciples were (John 7:39; 16:7), nor had Jesus' disciples yet been instructed in the Divine Trinity and the redemption wrought by the death of Christ, which are essential elements in the future baptism of water and the Spirit (Matt. 28:19; Rom. 6:3ff.). Hence this rite, too, was only a symbol like that of John. That is why John continued to administer his baptism at Ainon near Salim even after the disciples of Jesus began to baptize, while if they had been baptizing in water and the Spirit, he would have had to stop.

Nevertheless, one day a kind of dissension did arise. The disciples of John and a certain Jew began to argue "concerning purification." Perhaps this Jew thought the rite administered by the disciples of the Galilean Rabbi more purifying than that of John. The latter's disciples were indignant and running to their master they told him of the supposedly rival activity of Jesus: "Rabbi, he who was with thee beyond the Jordan, to whom thou hast borne witness, behold he baptizes and all are coming to him."

John's impetuous disciples perhaps expected him to burst into jealous invective, but instead they heard him speak in a tone of joyous consolation: "No one can receive anything unless it is given to him from heaven. You your-selves bear me witness that I said: I am not the Christ [Messiah], but have been sent before him. He who has the bride is the bridegroom; but the friend of the bridegroom, who stands [present] and hears him, rejoices exceedingly at the voice of the bridegroom. This my joy, therefore, is fulfilled. He must increase, but I must decrease" (John 3:27–30).

This was John's last testimony. A few weeks later, probably in May, the austere censor of the court scandal was imprisoned in the Machaerus.

It is hardly possible that the Pharisees had no share, indirect at least, in this imprisonment. The Synoptics attribute it to John's censure of the royal couple, while Flavius Josephus ascribes it to his popularity, which was not relished by the authorities. Both reasons are good and dovetail perfectly. But the fourth Gospel suggests a third: "The Pharisees had heard that Jesus made and baptized more disciples than John" (John 4:1), and so Jesus left Judea and returned to Galilee. Thus Jesus feared that His popularity, greater than John's, would expose Him to the jealousy of the Pharisees, hence He went away. Had John, then, fallen victim to this jealousy?

Nothing tells us so explicitly; but the Synoptics, too, give us to understand that Jesus left Judea as soon as John's imprisonment became known. This, then, was the trap that closed on John thanks to the activity of the Pharisees as well as to his courage in openly rebuking the court.

If John was still at Ainon near Salim, he was not in Herod's territory, but in that of the free city of Scythopolis, which formed part of the Decapolis. But Scythopolis was wedged in between the two arms of Antipas's territory, Galilee and Perea, and so it would be easy to draw him within Antipas's jurisdiction on some pretext presented by obliging go-betweens. Later, as we shall see, the Pharisees play the go-between again but in reverse.

In the secret dungeons of the Machaerus, John languished through long exhausting months of waiting.

The Samaritan Woman

To return to Galilee, Jesus chose the road that ran through the center of Palestine and therefore across Samaria. He could have taken the road to the east, which followed the Jordan, but according to Flavius Josephus the former was the one more often taken by Galileans traveling to and from Jerusalem.

At a certain point the road entered a narrow valley formed by Mount Ebal on the north and Mount Garizim on the south. A short distance before entering the valley from the east, there was a spot famous in the history of the Hebrew patriarchs, the site of "Jacob's Well," which is still standing. A few hundred yards within the valley on the right lay the ancient city of Sichem, which in Jesus' time was falling into decay and had very few inhabitants.

Having left Judea, then, Jesus "came to a town of Samaria called Sichar, near the field that Jacob gave to his son Joseph. Now Jacob's well was there. Jesus, therefore, wearied as he was from the journey, was sitting at the well. It was about the sixth hour" (John 4:5–6), that is, about noon, and it is probably the month of May. Jesus, hot and tired, is resting alone near the well, while his disciples go into the adjacent town to buy food.

A Samaritan woman comes from the settlement to draw water at the well. Jesus says to her: "Give me to drink." The woman answers haughtily: "How is it that thou, a Jew, dost ask drink of me, who am a Samaritan woman?" She

Sichem, the well of the Samaritan woman

emphasizes how humiliating it is that a man and a Jew should be in such need that he must ask a woman and a Samaritan for help. Jesus answers: "If thou didst know the gift of God, and who it is who says to thee: Give me to drink, thou, perhaps, wouldst have asked of him, and he would have given thee living water."

Like Nicodemus, the woman perceives that there is something in the words that she cannot grasp, and so she sticks to their literal meaning, though she begins to speak with a little more respect: "Sir, thou hast nothing to draw with, and the well is deep; whence then hast thou living water?" The observation is legitimate. The well today is over ninety feet deep, one of the deepest in all Palestine, although in Jesus' day its depth may have been somewhat less. And she completes her remark with a historical consideration: "Art thou greater than our father Jacob, who gave us the well, and drank from it, himself, and his sons, and his flocks?"

But Jesus replies: "Everyone who drinks of this water, will thirst again. He, however, who drinks of the water that I will give him, shall never thirst; but the water that I will give him shall become in him a fountain of water, springing up into life everlasting." The woman is still fluttering close to earth: "Sir, give me this water, that I may not thirst, or come here to draw."

Jesus must explain and help with a "sign." Therefore, He says to the woman: "Go, call thy husband, and come here." Both Hebrew and Aramaic said "man" for "husband." The woman plays on the double meaning of the word and says unabashed, "I have no man." Jesus disregards the ambiguity and takes the woman's answer in its less lovely significance: "Thou hast said well: I have no husband. For thou hast had five husbands, and he whom thou now hast is not thy husband. In this thou hast spoken truly." Her "man" at the time, then, was not her "husband," and probably not all his predecessors had been husbands either. In short, the Samaritan woman was not a model of chastity.

The "sign" Jesus offers produces a good effect. Upon seeing her guilty secrets thus discovered, she exclaims: "Sir, I see that thou art a prophet!" But this discovery and her exclamation testify to the superiority of this man who was one of the hated Jews; hence she turns the conversation to the reason for this hatred — and also to avoid the touchy subject of her private life: "Our

A Samaritan woman at Jacob's Well

fathers adored [God] on this mountain, and you say that at Jerusalem is the place where men must adore."

Mount Garizim towers above the heads of the two speakers; but the unknown Jew is returning from Jerusalem where He has certainly adored God in the Temple of Yahweh. What then does He, a prophet, think of this agelong dispute between Samaritans and Jews?

Jesus considers the woman's words almost entirely from a historical point of view, as though they represent what is now an idle question. Even so, however, He speaks as a Jew, favoring the Jews against the Samaritans. But He turns immediately from the past to the present, in which the old rivalries no longer have any reason for being: "Woman, believe me, the hour is coming when neither on this mountain nor in Jerusalem will you worship the Father. You worship what you do not know; we worship what we know; for salvation is from the Jews. But the hour is coming, and is now here, when the true worshipers will worship the Father in spirit and in truth. For the Father also seeks such to worship him. God is spirit, and they who worship him must worship in spirit and truth." The prophet has given His answer. From now on the worship of God will not be bound to Mount Garizim nor to the hill of Jerusalem nor to any other place on earth, but only to the condition that it be offered "in spirit and truth."

The woman now realizes that she is in an unfamiliar sphere. Not Garizim, not Jerusalem, but spirit and truth! What world is this? Certainly not the petty world in which Samaritans and Jews are forever quarreling. Nevertheless, she perceives intuitively that these are visions of the future, to be fulfilled only in the blessed days of the Messiah. Hence her bewildered thought retreats to those days, and though she does not dare to contradict this unknown prophet, she exclaims: "I know that the Messiah is coming and when he comes he will tell us all things." Jesus answers: "I who speak with thee am he!"

The Samaritans were in fact expecting the Messiah, and their descendants today are still waiting for him. They call him *Taheb (Shaheb)*, "he who returns," or "he who recalls (to good)." He is pictured as a reformer, like Moses, who will resolve all doubts, compose all differences, and establish a reign of happiness that will last a thousand years after his death.

Now, it is precisely to this woman of a race hostile to the Jews that Jesus reveals Himself as the Messiah, though He later commands His disciples not to disclose this fact (Matt. 16:20). Yet in this very Samaritan hostility lies the secret of His preference. The announcement would hardly arouse among them the political enthusiasm it would most probably have excited among the Jews, a thing Jesus wanted to avoid at any cost.

While Jesus is exchanging the last of these words with the Samaritan woman, His disciples return from the town with the food they have bought and approach the well. When the woman hears Jesus declare He is the Messiah, she does not dare to answer Him. Leaving her water jar at the well, she runs into the town, shouting to everyone she meets: "Come, and see a man who has told me all that I have ever done! Can he be the Christ?"

The disciples do not venture to ask Jesus the reason for that unusual conversation though they wonder at it, since the Jewish rabbis avoided speaking to women in public, even their own wives. Somewhat disconcerted, they approach the Master only after the woman runs off.

"Rabbi, eat," they say to him, offering the food they have brought. By way of answer, Jesus continues the metaphor He has used in His conversation with the woman. He is nourished on spiritual food above all, and this is doing the will of Him who has sent Him to accomplish His work. He is the reaper of a spiritual harvest. At the end of December when the sowing was finished, the Palestinian farmers used to exclaim with relief: "Another four months and the harvest will be ready!" It was a kind of proverb, for the reaping took place in April or May, after four months of rest. But Jesus shows that the proverb has no meaning so far as His spiritual harvest is concerned. It is ripe and ready, nor can it wait. Hence the reapers must be ready, too, even though they have not done the sowing.

And a few sheaves of the spiritual harvest were gathered immediately. The busy garrulousness of the woman brought many Samaritans to the well to see the Jewish prophet. They must have been won at His very first words, for they invited Him to stay with them for a time. And they were Samaritans — men who preferred to beat until they drew blood or to murder outright the Jews traveling through their territories and who later refused hospitality to Jesus' own disciples (Luke 9:52–53). But this time, or rather these Samaritans of Sichar were gracious, for they had undoubtedly been tamed by the personality of the prophet. Jesus accepted the invitation and "he stayed there two days. And far more believed because of his word. And they said to the woman: We no longer believe because of what thou hast said, for we have heard for ourselves and we know that this is in truth the Saviour of the world" (John 4:42).

Return to Galilee and the First Part of the Ministry There

After the two days at Sichar, Jesus returned to Galilee. John gives us the reason (4:44) in these words: "For Jesus himself gave testimony that a prophet hath no honor in his own country."

At first the Galileans welcomed Jesus. Several of them had witnessed the things He had done in Judea and talked about them on their return home, thereby exciting the pride of the prophet's fellow countrymen.

When Jesus arrived again in Cana, the town of His first miracle, He was sought out immediately because of His fame as a wonder-worker. The son of an official of the royal court lay seriously ill at Capernaum, and the father, as soon as he heard of Jesus' arrival, hurried to Cana and besought Him to come down at once and heal the boy, who was at the point of death. Jesus seemed reluctant to grant his plea, and His chief concern being for His own mission, He answered: "Unless you see signs and wonders, you do not believe!" The anguished father was concerned only with his dying son and he insisted: "Sir, come down [to Capernaum] before my child dies!" To be certain of the cure, he wanted Jesus to go there personally, like a physician. Jesus answered him: "Go thy way; thy son lives!" The firmness with which these words were uttered inspired equal firmness of faith in the father's heart. It was now "the seventh hour" or about one o'clock in the afternoon, but after the journey of the morning from Capernaum to Cana, a distance of more than twenty miles, he could not wear out the men and beasts in his escort by setting out immediately on the return. Hence he did not leave until the next morning. As he approached Capernaum, his servants came to meet him to tell him that the boy was better. Asked at what hour they had begun to notice the improvement, they answered: "Yesterday, at the seventh hour, the fever left him."

The careful John (4:54) points out that this was Jesus' second miracle, also in Galilee like that of Cana, but exclusive of the sojourn in Judea.

Having returned to Galilee, Jesus immediately began His mission "preaching the gospel of the kingdom of God, and saying: The time is fulfilled and the kingdom of God is at hand; repent and believe in the Gospel" (Mark 1:14–15).

He gradually visited practically all the centers in Galilee, because we are told that He "taught in their synagogues" and that "all" listened to Him and did Him honor, not perhaps without some feeling of local pride (Luke 4:14–15). Nevertheless, He stayed longest and most frequently at Capernaum. There is much to favor the supposition that He visited Nazareth as well. But the episode of His preaching in the synagogue there, which ended in His being driven from the village, must have occurred at the end of His activity in Galilee because on that occasion there is explicit mention of the miracles He had already wrought in Capernaum (Luke 4:23). Hence, though Luke places the incident at the beginning, the sequence followed by the other two Synoptics is to be preferred (Matt. 13:54–58; Mark 6:1–6).

In the towns He visited, Jesus spoke mainly in the local synagogue. Every tiny village in Palestine had one, and there the inhabitants gathered without fail on the Sabbath and sometimes even on other days. The synagogue not only provided an audience, but it also furnished the occasion for speaking in full conformity with traditional customs, since, after the reading from the Scriptures, the ruler of the synagogue would invite someone present to give the usual instruction and exhortation. It is natural that Jesus should have volunteered frequently on such occasions, for they were well suited to His purpose. At other times, however, He spoke in the open or in some private home or when a crowd had gathered about Him.

His listeners were rapidly growing in number because they had noticed that He "was teaching them as one having authority, and not as the Scribes" (Mark 1:22; Luke 4:32; cf. Matt. 7:29). Even the people, by virtue of their simple common sense, noticed a profound difference between the teachings of Jesus and those of the scribes. The latter always took refuge in the ancients, and it was their ideal to transmit, without adding or omitting anything, the teachings they had received. Jesus, on the other hand, was opening treasures to which He alone had the key and over which He only "had authority," and He did not hesitate to contradict the teachings of the ancients when He thought it necessary to perfect them. "It was said to the ancients … but I say to you …" (Matt. 5:21ff.). The scribes were the voice of tradition. Jesus was His own voice, and He claimed the right both to approve the tradition and to reject or correct it.

Capernaum and Elsewhere

And if the new preacher had "authority" in matters of doctrine, He showed He had no less authority over nature, working extraordinary "signs"; and since this second authority confirmed the first, it also attracted the attention of the multitudes, who must have reasoned something like Nicodemus on this point: "No one can work these signs … unless God be with him."

In Capernaum, one Sabbath day, after He had preached in the synagogue, Jesus publicly cured a demoniac, who, at His words, first gave forth convulsive cries and then was freed of the obsession. The people who had heard the preaching and witnessed the deliverance of the demoniac wondered at both among themselves. "What is this? A new teaching with authority! He commandeth even the unclean spirits and they obey him!" (Mark 1:27).

While these exclamations are still reechoing, Jesus leaves the synagogue and goes immediately to the home of the brothers Simon Peter and Andrew, where He finds Peter's mother-in-law lying ill. Luke, the physician-evangelist, notes that she was the victim of a "great fever" (Luke 4:38), which, in the technical terminology of the time, was different from the "little fever." With Jesus are James and John, and certainly others as well, who witnessed the cure of the demoniac and now beg Jesus to help this poor, sick old woman. He bends over her pallet, takes her by the hands, and lifts her up, in complete good health once more. She feels so well the moment she rises that she immediately bustles about to prepare something for her extraordinary guest and wait upon Him.

The town is still talking of the cured demoniac when the news spreads that Peter's mother-in-law also has been healed. To have a man like that in town and not profit by His presence would be more than stupid. But it is the Sabbath, and nothing can be carried on that day nor is it lawful to walk more than a limited distance. Well, they will wait until sunset, when the Sabbath rest ends, and then it will be permissible to carry the sick to Him.

That evening, in fact, demoniacs and sick people of every description were assembled before Peter's house, and Jesus, "laying his hands on every one of them, healed them. And the devils went out from many, crying out and saying: Thou art the Son of God. And rebuking them he [Jesus] suffered them not to speak because they knew that he was the Christ [Messiah]" (Luke 4:40–41). The same Jesus who had declared to the Samaritans that He was the Messiah, here, in the land of the Jews, did not permit the same declaration to be made by a reliable witness to the fact, the devil. But here there was the danger that did not exist on the first occasion, namely, that those present, following the current fashion, might consider the Messiah a political leader. Jesus was preaching not a kingdom of the world or of men but the Kingdom of Heaven and of God.

In the beginning, then, that is, during this first period of His ministry in Galilee, He continued the preaching of His precursor John, declaring only that the Kingdom of God was at hand (Matt. 4:17; Mark 1:15). He spoke of the kingdom but not of its head, of the institution but not of its founder. Later, when He has gathered about Him a small nucleus of followers who understand at least in a general way that His kingdom is not political and that its founder is a spiritual king, to these He confides that He is the Messiah, though He commands them too, in the beginning, not to reveal this secret to others.

The evening of that Sabbath day was a laborious one, but Jesus was at last able to retire into Peter's house. On the following morning, long before dawn, He went out to a solitary place to pray. Soon afterward visitors from the town began to arrive seeking favors of the wonder-worker and wanting to beg Him never to go away from them again. Peter and the other members of the family, not finding Jesus in the house, began to search for Him. At length they found Him and told Him what all hoped and desired of Him, but He answered that He must announce in other places as well the good tidings of the Kingdom of God, that it was for this He had been sent.

And He began once more to travel here and there throughout Galilee, having probably none of His disciples with Him.

The Choosing of the First Four Apostles

At this point, Luke (5:1–11) tells of the calling of the four principal disciples, Simon Peter and Andrew his brother, John and his brother James. Matthew and Mark record this much more briefly at the beginning of Jesus' ministry in Galilee, immediately after He has heard of the imprisonment of John the Baptist. Luke's order seems the more likely from the chronological viewpoint. It should be noted that neither Matthew nor Mark speaks of any previous association between Jesus and these four men, whereas Luke has mentioned and John has described their relations. Besides, this summons presupposes that Jesus had begun His preaching some time before, since there is a great crowd thronging about Him anxious to see and hear Him; this would not be easy to explain if the incident occurred during the first days after Jesus' return to Galilee. Hence it must have taken place when Jesus had been preaching for some time and had already won a large following in Galilee.

One morning on the western shore of Lake Tiberias, Jesus found Himself surrounded by a multitude anxious to hear Him speak. But the crowd was so great that in order to hold their interest and at the same time be heard more easily, He had recourse to a very practical expedient. When the lake is calm, it is almost motionless, nor is there the least ripple of sound to keep one from hearing anyone speaking in a loud voice. Hence, from a boat a few yards out from the shore, one could speak very effectively to a crowd gathered on the beach to listen.

That is what Jesus did. There were two small boats nearby, whose owners were busy washing their nets. One of these was Simon Peter. This suggests two probabilities: that the incident occurred near Capernaum and that at the time Peter had suspended his intermittent following of Jesus, returning to his trade with his brother Andrew in order to provide for his family. When Jesus finished speaking from His floating pulpit, He was careful to reward the one who had furnished it. Turning to Simon, He told him to row out on the lake and cast his nets.

Lake Tiberias

Jesus' invitation must have seemed to Peter an unwitting irony. That very night had been a wretched one, and Simon and his companions had labored hard without catching anything, and if the fishing had been bad at night, it would be still worse by day. But since the Master told him to cast his nets, he would not refuse. And so the nets were cast. Suddenly, however, they began to pull in so much fish that the rigging could not support the weight and the nets began to break under the strain. Peter shouted to his companions in the other boat, which was idling by, to come and help, and

The modern city of Tiberias with the lake in the background

so they did, but they worked a long time, loading both boats with fish, so that they almost sank.

Lake Tiberias was in ancient times, and still is today, very rich in fish. But in every age, the fishermen of Tiberias have also had days and nights of bad luck when it seemed that all the fish in the lake had gone off to other waters. Was the lucky draft that day mere chance? Simon, an expert fisherman, did not think so. Nor was he the only one, for the fishermen in the other boat, James and John, were astonished at the haul. The impulsive Simon threw himself at the feet of Jesus, exclaiming: "Depart from me, for I am an unworthy sinner!" But Jesus answered: "Do not be afraid. From now on you will be a fisher of men."

When they had all come to land, Jesus extended the same invitation to James and John, who with their father Zebedee were partners[11] of Simon and his brother Andrew. And the two pairs of brothers left their boats and all things, and from that day they were constantly with the Master.

---

[11] The term is a technical one. Since fishing with large nets required a great many men and tools, a number of fishermen formed a company; one furnished the boat, another the nets or other implements, and another his labor. The profit was divided among the "partners" in proportion to their contribution.

Other Miracles; First Difficulties

Jesus continued His ministry in Galilee, and the Synoptics present several of its episodes without offering a very definite picture of the time sequence. But as the fame of the new prophet spread, difficulties began to arise, first from the Pharisees, then from other sources as well.

Once, perhaps shortly after Jesus had chosen the first apostles, a leper approached and, falling at His feet, said to Him simply: "Lord, if thou wilt thou canst make me clean!" (Luke 5:12). The lepers in ancient Israel were the object of extreme horror. The Mosaic Law excluded them from all human intercourse, and they were obliged to live in isolation in lonely places and to shout, "Away! Unclean! Unclean!" (Lam. 4:15) whenever a wayfarer approached. In recompense for this warning, some food was sent out to them in their solitude, but aside from this, society wanted nothing to do with them; they were the very incarnations of impurity, the victims of the extreme wrath of Yahweh. Not rarely, however, the lepers violated the quarantine, just as this leper did when he came to Jesus. Certainly he had heard of Jesus and of the miracles He wrought for all kinds of sufferers. Who knew but what the Galilean prophet, kind and powerful as He was, would do something for him, too, in his extreme misfortune?

His case, however, was so frightening that he did not even dare to express what he had come to implore; he could only express his confidence in the One he besought. Jesus "had compassion" on him and his recklessness, which had impelled him to break the law and come among clean men. So He "stretched forth his hand," and then, to the horror of any who may have been watching Him, He touched that leprous mass of puss and stench. And answering the man's thought rather than his words, He said: "I will. Be thou made clean!" (Mark 1:41). And the leper was instantly made clean. Jesus immediately sent him away, however, because as usual He wished to avoid the enthusiasm of the people, and He bade him sternly not to tell anyone what had happened. At the same time, He reminded him to fulfill what the Mosaic Law required in the rare instances of a leprosy cure — to present himself to the priest and declare his cure and offer the prescribed sacrifice of purification. This was on Jesus' part an act of deference toward the Law and a kind of compensation for the violation the leper had committed against it. The cured man probably fulfilled the legal requirements later, but he began by disobeying Jesus and spreading the news of what had happened. After all, even had he kept silent, his face would have spoken for him, for it was now the face of a healthy, normal man.

The consequences of this news were not long in coming. Other crowds ran to the wonder-worker to hear Him and other unfortunates thronged to be cured, "so that he could no longer openly enter a town, but remained outside in desert places" (Mark 1:45). And He "was in retirement in the desert and in prayer" (Luke 5:16).

Later, when the excitement had abated, Jesus went back to Capernaum. His popularity had put the scribes and Pharisees on the alert, and unable as yet to form a definite judgment of this new prophet, they began to watch Him as they had John the Baptist. Hence, during the sojourn in Capernaum we find Jesus in a house teaching, and "there were also Pharisees and doctors of the Law sitting by, that were come out of every town of Galilee, and Judea, and Jerusalem" (Luke 5:17). It is significant that they had come even from Jerusalem to watch Him. Apparently, however, their attitude was not aggressive; they seem to have been there only to learn like the others who had filled the house. While Jesus was speaking, a group of men tried to open a way through the crowd jamming the entrance. They were carrying a paralytic on a pallet, and they hoped to lay him before the Master. But no one in that closely packed multitude would budge to let them by. They had to act quickly. The Master might end His discourse at any moment and retire to some unknown place to pray as He usually did. So while Jesus was still speaking in the main room of the house, the paralytic suddenly came floating down from the ceiling, pallet and all. What had happened? The sick man's bearers had indeed been quick about their business. The houses of the poor in Palestine generally consisted of only one floor roofed with a terrace of packed earth. They had mounted to this roof by the outside stairway, removed the earth, displaced one or two boards or small beams, and there was an opening big enough to allow the pallet and its burden to be lowered with ropes. Naturally, at the unexpected appearance of this new listener, Jesus' preaching stopped. His first reaction was one of admiration for the faith of those men and their charge; then, turning to the paralytic, He said to him only: "Son, thy sins are forgiven thee!"

The Hebrew word for *sin* may mean either the sin itself or its consequences; and one of the principal consequences of sin, according to the Hebrews, was physical deformity, especially if it was serious and chronic. In which sense did Jesus use the term? Probably His words included both the invisible moral guilt and the visible consequence. But no sooner were they spoken than "the Scribes and Pharisees began to argue, saying: Who is this man who speaks blasphemies? Who can forgive sins but God only?" (Luke 5:21). Evidently the objection concerned only one meaning of the word, that of moral guilt, the remission of which could not be ascertained physically by anyone. But there was the other meaning, too, that of bodily illness; and here it was possible to see what happened, and all could judge for themselves whether Jesus had spoken recklessly. Jesus answered His critics by performing a physical cure in proof of the invisible remission. "But Jesus knowing their thoughts, answered and said to them: What are you arguing in your hearts? Which is easier, to say, 'Thy sins are forgiven thee,' or to say, 'Arise and walk'?" The challengers must have understood immediately that they were cornered, for their challenge had been accepted. Jesus' question must have been followed by the embarrassed silence of people afraid to say any more for fear of making matters worse. Receiving no answer, He continued: "But that you may know that the Son of Man has power on earth to forgive sins" — and at this point He turned to the paralytic — "I say to thee, arise, take up thy bed and go to thy house!" And the sick man rose to his feet, rolled up his pallet, and walked off. All present were astounded, but we do not know exactly how the Pharisees reacted. Probably they thought this was not a fair reply to an elegant question of Jewish theology, but in any case, they certainly did not give Jesus the right of it.

In fact, they did not relax their vigilance. Shortly after the cure of the paralytic, a different kind of incident occurred. As Jesus was passing through Capernaum He saw a publican, Levi, son of Alpheus, sitting in the tax collector's place, receiving payments, giving receipts, and gathering far more curses than coins. Perhaps this publican knew Jesus by reputation, or he may have been personally acquainted with Him and cherished some veneration for Him. He may even have nourished a kind of envy for Jesus' disciples, poor but blessed and beloved by the people, while he, with his little piles of gold and silver before him, was regarded as some sort of mangy dog. The fact is that Jesus, as He passed, looked at him and said only: "Follow me!" The words were a spark touched to tinder. As soon as the publican heard them, "leaving all things, he arose and followed him" (Luke 5:28). This publican, according to the prevailing custom, had besides the name Levi that of Matthew, meaning gift of God. He is the author of the first Gospel.

Now, this new follower of Jesus, who had so promptly renounced his social status, did not immediately renounce its material advantages but used them to honor his new Master. Being a wealthy man, he gave a magnificent banquet to which he invited Jesus and His disciples, and right beside them he sat his own former colleagues, that is, "many publicans and sinners" as he says himself (9:10; Mark 2:15). The very fact of such mixed company seemed offensive to the scribes and Pharisees, who were still busy with their watching. Highly scandalized, they refrained from entering the house of that sinner in order to avoid contamination, but at the door they approached the disciples of Jesus and remarked: "How does this happen? You and your Master lower yourselves to eat and drink in company with publicans and sinners? Where is your self-respect? Where is your legal purity?"

The remarks reached Jesus, who answered for all of them: "It is not the healthy who need a physician, but they who are sick. But go and learn what this means: I desire mercy, and not sacrifice. For I have come to call sinners, not the just." The words Jesus quotes are from the prophetic writings (Hos. 6:6), which shows that Jesus' teaching was linked with that of the ancient prophets, who were much more concerned with the spiritual formation of their people than with the ritual formalities, just as John the Baptist had been.

Naturally the Pharisees were not persuaded by this reply, which appealed to one of the most dangerous pronouncements of the already dangerous prophets. Taken literally, it would abolish the whole Law of Moses and all the observances of the Jewish religion. And then what could save the vast fortress of rabbinic legislation, the supreme delight of God and of men? And, incidentally, what was Jesus' opinion of the pious practices of the Pharisees, like fasting? On this point, those who were spying on Jesus found support among certain disciples of John the Baptist who were jealous of the new Master. One day they came together and asked Jesus: "How is it that we, the disciples of John and the Pharisees both, fast frequently, but you and your disciples eat and drink?" How can they win holiness before God and power among the people if they do not become thin and gloomy with fasting? Jesus answered: "Can the wedding guests [i.e., the "friends of the bridegroom"] mourn as long as the bridegroom is with them? But the days will come, when the bridegroom shall be taken away from them, and then they will fast" (Matt. 9:15). The answer turns on the person of Jesus Himself though it defends the disciples: for them the time will surely come for mourning and fasting, but it is not the present, in which the Master is among them as the bridegroom among his groomsmen. The answer should have been at least partially understood by all who heard it. Only recently John had been violently taken from his disciples and had left them in mourning, and Jesus predicts a like fate for His own followers.

After all, why insist so much on the material fast? Though it had assumed supreme importance among the Pharisees (without producing great spiritual results), it had not been so important in the ancient Law. If the spirit was to be festively clothed, then it was necessary to change its garment completely, not mend the old: "No one puts a patch of raw cloth on an old garment, for the patch [being stiff] tears away from the garment and a worse rent is made. Nor do people pour new wine into old wineskins, else the skins burst, the wine is spilt, and the skins are ruined. But they put the new wine into fresh skins, and both are saved" (Matt. 9:15–17).

Principles like these must have convinced the Pharisees, who certainly were not imbeciles, that the new Rabbi would never associate Himself with the school of any of the great teachers of "tradition." Nevertheless, they or others continued to shadow Him if only to catch Him in new assaults against their "tradition."

The opportunity soon came. Several weeks had passed since the conversation with the Samaritan woman, which had taken place in May. Hence, the harvest was good and ripe, even in Galilee, and here and there the reaping had perhaps already begun. On a certain Sabbath, while Jesus and His disciples were crossing a field, one or two of them felt hungry; so they began to pluck the ears of wheat and, crumbling them in their hands, they ate the kernels. This was a violation of the Sabbath, because reaping was one of the thirty-nine categories of work prohibited on the Sabbath, and according to the rabbis, rubbing the ears between the hands was a kind of reaping. Having taken the culprits by surprise in this flagrant misdemeanor, His critics confronted Jesus: Do you not see? They are doing what is unlawful on the Sabbath day! Jesus answered them with a discussion of the principle of lawful exception to the Sabbath rule. He reminded them that David, when he fled hungry, entered the tabernacle of Yahweh with his companions, and they ate the "loaves of proposition," which only the priests might eat lawfully. From this it was natural to proceed to a consideration of the Sabbath itself. Going back to the basic principle involved, Jesus declared: "The Sabbath was made for man, and not man for the Sabbath," the exact opposite of what the Pharisees ordinarily thought. And he concluded: "Therefore the Son of Man is Lord even of the Sabbath" (Mark 2:27–28). The relationship expressed in the "therefore" is important. The Sabbath was made for man and *therefore* He who had but recently demonstrated His authority over the sins of man had authority over the Sabbath as well.

But the Pharisees were too jealous of their Sabbath to let the matter rest with the statement that Jesus was lord of that too. This time there was no visible proof as there had been in the case of the paralytic's sins. It came shortly afterward, however.

It was again the Sabbath and Jesus had gone to a synagogue to preach as was His custom. And here the Pharisees who were still spying on Him were presented with an excellent opportunity to corner Him on the matter of the Sabbath precept. A man with a withered hand had come to the synagogue, and the miracle-worker might possibly be tempted to cure him. They were not content just to watch, it seems, for certain ones set themselves to lead Him on (Matt 12:10), asking Him if it was lawful to cure on the Sabbath. This was a broad question, but there was the rule that except in immediate danger of death, any cure or medical treatment was forbidden on the Sabbath.

As in the case of the paralytic, Jesus did not enter into discussion but furnished a visible proof of the lawfulness of healing on the Sabbath. Who, according to the Pharisees, had established the precept? God, certainly. Who was the Lord of all natural laws? God, certainly. Then if a natural law is suspended on the Sabbath, that is God's work.

This was the reasoning of Jesus' answer, but He expressed it by action rather than words.

"But he said to the man with the withered hand: Arise and stand forth into the midst. And he arose and stood forth. Then Jesus said to them: I ask you, is it lawful on the Sabbath to do good or to do evil, to save a life or to destroy it?" (Luke 6:8–9). "But they kept silence. And looking round upon them with anger, and being grieved at the blindness of their hearts, he said to the man: Stretch forth thy hand! And he stretched it forth, and his hand was restored." Then the Pharisees answered in their own fashion, for they "went out and immediately took counsel how they might do away with him" (Mark 3:4–6). But He, aware of their scheming, retired from the place, as He had when He heard of John's imprisonment, and many followed Him (Matt. 12:15).

The Twelve Apostles

Against the horizon of Jesus' life, a cloud, still quite distant but foreboding certain storm, was by now clearly outlined; it was the cloud of the Pharisees. There was no mistaking the outcome, for the recent case of John the Baptist was clear example of the fate of anyone caught in that storm. Hence Jesus provides a shelter, not for Himself but for His work.

Six or seven months had passed perhaps since the beginning of His public life, and His ministry in Galilee had won Him many enthusiastic followers. From among them He would choose the foundation stones of His spiritual edifice. These He would set in place and then begin to raise up the house that should resist the tempest to come.

Among Jesus' customary followers, some were already bound to Him with a particular loyalty; these were Simon Peter and Andrew, James and John the sons of Zebedee, then Levi or Matthew, Philip, and Nathaniel or Bartholomew. Their number was increased by five others who certainly had been following Jesus for some time, although we are not told when or how they became associated with Him. Mark (3:13–19) and Luke (6:12–16) record the choosing of the Twelve before the Sermon on the Mount, and this is undoubtedly correct. Matthew (10:1–4) lists the Twelve after the Sermon on the Mount on the occasion of their temporary mission in the cities of Israel, but it is evident that they had been chosen earlier.

As at the beginning of His public life, so before this act, unique in His ministry, Jesus "went out to the mountain to pray, and continued all night in prayer to God. And when day broke, he summoned his disciples, and from these he chose twelve [whom he also named apostles]" (Luke 6:12–13).

In Greek the word *apostle* meant "one sent." In civil life, an "apostle" was one sent to arrange a marriage or divorce or to deliver a legal decision. The Sanhedrin in Jerusalem had its "apostles," too, messengers sent with information to the various outlying communities.

But the ordinary "apostles" of Judaism (except the prophets and others who showed special marks) and the apostles instituted by Jesus had nothing in common except the name. The former were simply agents representing a certain person in a specific affair, or they might be the bearers of messages or letter carriers; they were "apostles" in the strict sense of the term, but they did not form a true juridical institution. The latter, however, did constitute a specific and permanent institution, while they were "sent" in a true and much higher sense, for they were to be the actual and spiritual bearers of the "good tidings."

The number twelve had an evident analogy with the twelve sons of Israel and the twelve tribes descended from them to form the chosen nation of Yahweh. Since the house of Israel now threatened not to receive the Messiah, the new house He instituted in place of the old would also be directed by twelve spiritual tribal heads. The first generation of Christians so cherished the number twelve chosen by Jesus that they not only included unfailingly the name of the traitor Judas, but when he came to die, the first concern of the chief of the twelve, Peter, was to choose a new disciple in his place and thus complete the sacred number once more. In fact, the New Testament calls them the "Twelve" (thirty-four times) much more frequently than "apostles" (four times).

The list of the Twelve is given four times, in each of the Synoptics (Matt. 10:2–4; Mark 3:16–19; Luke 6:14–16) and in the Acts (1:13). No list is completely identical with another, not even the two that belong to the same author, namely, in the Gospel of Luke and in the Acts. But there are these constant similarities: Simon (Peter) is always named first and Judas the traitor last (except in the Acts when he has already died); the names are always arranged in three groups of four, Simon invariably heading the first group, Philip the second, and James son of Alpheus the third. The list as given by Matthew follows:

Simon, who is called Peter

Andrew, his brother

James, the son of Zebedee

John, his brother

Philip

Bartholomew

Thomas

Matthew, the publican

James, the son of Alpheus

Thaddeus

Simon the Cananean

Judas Iscariot, the traitor

The names vary in the third group only, due no doubt to the frequent Jewish custom of having two names. Instead of Thaddeus, which in some manuscripts is written *Lebbeus*, there appears a *Jude* [son] of *James*, but it is the same person. The patronymic *of James* served to distinguish him from the traitor Judas, as the epithet *the Cananean* served to distinguish the second Simon from Simon Peter. The adjective *Cananean* appears in some lists translated *Zealot*.

If Bartholomew is really Nathanael, the first six in the list are already known to us, and so is the eighth, Matthew. Of the others we know that James son of Alpheus, or James the Less (the "Greater" is James son of Zebedee), was the son of a certain Mary and that his brothers were Joseph, Simon, and Judas (cf. Mark 15:40; Matt. 13:55; 27:56) and that he was called the "brother of the Lord." Probably this last fact is the reason why he has first place in the third group. The name *Thomas* is the Greek transliteration of the Aramaic *toma*, which means "twin." The traitor Judas is distinguished by the epithet "Iscariot." It almost certainly refers to the city in Judea named Qeriyyoth from which Judas's ancestors had come. In Mark's list (3:17) we read that Jesus called the two brothers James and John, "sons of thunder." This name was not bestowed on the young men at this time of the apostles' selection, but only later, after various incidents in which they had displayed the impetuous nature that prompted it.

As for the social position and education of the Twelve, we may conclude from hints in their later conduct that they belonged in general to that class a little below the middle class of small proprietors and quite a bit above the lowest class of proletarians. Its position may be compared in general, although not exactly, to that of our small tradesmen or ordinary wage earners.

All of them worked at some manual labor, such as fishing, but then this was common also among the rabbis dedicated to the study of the Law. Nor did it represent so stern an economic necessity in those days as it does with us. The general way of life permitted them to stop working for several days at a time, and this was particularly true of those whose economic position was a little more solid, like that of the family of Zebedee, for instance, who operated a rather large fishing business. It is not too hardy to suppose that Jesus' family was less comfortable, financially, than those of all or most of the apostles.

Many in this modest category were intensely interested in spiritual problems, especially those in any way related to religious and national issues. They voluntarily left the humble comforts of their homes to take part in a discussion, to listen to a celebrated teacher, or to follow for several days in a row some popular leader. What they learned in these gatherings they cherished in their memories, the favorite archive of the Semitic people, and it furnished the material for continued private reflection and frequent group discussions as well, forming the principal cultural heritage of this particular class. They read and wrote little, but that does not mean that they were all illiterate.

This in general was the social and cultural background of the Twelve chosen by Jesus, although one or two of them may have been in some ways more favored than the others.

Naturally the apostles were of varying temperaments. Andrew seems to have been of a rather calm nature, resembling very little his impetuous brother Peter. The two "sons of thunder" were not much like the mistrustful and diffident Thomas. All of them, when they became Jesus' disciples, were certainly afire with love and enthusiasm for Him, but within their own respective personalities they were much the same as other men, and taken together, they more or less represented all of humanity. That is why there had also to be a traitor among them.

The Sermon on the Mount

The public choosing of the Twelve would have meant little had it not been followed by a spiritual vocation, that is, by a fuller instruction in Jesus' teachings. Notwithstanding their affection for the Master, the apostles must have known very little of His thought, and they would have been much embarrassed had some learned Pharisee challenged them to a complete, precise exposition of His doctrines. They had seen Him work miracles to help the afflicted, and they had heard Him preach as one "having authority" and affirm principles of justice and goodness; they themselves had felt dominated and attracted by Him, and they loved Him deeply. And that was all they would have been able to say.

Besides, the people, too, needed an exposition of the basic principles of Jesus' teaching, for the crowds that had occasionally heard Him preach must have had much vaguer notions regarding it than the apostles had. The increasing hostility of the scribes and Pharisees also called for the laying down of a definite program, so that Jesus' position and theirs might be more clearly defined for the people.

The Sermon on the Mount filled all these needs.

Jesus was by now well-known not only in Galilee but also beyond its borders. With the surprising rapidity with which news traveled by mouth throughout the Semitic world, His fame had spread to the south through Judea and Idumaea, both Jewish regions, to the Greek Decapolis in the east and to the great Mediterranean centers of pagan Phoenicia in the west. Groups of people kept coming from these countries to the Galilean prophet, to see Him and to "listen to him," but also and especially to "be healed of their diseases" (Luke 6:18). "For he healed many, so that as many as had ailments were pressing upon him to touch him" (Mark 3:10). The waves of people followed one after the other increasing in number until one day Jesus thought it was time to set His program before the multitude and His chosen Twelve together.

All three Synoptics set the Discourse on "the mountain," with the definite article but with no further description. Hence it was one of the hills of Galilee. The tradition that has chosen what is today called the "Mount of the Beatitudes" has several not inconsiderable arguments in its favor. The "mountain" is the hill, about five hundred feet high, on the western shore of Lake Tiberias about eight miles from Tiberias and two from Capernaum. Jesus did not deliver the Discourse on the very top of the hill, but somewhat further down on a level place on the southwest slope.

We have two reports of the Sermon, Matthew's and Luke's, but they present a number of differences, chiefly in the amount and arrangement of material. Matthew's account is about three and a half times as long as Luke's, but in other episodes of Jesus' life Luke records ample excerpts of the Sermon as given by Matthew.

The fact that Luke assigns these statements to other circumstances is important. Not only do we find this true of Mark, who omits the entire Sermon but records separate parts of it here and there, but we also unexpectedly find it in Matthew himself, for he has Jesus repeat certain maxims of the Sermon on other occasions (compare Matt. 5:29–30 with 18:8–9 and 5:32 with 19:9). This is not surprising if we keep in mind what we have already observed regarding both the evangelists' direct dependence on the living catechesis of the Church and their respective aims and methods. On this last point we must remember particularly that Matthew is the one who writes with "order"; Luke the one who proposes to set forth "in order."[123]

The possibility is even greater that the Sermon on the Mount as Jesus gave it was much longer than either of the two versions we now possess. Matthew's, the longer, could be delivered as a sermon today in about twenty minutes, and if we add the few verses peculiar to Luke, we lengthen it by only three or four minutes more. This would certainly not be a very long discourse for the crowds who came from distant places to listen to Jesus. So it is quite probable that the early oral catechesis gave a much fuller account of this discourse than we possess today and that, while Mark omitted it altogether, the other two Synoptics reproduced only the parts of it that suited their aims.

In conclusion, Matthew's account seems nearer to the form the Discourse had in the early catechesis and is therefore more suitable as the basis of our discussion.

The Sermon on the Mount may be compared to a majestic symphony, whose clear basic themes are resolutely proclaimed with full orchestra in the very first measures. And they are the most unexpected, the most unheard-of themes in all this world, totally unlike any others ever played, and yet the most natural and spontaneous of all to a well-trained ear. And in truth, until the Sermon on the Mount, all the symphonies of the sons of men, though they varied in kind, were alike in proclaiming that blessedness for man was good fortune, that satisfaction came with satiety, that pleasure was the satisfaction of desire and honor the product of esteem. On the other hand, in its very opening harmonies, the Discourse on the Mount announces that man's

---

[12] It is to be noted that Jesus spent the night in prayer and chose His apostles on the mountain (cf. Mark 3:13; Luke 6:12–13), that is, on the higher part of the mountain less accessible to the multitudes. According to Matthew, the Sermon was given "up the mountain" (5:1), but after Jesus "coming down with them ... took his stand on a level stretch," according to Luke (6:17). It is easy to imagine this level place on the slope or at the foot of the hill, which Matthew includes in the term *mountain*, and so the two pieces of information complete each other. The level place indicated by tradition fits both designations very well.

blessedness resides in misfortune, satisfaction in hunger, pleasure in unfulfill-ment, and honor in disesteem, all ultimately to resolve into the reward that awaits him in the future.

In this sense of being contrary to common opinion, the Sermon on the Mount is the most complete paradox ever asserted. No discourse on earth was ever more subversive, or better, reversive than this. White is not called dark or gray but altogether black, and black is shining white. What has always been a good is now assigned to the category of evils, and an evil is called a good. And this reversal of things is presented with a tone of crisp, concise command justi-fied by the authority of the speaker alone: This is so, because I, Jesus, tell you it is so; others have told you white, but I tell you black; fifty has been prescribed, but that is only partly good, and I, Jesus, prescribe the whole hundred.

And what are the sanctions of this new order of things? It has no human sanctions, only divine ones; no worldly sanctions but entirely supraworldly.

The poor are blessed because theirs is the Kingdom of Heaven, not a king-dom on earth. The sorrowful are blessed because they shall be comforted, but in a distant and unspecified future. The clean of heart are blessed because they will see God, not because their purity is to be praised by men. Thus, the new order has a true basis only for those who accept and await the Kingdom of Heaven.

Finally, the Sermon on the Mount does not ignore historical fact, but fits in with past and contemporary Hebraism on many essential points. The Mosaic Law is not abolished, but integrated and perfected; it is kept as a kind of first floor to which an upper story is added. The chief concern is always for the moral and the spiritual rather than for the material act in itself. Not even the economic and financial question is slighted, but it is given a new setting in an act of faith, in a vision of the providence of God. Love governs all, in its twofold expression toward God and toward men. God is the Father of the whole human family who knows when His children are hungry and requires only the tribute of their persistent prayer for bread. All men, children of the supernatural Father, are brothers one of another. So important is the love we must bear our fellow men that not even our love for God is true unless it is accompanied by this other love. God is not pleased with offerings from one whose conscience toward his brother is not at peace.

The Sermon on the Mount follows a quite clear outline, especially in Mat-thew's version. The prologue, which plunges into the very heart of the matter, is represented by the beatitudes (5:3–12).

This astounding prologue presents the general spirit of Jesus' program, or the Messianic Law. It concludes with the announcement that this spirit must be as a salt to preserve the entire world from corruption and as a light to illumine all the earth (Matt. 5:13–16; in other context, Luke 14:34–35, and 8:16, 11:33). But immediately after this glance toward the future, the Discourse turns back and faces the question of the relationship between past and future where the Hebrew Law is concerned. The outline follows:

Jesus does not destroy the Law but renews it, in part abrogating and in part retaining and perfecting it (Matt. 5:17–20). The Messianic Law perfects the Mosaic Law in the precepts regarding fraternal peace and concord, chastity, matrimony, the taking of oaths, revenge and charity (5:21–48). It surpasses by far the practice of the Pharisees with regard to almsgiving, prayer, and fasting (6:1–8). It is the one true treasure for those who accept it and frees them from all other solicitude (6:19–34). It demands more perfect charity and more constant prayer (7:1–12). It is a narrow gate but a protection against false prophets, and it induces good works (7:13–23). In short, the New Law is a house built on living rock and will withstand the floods and tempests that beat against it (7:24–27).

Even this sketchy summary makes it clear that the Sermon on the Mount is intended, among other things, to counterbalance the Law of Moses, which it does not destroy but perfects. This is also reflected by the setting in which the Discourse was delivered. Just as Moses, assisted by the ancients of the nation, had promulgated the Old Law on Mount Sinai in the presence of the people, Jesus, attended by the twelve apostles, promulgated the New Law on a hill in Galilee in the presence of the multitude.

The Sermon on the Mount is popular in style and Oriental in expression. It contains no subtleties or abstractions but abounds in concrete examples, which have always been dear to the people and from which they are expert in extracting the general rules. Typical Oriental exaggerations are frequent, but the audience knew how to give them their true value. For the audience, phrases like, "If thy right hand scandalize thee, cut it off, and cast it from thee," or "if one strike thee on thy right cheek, turn to him also the other," added flavor to the discourse. But Jesus' first followers never did cut off their right hands or offer the left cheek for the simple reason that they understood the way men spoke in their country and besides they had good common sense.

The rest of the Discourse follows (Matt. 5):

> You are the salt of the earth; but if the salt loses its strength, what shall it be salted with? It is no longer of any use but to be thrown out and trodden underfoot by men.

You are the light of the world. A city set on a mountain cannot be hidden. Neither do men light a lamp and put it under the measure, but upon the lamp-stand, so as to give light to all in the house. Even so let your light shine before men, in order that they may see your good works and give glory to your Father [he who is] in heaven.

Do not think that I have come to destroy the Law or the Prophets. I have not come to destroy, but to fulfill. For amen I say unto you, till heaven and earth pass away, not one jot or one tittle shall be lost from the Law, till all things have been accomplished. Therefore whoever does away with one of these least commandments, and so teaches men, shall be called least in the kingdom of heaven. But whoever carries them out and teaches them, he shall be called great in the kingdom of heaven. For I say to you that unless your justice exceeds that of the Scribes and the Pharisees, you shall not enter into the kingdom of heaven.

You have heard that it was said to the ancients: "Thou shalt not kill"; and that whoever shall murder shall be liable to judgment. But I say to you that everyone who is angry with his brother, shall be liable to judgment; and whoever says to his brother "Raca," shall be liable to the Sanhedrin; and whoever says, "Thou fool!" shall be liable to the fire of Gehenna. Therefore, if thou art offering thy gift at the altar, and there rememberest that thy brother hath anything against thee, leave thy gift before the altar and go first to be reconciled to thy brother, and then come and offer thy gift.

Come to terms with thy opponent quickly, while thou art with him on the way; lest thy opponent deliver thee to the judge, and the judge to the officer, and thou be cast into prison. Amen I say to thee, thou wilt not come out from it until thou hast paid the last penny.

You have heard that it was said: "Thou shalt not commit adultery." But I say to you that anyone who even looks with lust at a woman has already committed adultery with her in his heart. So if thy right eye is an occasion of sin to thee, pluck it out and cast it from thee; for it is better for thee that one of thy members should perish than that thy whole body should be thrown into hell. And if thy right hand is an occasion of sin to thee, cut it off, and cast it from thee; for it is better for thee that one of thy members should be lost than that thy whole body should go into hell.

It was said, moreover: "Whoever puts away his wife, let him give her a written notice of dismissal." But I say to you that everyone who puts away his wife, save on account of immorality, causes her to commit adultery; and he who marries a woman who has been put away commits adultery.

Again you have heard that it was said to the ancients: "Thou shalt not swear falsely, but fulfill thy oaths to the Lord." But I say to you not to swear at all: neither by heaven, for it is the throne of God; nor by the earth, for it is the footstool of his feet; nor by Jerusalem, for it is the city of the great King. Neither do thou swear by thy head, for thou canst not make one hair white or black. But let your speech be: "Yes [if it is] yes," "no [if it is] no" and whatever is beyond these [words] comes from the evil one.

You have heard that it was said: "An eye for an eye," and "a tooth for a tooth." But I say to you not to resist the evildoer; on the contrary, if someone strike thee on the right cheek, turn to him the other also; and if anyone would go to law with thee and take thy tunic, let him take thy cloak as well; and whoever forces thee to go for one mile, go with him two [miles]. To him who asks of thee, give; and from him who would borrow of thee, do not turn away.

You have heard that it was said: "Thou shalt love thy neighbor, and shalt hate thy enemy." But I say to you: Love your enemies, do good to those who hate you, and pray for those who persecute and calumniate you, so that you may be children of your Father [he who is] in heaven, who makes his sun to rise on the good and the evil, and sends rain on the just and the unjust. For if you love those who love you, what reward shall you have? Do not even the publicans do that? And if you salute your brethren only, what are you doing more than others? Do not even the pagans do that? You therefore are to be perfect, even as your heavenly Father is perfect.

Chapter 6:

Take heed not to practice your good [justice] before men, in order to be seen by them; otherwise you shall have no reward with your Father [who is] in heaven. Therefore when thou givest alms, do not sound a trumpet before thee, as the hypocrites do in the synagogues and in the streets, in order that they may be honored by men. Amen I say to you, they have had their reward. But when thou givest alms, do not let thy left hand know what thy right hand is doing, so that thy alms may be given in secret; and thy Father, who sees in secret, will reward thee.

Again, when you pray, you shall not be like the hypocrites, who love to pray standing in the synagogues and at the street corners, in order that they may be seen by men. Amen I say to you, they have had their reward. But when thou prayest, go into thy room, and closing thy door, pray to thy Father [who is] in secret; and thy Father who sees in secret will reward thee.

But in praying, do not multiply words, as the pagans do; for they think that by saying a great deal, they will be heard. So do not be like them; for your Father knows what you need before you ask him. In this manner therefore shall you pray:

Our Father who art in heaven	(Luke 11:2–4)
hallowed be thy name,	Father,
Thy kingdom come,	hallowed be thy name.
thy will be done,	Thy kingdom come.
on earth, as it is in heaven.	
Give us this day our daily	Give us this [every] day our daily
[necessary] bread	[necessary] bread.
And forgive us our debts,	And forgive us our sins,
as we also forgive our debtors	for we also forgive everyone
	who is indebted to us.
And lead us not into temptation,	And lead us not into temptation.
but deliver us from evil.	

For if you forgive men their offenses, your heavenly Father will forgive you your offenses. But if you do not forgive men, neither will your Father forgive you your offenses.

And when you fast, do not look gloomy like the hypocrites, who disfigure their faces in order to appear to men as fasting. Amen I say to you, they have had their reward. But thou, when thou dost fast, anoint thy head and wash thy face, so that thou mayest not be seen by men to fast, but by thy Father who is in secret, and thy Father, who sees in secret, will reward thee.

Do not lay up for yourselves treasures on earth, where rust and moth consume, and where thieves break in and steal; but lay up for yourselves treasures in heaven, where neither rust nor moth consumes, nor thieves break in and steal. For where thy treasure is, there thy heart also will be.

The lamp of the body is the eye. If thy eye be sound, thy whole body will be full of light. But if thy eye be [in] evil [state], thy whole body will be full of darkness. Therefore if the light that is in thee is darkness, how great is the darkness itself?

No man can serve two masters; for either he will hate the one and love the other, or else he will stand by the one and despise the other. You cannot serve God and mammon. Therefore I say to you, do not be anxious for your life, what you shall eat; nor yet for your body, what you shall put on. Is not the life a greater thing than the food, and the body more than the clothing? Look at the birds of the air; they do not sow, or reap, or gather into barns; yet your heavenly Father feeds them. Are not you of much more value than they? But which of you by being anxious about it can add to his stature [or age] a single cubit? And as for clothing why are you anxious? See how the lilies of the field grow; they neither toil nor spin, yet I say to you that not even Solomon in all his glory was arrayed like one of these. But if God so clothes the grass of the field, which today is alive and tomorrow is thrown into the oven, how much more will he clothe you, O you of little faith? Therefore do not be anxious, saying: "What shall we eat?" or "What shall we drink?" or "What are we to put on?" (for after all these things the Gentiles seek); for your Father knows that you need all these things. But seek first the kingdom of God and his justice, and all these things shall be given you besides. Therefore do not be anxious about tomorrow; for tomorrow will have anxieties of its own. Sufficient for the day is its own trouble.

Chapter 7:

Do not judge [condemn] that you may not be judged [condemned]; for with what judgment you judge, you shall be judged; and with what measure you measure, it shall be measured to you. But why dost thou see the speck [that is] in thy brother's eye, and yet dost not consider the beam [that is] in thy own eye? Or how canst thou say to thy brother, "Let me cast out the speck from thy eye"; and behold, there is a beam in thy own eye? Thou hypocrite, first cast out the beam from thy own eye, and then thou wilt see clearly to cast out the speck from thy brother's eye.

Do not give to dogs what is holy, neither throw your pearls before swine, or they will trample them under their feet and turn [against you] and rend you.

Ask, and it shall be given you; seek, and you shall find; knock, and it shall be opened to you. For every one who asks, receives; and he who seeks, finds; and to him who knocks, it shall be opened. Or what man is there among you, who, if his son asks him for a loaf, will hand him a stone; or if he asks for a fish, will hand him a serpent? Therefore, if you, evil as you are, know how to give good gifts to your children, how much more will your Father [who is] in heaven, give good things to those who ask him!

Therefore all things whatever you would that men should do to you, even so do you also to them; for this is the Law and the Prophets.

Enter by the narrow gate. For wide is the gate and broad is the way that leads to destruction, and many there are who enter that way. How narrow [is] the gate, and close the way that leads to life! And few there are who find it.

Beware of false prophets, who come to you in sheep's clothing, but inwardly they are ravenous wolves. By their fruits you will know them. Do men gather grapes from thorns, or figs from thistles? Even so, every good tree bears good fruit, but the bad tree bears bad fruit. A good tree cannot bear bad fruit, nor can a bad tree bear good fruit. Every tree that does not bear good fruit is cut down and thrown into the fire. Therefore, by their fruits you will know them.

Not everyone who says to me, "Lord, Lord," shall enter into the kingdom of heaven; but he who does the will of my Father [who is] in heaven shall enter the kingdom of heaven. Many will say to me that day, "Lord, Lord, did we not prophesy in thy name, and cast out devils in thy name, and work many miracles in thy name?" And then I will declare to them, "I never knew you. Depart from me, you workers of iniquity!"

Everyone therefore who hears these my words, and acts upon them, shall be likened to a wise man who built his house on rock. And the rain fell, and the floods came, and the winds blew and beat against that house, but it did not fall, because it was founded on rock. And everyone who hears these my words and does not act upon them, shall be likened to a foolish man who built his house on the sand. And the rain fell, and the floods came, and the winds blew and beat against that house, and it fell, and was utterly ruined.

With this simile of the house, in both versions, the Sermon on the Mount comes to a close. If one who heard and practiced its precepts was like one who builds a house on rock, then this is true even more so of Jesus, when He spoke it so far as the aims of His ministry were concerned. For as we have said, He, too, was building a shelter against the gathering storm. He had chosen and set in place twelve foundation stones, according to the number of the tribes of Israel, and other smaller stones were represented by the many other Israelites who were following Him. Now He was cementing all together with a teaching that was in part the ancient teaching of Israel and in part His own. There was more building still to be done and many places remained to be smoothed and finished, but the frame of the house was firmly erected in the Sermon on the Mount.

What does this Sermon represent in the general teaching of Jesus? It is not elaborate enough to be considered a code, nor is it even a summary, because it leaves too many doctrines of prime importance yet to be stated. The Sermon, for example, does not mention the redemption wrought by the death of Christ, Baptism, the Eucharist, the Church, or the end of the world, and without these we do not have a true historical picture of Christ's teaching. Nor is the Discourse, strictly speaking, a refutation of Pharisaic teaching or, better, a correction and perfection of Judaism, although these things are included in its purpose. Actually, the Sermon on the Mount is the description of the "change of mind" that both Jesus and John the Baptist had already been preaching as the prerequisite for the fulfillment of the Kingdom of God. And what "change of mind" could possibly represent so complete a subversal and reversal of ideas as this? The Sermon, then, rather than a "code," is the spirit that will later animate a whole new code; it is the central idea around which a full rich commentary will later develop.

The Centurion of Capernaum and the Widow of Naim

Shortly after the Discourse, Jesus returned to Capernaum. There was a centurion garrisoned there, probably in the mercenary troops of Herod Antipas and not in any Roman detachment. He was a pagan but kindly disposed to Judaism; he had, in fact, built the synagogue of Capernaum at his own expense. His goodness of heart is further evidenced by the fact that he was devotedly fond of his slave, whom he treated more as a son than a servant. Now this slave was on the point of death. The grief-stricken centurion, who must have tried all the known remedies in vain, knew Jesus by reputation. Having lost all hope in physicians, he thought of the miracle-worker, but he did not quite venture to present his

Ruins of the synagogue in Capernaum

plea to him, perhaps because he did not know him personally. He appealed therefore to the prominent Jews of the city to beg Jesus to do something for the dying man. The Jews earnestly recommended that Jesus grant the centurion's request: "He is worthy that thou shouldst do this for him, for he loves our nation and himself has built us our synagogue" (Luke 7:4–5).

Jesus, Himself a Jew, was naturally touched by the Jewish appeal in the request. So with the messengers He set out immediately for the centurion's house. It was already in sight when they were met by other messengers sent by the centurion. He felt a certain hesitancy, prompted by scruple and respect. His was a pagan house, and a practicing Jew could not enter it without being defiled. Would not the famous Jesus feel some repugnance about entering it, or would He not suffer some loss of respect among His coreligionists? Hence the second group of messengers tactfully suggested to Jesus in the words of the centurion: "Lord, do not trouble thyself; for I am not worthy that thou shouldst come under my roof; this is why I did not think myself worthy to come to thee. But say the word, and my servant will be healed. For I too am a man subject to authority, and have soldiers subject to me; and I say to one: 'Go,' and he goes; and to another: 'Come,' and he comes; and to my servant [slave]: 'Do this,' and he does it" (Luke 7:6–8). The centurion was trying to explain and justify his deference toward Jesus with his own soldier training. He was well acquainted with military discipline, and he exercised it over his soldiers. Hence, Jesus was not to humble

Himself to come into his house; let Him speak a single word and His command would be executed by the forces of nature that were conquering the dying man.

"Now when Jesus heard this he marvelled, and turning to the crowd that followed him, said: Amen I say to you, not even in Israel have I found so great a faith!" The order asked of Him was immediately given, and the sick man was cured instantly. But this, in the Gospel narrative, seems to take second place; what we remain conscious of most is the "great faith."

Luke follows this episode with the account of Naim. The present-day village — called Nain — is on the slopes of Little Hermon, about eight miles from Nazareth and thirty from Capernaum by the modern highway. Today it consists of a handful of pitiful little houses and numbers less than two hundred inhabitants. It was certainly in a better state in Jesus' time, but it was just as tiny a village and seems to have had only one gate in its walls.

To this hamlet Jesus came one day with His disciples and a great crowd of people. As He was about to enter the gate, along came a funeral procession, on its way, no doubt, to the cemetery, which is still to be seen a short distance from the dwellings. A young man was being carried out for burial, the only son of his widowed mother, who was following the bier. It was a particularly pitiful case, and perhaps that explains why "a large gathering from the town was with her" (Luke 7:12). For the physician-evangelist, the whole mournful procession is personified in the weeping mother, and Jesus sees no one but her. "And the Lord, seeing her, had compassion on her, and said to her: 'Do not weep.'" The poor woman had probably heard those words a thousand times that day, but they had been just words. Jesus goes further: "And he went up and touched the stretcher; and the bearers stood still. And he said: 'Young man, I say to thee, arise.' And he who was dead, sat up, and began to speak. And he gave him to his mother."

The Message of John the Baptist

Meanwhile in the dungeon of Machaerus, John the Baptist was as restless as a caged lion. As time passed, his spirit was consumed the more with the fervor of his hope. He had been born and he had lived to be the precursor of the Messiah, nor had he stolen a single day away from that mission. Now human tyranny might cut off his life at any time, and still he did not see his mission crowned by an open and solemn manifestation of the Messiah. This waiting was much harder for the prisoner than the sword of Antipas dangling over his head.

He was not, however, completely isolated. The tyrant, who nourished a superstitious veneration for John, permitted him to receive the disciples who had remained faithful to him even after Jesus began His public ministry, some of whom nourished a resentment toward Christ. Through these visitors, the prisoner followed the progress of Jesus' ministry and the extraordinary happenings that accompanied it. But this information increased the yearning anxiety of his waiting. The visitors told him that the new Rabbi worked miracles, yes, but had never proclaimed Himself the Messiah; in fact, He rebuked those who so proclaimed Him and fled every occasion when the crowd seemed about to declare Him such. Perhaps the prisoner wondered if his mission as precursor was truly ended or whether even from his prison there was not something he must yet do to have Jesus recognized as the Messiah. Why did Mary's son delay so long in asserting who He was? Only with His solemn declaration would John's mission come to a close; without it, he would be the precursor of one who failed to appear. What could he still do from his prison? How could he impel Jesus to make the declaration that he was yearning to hear and at the same time urge on toward Jesus his own reluctant disciples?

One day the prisoner came to a decision. From the Machaerus he dispatched two of the disciples to Jesus to ask him this question: "Art thou he who is to come, or shall we look for another?" (Luke 7:19–20). The expression "he who is to come" denoted for the Jews the Messiah who "was to come," whose distant heralds had been the prophets and whose immediate precursor John the Baptist claimed to be.

The question, therefore, required a specific declaration both from Jesus, to whom it was addressed, and from John's disciples, who were asking it. Jesus could not publicly deny His messianic nature, of which John was absolutely certain. The disciples who brought John's question, when they heard from Jesus' lips what they had heard of Him from their own revered John, could no longer fail to become His followers.

Jesus did not answer as He was expected to. He did not say the "no" that was impossible, but neither did He reply with a clear, explicit "yes." When the messengers stated their question "in that very hour he cured many of diseases, afflictions and evil spirits, and to many who were blind he granted sight. And he answered and said to them: Go and report to John what you have heard and seen: the blind see, the lame walk, the lepers are cleansed, the deaf hear, the dead rise, the poor have the gospel preached to them. And blessed is he who is not scandalized in me" (Luke 7:21–23). In short, Jesus answered not with words but with actions. Now, these miraculous actions appealed to prophetic words of the past, for Isaias had predicted that in the time of the Messiah the blind would see, the deaf hear, the lame walk, and the poor would receive the good tidings. If Jesus verifies with His works the messianic prophecies, then those works proclaimed Him the Messiah. But the explicit proclamation from His lips was not forthcoming.

Yet, though He did not answer John's respectful invitation, Jesus was pleased by it. Immediately after the departure of the messengers, to show that the precursor was not among those who would be scandalized in Him, Jesus spoke of John in terms of highest praise, declaring him "more than a prophet," second to none "among those born of woman," the precursor of the Messiah according to the prophecy of Malachias. But while the poor and the publicans had accepted John's preaching and received his baptism, most of the scribes and Pharisees had hung back, bringing to naught "God's purpose concerning themselves" (Luke 7:30). And here Jesus adds a similitude: "'To what then shall I liken the men of this generation? And what are they like? They are like children sitting in the market place, calling to one another and saying, 'We have piped to you, and you have not danced; / We have sung dirges, and you have not wept.'" The figure is drawn from the customs of the time. The children in Palestine used to play in the marketplace imitating the social habits of their elders, including their wedding and funeral processions. In the first instance, some would play or pretend to play the flute, while the others were supposed to dance, pretending that they were the "friends of the groom." In the latter instance, some would imitate the lamentations of the professional mourners while their playmates were supposed to weep like the relatives of the deceased. But sometimes the game did not go according to schedule; the children supposed to dance or weep did not show proper enthusiasm for their roles, and then followed the usual childish arguments. Jesus Himself explains the comparison: "For John the Baptist came neither eating bread nor drinking wine, and you say: 'He has a devil.' The Son of Man came eating and drinking, and you say: 'Behold a man who is a glutton, and a wine-drinker, a friend of publicans and sinners'" (Luke 7:33–34).

The Pharisees had not accepted John's preaching because, among other things, he was too rigorous. But when Jesus appeared, His preaching was rejected also on the pretext that He ate like other men, let His disciples eat when they were hungry, and treated with publicans and sinners. Hence, whether one played the flute or wailed a funeral chant, the game could not be played with the Pharisees simply because they did not want to play it. Yet it was going to be well played just the same, for "wisdom [divine] is justified by [all] her children."

The Penitent Woman

At this point Luke, the "scribe of Christ's mercy," records an episode that illustrates His gentleness.

The Pharisees continue to watch Jesus, but their vigilance need not always be aggressive; in fact, sometimes it is shrewder to cloak it with seeming friendliness. For this reason a Pharisee, with the common name of Simon, invites Jesus to dinner. According to the custom of the time, the dinner is held in a room with a U-shaped table in the middle. The guests recline on small divans arranged like rays around the table, while the servants pass the food from the other side of it. Hence each is leaning on one elbow with his head toward the table, while his feet extend somewhat beyond the end of the divan away from it. There are several guests at Simon's dinner, and it probably is not being given especially for Jesus. In any case, Jesus has not received the honors ordinarily given a prominent guest, who had his feet washed as soon as he entered, was embraced and kissed by the master of the house, and had his head sprinkled with perfume before he sat down. Jesus notices the omissions but says nothing and takes His place at table.

But when the banquet is at its height, a woman enters the room with the servants. She goes straight to the divan of Jesus, kneels at the foot of it, the end farthest from the table, and bursts into tears so abundant that they trickle down upon the feet of Jesus. Unwilling that those feet should be lined with her grief and having no cloth with which to wipe them, she proceeds, with great deference, to loosen her hair and dry them with that. Then she kisses them over and over again and sprinkles them with the ointment from the little alabaster vase she has brought with her to anoint the head of the man she so revered. This all takes place without a word spoken either by the woman or by Jesus. Perhaps a thin smile marks Simon's face. The examiner feels he has already tested and judged his candidate; as he watches the incident, he says to himself: "This man, were he a prophet, would surely know who and what manner of woman this is who is touching him, for she is a sinner!" (Luke 7:39).

For the Pharisees the term *sinner* had various meanings: it might denote an immoral woman or merely a woman who did not observe the Pharisaic precepts. We may suppose that this woman was a person of doubtful reputation, for had she been a public sinner, the Pharisee's servants would hardly have permitted her to enter. The unnamed woman already knew Jesus at least by sight; she may have heard Him speak those words that summoned everyone to a "change of mind" and yet were so kind and comforting to the most sinful. She had been deeply shaken by the consciousness of her miserable life;

but then, comforted by the hope those same words aroused, she had come to believe in a new life. And now, to begin it, she presented herself before the One who had given it to her to show Him her change of heart in a manner that was exquisitely feminine.

Perhaps Jesus noticed the smirk on Simon's lips; certainly He read the disapproval in his thoughts and so He turned quietly to speak to him: "Simon I have something to say to thee!" And Simon, with some condescension: "Please speak, Master!" And Jesus: "There was once a money-lender who was to collect five hundred denarii from one debtor, and from another a sum ten times less, fifty denarii. But since neither of the two could pay and the creditor was a kindhearted man, he forgave both their debts. Now which of these two debtors do you think, Simon, would be more grateful to this generous creditor and love him more?" And Simon answered: "I suppose the man who had more forgiven him." The answer was as elementary as it was correct. Jesus then replied:

> Dost thou see this woman? I came into thy house; thou gavest me no water for my feet; but she has bathed my feet with tears, and has wiped them with her hair. Thou gavest me no kiss; but she, from the moment she entered, has not ceased to kiss my feet. Thou didst not anoint my head with oil; but she has anointed my feet with ointment. Wherefore I say to thee, her sins, many as they are, shall be forgiven her, because she has loved much. But he to whom little is forgiven, loves little. (Luke 7:44–47)

The sinner was forgiven much because she loved much; but if she loved much, the reason, in its turn, was that she sought and almost anticipated the forgiveness of much. It was one love; it first impelled the sinner to seek the forgiveness of which it was the cause, and then confirmed the forgiveness and was its effect, as in the case of the debtor in the parable. Simon, being a good Pharisee, has little exteriorly to be forgiven but also has little love in his heart. Now for Jesus, sins are certainly an obstacle to one's entrance into the Kingdom of Heaven, but sins can be forgiven. The insurmountable obstacle, on the other hand, is the lack of desire to enter, the lack of love. A Pharisee, though he were set on the very threshold of the kingdom, would probably not enter it because he was satisfied with himself and would feel no impulse to take those extra steps that would bring him inside. But a harlot, once she saw herself as she really was, would feel an utter loathing of herself and run a thousand miles to enter the kingdom, sped on her way by love.

When He finished speaking with Simon, Jesus turned to the woman and said to her: "Thy sins are forgiven." We do not know how Simon reacted to this; we are told only that the other guests, who were of the same stamp as he, began to say to themselves: "Who is this man, who even forgives sins?" The Pharisees present who had witnessed the incident of the paralytic let down through the roof had asked themselves the same question, and Jesus had silenced them with a miracle. This time there was no miracle because there was no reason why Jesus should perform one every time the geese who had undertaken to guard some hypothetical capitol of orthodoxy began to cackle.

He preferred to confirm the woman in her new way of life, and so He said to her: "Thy faith has saved thee. Go in peace!" Peace and love were the same thing.

The Ministry Day by Day

Immediately after the account of Simon's banquet, Luke adds: "And it came to pass afterwards, that he himself was journeying through towns and villages, preaching and proclaiming the good tidings of the kingdom of God. And with him were the twelve" (Luke 8:1). These words may be taken as a summary of Jesus' activity in Galilee until the second Pasch of His ministry. Jesus led the life of a traveling missionary, journeying from region to region and from town to town, preaching in public and private, in synagogues and houses, and confirming His preaching with miracles. The crowds thronged to Him, attracted not only by the effectiveness of His teachings but even more by the immediate benefit of His miracles.

Jesus was not journeying alone; with Him was a small group of persons who had dedicated themselves to Him, as well as a constantly changing trail of people animated by a variety of motives.

Among those devoted to Him were first of all the twelve apostles. And there certainly were other disciples who were bound to the Master by particular ties of affection. But in that life of continuous traveling, Jesus and His helpers needed material assistance to take care of their daily wants, especially since this constant ministry left them no time to provide these things themselves. For this reason, the careful Luke adds that with Jesus there were also "certain women who had been cured of evil spirits and infirmities; Mary who is called Magdalene, from whom seven devils had gone out, and Joanna, the wife of Chuza, Herod's steward, and Susanna, and many others who used to provide for them out of their means" (8:2–3). We do not need to suppose that all of these were constantly with Jesus in His travelings;

probably they had some arrangement for taking turns in attending to the needs of the missionaries.

Of the women mentioned here, Joanna and Susanna are named only by Luke, while Mary Magdalene is mentioned also by the other evangelists. The epithet, "Magdalene," indicates that she came originally from Magdala, on the western shore of the lake, and hence was a native of Galilee and not of Judea. The statement that "seven devils had gone out" from her means only that Jesus had freed her from some powerful diabolical obsession, but the Gospel narratives do not furnish any basis for supposing that she had been a public sinner and much less the anonymous penitent at Simon's banquet.

Besides this group of faithful followers, there also swarmed about Jesus a train of people, some of them definitely hostile, like the Pharisees, and some diffident or at least uncertain about him. Mark incidentally gives us a brief bit about the latter (3:20–21). During a short trip that Jesus made at this time, probably to some town between Capernaum and Nazareth, He "came to the house, and again a crowd gathered so that they [Jesus and His disciples] could not so much as take their food." It was the customary rush of people, but this time it was more inconvenient than usual because there was so little room. Now this constant thronging of the people about Jesus, as well as His tireless activity, had attracted the attention of neutral and indifferent persons as well, who felt neither the devotion of His disciples nor the antipathy of the Pharisees. And they also had expressed their opinion of Jesus, "for they said he is beside [out of] himself."[13][4]

Although this expression could be disparaging, it was not necessarily so by any means. One who is abnormal mentally could be "out of himself" but so could a perfectly normal person completely possessed by a wise and holy enthusiasm. These indifferent neutrals, then, got out of the difficulty with this equivocal opinion of Jesus, referring only to what was clearly evident, namely, His incessant missionary activity, which implied a state of mind that was not usual. The remark reached the ears of Jesus' relatives, and when they learned that He was in a house nearby, practically besieged by the crowd, "his [own people] ... went out to lay hold of him, for they said: He is beside himself." The expression "his own people" unquestionably refers to Jesus' kin, some of whom we know did not look on Him too favorably; but that is not enough to ascribe to them the opinion "he is beside himself," because the main verb, "they said," could just as well be an impersonal ("it was said," "people said")

---

[13] See note on Mark 3:21 in Confraternity version.

as it is elsewhere in Mark (3:30, etc.). Whoever expressed the opinion, Jesus' relatives probably came in all kindliness to do Him a service.

Thus regarded as "out of himself," Jesus answered precisely as He was regarded, namely, as a person totally consecrated to a sublime moral ideal. Right after the above information, Mark describes His discussion with the Pharisees regarding Beelzebub and the matter of casting out devils, but then he immediately brings Jesus' relatives back on the scene together with Mary, His Mother. The incident would lead us to believe that the two references here to Jesus' kin belong to the same episode. Jesus is still being besieged by the throng in the house when He is told that His Mother and "brethren" are outside anxious to speak with Him but unable to enter. So the heroes of mediocrity, to prevail upon Jesus, had counted on Mary's authority, which had proved so effective at the wedding in Cana. This does not mean that Mary agrees with them; if she came, it was partly because a woman of Palestine could hardly exclude herself from the decisions made by the head of the family who claimed to be acting for the good of a kinsman, and partly because she could have had reasons of her own for wanting to see her son again; she may even have wanted to be there to intervene when their relatives met Him. When Jesus was informed of the visit, He answered that his mother and brothers were all those who heard and did the will of God, and with a gesture He indicated the listeners packed so closely around him. Mary must have found this answer very similar to the one her twelve-year-old son had given her in the Temple, and so she laid it, too, in the treasury of her heart to ponder with the other things.

The Calming of the Tempest; the Gerasene Demoniac

We are given only a few particulars of Jesus' activity in Galilee. To this period certainly belongs the day He devoted to parables, which we will discuss in the following chapter. The other episodes recorded are the following.

Possibly on the evening of the day of parables (cf. Mark 4:35) Jesus, who had been speaking to the crowds on the western shore of Lake Tiberias, entered a boat with His disciples and told them to make for the opposite shore. The departure seems to have been sudden. Perhaps Jesus was again trying to escape the demonstrations of the crowd that had been listening to Him. The crossing is only a matter of a few miles but it can be dangerous, especially toward nightfall, because cold winds come tumbling suddenly down from the snowy heights of Hermon and blow up extremely violent storms. This is what happened that evening. Jesus, wearied from the long day, went to sleep in the stern of the boat. Mark (4:38), who must have heard Peter tell the story many times, even mentions the cushion on which Jesus laid His head. Mark is, besides, the only one who tells us that other boats were sailing along with that of Jesus. Suddenly a gale strikes the lake, and before long Jesus' boat begins to ship water and is in danger of sinking. Its crew try to maneuver it to safety but all in vain, and from one minute to the next the lake may close over them; yet Jesus continues to slumber peacefully in the stern. The disciples cannot understand how He can sleep through the raging fury, but they hesitate between their desire not to disturb Him and their terror of impending disaster, between their respect for the Master and their instinctive habit of turning confidently to Him for help. But after a little they are convinced that they simply have to waken and warn Him so that He may somehow save Himself as well as them. So they shout: "Master! We are perishing! Save us!"

Jesus awakens and sees the disturbance in the elements and also in His disciples' hearts. Turning to the winds, He commands them to be silent, and instantly there follows a great calm. Then to those troubled hearts, He exclaims compassionately: "What are you afraid of? You still have little faith!" But they are troubled now in a different way and begin to ponder: Who, then, is this that even the winds and the sea obey Him?

In the calm, the boat slid quickly to land, and Jesus and His disciples disembarked, undoubtedly on the eastern shore of the lake almost opposite Capernaum or Magdala; but the name of the place varies in the Synoptics. Matthew calls it the "region of the Gadarenes," Mark "of the Gerasenes," Luke of the "Gergesenes" or more probably the "Gerasenes." The two adjectives to be considered, "Gadarene" or "Gerasene," refer respectively to the two cities of Gadara and Gerasa, both belonging to the Decapolis in Transjordan. Both, however, lay to the south of the lake and, Gerasa especially, at a great distance from it; hence it is hardly possible that their territories extended to the lake shore. But if we consider only the adjectives themselves, it is not impossible that the inhabitants of the western shore should indicate the opposite shore by using the name of the most important cities in the direction toward which they were facing.

At any rate, here on the eastern shore of the lake, on a certain day after the night of the tempest, an incident occurred that is narrated by all three Synoptics; Matthew gives us the briefest account of it and Mark the fullest. Matthew's short summary, however, does tell us that there were two demoniacs, and not one as we should suppose from Mark and Luke. It is the same incident certainly in all three. Mark and Luke concentrate on the principal actor in the strange scene and do not even mention the lesser one. Matthew, though more concise in his treatment, records them both.

A demoniac then came rushing to meet Jesus. He was a wild and savage creature who lived among the tombs and wandered naked through the countryside. He had the strength of a monster and had repeatedly broken the ropes and chains with which the people tried to bind him. Sometimes he would set up a wild howling and at others he would beat himself with stones; and such was the terror he inspired that no one would travel through the district where he wandered. When he saw Jesus in the distance, he ran to meet Him, but instead of attacking Him, he fell prostrate before Him, shrieking: "What have I to do with thee, Jesus, Son of the Most High God? I adjure thee by God, do not torment me!" (Mark 5:7). It was the poor brutish creature speaking, but Jesus answered the one who was within the man and had so brutalized him. For Jesus said: "Begone, foul spirit, out of the man!" This was not so much a command as an announcement; Jesus, in fact, immediately questioned the degrading spirit: "What is thy name?" And it answered: "My name is Legion, for we are many."

The word *legion* was never spoken then in Palestine or elsewhere without inspiring a vague fear. That multitude of armed men, welded into such wonderful compactness as to form an invincible war machine, seemed a superhuman institution. At the time of Jesus, the Roman legion varied between five and six thousand men. Here the word is obviously used to denote in general a large and compact crowd.

After this confession, the troop of spirits "urgently pleaded" with Jesus not to "send them away out of the country," meaning certainly the surrounding district. But Luke (8:31) substitutes here their logical destination, for he says the demons besought Jesus not to send them "into the abyss." The plea was bolstered with a concrete suggestion: "Now a great herd of swine was there on the mountainside feeding. And the spirits kept entreating him, saying: Send us into the swine that we may enter into them. And Jesus immediately gave them leave. And the unclean spirits came out and entered into the swine; and the herd — in number about two thousand — rushed down with great violence into the sea, and were drowned in the sea" (Mark 5:11–13). The presence of a herd of swine confirms the impression that we are now out of Jewish territory, because in Palestine itself the prescriptions of the Law were such that no one raised these animals, considered unclean; hence, here they seem a fitting refuge for the unclean spirits. When the swineherds saw what happened, they took to their heels and raced to the neighboring town to report the adventure and to persuade their masters that they were not to blame for the loss of the herd. Out came the people from the city to see what had really taken place, and they found the notorious demoniac "sitting" quietly near Jesus, "clothed, and in his right mind." And their questions were answered with the detailed account of eyewitnesses. These Greeks did not in the least doubt the prodigy; in fact, precisely because they did believe it, they began to worry about the future. Practical men that they were, they could not help reflecting that with a wonder-worker of that power traveling through their territories, anything might happen. Hence, turning to Jesus, "they began to entreat him to depart from their district." Jesus consented and went back to His boat, but the man who had been healed wanted to be received among His followers. Jesus, however, bade him return to his own family and make known how great the favor he had received from the Lord. And he obeyed and departed and began to publish in the Decapolis all that Jesus had done for him. And all men marveled.

The Daughter of Jairus; the Woman with a Hemorrhage; the Two Blind Men

Having recrossed the lake, Jesus returned to Capernaum, where the "crowd welcomed him, for they were all waiting for him" (Luke 8:40). Waiting perhaps more anxiously than all the rest was a prominent Jew of the city, named Jairus, the ruler of the synagogue. As soon as he learned of Jesus' arrival, he ran "and fell at his feet, and entreated him much, saying: 'My [little] daughter is at the point of death; come, lay thy hands upon her, that she may be saved and live'" (Mark 5:22–23). Luke's account adds that the dying girl was about twelve years old and Jairus's "only" daughter.

Jesus sets out immediately with the distraught father, followed, naturally, by a great crowd, which surges about the wonder-worker — pushing, shouting, pleading, and kissing His garments, while others try valiantly to clear a path for Him. As they proceed, Jesus suddenly stops and looks about Him, asking: "Who touched me?"

They are all puzzled by the question, not knowing exactly what He means, while Peter and the other disciples voice their perplexity: "Master, the crowds throng and press upon thee" (Luke 8:45). But Peter's explanation explains nothing; the Master replies that He has felt a power go out from Him at the touch of some person. And indeed a humble little woman comes forward trembling to fall at Jesus' feet and tell the crowd what has happened.

The woman had been suffering from hemorrhages for twelve years and "had suffered much at the hands of many physicians, and had spent all that she had, and found no benefit, but rather grew worse." Mark's blunt information is quietly condensed by Luke.

There were indeed a number of cures for this particular ailment, and the rabbis, who were often physicians as well, have handed down to us a sizable list of prescriptions, some of them possible, some clearly absurd. This woman had tried them all, for she "had spent all her substance," without obtaining relief. Having lost faith in medicine, she found medicine in faith. The Jesus everyone was talking about would certainly be able to cure her. So firmly did she believe this that she kept repeating to herself: "If I touch but his cloak, I shall be saved." Confident as she was, she did not presume to touch the person of the wonder-worker, but only His garment, or perhaps only the border or fringe that every practicing Israelite had to have at the corners of his cloak. With the courage of her faith, the woman had secretly touched the border of Jesus' cloak and felt herself cured on the instant.

And the Physician approved the medicine she had chosen, for turning to her, He said: "Daughter, thy faith has saved thee. Go in peace, and be thou healed of thy affliction!"

This incident was ended, and Jesus was about to proceed to the house of Jairus when there came others to announce to the poor father: "Thy daughter is dead, do not trouble the Master!" Jesus hears the message and, almost as if continuing His words to the woman on faith, He says to Jairus: "Fear not, only believe, and she shall be saved!" They soon reach the house, but Jesus permits no one to enter except His favorite disciples, Peter, James, and John, and the parents of the dead child. The customary flute players and mourners have already gathered, but Jesus tells them their presence is unnecessary: "Why do you make this din, and weep? The girl is asleep, not dead." The mourners think this play on words bad taste in the presence of the corpse, and they answer with scorn and sarcasm. Between the reality lying before them and the firm confident words of the wonder-worker whose help they have invoked, the parents of the girl stand bewildered. Jesus urges them, with His three disciples, into the dead child's room after everyone else has left it. Then Jesus walks up to the little girl, takes her cold hand in His, and speaks only two words. The disciple of Peter, who witnessed the scene, has preserved these words in their original form: *Telita qumi*, which means, "Girl, arise!" Their effect is described by the physician-evangelist: "And her spirit returned, and she rose up immediately. And he [Jesus] directed that something be given her to eat. And her parents were amazed, but he charged them to tell no one what had happened." This is what Jesus usually did, as we have seen; but these parents who had been made glad again could not, with all the good will in the world, obey Jesus except to the tiniest extent. The very presence in their house of the little daughter whom all had seen depart for the next world, and who had so suddenly returned from it, spoke for them. Indeed, the realistic Matthew concludes the episode with the words "and the report of this [event] spread throughout all that district" (9:26).

The miraculous teachings of faith did not end with the woman's cure and the little girl's return to life. As Jesus left Jairus's house, two blind men followed Him, unfortunates of a sort that must have been as numerous in ancient Palestine as they are today. When they heard about the miracles just performed, they saw a ray of hope for themselves, and having been led to Jesus, they began to follow Him, crying out repeatedly and tenaciously: "Have pity on us, O Son of David!" Given Jesus' habitual prudence, that title could not have pleased Him very much, for it was a messianic epithet usually denoting the great One to come and so was doubly dangerous at the moment, when the people were still excited over the miracles He had just wrought. Jesus did not even glance in the direction of the insistent cry, but it continued nevertheless. He finally entered the house where He lived, certainly in Capernaum, and the two beggars went right in after Him.

After all, the persistence of these two blind men was nothing but faith, the same faith that Jesus had praised in the sick woman and Jairus. Besides, once inside the house the messianic epithet was no longer dangerous, and so Jesus began to talk to the two. His first and perhaps His only question to them concerned their faith. "Do you believe that I can do this to you?" The two naturally answered: "Yes, Lord!" Then Jesus touched their eyes, saying: "Let it be done to you according to your faith." And the two blind men were able to see. Then Jesus commanded them with the greatest earnestness not to tell anyone what had happened; but they, going out with the light in their eyes and in their hearts, spoke of it throughout all that region.

The Mission of the Twelve Apostles

In between these events Jesus continued in all of Galilee "preaching and proclaiming the good tidings of the Kingdom of God." But meanwhile, the multitudes were growing, and despite the cooperation of the Twelve, the responsibilities were growing too. And Jesus, "observing the crowds ... felt compassion for them, because they were harassed and scattered like sheep

A flock of sheep in the hills of Judea

that have no shepherd. Then he said to his disciples: The harvest [indeed] is abundant, but the laborers are few. Pray, therefore, the Lord of the harvest to send forth laborers into his harvest." And calling to Him His twelve disciples, "he gave them authority over unclean spirits, so as to cast them out, and to cure every kind of disease and infirmity" (Matt. 9:36–10:1). Invested with this power, the Twelve were sent out alone without the Master, like a select detachment on a special mission with definite instructions.

Their mission was to announce that the Kingdom of God was at hand, as John the Baptist had done and as Jesus had too. But this detachment was sent ahead into districts not yet covered, which, however, were still to be districts belonging to Israel; for to Israel first among all nations the good tidings of salvation had been promised by the ancient prophets. In proof of their tidings and by virtue of the power they had just received, they were to cure the infirm, cleanse lepers, drive out unclean spirits, and even raise the dead to life. Theirs was the mission of Jesus, transmitted now from one to twelve, but with the same purpose and methods.

In practical matters, too, they followed Jesus; that is, theirs was a complete indifference to political subjects, financial considerations, and economic worries of any sort. The spiritual revenues with which the Kingdom of God was accredited were the proofs of its solvency, namely, curing the sick, cleansing lepers, casting out devils, and raising the dead. But just as the bankers to whom this credit was entrusted had received it gratis, so were they to share it gratis: "freely you have received, freely give" (Matt. 10:8).

Any economic worries were equally forbidden the heralds of the Kingdom of God, except for what was strictly indispensable.

Finally, the messengers were to set out two by two to help and to watch each other, and in their journeyings they were to be distinguishable from other wayfarers for several reasons.

In the first place, the usual travelers were likely to have a donkey. Before their departure, they packed some food, wound some coins in their belts or turbans, and took along a second tunic to protect them from the cold or to provide a change of clothing after a storm, a pair of stout sandals to carry them over the rough roads, a knotted staff for self-defense, and a wallet to hold other lesser provisions for the journey.

Now, the very lack of all these accessories was to distinguish the Twelve sent by Jesus from all other travelers: "Do not keep [take] gold, or silver or [copper] money in your girdles, no wallet for your journey, nor two tunics, nor sandals nor staff" (Matt. 10:9–10). Mark (6:8–9) adds that they are to take no provisions (bread) with them, but says they are to be shod with sandals and are to carry "a staff only."

The Twelve were not even to be concerned about lodgings. When they reached a cluster of dwellings, they were to seek out some worthy householder and stay with him, without moving from one house to another.

Their time was to be employed solely in their mission. Almost certainly, the Twelve, like the seventy-two a little later, were forbidden to lose time in greeting those they met along the road (Luke 10:4). In the Orient, the "greeting" exchanged between travelers, especially if they met in lonely places, could last for hours on end, drifting off into all sorts of discussions. Even today the Bedouin who approaches the ticket window in a railway station for the first time often feels that he must ask the ticket clerk first if he is well, if his children are growing strong and sturdy, if his flocks or his harvest are satisfactory, and only after furnishing these and other evidences of his good breeding does he ask for his train ticket. The messengers of the Kingdom of God were to do without these polite conventionalities, for more important things pressed.

If some town should not receive the messengers of the Kingdom of God or should pay them scant attention, they were to leave it without protest, but they were at the same time to show that the responsibility lay entirely with the townsmen. Hence, as they left, they were to make the symbolic gesture of shaking the dust of the place from their feet.

With these instructions, the Twelve departed. It is probable that Jesus also set out at the same time but not with them (cf. Matt. 11:1). Their journey could not have lasted more than a few weeks, toward the beginning of the year 29, and we are not told its result. We learn only in general that the missionaries preaching the change of mind "cast out many devils, and anointed with oil many sick people, and healed them" (Mark 6:13). Their preaching of the Kingdom of God, then, is accompanied by miraculous signs as Jesus' is, for the cures here mentioned are unquestionably presented as miracles, even though an anointing with oil is listed among them. Oil was in those days a common medicament, but here the context clearly shows that it was not used as an ordinary treatment but a symbol, at the most, of a higher and a spiritual cure. Later, when Christianity is fully established, the anointing with oil will be a specific and permanent rite.

The Death of John the Baptist

About the time of this journey of the apostles, perhaps between February and March of the year 29, John was executed. About ten months had passed since his imprisonment and many more would have been allowed to pass still had it not been for an unforeseen event. Antipas did not desire his death, but Herodias did desire it, and her feminine shrewdness and rancor prevailed.

Now she pounced on the occasion offered by the celebration of Antipas's birthday. It was a formal celebration, and the ancients of the whole tetrarchate had been invited, influential and wealthy people but provincials, very anxious to keep "in the know" and to admire the latest refinements of metropolitan society. The situation was extremely convenient for Herodias, because she possessed the means to set these poor provincials gaping with wonder and at the same time to obtain what she so passionately desired. She had with her Salome, the daughter of her real husband in Rome, who, in the high society of the city, had learned to dance enchantingly. The mother played on her daughter's vanity and the girl responded wonderfully.

Introduced into the banquet chamber at just the right moment when the fumes of wine and lust had already befogged the guests, the dancer's shimmering legs whirled her driveling spectators into delirium. Antipas literally melted with tenderness. Spectacles like this proved his court was truly up-to-date and superior to all other Oriental courts. Indeed, the monarch grew so soft and mellow that he called the breathless and perspiring little dancer to him and said to her: "Ask anything you wish and I shall give it to you!" And he made his promise sacred with an oath: "Whatsoever thou dost ask, I will give thee, even though it be half of my kingdom!" (Mark 6:23).

Between the delirious applause of the guests and the breathtaking offers of the king, our dancer might not have known how to answer. But her mother had foreseen this moment and had told her what to do. The maternal warnings rescued her perplexity, and off she ran to consult Herodias, who was at banquet in the room reserved for the women. The practical lady perceived that her man had fallen into the trap and she had won her play. So, fondling her little dancer, she said to her crisply: Ask for one thing only, "the head of John the Baptist."

This time, too, the girl behaved beautifully. "And she came in at once with haste to the king, and asked, saying: I want thee right away to give me on a dish the head of John the Baptist. And grieved as he was, the king, because of his oath and his guests, was unwilling to displease her. But sending an executioner, he commanded that his head be brought in a dish. Then he beheaded him in the prison, and brought his head on a dish and gave it to the girl; and the girl gave it to her mother" (Mark 6:25–28). Though she herself had no interest in it whatever, Salome carried the head, still warm and dripping with blood, to her mother, who was extremely interested in it. According to later information recorded by St. Jerome, the adulteress gave vent to her hatred by thrusting a bodkin through the tongue. Later the disciples of the martyred John succeeded in recovering his body and burying it.

Jesus Driven out of Nazareth

For some time now news had been coming to Antipas about Jesus, the extraordinary preacher who was exciting His subjects in Galilee. The memory of John the Baptist was still fresh, and the character and activity of the new prophet were extremely reminiscent of the prophet just dead. Hence the superstitious Antipas concluded that John had come to life again, assuming the form of Jesus, and was going about working miracles. From then on Antipas was very curious to see Jesus and discover for himself precisely what features the resuscitated John had assumed (Luke 9:9).

But Jesus had no desire to make the acquaintance of John's adulterous assassin. This was about the time when He sent his Twelve on their journey, and while they worked in a wider area, Jesus reserved for Himself a more restricted but also a much more difficult region. After raising the daughter of Jairus to life, He left Capernaum (cf. Mark 6:1) and chose to make a special visit to

Nazareth because He knew that resentments against Him were brooding in His native village. This had not been so in the beginning. Upon His return from Judea, He had received ovations in Nazareth, too, but since then His fellow townsmen's feelings toward Him had changed, and the superciliousness of some of His relatives must have had something to do with it. But what offended the local pride of the Nazarenes most deeply was Jesus' preference for Capernaum, now become His customary dwelling place.

The Nazarenes could not forgive Jesus for having, practically speaking, abandoned His own village, especially since in Capernaum He had done these extraordinary things that all of Galilee was talking about. Did Nazareth lack sick people to heal, or lame to straighten, or blind to give light to? Why deprive His own town of so many benefits, benefits that would also redound to the glory of the village now scorned so much? This sour temper on the part of Jesus' fellow townsmen must have constituted a barrier against His preaching too.

If he could get along without His hometown, then His town could get along without His preaching.

Was He not the son of Joseph the carpenter? Was His Mother not Mary, whom they all knew? Were not His brothers James, Joseph, Simon, and Judas? And were not His sisters well-known in the town? They were all ordinary people, not one whit better than anyone else. Where did He get His learning then? Was not the wonder of it perhaps due to the fact that people were easily impressed who did not know Him and had not watched Him grow from babyhood to manhood like everyone else, as the Nazarenes had?

There were, of course, the miracles; but there was some question about these too. Anyone who can work miracles works them everywhere, at home and abroad. In fact, if He were to show any preferences, it would be His own town and friends. Instead, this strange Nazarene worked miracles everywhere but in Nazareth. He was like a doctor who can cure others but is unable to cure his own family or himself.

The comparison caught on and was repeated with all the petulance characteristic of little towns. The most hotheaded among them took occasion to say to Jesus' face: "Physician, heal thyself! As great things as we have heard done in Capharnaum, do also here in thy own country!" (Luke 4:23). Jesus answered by trying to enlighten and convince them, observing that no one is a prophet in his own country. He did perform some miracles, healing the sick, but only a few, not because this village was called Nazareth rather than Capernaum but "because of their unbelief" (Matt.

13:58). What they lacked here indeed was precisely what had triumphed only recently with the daughter of Jairus, the woman with the hemorrhage, and the two blind men.

The final clash came when Jesus made a formal and almost official attempt to shake His townsmen out of their complacency at the Sabbath gathering in the synagogue. His enemies must have gone to the assembly with the intention of challenging Him. The scent of battle was in the air; Jesus would be there, and they would have a chance to corner Him.

Jesus did indeed come, and the meeting proceeded according to rule. This time Jesus gave the instruction after the reading of the "Prophets," and it is not too hardy to suppose that the ruler of the synagogue presiding over the meeting purposely invited his much-discussed townsman to give the instruction in order that He might have plenty of opportunity to explain Himself. Jesus mounted the pulpit.

> The volume of Isaias the prophet was handed to him. And after he opened the volume, he found the place where it was written:
>> The Spirit of the Lord is upon me;
>>> because he has anointed me;
>> To bring *good tidings* to the poor he has sent me,
>>> to proclaim to the captives release,
>>> and sight to the blind;
>> To set at liberty the oppressed,
>>> to proclaim the acceptable year of the Lord....
> And closing the volume, he gave it back to the attendant and sat down. And the eyes of all in the synagogue were gazing on him. But he began to say to them: Today this scripture has been fulfilled [which has resounded] in your hearing. (Luke 4:17–21)

This was the beginning of Jesus' discourse; the rest of it unfortunately has not been preserved for us. Certainly He applied to Himself at length the passage He had just read, showing how, with His works, He completely fulfilled the ancient prophecy concerning the proclamation of the "good tidings." His exposition was effective, and this time, too, the speaker seemed as one "having authority" so that all wondered. But at the root of their very admiration was the fuel of scandal. Was not this the lowly son of the carpenter? If He had worked so many miracles elsewhere, which He Himself cited in His discourse, why did He not perform some there among His own townsmen? These questions, not uttered in the synagogue, were loudly muttered outside when the gathering was over. His listeners argued pro and con; then they confronted the speaker directly. They invited Him once more to answer these questions and remember above all that He was a Nazarene. Did He really wish to win His countrymen over to His teachings? Well, then, let Him work a few convincing miracles right there in the public square and they would give themselves to Him body and soul: "Physician, heal thyself!"

Jesus answered as He had before. Let them beware of verifying for Nazareth the principle that no prophet is accepted in his own country. For Him, Jesus, Nazareth and Capernaum and every other Israelite town were the same. There were many widows in Israel at the time of the prophet Elias, yet God sent him to a widow who was not an Israelite. And in the time of the prophet Eliseus there were many lepers in Israel, yet God sent the prophet to the leper Naaman, who was a Syrian (Luke 4:25–27).

Jesus' answer was a warning, but His ill-disposed interlocutors interpreted it as an insult. So He declared that He did not need Nazareth and that He was ready to choose any other town at all in its place, even outside of Israel! How did this carpenter's son get so high and mighty? Let Him learn to be a little grateful to the village that had raised Him! He must be driven out of the town and in such a way that He would never want to come back.

The outburst of violence was sudden, as it always is among excited mobs. They were still muttering there near the synagogue when someone probably began to shout against the unworthy Nazarene: Drive the fellow out! Death to the traitor! The few who were on Jesus' side probably shrank back in terror, the others "put him forth out of the town, and led him to the brow of the hill, on which their town was built, that they might throw him down headlong. But he, passing through their midst went his way" (Luke 4:29–30).

Why did not the Nazarenes carry out their intention? We do not know. Perhaps at the last minute those who favored Jesus recovered their courage and intervened. Or perhaps the hotheads themselves, at the fatal moment, recovered their senses and contented themselves with the threat they had given Him. Nor are we to exclude the possibility that the superior force of Jesus' own personality quelled the rioters so that He was able to escape them. We are not told, either, the precise place where this occurred. A small peak is pointed out today called Jebel el-Qafse, which rises about nine hundred feet above the valley of Esdraelon and is known today as the "Hill of the Precipice." But this place is about two miles from ancient Nazareth, which is too far away for an excited mob that had resolved on summary execution. In the actual vicinity of the ancient village there must have been steep drops that would be very well suited to their violent purpose. Hence some have thought, with fair likelihood, of a drop about thirty feet high near the modern Greek Catholic Church, which is situated on the old site of the ancient synagogue. Pious Christian meditation later contemplated what Mary must have felt on that occasion, and a chapel situated in the direction of the "Hill of the Precipice" received in the Middle Ages the name *Our Lady of the Spasm* in memory of Mary's fear when she saw her son in danger.

Valley of Esdraelon

Chapter 11

∞

The Day of Parables

The Parable

During this part of His ministry in Galilee, probably on the very day when He calmed the storm, Jesus gave that abundant instruction that we may designate as the day of parables.

Unquestionably He had used certain elements of the parable in His earlier discourses, including the Sermon on the Mount. But this day was dedicated in a particular way to the true parable, as we glean from the short introductions with which all three Synoptics preface it (Matt. 13:1–3; Mark 4:1–2; Luke 8:4; cf. Mark 4:35). It is almost certain, too, that as in the Sermon on the Mount, the evangelists, in recounting the preaching of this day, recorded parables Jesus gave on other occasions (Matthew) or transferred the parables given on this day to other episodes (Luke).

The parable is a literary device that uses an imaginary but entirely plausible and likely fact to illustrate a moral and religious truth.

Substantially, it is a comparison. It may be simple or complicated depending on the subtlety of concept and comprehension on the part of its author or listeners. For instance, if the schoolteacher's task is compared simply with the gardener's, then we have a parable. If the comparison is carried out to fine details, the little plants in the garden symbolizing the pupils; the flowers and fruits, the various promotions and prizes, and so on, then the comparison becomes symbolic as well, or rather it becomes an allegorical parable. If the school itself is never mentioned but only the plants, flowers, spade, shears, and so forth are spoken of, then we have pure allegory, or a sustained metaphor. It is clear, however, that while pure allegory sustained for any length is both difficult and rare, it is easy for the simple parable to border on the allegory and use certain of its features.

The parables of Jesus follow these general rules.

Simple and precise, they are based on the most humble realities, but they mirror with crystal clearness the most sublime concepts. They are easily understood by the unlettered and offer abundant meditation to the learned. Absolutely free of any literary device or artifice, yet for sheer power they surpass by far the most elaborate of them. They do not startle but they persuade; they are not only winning but convincing.

The Purpose of the Parables

The purpose of Jesus' parables is to introduce the Kingdom of God, or Heaven. In the Sermon on the Mount He had spoken of the moral prerequisites for entrance into that kingdom. Now it was necessary to take another step forward, to speak of the kingdom itself, of its nature, of the members who should compose it, of the manner in which it was to be realized and established. In this regard, too, Jesus' method was essentially a gradual one.

The reason for this is to be found in the important historical circumstance already mentioned — namely, the acute expectation by the Jews of a political-messianic kingdom. To speak to these crowds of a Kingdom of God without explaining and clarifying would be to flash before their excited fancies the vision of a celestial omnipotent king, surrounded by phalanxes of armed men, or better, legions of warring angels; a being who should carry Israel from victory to victory and finally to dominion over all the earth. Yet it was to these inflammable multitudes that Jesus had to speak of the object of their enthusiasm, and to speak in a manner that would at the same time attract and disenchant them. The Kingdom of God was unquestionably to come — in fact, it had already begun to be realized; but it was not their "kingdom." It was Jesus' kingdom and quite different. Hence His teaching was to open their eyes to the truth and to shut them to their fantastic dreams. Extreme caution was necessary, because Jesus was treading volcanic ground that might explode at any minute; and it was His compassionate prudence that induced Him to use the parable.

Even if the parable were not understood immediately, there was still another resource. Jesus' parables were spoken in public both to people who were well-disposed and to others who were not, that the gate to the kingdom might be open to all. Mercy and prudence both required the veil of the parable, but the veil could always be removed by speaking to the author of the parables in private. Since Jesus wished truly to spread His kingdom, He would not refuse to speak clearly when consulted in private.

The Parables of the Kingdom

The day of the parables was spent near Capernaum on the shore of the lake. Since a great crowd was gathered, Jesus did as He had done before: He climbed into a boat, and having pushed out a little into the lake, He spoke to the people lining the shore.

The first parable recorded on this day is that of the sower and his seed. In the hilly and broken Galilean terrain, small plots of more likely ground here and there on the slopes and in the hollows were chosen for cultivation. After preparing his ground, the sower went out at the first rains, about November, going from plot to plot with his seeds of wheat or barley. Now, the progress of the Kingdom of Heaven resembles that of the sower of Galilee.

The sower goes out carrying against his hip the sack full of seeds, and when he reaches the ground he has prepared, he begins to sow. But in Palestine everyone cuts across the fields to get from one place to another, and small paths soon traverse even those patches that have been freshly plowed. Hence some of the seed falls on these pathways, where the birds soon pick it up or the passersby trample it underfoot. Another some falls on rocky ground, where there is only a light sprinkling of good soil, and there in the heat it quickly begins to sprout; but since there is not enough earth for it to root properly, a few days of bright sunlight are enough to wither it. Another some falls on soil that is deeper but not properly prepared, and so weeds and thorns grow up with the seedlings and eventually choke them. Finally, the rest of the sack is emptied on good ground, and there the sowing yields thirtyfold and sixtyfold and a hundredfold depending on the soil. This everyday occurrence Jesus narrates as the adventure of one particular sower and thus composes a parable. He concludes by saying: "He who has ears to hear, let him hear!"

Later, however, He explained the parable to the disciples who asked Him to do so. The seed was the word of God, that is, the announcement of the Kingdom of Heaven. The seed that fell on the pathways and was eaten by the birds represented the message as it was received by ill-disposed hearers, who barely listened with their ears and not with their hearts, and immediately Satan came and took it away from them. The seed fallen on rocky ground represented the superficial listeners, who accepted the message with joy at the moment but forgot it at the first difficulty they encountered. The seed fallen among thorns and thistles represented the hearers enveloped in the passions and cares of this world, who kept the good tidings in their hearts for a little while but then let their materialistic desires and anxieties stifle it. Finally, the seed fallen on good ground represented those who received the good tidings in hearts that were well-disposed and cherished it so that they yielded fruit in varying abundance according to their dispositions.

The average Jew who was expecting a political-messianic kingdom would not have understood the true meaning of this parable. For the average Jew was expecting a resplendent conqueror-king, and here the founder of the kingdom is not even mentioned. He was expecting the kingdom, fully established and ready for him, to descend from the clouds of Heaven midst the rumble and crash of awesome portents, and here the kingdom was presented as rising silently from the earth midst obstacles of every kind. He was awaiting the vindication of his nation and victory over the pagans, and here instead mention is made only of the hidden formation of the spirit, of victory over the passions and mundane interests. The average Jew, therefore, could see and could not see through the parable. The more tenaciously attached he was to his old concepts and beliefs, the more dense would be his heart and the deafer his ears, and he would reject the complete "change of mind" to which the parable cautiously invited him.

But the Kingdom of Heaven finds obstacles to its realization even where it has been well received, and this fact is illustrated in the second parable.

A man sowed good seed in his field. He had prepared his ground well and done his sowing in good season, and he could confidently await his harvest. But a neighbor of his, who had an old spite against him, came at night and scattered in his field an abundance of darnel weed. Among farmers this was a typical way to pay off a grudge and is specifically considered in Roman law. Even when it has begun to sprout, the darnel weed cannot be distinguished from the wheat, and the difference between them is seen only when they begin to ear; by that time it is too late to pull up the darnel, and the wheat has already suffered. In the parable, too, the trick was not discovered until the crop had begun to ear. And then the laborers went to the master and said to him: "Sir, didst thou not sow good seed in thy field? How then does it have weeds?" And the master immediately surmised where the weed had come from and exclaimed: "It is my enemy that has done this." The workers then suggested: "Shall we go and gather it up and give the crop more room?" But the master replied: "No, because in gathering up the darnel you may also root up the wheat; rather let them both grow until the harvesting, and then I shall tell my harvesters first to gather up the weeds in bundles and throw them into the fire, and then to gather the wheat into my barn."

We also have the explanation of this parable that Jesus gave His disciples (Matt. 13:36–43). He who sows the good seed is the Son of Man, and the field is the world. The enemy who sows the spite crop is the devil, and the harvesting is the end of the present "age" or world. At the end of the world, the Son of Man will send His angels, who, like the harvesters with the weeds, will cast out of His kingdom all those who have done evil and given scandal, throwing them into the furnace of fire, and the just will shine resplendent as the sun in the kingdom of the Father.

The second parable, then, showed that the kingdom preached by Jesus would contain both the good and the bad, the good deriving from the Son of Man and the bad from the devil. This coexistence of good and evil would be tolerated in view of the full triumph of the good, which was to take place only when the present world passed into the world to come. Hence the kingdom was a kind of bridge, joining the two "ages" or worlds.

The parable that only Mark gives (4:26–29) resembles in part the one given above. The Kingdom of God is like a man who has sowed his field. Whether he sleeps or wakes, by day or by night, whether he thinks of his crop or not, it sprouts and grows, and finally it puts forth ears and ripens, because it has an inner life and energy of its own; this, however, must unfold gradually and run its complete regular cycle.

Hence, the good tidings preached by Jesus would run its regular course, developing in extent and depth within the spirits of men, without the sudden cataclysms anxiously awaited by the multitudes, in virtue of that inner force with which it was imbued from on high.

The parable of the mustard seed also demonstrates that the Kingdom of God is to begin without any exterior display.

The mustard is very common in Palestine, and although it is an annual plant, it may become, under favorable conditions, a bush some ten or twelve feet high. Yet its seeds are the very tiniest kernels, so that in Palestine even today they are proverbial for things that are barely visible: "Small as a mustard seed." Now this disproportion between the tiny seed and the size of the plant, which is the largest of all leafy shrubs, furnishes Jesus with a picture of the actual disproportion between the beginnings of the Kingdom of God, humble and silent, and its subsequent expansion, which will be greater than that of any other.

Here, too, we have a complete rejection, in fact, a specific reversal of the prevailing Jewish concepts of the time.

Similar to this is the parable of the leaven. In the evening the housewife fills her kneading trough with three full measures of flour and works into it a handful of leaven. The next morning, when she uncovers her trough, she finds that the small handful of leaven, in its hidden nightlong growth, has transformed the whole mass of dough, which is now a hundred times larger.

Here, too, we have demonstrated the actual disproportion between the beginnings of the kingdom, represented by the leaven, and its full development, represented by the mass of raised dough. But even clearer here is the allusion to the silent spiritual nature of the kingdom, which will spread not by force of arms, money, or political ideologies, but by the hidden conquest of minds and hearts, like a mysterious leaven.

Other parables, which Jesus probably gave His disciples privately, are recorded very briefly.

The Kingdom of Heaven is like a treasure hidden in a field. It was the custom, during the various political upheavals of the time, to hide precious objects in convenient places in the country to keep them from becoming soldiers' booty. But sometimes the owner of the treasure died before he had recovered it, and later some wayfarer or peasant working the field came upon it. Naturally, the first thing the lucky man tried to do was buy the field, saying nothing about what he had found in order that he might become the legal owner of the treasure. In Jesus' parable, the lucky finder, as soon as he is certain that he has come upon a treasure, covers it up again so that no one else may discover it. Then, rejoicing secretly, he sells all that he has to scrape together enough to buy the field. In short, he stakes everything for everything, because he is certain that the everything he leaves behind is worth much less than the all he is acquiring.

This is what happens when one has come to know and value the Kingdom of Heaven. He will leave every good he has to acquire this supreme good (Matt. 13:44).

The same teaching is expressed in the brief parable of the pearl. A merchant searches at great length for a fine pearl, one of those celebrated in antiquity for their value such as the two huge pearls of Cleopatra mentioned by Pliny. When he has found one of great rarity, then he sells all that he has to buy it (Matt. 13:45–46).

Similar to the parable of the darnel weed is the short one of the fishnet, based on an everyday occurrence along the shores of Lake Tiberias. The Kingdom of Heaven is like a great net cast into the water and then drawn forth full of fish of all kinds. The fishermen sort their catch, putting the good fish in baskets and throwing away the bad. Similarly, at the end of the world, the angels will separate the wicked from the just and put them into the furnace of fire (Matt. 13:47–50).

This separate conversation with His disciples, which closed the day of the parables, was sealed with another short parable. When He had finished speaking, Jesus asked His disciples: Have you understood all this? And they answered yes. "Well then," He added, "every scribe who becomes a disciple in the Kingdom of Heaven is like the householder who brings out of his storeroom things that are new and things that are old." These disciples who are destined to continue the Master's work, therefore, were to act according to the principle He Himself had laid down in the Sermon on the Mount, namely, that He had come not to abolish the Old Law but to complete and perfect it. The things that were old were to be completed and perfected by the things that were new.

Chapter 12

∞

From the Second Pasch to the
Last Feast of Tabernacles

The First Multiplication of the Loaves

Meanwhile some time had passed and it was probably mid-March. Hence, "the Pasch, the festival day of the Jews, was near at hand" (John 6:4), the Pasch of the year 29 and the second Pasch of Jesus' public ministry.

At this point the apostles return from their missionary journey and at about the same time comes the news of John the Baptist's death. The apostles, worn out from the labors they had just undergone, were so besieged by the crowds swarming about them that "they had not so much as time to eat" (Mark 6:31). Jesus, on His part, had been deeply saddened by John's tragic death, and so He took His returned missionaries and left Capernaum in search of rest for them and solitude for Himself; and "they got into the boat, and went off into a desert place apart" (Mark 6:32). It was near the town of Bethsaida, which the tetrarch Philip had rebuilt and named Julia (Bethsaida-Julia) in honor of the notorious daughter of Augustus, and it was the native city of the two pairs of brothers, Peter and Andrew, and James and John.

It seemed a very suitable place. It was not under the jurisdiction of Antipas, but of Philip, and hence Antipas could not take any steps against Jesus; besides, the town was situated on the other side of the Jordan a little above its entrance into the lake, and to the east lay a stretch of almost uninhabited country where they might rest and be alone. Finally, from the vicinity of Capernaum it could be reached easily by boat.

But Jesus' departure with His little group of apostles was noticed by the crowds around Capernaum, and from the direction in which the boat made off they were able to guess its destination. Then many of them took to the roads along the northern curve of the lake, crossed the Jordan where it flows into the lake, and thus succeeded in reaching the other shore before Jesus' boat did. When He landed in the desert place beyond Bethsaida-Julia, the crowds were already waiting for Him.

The multitudes immediately dispelled all hope of rest and solitude, especially since Jesus, as soon as He saw all those eager people, "had compassion on them" and began to cure miraculously the infirm and to speak to all of them of the Kingdom of God. Meanwhile the hours passed and the day "was now far spent" (Mark 6:35).

The crowds, forgetful of everything else, showed no signs of leaving. Hence the practical-minded apostles approached Him and pointed out that since they were in a desert place and the hour was late, it would be well to dismiss the people that they might scatter through the nearest towns and find food and lodging. Jesus answered: "You yourselves give them to eat!"

The answer seemed strange indeed. They had no bread and perhaps not even money to provide it. Philip did some quick figuring and observed that even if they could find two hundred silver denarii (some forty dollars) worth of bread, it would barely furnish a good mouthful apiece. Jesus did not answer Philip's mathematics, but changing His tone, He asked: "How many loaves have you?" Andrew, Peter's brother, answered: "There is a young boy here who has five barley loaves and two fishes"; but he, too, feels obliged to point out, "What are these among so many?" And Jesus did not answer Andrew's reckoning either.

All around, as far as the eye could see, stretched the meadow, its verdure in the bright vigor of the Paschaltide. All of a sudden, Jesus ordered the apostles to have the crowds recline on the grass, and they did so in groups of fifty or a hundred. But no one could yet fathom the reason for the command. To recline on divans was customary at banquets, but what food could possibly be served there to guests lying on the grass? Jesus, however, "took the five loaves, and the two fishes and, looking up to heaven, blessed and broke the loaves, and gave them to his disciples to set before the people; and the two fishes he divided among them all. And all ate and were satisfied." The traditional Jewish procedure at banquets had been observed in the reclining and also in the prayer at the beginning and the breaking of the bread, both of which were the duty of the father of the family; and it was also observed at the end when the leftovers were gathered up, as they were at the end of every Jewish meal: "And they gathered up what was left over, twelve baskets full of fragments, besides what was left over of the fishes." Since the crowd had been divided into groups, it was easy to calculate their number: "Now those who had eaten were five thousand men" (Mark 6:41–44). Matthew confirms the number five thousand, but as a former tax gatherer he is a little more accurate and adds "without counting the women and children" (Matt. 14:21).

In the Sermon on the Mount Jesus had admonished His listeners: "Do not be anxious saying: 'What shall we eat?' or 'What shall we drink?' or 'What are we to put on?' ... For your Father knows that you need all these things. But seek first the kingdom of God and his justice, and all these things shall be given you besides"; the truth of the admonition was proved on the meadow outside Bethsaida. Those people throughout the long day had been seeking the "kingdom and his justice," or the bread of the spirit, and without thinking about it at all they had found bread for their bodies. But this material bread was a secondary adjunct in the scene we are witnessing; the unusual thing about that particular day was the whole-souled search for the kingdom and its triumphant expansion.

We should expect the crowds, however, to be much more impressed by the material reality than by anything else. Throughout the day they had heard about the "kingdom," and were moved by what they heard, and now they watched the food for their bodies multiply in the hands of this "kingdom's" preacher. Their conclusion was simple and immediate and in perfect keeping with their messianic expectations. This was the awaited Messiah; His power revealed Him as such. From a conclusion so clear and compelling the impetuous Galileans moved at once to action: "When the people, therefore, had seen the sign [miracle] which Jesus had worked they said: This is indeed the Prophet who is to come into the world! So when Jesus perceived that they would come to take him by force and make him king, he fled again to the mountain" (John 6:14–15).

Here we have sheer historical reality, the reality Jesus had long Himself alone foreseen and chosen to avoid by the prudence of His conduct.

On that evening, too, Jesus had forearmed Himself against the danger. As soon as the meal was over, even before His zealous electors had decided to proclaim Him king, He obliged "his disciples to get into the boat and cross the sea ahead of him while he himself dismissed the crowd" (Mark 6:45). In other words, having noticed the crowd's excitement and realizing their intentions, Jesus first protected His disciples by sending them away and then stayed there alone in order the better to handle His excited political messianists. As the other evangelist tells us, He did exactly what He had done on other occasions, namely, He passed secretly from their midst. A good part of the night He spent on the mountain in prayer (Matt. 14:23), and in the meantime the disciples were sailing toward Capernaum.

Jesus Walks on the Water;
Discourse on the Bread of Life

It was already night when the boat left the shore. Before embarking, the disciples probably lingered a while hoping that Jesus would join them, but when He did not come and it was already late, they set sail.

That is what the Master had bidden them to do, and they obeyed, but they were not too happy about it both because He was not with them and because that journey by night was neither safe nor pleasant. Lake Tiberias, as we have seen, is subject to sudden and violent storms. And on this particular night a storm blew up. Surprised by the wind that caught them broadside and pushed them south instead of west, the disciples furled the sail and took to the oars. But the waters were so rough that the boat made little progress, and by a little after three in the morning, they had gone only about three miles. A good third of the crossing perhaps lay still ahead of them, and their weariness must have affected their dispositions.

All of a sudden, through the mist and spray they saw a man walking on the waters a short distance from the boat. A shout from one of the rowers and all looked where he was pointing. Unquestionably it was a human figure. The man seemed to be walking in the same direction as the boat and trying to pass it. But no, he turned and came toward them. Then all of them "were greatly alarmed, and exclaimed: It is a ghost! And they cried out for fear. Then Jesus immediately spoke to them saying: Take courage! It is I! Do not be afraid!" (Matt. 14:26–27). If it was truly He, there was nothing to wonder at; He who a few hours before had multiplied the loaves and fishes could very well walk on the water. But was it truly He? Peter wanted to be sure: "Lord, if it is thou, bid me come to thee over the water!" And Jesus answered: "Come!" Peter climbed out of the boat and strode across the water until he came to Jesus. The experienced fisherman had never traveled the lake in that fashion before, and it was his experience that betrayed him; for when he found himself in the midst of those tumbling waves, the enthusiastic faith that helped him out of the boat suddenly deserted him, and he was only the expert fisherman once more and therefore afraid. His fear began to pull him underwater, and in terror he shouted: "Lord, save me!" And Jesus at once stretched forth His hand and took hold of him, saying to him: "O thou of little faith, why didst thou doubt?" And both then climbed into the boat, the wind subsided, and they soon reached their landing place.

During the remaining brief and now tranquil sail, a stunned bewilderment fell upon the little boat. The travelers threw themselves at the feet of the new messenger, exclaiming: "Truly thou art Son of God!" They did not say He was *the* "Son of God" par excellence, the Messiah, but they certainly were proclaiming Him an extraordinary man to whom God had been most generous with His favors. But somehow there was still a blind spot. When they tried to piece this new miracle together with all the others into some sort of picture that would explain them all, our travelers, their stomachs filled with the miraculous bread and their eyes feasting on the supposed ghost, could not come to any clear judgment. They repeated to themselves exactly the same reasoning the crowds had arrived at a few hours before. If this man knows how to work such miracles, why does He not make up His mind to show He is the powerful "messianic king" of Israel? "And they were far more astonished within themselves; for they understood not concerning the [matter of the] loaves, for their heart was blinded" (Mark 6:51–52).

They landed at Gennesaret, about two miles south of Capernaum. They probably avoided the latter city in order to avoid the usual noisy and dangerous demonstrations. Jesus' arrival was noticed immediately, however, and as usual the sick and the suppliant throughout the vicinity began to gather around Him, "and as many as touched him were saved" (Mark 6:56).

Meanwhile, many from the region of Capernaum had stayed at Bethsaida where the loaves were multiplied. When morning came, some of them took advantage of the boats that had come there to fish and got passage back to Capernaum, while others went off in other directions.

Those who came to Capernaum began to search for Jesus, perhaps hoping still to proclaim Him king and force Him either to accept the title or refuse it openly. They did find Him, but probably only after two or three days during which Jesus had been staying in the region of Gennesaret. Then, meeting Him perhaps along the way, they attempted to engage Him in discourse and asked: "Rabbi, when didst thou come here?" (John 6:25).

This question begins the famous discourse on the Bread of Life, which only John records (6:25–71). The question veiled an ulterior motive, and it is to that that Jesus replies, saying: "Amen, amen I say to you, you seek me, not because you have seen signs, but because you have eaten of the loaves and have been filled." The "signs" were the miracles wrought by Jesus in proof of His mission, and as such they would be effective "signs" insofar as they induced the spectators to accept that mission. Yet though these people had witnessed many miracles, they had not accepted them as signs; they had enjoyed the material benefit to be derived from them, but they remained impervious to the spiritual benefit. Hence Jesus continued: "Do not labor for the food that perishes, but for that which endures unto life everlasting, which the Son of man will give you. For upon him the Father, God himself, has set his seal." The seal was the most important instrument in a king's chancellery. Only a little while before, Jesus' listeners had tried to elect Him "king"; but what kind of king would He have been after that election? He had received His authority not from men but from the "Father, God." His questioners replied: "What are we to do, in order that we may perform the works of God?" And the question clearly referred to Jesus' exhortation to "labor for the food that endures unto life everlasting." Jesus answered: "This is the work of God, that you believe in him whom he has sent"; that is, that you believe in Him even when His word disappoints your hopes and dispels your dreams, that you believe in His kingdom even if it is a complete denial of yours.

But they persisted: "What sign, then, dost thou, that we may see and believe thee? What work dost thou perform? Our fathers ate the manna in the desert, even as it is written: Bread from heaven he gave them to eat" (Exod. 16:4; Ps. 77[78]:24). Two things were implicitly compared in this reference: the work of Moses, on the one hand, with its "sign" or seal, the manna from Heaven; and the work of Jesus, on the other, with its most recent "sign," the multiplication of the loaves at Bethsaida. Jesus' questioners seem to prefer the former. The other signs Jesus has wrought are not even considered, almost as if they had no value as proof. The question is a reproach to Jesus and sets Him second to Moses. If He wished to create faith in His invisible and intangible "kingdom," then let Him work "signs" equal, at least, to those of Moses.

The discussion has brought them to a crossroad, and a choice must be made between the two terms of the comparison: Moses and his work on the one hand, Jesus and His "kingdom" on the other. Which of these two is the greater? This is the crux of the question, and Jesus faces it squarely: "Amen, amen I say to you, Moses did not give you the bread from heaven. For the bread of God is that which comes down from heaven and gives life to the world." The judgment of Jesus' challengers has been reversed. Jesus is greater than Moses as Heaven is greater than earth. Jesus, not Moses, "comes down from heaven and gives life to the world"; it is He who is truly the "bread from heaven." The exposition is interrupted for a moment by the exclamation: "Lord, give us always this bread!" — the twin of the Samaritan woman's request for living water, which shows that in both cases Jesus' listeners still had their minds on material things. And Jesus answered: "I am the bread of life. He who comes to me shall not hunger, and he who believes in me shall never thirst. But I have told you that you have seen me and you do not believe." And with further assertions by Jesus in this vein (John 6:37–40), the first part of the discourse comes to a close.

There must have been a great deal of discussion in the city concerning Jesus' statements; and people must have desired to hear Him explain them further. The opportunity was offered Him to clarify His words at the next meeting in the synagogue, because the statements that follow were made while He was "teaching in the synagogue at Capharnaum" (6:60).

The Jews (that is, the countrymen of Jesus who rejected this teaching) were now murmuring against Jesus "because he had said: I am the bread that has come down from heaven. And they kept saying: Is this not Jesus the son of Joseph, whose father and mother we know? How, then, does he say: I have come down from heaven?" After a few more general observations, Jesus came back to the question of the bread: "I am the bread of life. Your fathers ate the manna in the desert, and have died. [Rather] this is the bread that comes down from heaven, so that if anyone eat of it he will not die. I am the living bread that has come down from heaven. If anyone eat of this bread he shall live forever; and the bread that I will give is my flesh for the life of the world." At these words, the "Jews," unfriendly to begin with, had much more reason than Nicodemus and the Samaritan woman to be dumfounded. Jesus had spoken to the latter of being "born again of the Spirit" and of water "springing up unto life everlasting," but these expressions could be taken figuratively, just as the phrase, "bread of life," could be taken in a figurative sense, too, the first time Jesus used it and applied it to Himself. But Jesus did not confine Himself to that first time. He came back to the very same expression, and as if to preclude any possible symbolic interpretation, He declared that this bread was "his flesh" given for the life of the world. So specific a definition was not permissible in a metaphorical discourse; when He spoke of His flesh as bread, Jesus was not using a symbol. That is the way His audience in the synagogue at Capernaum reasoned, with perfect logic; and they began to argue with one another: "How can this man give us his flesh to eat?" It was indeed a solemn and decisive moment. It was now up to Jesus to define His meaning and to make it crystal clear whether His words were to be taken as metaphor or as a plain and genuine statement of fact.

And Jesus' answer was crystal clear. Having heard His listeners' objections, He continued:

> Amen, amen, I say to you, unless you eat the flesh of the Son of man, and drink his blood, you shall not have life in you. He who eats my flesh

and drinks my blood has life everlasting and I will raise him up on the last day. For my flesh is food indeed, and my blood is drink indeed. He who eats my flesh and drinks my blood, abides in me and I in him. As the living Father has sent me, and as I live because of the Father, so he who eats me, he also shall live because of me. This is the bread that has come down from heaven; [it shall] not [be] as [it was with] your fathers [who] ate the manna, and died. He who eats this bread shall live forever.

With this explanation, Jesus' audience no longer had the least doubt. The words they had just heard may have been "hard," but they could not have been more clear or more precise. Jesus had plainly repeated that His flesh was true food and His blood true drink, and that to have eternal life it was necessary to eat of that flesh and drink of that blood. It was impossible to find any ambiguity in His words, and in fact the hostile "Jews" did not find any. Nor did "many" of His own disciples find them ambiguous; they were scandalized by them. "Many of his disciples, therefore, when they heard this, said: This is a hard saying. Who can listen to it?" The adjective *hard* here means "repugnant," "sickening," indicating one could not "listen to it" without a certain feeling of revulsion. Evidently their thoughts were literal and suggested something of a cannibal nature.

Actually, Jesus did not specify the manner in which His flesh was to be eaten and His blood drunk; but even before the possibility of that very literal interpretation and the ensuing scandal, He did not withdraw a single word. Knowing "that his disciples were murmuring at this, [He] said to them: Does this scandalize you? What then if you should see the Son of man ascending where he was before? It is the spirit that gives life; the flesh profits nothing; the words that I have spoken to you are spirit and life." Jesus considered this last sentence sufficient to dispel the literal fear of some form of cannibalism: His words were spirit and life. But these same words retained their full literal significance with no metaphorical implications whatever. The indispensable thing was to have faith in Him, and the last confirmation of this faith would be to see the Son of Man ascending into Heaven, whence He had descended as the living bread — heavenly bread, heavenly flesh.

Notwithstanding this added explanation, the disciples' reaction was not merely vocal: "From this time [on] many of his disciples turned back and no longer went about with him." But the twelve apostles remained faithful. One day, when a number had already gone, "Jesus therefore said to the Twelve: Do you also wish to go away? Simon Peter answered him: Lord, to whom shall we go? Thou hast words of everlasting life, and we have come to believe and to know that thou art [the Holy One] of God" (John 6:67–69).

It is not mere chance when a writer like John so arranges his words that the Twelve "believed" and *then* "knew."

John does not return to this subject again, and the promise of the Bread of Life is not fulfilled throughout the rest of his Gospel, because he is the only evangelist who does not recount the institution of the Eucharist. John omits the institution of the Eucharist because it had already been narrated by all three Synoptists and his listeners were well acquainted with it; he records the promise instead because the Synoptists had omitted it.

The Paralytic of Bethsaida

These things had occurred in Galilee before the Pasch. It is also very possible that the Pasch had come and gone while they were happening.

Going back now to chapter 5 of John, we find that Jesus has gone up to Jerusalem for an unnamed "festival day of the Jews." This may have been the Pasch, but more probably it was the Pentecost of the same year, 29, toward the end of May.

At the northern end of Jerusalem, just outside the city walls, a new quarter was developing which — as often happens in such cases — had a double name, the general epithet "New City" and a specific name Bethsaida. In this quarter near the old city gate, which was called Probatica, or Sheepgate, there was a kind of pool likewise named Bethsaida. In it were gathered the waters of an underground spring that flowed only intermittently. Special curative powers were attributed to these waters, especially if a sick person managed to bathe in them as soon as the new flow of water began to bubble. Hence porticoes had been constructed around the four sides of the pool with a fifth across the center. In these porticoes "were lying a great multitude of the sick, blind, lame, and those with shriveled limbs, waiting for the moving of the water."

One day as Jesus was walking through this pitiful convention of miseries, He stopped before a man lying on a pallet. The man had been paralyzed for thirty-eight years, and he continually had himself brought to the pool in the hope of obtaining a cure. Unexpectedly, Jesus said to him: "Do you wish to be cured?" Naturally the poor man thought of the water; he explained that he was never the first to enter it because he could not move and had no one there to push him in ahead of the others when it began to bubble. Jesus made no answer to this complaint but instead commanded the man: "Rise, take up thy pallet and walk!" And "at once the man was cured; and he took up his

The Pool of Bethsaida

pallet and began to walk" (John 5:8–9). Now, it was the Sabbath day, and so when certain zealous Jews saw this scandalous performance, they went up to the cured man and indignantly pointed out that he could not carry a pallet on the Sabbath. The man's answer was natural: "He who made me well told me to take up my pallet and walk." And they retorted: "Who is this fellow?" The man did not know because he did not know Jesus, and Jesus had slipped away to avoid the crowd gathering at the news of the miracle.

A little later, however, Jesus met the cured man in the Temple and spoke a few words of exhortation to him. Then the man, fearing perhaps that the Pharisees would judge him Jesus' accomplice, went and told them the identity of his healer. "And this is why the Jews kept persecuting Jesus, because he was doing these things on the Sabbath" — hence not only because He commanded the man to carry his pallet, but also because He worked the cure. The Pharisees of Jerusalem shared completely the views of their Galilean colleagues, expressed on the occasion of the cure of the man with the withered hand. But Jesus, entering into discussion with them, answered: "My Father works even until now, and I work. This, then, is why the Jews were seeking the more to put him to death; because he was not only breaking the Sabbath, but was also calling God his own Father, making himself equal to God." There was no lack of intelligence or sharp-wittedness among those people. They had caught His meaning perfectly, but since His conclusion, confirmed by the miracle, knocked down one of the pillars of Pharisaic casuistry, both the reasoning and its conclusion had to be rejected.

Jesus then talked at some length in defense of His mission. In the first part of His discussion (John 5:19–30) He illustrates His equality with the Father and His consequent office as dispenser of life and universal judge. In the second part (31–47) He lists the testimonies that prove His mission though the Jews continue to misread them.

Jesus' long discourse (which should be read directly in the text) did not at all convince the Jews, and they had recourse to arguments of quite another kind. They decided that this bothersome worker of miracles must be done away with. Thus, "after these things Jesus went about in Galilee, for he did not wish to go about Judea because the Jews were seeking to put him to death" (John 7:1, referring to 5:47).

The "Tradition of the Ancients"

By moving to Galilee, Jesus put Himself beyond reach of the Pharisees of Jerusalem, but they did not abandon the game on that account. Up there in Galilee they could not lord it as they did in Jerusalem, but they could always do something; for example, they could dog Jesus and pick up new charges to bring against Him. In fact, when He returned to Galilee, "the Pharisees and some of the Scribes who had come from Jerusalem gathered about him" (Mark 7:1). The tactics these delegates chose were to pester the unmanageable Rabbi with criticisms concerning His conduct, both to humiliate Him personally and to discredit Him among the people. They noticed that His disciples did not wash their hands before eating — a serious violation of the "tradition of the ancients," a terrible misdemeanor equivalent (according to rabbinic opinion) to "frequenting a harlot," and the penalty it cried out for was being "uprooted from the world." As soon as the official critics discovered this crime, they denounced it to the Rabbi as responsible for His disciples.

Jesus accepts the challenge, but He rises from the particular to much more general considerations. All this washing of hands and dishes has been prescribed by the "tradition of the ancients" — very well. But the ancients are not God, and their tradition is not the law of God, which is infinitely greater. Hence it is necessary first to obey the law of God. There was this case, for instance. The law of God, or the Ten Commandments, prescribed that men honor their fathers and mothers and hence aid them materially when necessary.

The rabbis, on the other hand, established the rule that if an Israelite decided to offer a certain object to the Temple, that offering could go nowhere but into the Temple treasury. In such instances it was sufficient to pronounce the word *Corban* (sacred "offering"), and the object so designated became holy Temple property. It often happened, therefore, that an ill-disposed son declared all his possessions *Corban* and so, though they might be dying of hunger, his father and mother could touch nothing belonging to him. He meanwhile could continue to enjoy the goods he had so consecrated (this also was permitted by the rabbis) until he actually consigned them to the Temple, or else he managed to find some means of avoiding their donation to the treasury (and there was no dearth of rabbinic loopholes on this point either).

This being the case, Jesus answered His hecklers: "How nicely you set aside the commandment of God in order to observe your tradition! For Moses said: Honor thy father and thy mother, and, He who curses father or mother let him surely die. But you say: If a man says to his father or mother: Whatever support thou mightest have had from me now is Corban [he must maintain it]; and so you no longer allow him to do anything for his father or mother, thus annulling the word of God by means of your tradition which you have handed down" (Mark 7:9–13). And He refers to other cases that do not enter into the discussion: "and many similar things you do." The conclusion is based on a passage in Isaias: "Hypocrites! Well did Isaias prophesy of you, saying: This people honors me with their lips, but their heart is far from me; but in vain do they worship me, teaching for doctrines the precepts of men" (Matt. 15:7–9).

The Pharisees had been answered, and they do not seem to have made any further reply. But Jesus was solicitous for the crowds who had been listening and whose heads were crammed with Pharisaic prescriptions regarding the purity or impurity of foods, so turning to them, He continued: "Hear me, all of you, and understand! There is nothing outside a man that, entering into him, can defile him; but the things that come out of a man, these are what defile a man" (Mark 7:14–15). As on other occasions, Jesus here turned the prevailing concept upside down and the Pharisees were scandalized. The disciples themselves did not understand clearly the full force of this reversal of values, so when they were alone with Jesus, they asked Him to explain it. The explanation was elementary; that which enters into a man does not reach his heart, which is man's true sanctuary, but his belly. But from the heart of man come evil thoughts, adulteries, blasphemies, and the whole long procession of evil actions, which alone have power to defile a man.

For Jesus, therefore, man is essentially spirit and a rational creature; all the rest in him is accessory and subordinate to that superior essence.

Jesus in Phoenicia and the Decapolis; the Second Multiplication of the Loaves

The Gospel narrative here becomes sketchy again and unexpectedly tells us that Jesus is in the district of Sidon and Tyre, or Phoenicia. This is the first time He has left Palestine, perhaps since His birth, except for the flight into Egypt during His infancy. Why has He left it now? Probably to avoid the persecutions of the Pharisees from Jerusalem who were trailing Him, and to take refuge for a while in a place where He would be unknown and undisturbed and could take thought for His disciples, who still had so much need of spiritual formation.

But in Phoenicia, as in Bethsaida, the hope of peace and quiet soon vanished. Even those pagan regions bordering on Palestine had heard of Jesus as a great wonder-worker. So many self-styled miracle-workers were wandering about the pagan world of that time that it was not difficult to include among them the Galilean prophet as well.

These must have been more or less the sentiments of a woman of Tyre who approached Jesus, prompted by maternal solicitude. Her "little daughter" — as Mark calls her — was oppressed by an unclean spirit, and the mother now put her hope in Jesus. She makes her request but receives no answer. The unhappy mother is persistent, and she follows Jesus and His disciples down the street beseeching in a loud voice: "Have pity on me, O Lord, Son of David!" Jesus continues to pay no heed to her; but after a little, the disciples, annoyed by the unwanted publicity they are getting, tell Jesus to send her away, thus implicitly inviting Him to grant her request. Jesus answers dryly that He has been sent only to the lost sheep of the house of Israel. But the woman repeats her plea. Jesus then answers her sternly: "Let the children first have their fill, for it is not fair to take the children's bread and to cast it to the dogs." The privileged "children" are the Jews, and the dogs are the pagans. The severity of His words is almost like a bitter medicine that provokes the reaction that leads to cure. The woman reacts by answering again as an imploring and suppliant mother: "Yes, Lord; for even the dogs under the table eat of the children's crumbs!" Hers was the reaction of faith, and for Jesus faith meant salvation; hence He said: "O woman, great is thy faith!" (Matt. 15:28). "Because of this answer, go thy way; the devil has gone out of thy daughter" (Mark 7:29).

The mother believed directly, and returning home found her little girl lying quietly on her bed, entirely freed of the obsession.

From Tyre, Jesus proceeded north, as far as Sidon, then turned toward the east and traveled through the Decapolis, returning finally to the neighborhood of the Lake of Tiberias (Mark 7:31). Of this rambling journey, which probably afforded Jesus the privacy with His disciples He had not found at Tyre, only one episode has been handed down to us and that by Mark (7:31–37) alone.

A deaf-mute was brought to Jesus with the earnest request that He lay His hands upon him. Jesus took the man apart from the crowd, put His fingers in the deaf ears, and with a bit of His own saliva touched the tip of the man's tongue. Then He looked up to Heaven, sighing, and at last said: " *'Ephphetah,'* " that is, "Be thou opened!" The deaf-mute was cured instantly, and Jesus then enjoined him not to speak of what had happened; but this time, too, His command was hardly obeyed.

Why, instead of working an immediate cure as He had in other instances, did Jesus preface this one with these preliminary actions? We may suppose that since Jesus was in the pagan country of the Decapolis, it was somehow expedient to use this kind of symbolic preparation for reasons that now escape us. At the same time, it is probable that since the deaf-mute could not hear Jesus' words, Christ used these material acts just to excite in him the lively faith He always required of those asking a miracle of Him.

At this point, Matthew and Mark record a second multiplication of loaves that closely resembles the first and also took place on the eastern shore of Lake Tiberias.

Great crowds throng to Jesus and stay with Him for three days, during which time their food is all consumed. Jesus has compassion on all these people and is unwilling to send them away hungry for fear they may faint from weakness along the way. The disciples point out that there is no way to get food in this desert place. Jesus asks how many loaves of bread there are available, and they answer: "Seven, and a few little fishes" (Matt. 15:34). As in the first instance Jesus takes the food, breaks it, and has it distributed. All eat until they are filled, and seven baskets of fragments are gathered up afterward. Those who had eaten were "four thousand men apart from women and children" (Matt. 15:38).

Both Synoptists who relate this incident also record the first multiplication of the loaves and thus explicitly treat them as two distinct episodes. That is more than sufficient to prove that the early catechesis of the apostles, who witnessed these things, treated of two separate events. The two episodes, similar as they are, differ both as to the time of occurrence and the numbers fed. Their similarities are easily explained by the similar circumstances in which they took place. And if Jesus chose twice to provide miraculously for the material needs of the multitudes seeking the Kingdom of God, it was to confirm ever more strongly the admonition of the Sermon on the Mount: "Seek first the kingdom of God and his justice, and all these things shall be given you besides." Since the urgent human need for food was concerned here, it was not amiss to have two practical examples instead of one.

After the performance of this miracle, Jesus went back into the boat and came to land on the western shore of the lake at a place that Matthew (15:39) calls *Magedan* and Mark (8:10) *Dalmanutha*. The names are entirely unknown, and we do not know to what places they refer.

The Sign from Heaven; the Leaven of the Pharisees; the Blind Man of Bethsaida

As soon as Jesus returned to Galilee, up popped the vigilant worthies on His trail again. The Pharisees, accompanied this time by Sadducees, entered into discussion with Him and asked Him for a definite proof of His mission, that is, for some portent from Heaven. This indeed would be the incontrovertible proof, which would persuade even them absolutely — not this business of curing the lame, raising the dead, and multiplying loaves of bread! What they wanted was some beautiful globe to come floating down from Heaven, or the sudden blacking out of the sun. Then, yes, Jesus would win His case without question.

The request was not a new one. The messianic "sign" par excellence was, in the common opinion, some astronomical and meteoric portent. No other could have the value of certain proof precisely because it would not be what everyone was expecting to see.

But because this expectation was distorted and unworthy, Jesus did not satisfy it. When He heard the request, He sighed deeply, and this was His real answer, compounded of pity and regret. And then He added: " 'Why does this generation demand a sign? Amen I say to you, a sign shall not be given to this generation.' And he left them, and getting back into the boat crossed the sea" (Mark 8:12–13).

Their departure was so sudden the disciples forgot to get the necessary provisions, and during the crossing they were bemoaning the fact that they had only one loaf of bread. Jesus, hearing them, said: "Beware of the leaven of the Pharisees and of the leaven of Herod!" The mention of Herod Antipas is certainly due to the preceding discourses or events. It is probable that there were some of his agents among those who had just been in discussion with Jesus, or that the Pharisees themselves acted on his behalf. The very suddenness of Jesus' departure might indicate that He wished to take Himself beyond reach of the malicious inquiries of both parties. The disciples, however, whose stomachs were articulately empty, could not see what "leaven" had to do with the Pharisees or Herod. Jesus, reminding them of the two multiplications of the loaves, exhorted them not to worry about material bread but to keep far away from the aforementioned "leaven." Then they understood that He was referring to the doctrines of the Pharisees and the wiles of Herod, which permeate the spirit as leaven permeates the dough.

The hostility encountered on the western lake shore (which must have been much more serious than its scant mention by the evangelists would imply) had induced Jesus to go back to Bethsaida, perhaps because He was seeking souls better disposed. But nothing of what took place there is handed down to us either, except for a cure recorded only by Mark (8:22–26):

> They brought him a blind man and entreated him to touch him. And taking the blind man by the hand, he led him forth outside the village; and applying spittle to his eyes, he laid his hands upon him, and asked him if he saw anything. And the man looked up, and said: "I see men, as though they were trees but walking about." Then again he laid his hands upon the man's eyes, and he began to see, and was restored, so that he saw all things plainly [from a distance]. And he [Jesus] sent him away to his house.

In this vivid description we watch a true gradual cure. Perhaps the man had not been blind from birth, because he immediately recognizes the forms of men and trees; but his vision is clouded and confused at first, and then perfect. Why is the cure gradual? We may repeat here the observations regarding the deaf-mute, whose cure is somewhat similar to this one. But we can offer no more than conjectures.

At Caesarea of Philip

From Bethsaida, Jesus went toward the north, drawing still further away from Jewish districts, until He came to the region of Caesarea Philippi. In that predominantly pagan country, He and His disciples were disturbed neither by crowds nor by the intrigues of Pharisees and politicians. It was, therefore, a kind of retreat for them.

The disciples, after all, represented the best fruit of His work. Some of them may have been rough or rustic or hardheaded. All of them probably showed more or less influence of the narrow ideas prevailing among their race, but they were men of great heart, sincerely fond of their master and full of faith in Him. The crowds usually pressing about Jesus did not have these merits. Hence Jesus preferred His disciples, and He took special care of their spiritual formation with a view to the future.

And now after a year and a half of activity, He could discuss with them in confidence the matter most delicate for Him and most obscure perhaps for them, namely, His messianic identity. This teacher so beloved, this wonder-worker so powerful, this preacher so forceful — was He truly the Messiah foretold to Israel, or was He only a later prophet endowed with extraordinary powers? Was He *a* son of God, or was He *the* Son of God? Certainly the disciples had pondered this question. But if they felt inclined to answer that He was truly the Messiah, the Son of God, they were kept from doing so by the extreme care Jesus Himself had taken that no such statement be pronounced aloud. What was the reason for His reluctance? This was a difficult point for the disciples, but they were no doubt confident that the Teacher knew more than they about it, and they trusted and waited until it should be clarified in time.

Jesus now considered that the time was come. Their long intimacy with Him had opened the disciples' eyes with regard to many things. Besides, here in pagan territory there was not the danger of riotous demonstrations and outbursts of nationalism when the disciples should become certain that Jesus was the Messiah and speak of it freely among themselves. It is also probable that during these days of quiet retreat Jesus prepared His disciples spiritually to receive the confidence, pruning from the figure of the Messiah of Israel any of the political accessories He might still be wearing in their imaginations. Finally, He went apart to pray alone as He usually did in the most decisive moments of His mission.

Now they had set out together again and were walking toward Caesarea Philippi. They were already in sight of the city (Mark 8:27), and before them rose the majestic rock crowned by the temple of Augustus.

Undoubtedly in reference to previous conversations, Jesus suddenly asked His disciples: "Who do men say that I am?" They answered, all talking more or less at once: "I have heard them say that you are John the Baptist." "There are those who say you are Elias!" "Some say you are Jeremias!" Still others quoted the vague notion that Jesus was one of the ancient prophets come to life again. The opinions were numerous, but Jesus did not stop to discuss them. He asked what others thought simply to introduce the important question, namely, the personal opinion of the disciples concerning Him. When they had finished, Jesus "said to them: But who do you say that I am?"

No doubt the disciples gasped when they heard the question, which touched them deeply, and realized that Jesus was introducing a subject He had jealously avoided until then. There must have followed a silence that was more the speechless reluctance of joy than actual hesitancy — not unlike the silence of a girl who has just been proposed to by the man she has long loved secretly. And they stopped dead in the middle of the road, mute with an eloquent silence, their eyes fixed on the temple of Augustus towering over the city and the countryside from the peak of the rock.

After a few moments, their silence was translated into words by Simon Peter, nor could anyone have done it but he, the most impetuous of all that loved Jesus dearly: "Thou art the Christ, the Son of the living God." His expression of their reverent silence was a perfect one; this was plain to see in the happy assent on their bearded faces, telling the joy they had so long repressed.

Jesus glanced swiftly from one face to another; then He turned to the disciple who had answered Him and said: "Blessed art thou, Simon Bar-Jona [that is, "son of Jona"] for flesh and blood has not revealed this to thee, but my Father in heaven!" Simon's declaration was completely confirmed by Him it most concerned, and all present felt their own secret faith confirmed as well. There must have followed another brief silence, in which they looked again perhaps toward the temple up there on the rock. Then Jesus continued: "And I say to thee, thou art Peter, and upon this rock I will build my Church, and the gates of hell shall not prevail against it. And I will give thee the keys of the kingdom of heaven; and whatever thou shalt bind on earth shall be bound in heaven, and whatever thou shalt loose on earth shall be loosed in heaven" (Matt. 16:16–19).

Jesus had called Simon "Peter," or "Rock," before this, but the reason for it was not given them. Now the epithet is explained, and it is all much clearer as they stand there before that actual rock that supports the temple dedicated to the lord of the Palatine. The foundation rock of the spiritual temple that Jesus will build to the Lord of Heaven, namely, His Church, is to be the disciple who first declared Him the Messiah and truly the Son of God. Jesus' other words are just as clear in the light of the circumstances in which they were spoken. Hell corresponds to the Hebrew *Sheol*, as the dwelling of the wicked dead, the enemies of good and of the Kingdom of God; the "gates" of this satanic abyss, that is, its utmost strength, will not prevail against the edifice erected by Jesus and the rock that supports it.

The symbols of the keys and of binding and loosing are typically Semitic. Even today in Arab towns men go about the streets with a set of huge keys tied together with a small cord and dangling conspicuously on either side of the shoulder. They are landlords parading their authority in that fashion. The figure of binding and loosing (cf. Matt. 18:18) retains here the meaning it had among the rabbis of the time. The rabbis "bound" when they prohibited something and "loosed" when they permitted it.

Peter's office, then, is clearly defined. He will be the foundation of the Church, a foundation so unshakable that the powers of Hell will not prevail against it. He will also be the chief steward of this house, and its keys will be entrusted to him. Finally, he will dictate the laws of the house, prohibiting and permitting, and the judgments he pronounces on earth will be ratified in Heaven.

Jesus' reply to Simon Peter is so clear as to be dazzling. Yet, as we know, this very text has caused streams of ink to flow in absolute denial that Jesus ever conferred on Simon the office of foundation stone of the Church, trustee of its keys, and arbiter of its laws. Why has this been denied?

The early orthodox Protestants asserted that Jesus was not speaking of Simon Peter at all but of Himself, and that the rest of His statement refers to all the apostles collectively and to their faith. When He said, "Upon this rock I will build my church," and so forth, Jesus pointed to Himself even though He was speaking with and of Simon. This gesture supposedly solves the whole question: it is said to be evident from the context and in complete agreement with the words that follow, "and I will give *thee* the keys to the kingdom of heaven, and whatever *thou* shalt bind …". The reasoning here is perfect, provided we start with the premise that white means black.

The Messianic Idea Corrected

Jesus had now definitely proclaimed His Messiahship, but the announcement was still confidential; only the disciples received it. And as soon as Jesus had conferred Simon Peter's office upon him, He charged them "to tell no one that he was Jesus the Christ" (Matt. 16:20). Jesus did not consider the time ripe to spread the announcement, both because the populace had not yet been prepared for it and because the disciples themselves still had an imperfect notion of the nature of His messianism.

Hence, He began to correct and perfect their concept. "From that time Jesus began to show his disciples that he must go to Jerusalem and suffer many things from the elders and Scribes and chief priests, and be put to death, and on the third day rise again." How different from the splendid Messiah awaited by the people is this Messiah, who shuns recognition as such and predicts the suffering and violent death awaiting Him. The sharp warning is a hard blow for His disciples. The generous Peter, both by nature and from the new office just conferred on him, felt he must say something: "And Peter taking him aside, began to chide him, saying: 'Far be it from thee, O Lord! This will never happen to thee!' He turned and said to Peter: 'Get behind me, satan! Thou art a scandal to me, for thou dost not mind the things of God, but those of men.'" Satan was the tempter par excellence, and his name is here bestowed on the Rock of the Church and the chief steward of the Kingdom of Heaven. The reason for the rebuke, namely, the lingering desire for a conquering Messiah and a reluctance to accept the suffering one instead, was chargeable to his time more than to Peter personally, but it does show how necessary it was to correct the messianic concept even in the minds of the disciples closest to Jesus.

And the correction continued through a series of abrupt disillusionments. What did these disciples expect who were following the Messiah Jesus? To share a triumph, perhaps, and enjoy a life of magnificence with a conqueror? Jesus scatters these dreams, anticipating and belying their thoughts with statements rough as the slaps with which one tries to awaken a patient from drugged delirium. Those who would follow Him must deny themselves and take up their cross (Matt. 16:24). The allusion to the cross is naturally clearer after Jesus' death, but even now the disciples could understand it. Anyone who wants to follow Jesus is to consider himself already dead and then only will he live. By losing his life in the cause of Jesus and the "good tidings," he will be saved, but if he remains desperately attached to his life, he will lose it (Mark 8:35). In fact, what does it profit a man to gain the whole world if he lose his soul by failing to gain life eternal? What ransom can a man give for his soul (Mark 8:36–37)? Will there be some ashamed of Jesus and His "good tidings"? But when the Son of Man comes in the glory of His Father, surrounded by the angels, He will be ashamed of those who were ashamed of Him, and He will render to each one according to his conduct (Mark 8:38; Matt. 16:27).

For Jesus, the present life is transitory and has value only insofar as it is directed to the enduring life of the future. He, the Messiah, guides men toward eternal life through the harsh trials of our impermanent existence. Whoever does not want to follow Him, choosing instead this transient life, also chooses death.

All three Synoptics record here another statement that seems to have been pronounced on another occasion: "And he said to them: Amen I say to you, there are some of those standing here who will not taste death, till they have seen the kingdom of God coming in power" (Mark 8:39). With fine insight the Synoptists set this statement after the others that correct the messianic concept, for in substance it does the same thing. No political Messiah is to appear in a blaze of glory, but the kingdom of the suffering and murdered Messiah is to display in its coming such inner and exterior power that it will dispel forever all dreams of a political Messiah. And some of those present will not die before they have witnessed the unfurling of that power. In fact, some forty years later, that is, within the second "generation" according to Jewish reckoning, the Jerusalem of the messianic dreams has been destroyed and political Judaism cut down forever, while the "good tidings" of Jesus "is proclaimed all over the world" (Rom 1:8; cf. Col. 1:23).

The Transfiguration

As we might expect, the vigorous correctives Jesus applied to His disciples' hopes also depressed their spirits. Jesus remedied this with the Transfiguration, which took place "six days ["about eight days," according to Luke] after" He manifested that He was the Messiah.

The evangelists place this episode on "a high mountain" but neglect to give its name. A tradition dating back to the fourth century has settled on Tabor as the place of this event. For us today Tabor is not a "high mountain," being only about seventeen hundred feet above sea level. But for men in ancient times it could well represent a high enough mountain since it was completely isolated and most of Judea could be seen from its peak. As for the

Mount Tabor

distance between Tabor and Caesarea Philippi, it could have been covered easily in the six (or eight) days mentioned. Whatever the setting, the event took place as follows.

From among His dispirited disciples, Jesus took with Him three favorites, Peter and the brothers James and John, and led them up the mountain. The long road, the difficult climb, and the heat of the season must have wearied the travelers by the time they reached the top. They probably arrived at evening, because the three disciples lay down as comfortably as they could and started to go to sleep (Luke 9:32). Jesus, as was His custom at night, began to pray a short distance away from them. Suddenly a brilliant light flooded the faces of the sleepy disciples; they opened their eyes and there beheld Jesus "transfigured before them. And his face shone as the sun and his garments became white as snow" (Matt. 17:2). When the disciples, "heavy with sleep" (Luke 9:32), were fully awake and their eyes and minds adjusted somewhat to the dazzling splendor of the vision, they recognized Moses and Elias standing with the transfigured Jesus and speaking with Him of "his death which he was about to fulfill in Jerusalem" (Luke 9:31). The conversation lasted for a little and then Moses and Elias made as though to move away. But Peter, as usual, feels obliged to say something and he bursts out: "Master, it is good for us to be here! And let us set up three tents, one for thee, and one for Moses, and one for Elias!" We might be tempted to think the good Peter is remorseful that he has provided only a place for himself to sleep after the hard journey and neglected to do anything for Jesus. But the evangelist who is Peter's interpreter immediately adds the true explanation, which he had certainly heard from the lips of Peter himself, that he did not know what he was saying, they were so struck with fear (cf. Mark 9:6). Peter received no answer, for a radiant cloud enveloped them all, and "a voice out of the cloud said: 'This is my beloved Son, in whom I am well pleased; hear him!'" (Matt. 17:5). More terrified than ever, the three disciples threw themselves to the ground; but shortly afterward Jesus touched them, saying: "Arise and do not be afraid." They looked about and saw no one but Jesus, and He was as they always knew Him. The next day, as they descended the mountain, He commanded them: "Tell the vision to no one until the Son of man has risen from the dead!"

In a sense Jesus' Transfiguration balances His temptation. More directly, it remedies the depressing effect produced on the disciples by His reversal of their messianic notions, and at the same time it confirms that reversal. The Messiah Jesus, also splendid with radiance, speaks with Moses and Elias of

His death, which is about to occur in Jerusalem, as if it were the necessary bridge to the manifestation of His glory.

The remedy was undoubtedly successful in its effects on the disciples' spirits, but at the same time it created some uncertainties. Why were they forbidden to tell others of the vision? And to what future event did the permission to speak of it only after the Son of Man "has risen from the dead" refer? Was it then truly the eve of the world renewal and the resurrection of the dead mentioned in the ancient prophecies? But then why had Elias not come to stay — instead of appearing only in a vision — in order to prepare the way for the great rebirth? With this last question in mind the disciples began to interrogate Jesus: "Why then do the Scribes say that Elias must come first?" (Matt. 17:10). And Jesus answered: "Yes, Elias must come to prepare all things; but he has already come, and people have done to him all the evil they have wished. Thus also the Son of man must suffer and receive evil at their hands. Then the disciples understood that he had spoken to them of John the Baptist" (Matt. 17:13).

A Possessed Boy

They descended the slopes of the mountain and soon rejoined the other apostles waiting below, who were surrounded by a great crowd of people and some scribes with whom they were disputing.

As soon as Jesus came into view, one of the crowd approached Him, saying: "I have brought you my only son, who is possessed of a dumb evil spirit. And whenever it seizes him, it flings him down, bruising him sorely and he foams and grinds his teeth and his body becomes rigid. I have begged your disciples to drive out the spirit, but they could not." This failure had perhaps brought on the dispute with the scribes, who would not let the chance escape to say something malicious about the disciples and their absent master as well. But now He is there, and hearing the difficulty He exclaims: "O unbelieving generation, how long shall I be with you? How long shall I put up with you?" Then glancing about for the boy, He added: "Bring him to me!" (Mark 9:19). For Jesus, faith was the essential requisite for a miracle, and He deplored the lack of it in the scribes and the father of the boy as well as in the apostles, whose failure betrayed that their faith was weak and faltering.

The boy is brought to Jesus, but in the presence of the wonder-worker he is immediately seized with convulsions and falls violently to the ground, rolling and grunting and foaming at the mouth. Jesus questions the father, not to make a diagnosis but rather to underline for the benefit of all present the significance of the "sign" He is preparing to work and to induce them to reflect on their own lack of faith: "How long has this befallen him?" And the father answers: "From his childhood; and often the unclean spirit throws him into the fire or water. If you can do something, help us; have pity on us." The poor father's words still betray a slightly uncertain faith despite Jesus' lament in that regard. Hence, "If thou canst!" said Jesus to him. "Why, all things are possible to him who believes!" The little scene that follows these words is vibrant and lively. "At once the father of the boy cried aloud, and said with tears: 'I do believe; help my unbelief! So when Jesus saw that a crowd came running together, he rebuked the unclean spirit, saying to it: 'Thou dumb and deaf spirit, I command thee, go out of him and enter him no more.' Then shrieking and convulsing him violently it came out; and he became as if dead, so that many said: 'He is dead.' But Jesus, taking him by the hand, raised him, and he stood up." The physician-evangelist adds the delicate touch, he "restored him to his father."

The apostles could not help seeking the reason for their failure to perform the cure, so they ask Jesus in private: "Why could we not cast it out?" And Jesus replied: "Because of your little faith; for amen I say to you, if you have faith like a mustard seed, you will say to this mountain: Remove from here — and it will remove. And nothing will be impossible to you." Jesus had already spoken of the mustard seed in His parable; "this mountain" is perhaps Tabor, which loomed in front of them. As for the necessity of faith for miracles, Jesus had insisted on it many times in the past, but His lesson had borne little fruit.

Last Days in Galilee

After these events, Jesus was "passing through Galilee, and he did not wish anyone to know it" (Mark 9:30). Hence this journey was used exclusively for the spiritual formation of the disciples accompanying Him and not to spread the "good tidings" to the multitudes.

This formation soon required a new warning regarding the earthly lot of the Messiah to dispel more thoroughly the dreams of political messianism inbred in those Jewish souls: "The Son of man is to be betrayed into the hands of men, and they will kill him; and on the third day he will rise again." The effect of the warning showed how necessary it was, for the disciples "were troubled exceedingly" (Matt. 17:22–23), and Luke adds that "they did not understand this saying, and it was hidden from them, that they might not perceive it; and they were afraid to ask him about this saying" (9:45).

Later the group turned toward Capernaum, and they arrived there while the disciples, walking perhaps a little apart from Jesus, were busy in a serious discussion among themselves. Their arrival in town was immediately noted by the tax collectors, who hurried to make certain that Jesus had paid the tribute for the Temple in Jerusalem. All Israelites were obliged to pay annually a half shekel of silver (or a didrachma) for the upkeep of the Temple. This tax was usually collected before the Pasch, but in more distant localities like Galilee the collection might continue until, or be taken up instead, just before the feasts of Pentecost and of the Tabernacles. Since Jesus had been away from Capernaum for a long time and the feast of Tabernacles was drawing near, the tax collectors came to collect. They addressed Peter first, asking him: "Does your master not pay the didrachma?" And Peter with his usual impetuosity answered: "Certainly he does" — and he entered the house where Jesus was, to speak to Him about it. But Jesus spoke first: "What dost thou think, Simon? From whom do the kings of the earth receive tribute or customs; from their own sons or from others?" And Peter answered: "From others." Jesus replied: "The sons then are exempt."

The application of this statement to Jesus' case was clear enough. He was the Son of God and hence was not liable to tax for the earthly house of His heavenly Father. But Jesus continued: "However, that we may not give offense to them, go to the sea and cast a hook, and take the first fish that comes up. And opening its mouth thou wilt find a stater; take that and give it to them for me and thee" (Matt. 17:24–27). The stater was equivalent to a whole shekel or two didrachmas; hence it covered the tax for Jesus and Peter both.

In the Sermon on the Mount Jesus had exhorted His listeners to be concerned only for the Kingdom of God and His justice. This episode, like the two multiplications of the loaves, verifies His words. Perhaps at that moment the apostles' common purse held only a few coins. Jesus sends Simon to that Providence that supplies food to the birds and raiment to the lilies, and Providence promptly pays the note issued in its name in the Sermon on the Mount.

The errand given Peter here suggested in some way the discussion that the disciples were having among themselves when they arrived in Capernaum. This was perhaps revealed in their attitude or in some half-finished sentence, so Jesus questioned them directly: "What were you arguing about on the way?" (Mark 9:32ff.). The question embarrassed them; because they had been arguing about which one of them was the greatest in the Kingdom of Heaven. Each perhaps gave his own reasons for claiming that when the Master should be seated on His messianic throne, he and not his companion would have the seat of honor closest to it. After a short, embarrassed silence, one of them took courage and told Jesus they had been discussing who should be first among them.

As in the Sermon on the Mount, Jesus' answer is a complete reversal of ideas. The first, He said, was to be the least, the servant and slave of all. At that very moment a little child chanced to pass through the room, and Jesus called him to Him, fondled him, and set him in the midst of those grown men; then looking at them one by one He declared: "Amen I say to you, unless you turn and become like little children, you will not enter into the kingdom of heaven. Whoever, therefore, humbles himself as this little child, he is the greatest in the kingdom of heaven" (Matt. 18:3–4). Then Jesus went on to state that whoever should receive in His name a child like the little fellow He had given them as a model, received Him Himself, just as whoever received Him received the heavenly Father who had sent Him.

This broad criterion did not seem clear to John. Shortly before, he and the other apostles had deliberately hindered a man who was driving out devils in the Master's name. It was indeed permissible for him to use that Name in exorcism, but then he should have joined them, becoming a disciple as they had done. Since he had not chosen to join them, the apostles hindered him. Jesus disapproved their action; they should not have forbidden the man because whoever was not against them was for them (Mark 9:38–40).

There were other norms, too, that Jesus imparted to His disciples as the occasion presented itself in these days spent in their spiritual formation (Mark 9:41ff. and parallel passages).

Whoever gives a glass of water to Jesus' disciples because they are such will not be without his reward.

If anyone scandalizes one of these who, believing in Jesus, have become as little children, it will be better for that man that a millstone be tied around his neck and he be cast into the sea.

Care must be taken not to scorn those who are children in spirit, for their guardian angels constantly behold the face of the heavenly Father.

If a brother has sinned, he is to be reproved in secret. If he listens to the rebuke, then a brother has been won. If he refuses to listen, then one or two witnesses are to be sought in conformity with the precept in the Mosaic Law. If he remains obdurate, then he is to be referred to the Church. If he will not listen to the Church, either, then he is to be treated as a pagan or publican was treated by the Jews. And whatever the apostles, constituting the Church, shall bind or loose on earth shall be bound or loosed also in Heaven.

When two come together on earth to ask something of the heavenly Father, it will be granted to them. For wherever two or three are gathered in the name of Jesus, there, too, is Jesus in their midst.

But the rule to denounce the guilty and obdurate brother raised a difficulty in Peter's mind. "Lord, how often shall my brother sin against me, and I forgive him? Up to seven times?" (Matt. 18:21ff.). Jesus replies: "I do not say to thee seven times, but seventy times seven!" — proverbial for an unlimited number. According to Peter, one was to offer the other cheek, as the Sermon on the Mount commanded, only seven times. An eighth blow would nullify the precept. But according to the preacher of the Sermon, the eighth blow was still the first, and so the precept remained in force. And why?

Jesus explained why in a parable. There was a certain king, who one fine day decided to settle his accounts and called in his servants to give their reports. First came one who was to give him ten thousand talents, an overwhelming sum, amounting to more than twelve million dollars. The debtor naturally had no such sum at his disposal, and so the king, to recover at least a part of the amount, ordered his possessions to be sold and the debtor himself with his wife and children to be sold into slavery. The sentence was mild enough for ancient times, because the debtor and his family at least had their lives spared while the king lost the greater part of his money. But when he heard the sentence, the debtor threw himself at the king's feet and implored him with the heartbroken sincerity of a man ruined forever: "Have patience with me and I will pay thee all!" The king, a goodhearted man, took pity on him and immediately released him, forgiving him all his debt. The man might well breathe freely once more; he had escaped slavery and he had acquired ten thousand talents besides.

But this made him proud, and his pride blinded him. When he left that lucky audience, he met a colleague who owed him one hundred denarii, or a little more than twenty dollars. He no sooner saw him than he jumped on him, and grabbing him by the throat, almost as if to choke him, he began to shout: "Pay what thou owest!" This poor fellow threw himself at his feet exclaiming: "Have patience with me and I will pay thee all!" But the man would not listen, and he had him cast into prison. This grieved the other employees of the court, and they reported it to the king. Then the king summoned the debtor he had pardoned and said to him: "Wicked servant! I forgave you that whole enormous debt because you begged me to. Therefore, should you not have had pity on your fellow servant?" And in great anger the king had him thrown not into prison but to the "torturers," until he should pay all his debt.

And Jesus concluded: "So also my heavenly Father will do to you, if you do not each forgive your brothers from your hearts."

It seems this time the parable was so clear that the apostles did not ask Jesus for an explanation. The king is God; the alarming sum of money that the king forgave his servant are the many failings that God forgives man. The negligible sum the pardoned servant so brutally demanded of his colleague represents the little wrongs one man commits against another. Hence — and this is the lesson of the parable — God's pardon of man requires that he pardon his fellow man. It is the same thing Jesus taught earlier in the Lord's Prayer: "Forgive us our debts as we forgive our debtors."

Several months had now passed since the Pasch, and it was drawing toward autumn of the year 29. A year and a half, or about twenty months, had gone by since the beginning of Jesus' public ministry. Judging from the explicit information given in the Gospels, all the activity of these months had taken place in Galilee, with the exception of the trip to Jerusalem and the other journey into Phoenicia and the regions north of Palestine.

Unfortunately, looked at from the human point of view, the results of that activity showed a heavy deficit. The preacher of the "good tidings" had been driven out by His fellow townsmen of Nazareth. The villages along the lake shore, which He seemed to prefer, had gathered about the wonder-worker, only in order that their blind might see and their deaf hear, that their dead might be brought to life, and that they might have bread to eat. When it came to accepting the "change of mind" and the spiritual revolution required by the wonder-worker, most of those who had thronged about Him refused, and the seed that He had sown had fallen on the pathways and been trampled underfoot, or on the rock, or among thorns. What had sprouted from His sowing? Except for the slender sheaf of disciples — and even these were a long way from the full ripening of the harvest — we may reasonably suppose that those in all Galilee who sincerely accepted and adhered to the "good tidings" were few indeed. Humanly speaking, Jesus' work seemed to add up to failure.

Jesus felt this, and His heart grieved, especially since there was no time to insist further with the Galileans. He had now to try elsewhere. What more could He have done among those Galileans and especially in the towns along the lake that His harvest might have been more abundant? Nothing. And if the harvest was extremely small, did not the blame belong to those very towns He had loved so well? One day His sorrow and regret burst from His heart in poignant lamentation:

Woe to thee, Corozain! Woe to thee, Bethsaida! For if in Tyre and Sidon had been worked the miracles that have been worked in you, they would have repented long ago in sackcloth and ashes. But I tell you, it will be more tolerable for Tyre and Sidon on the day of judgment than for you. And thou, Capharnaum, shalt thou be exalted to heaven? Thou shalt be thrust down to hell! For if the miracles had been worked in Sodom that have been worked in thee, it would have remained to this day. But I tell you, it will be more tolerable for the land of Sodom on the day of judgment than for thee. (Matt. 11:21–24)

We are well acquainted with Bethsaida and Capernaum at this point, but there has been no other mention of Corozain, which occurs only here in all the Gospels. This unexpected mention is highly instructive, for it shows what gaps there are in the information concerning Jesus' activity that the evangelists have preserved for us. If Jesus names Corozain here particularly, singling it out for woe, then the town must have been the object of His care and affection no less than Bethsaida and Capernaum. Yet we know absolutely nothing about what He did there. Eusebius says that Corozain was two miles from Capernaum. In fact, about two miles north of the latter city, there is a place today called Keraze (or Kerazie), where the ancient synagogue has recently been discovered. Today, the whole place is deserted. In later times, this village, named in the Gospels only to be cursed, attracted the popular Christian fancy, which, having reflected over it for several centuries, decided it would be the country of the antichrist.

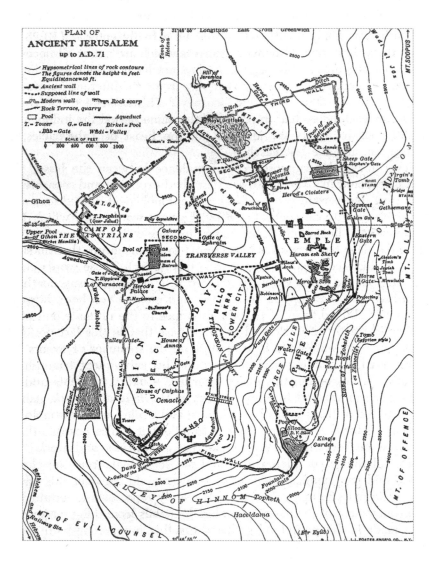

PLAN OF
ANCIENT JERUSALEM
up to A.D. 71

Hypsometrical lines of rock contours
The figures denote the height in feet.
Equidistance = 50 ft.
Ancient wall
Supposed line of wall
Modern wall   Rock scarp
Rock Terrace, quarry
Pool   Aqueduct
T. = Tower   G. = Gate   Birket = Pool
Bab = Gate   Wâdi = Valley

SCALE OF FEET
200 400 600 800 1000

Chapter 13

∞

From the Last Feast of Tabernacles
to the Last Feast of Dedication

The Feast of Tabernacles

As the summer of the year 29 drew to a close, the gay and popular feast of Tabernacles approached. If Jesus last visited Jerusalem for the feast of Pentecost, then He had been away from the Holy City about four months. His activity in Galilee during this period had yielded most disappointing results, and He decided to leave it. But where was He to go next? Those "brethren" who did not believe in Him enthusiastically recommended one destination. Jerusalem was the place to go to astonish the illustrious doctors with His works if He wanted definite results, instead of wasting miracles on the boorish mountaineers of Galilee (John 7:3–5).

Jesus, too, had thought of Jerusalem, but that suggestion from His "brethren," dictated by considerations far different from His, was a momentary obstacle to His plans. They were thinking that the feast of Tabernacles, to which great crowds thronged even from outside of Palestine, would be an opportune time for some spectacular manifestation on Jesus' part; He was thinking that precisely the danger of any such publicity was reason enough to reject their advice. So the "brethren," with other Galilean pilgrims, left for Jerusalem, and Jesus stayed a while longer in Galilee. Later, He, too, set out for the Holy City, "not publicly but as it were privately" (John 7:10).

Jesus chose the shortest route, that which crossed the center of Palestine through Samaria. The Samaritans, with their inveterate hatred of the Israelites, were quick to make the most of the opportunity offered to molest the pilgrims in every way, not hesitating even to wound and kill. It is true that Jesus in the past had found a welcome among the Samaritans, but only those of Sichar, and a year and a half before, so this former friendliness was not to be counted on very much. Hence, for precaution's sake, He sent some of the disciples ahead to find lodging in an unnamed village. But His fears were

Huts built for the feast of Tabernacles in Jerusalem

realized, for the Samaritans of the village, knowing that these were Galileans bound for Jerusalem, refused them hospitality. Whereupon, the two brothers, James and John, afire with zeal, remembered that they had received from Jesus the power to work miracles for the diffusion of the Kingdom of God; so they asked Him if he would permit them to call fire down from Heaven to burn those Samaritan blackguards to ashes. But He "turned and rebuked them.... And they went to another village" (Luke 9:55–56, Greek). Who knows but that the "other village" was Sichar?

Meanwhile the first of the Galilean pilgrims had arrived in Jerusalem, and its citizens, remembering what had happened a few months before at Bethsaida, immediately inquired if Jesus, too, had arrived: "Where is he?" And there was much whispered comment among the crowd concerning him. For some were saying: "He is a good man." But others were saying: "No, rather he seduces the crowd." Yet for fear of the Jews no one spoke openly of him" (John 7:11–13). Suddenly, when the eight days of the Tabernacles were half over, it became known that Jesus had arrived and had begun to teach in the Temple court. Both admirers and detractors ran to hear Him, all recognizing the power of His preaching.

But His detractors immediately posed a damaging question. No one could be truly learned and wise if he had not been trained in the schools of the great rabbis and scribes: "How does this man come by learning, since he has not studied?" There was reason to suspect the self-made teacher who in matters religious dared to deviate from "tradition." Jesus answered:

> "My teaching is not my own, but his who sent me. If anyone desires to do his will, he will know of the teaching whether it is from God, or whether I speak on my own authority. He who speaks on his own authority seeks his own glory. But he who seeks the glory of the one who sent him is truthful, and there is no injustice in him. Did not Moses give you the Law and [yet] none of you observes the Law? Why do you seek to put me to death?" The crowd answered: "Thou hast a devil! Who seeks to put thee to death?" Jesus answered and said to them: "One work I did and you all wonder. For this reason Moses gave you the circumcision — not that it is from Moses, but from the fathers — and on a Sabbath you circumcise a man. If a man receives circumcision on a Sabbath, that the Law of Moses may not be broken, are you indignant with me because I made a whole man well on a Sabbath? Judge not by appearances but give just judgment!" (John 7:15–24)

The discussion referred to the cure at Bethsaida and the objections then raised by the Pharisees. Jesus tried to make His opponents understand more deeply the true significance of the Mosaic Law, and the dispute continued, so that some of those in Jerusalem, who knew very well which way the wind was blowing, asked: "Is not this the man they seek to kill? And look, he speaks in public and they say nothing to him! Can it be that our elders have recognized he is truly the Messiah? But we know whence this man has come, but when the Messiah comes no one will know where he is from!"

It was indeed the common opinion that the Messiah was to be a descendant of David and be born in Bethlehem, but also that he would appear unexpectedly after being in absolute retirement for a long time in a place no one knew. But it was well-known where Jesus usually lived and so He could not be the Messiah.

Jesus, therefore, answered by appealing to His own heavenly origin and the authority of Him who had sent Him: "You both know me, and know where I am from. Yet I have not come of myself, but he is true who has sent me, whom you do not know. But I know him because I am from him, and he has sent me" (John 7:28–29). Jesus spoke these words in a loud voice, as though He were making a solemn declaration, and that is the way His adversaries took it. They interpreted it — and rightly — as a declaration of heavenly and divine existence. But for them such a declaration was blasphemy, and they therefore burst out in scandalized indignation and tried to carry out their old design and seize Jesus. "But his hour was not yet come" — observes the spiritual evangelist — and so no one succeeded in laying hands on Him. His enemies were, in fact, well counterbalanced by enthusiastic admirers; these took courage, and entering into the discussion, they observed: When the Messiah comes, will he perhaps work more miracles than this man works?

This answer was a recall to reality. The argument of the miracles, which simply *had* to be answered and was therefore as much of a target twenty centuries ago as it is today, produced a good effect, and "many believed in him." Nevertheless, Jesus' adversaries did not give in, but ran to the Temple magistrates to see if they could arrange a regular arrest. But the resolute attitude of Jesus' admirers must have dissuaded them from carrying out a procedure so dangerous since it might result in a riot. And while the guards were buzzing about Jesus, He was repeating to His enemies: "Yet a little while I am with you, and then I go to him who sent me. You will seek me and will not find me, and where I am you cannot come." Jesus is still alluding to His previous declaration of divine origin; His adversaries, who rejected that declaration, found themselves trying to understand an indefinite reference instead, and they wondered among themselves: Will He perhaps go into the Diaspora to teach the pagans there?

During the Octave of Tabernacles, meanwhile, there was the daily procession to the fountain of Siloe. On the last day, which was the most solemn, Jesus applied the ceremony to Himself and His teaching: "If anyone thirst, let him come to me and drink!" Earlier Jesus had spoken of a certain water to the Samaritan woman, and even six centuries before, a prophet spoke of the same water, attributing to God this lamentation:

> Two evils have my people committed:
> they have forsaken me, the fountain of living water,
> and have dug for themselves cisterns,
> broken cisterns that can hold no water!

This time, too, Jesus had spoken in the tone of solemn proclamation, and His words rekindled among the crowd the disputes of a few days before. Some of His admirers declared: "This man is truly the prophet!" And others: "He is the Messiah!" And His adversaries answered: "What Messiah can He be? Is Galilee going to give us a Messiah now? Is He not to come from Bethlehem, the descendant of David?"

The Temple guards tried again to seize Jesus, but they were stopped by His great spiritual magnetism. When they were rebuked by the magistrates and the Pharisees for not having arrested Him, they answered with beautiful simplicity: "Never has man spoken as this man!" (John 7:46). The Pharisees retorted sarcastically: Has He led you astray too? Has any one of the rulers or any of us Pharisees ever believed in Him? But this crowd, which does not know the Law, is everyone accursed!

The cautious Nicodemus also took part in the discussion. He had the courage to appeal to the Law, observing: "Does our Law judge a man unless it first give him a hearing, and know what he does?" But Nicodemus, too, received a sarcastic rebuke: "Art thou also a Galilean? Search the Scriptures and see that out of Galilee arises no prophet."

Jesus used still another circumstance of the feast to present Himself and His teaching. From evening of the first day of Tabernacles the outer court of the Temple was crowded with people bearing branches of palm, myrtle, and willow. As soon as darkness fell, the priests lit great lamps hanging from very high lamp holders, and immediately the crowd lit innumerable other lights of every kind. In the midst of this riotous illumination, the joyful festivities unfolded, chief among them the dances performed in the center of the court, while the Levites chanted hymns. The dances were executed principally by the dignitaries of the nation and the most famous doctors, who vied with one another to see who could dance the longest with a lighted torch in hand. The splendors of that gay night lingered in the eyes of the celebrating throng throughout the succeeding days, and on one of those days Jesus applied the ceremony to Himself.

One day, then, Jesus was in the Court of the Treasury, next to the Women's Court, and He said to the Jews: "I am the light of the world. He who follows me does not walk in the darkness, but will have the light of life." The Pharisees answered that no one was obliged to believe in Him, because He gave testimony of Himself and His testimony was not true. There followed a dispute in several installments (cf. John 8:20–21 with 8:30–31), which should be read in its entirety in the text. Jesus' fundamental assertions are the following.

The testimony of Jesus is guaranteed by His heavenly Father, but the Jews do not know the Father because they do not know Jesus. Meanwhile, time presses; Jesus will depart from the Jews forever, and they will die obstinate in their sin of not recognizing His mission. They are "from below" and of the world; Jesus is "from above" and not of the world. At this point, the Jews ironically ask Jesus the same question their special delegation had asked John the

Baptist, "Who art thou?" Jesus answers: "In the first place, [I am] precisely that which I tell you." The expression avoids the clear and definite assertion the Jews were waiting for as an excuse for using violence against Jesus, as indeed they do at the end of the discussion. Yet, continues Jesus, when the Jews "have lifted up the Son of Man" then they will know that He is "the Son of Man," the one who faithfully performed the mission received from the Father.

This total dedication to the will of the Father impresses many of His listeners, who believe in Him. To these new believers Jesus next addresses Himself, but others still hostile to Him challenge Him again. Jesus has said that by accepting His teachings they will achieve true liberty, which consists not in being the descendants of Abraham but in freedom from sin. Let the true descendant of Abraham do the just works of Abraham and not seek to kill Jesus, who has been sent by the heavenly Father. It is not enough to proclaim themselves the sons of God, as His adversaries do; they must also love Jesus and accept His teachings, because He "has come forth from God," being sent by Him. Whoever does not listen to the words of Jesus shows that he has for father the devil, who was a murderer from the beginning and the father of lies. If Jesus speaks the truth, why do they not believe in Him? Who can convict Him of sin? Whoever is of God listens to the words of God; that is why Jesus' adversaries do not listen to Him, because they are not of God.

At this point the conflict becomes more intense. The Jews resent the blows they have had to take, and they hit back, not with reasoned arguments but with insults:

"Are we not right in saying that thou art a Samaritan and hast a devil?" Jesus answered: "I have not a devil, but I honor my Father, and you dishonor me. Yet I do not seek my own glory; there is one who seeks [it] and who judges [of it]. Amen, amen I say to you, if anyone keep my word, he will never see death."

The Jews therefore said: "Now we know that thou hast a devil. Abraham is dead, and the prophets, and thou sayest: 'If anyone keep my word he will never taste death.' Art thou greater than our father Abraham, who is dead? And the prophets are dead. Whom dost thou make thyself?"

Jesus answered: "If I glorify myself, my glory is nothing. It is my Father who glorifies me, of whom you say that he is your God. And you do not know him, but I know him. And if I say that I do not know him I shall be like you, a liar. But I know him, and I keep his word. Abraham your father rejoiced that he was to see my day. He saw it and was glad." The Jews therefore said to him: "Thou art not yet fifty years old, and hast thou seen Abraham?" Jesus said to them: "Amen, amen I say to you, before Abraham came to be, I am." (John 8:48–58)

The discussion is ended. Jesus has proclaimed that He is before Abraham and consequently before all Hebraism, of which Abraham is the founder. Either they must accept His assertion and believe in Him, or they must declare Him later and inferior to Hebraism and therefore subject to its laws. Now, according to the Hebrew Law (Lev. 24:16), the blasphemer must be stoned; so the Jews, in whose opinion Jesus has blasphemed in declaring that He existed before Abraham, immediately start to apply the Law: "They therefore took up stones to cast at him; but Jesus hid himself, and went out from the Temple" (John 8:59).

The Adulteress

Also on the occasion of the feast of Tabernacles we have the episode of the woman taken in adultery, which is recorded right after the discourse on the living water and before the discourse on the light of the world (John 7:53–8:11).

Early one morning, perhaps during the Octave of the Tabernacles, Jesus came down from the Mount of Olives, crossed the Cedron, climbed back up the western path to Jerusalem, and entered the Temple. There the people gathered about Him in the outer court, and He sat down and began to teach. All of a sudden a group of scribes and Pharisees followed by a crowd of people burst into the court. They no sooner spy the circle of people listening to Jesus than they push their way through, interrupting Jesus' teaching. From the crowd trailing the scribes and Pharisees two or three men step forward dragging a woman after them, and they push her out into the empty space in front of the Teacher, where, disheveled and covering her face with her hands in shame, she sinks to the ground. The scribes and Pharisees then explain that the woman has been caught in adultery and has been arrested. She cannot deny the flagrancy of her crime, and so she must be punished according to the Law. Now Moses commanded in the Law that such women be stoned. What does the Master think of it? How should the culprit be treated?

The evangelist here points out that "they were saying this to test him, in order that they might be able to accuse him." This was unquestionably an excellent opportunity for the Pharisees. In the first place, dragging the trembling and weeping woman about the city they cut a magnificent figure as diligent custodians of the Law and guardians of morality. The Sanhedrin had to pass judgment on the sin; but what would have been the advantage of taking the woman directly to the Sanhedrin without all that noise and publicity? Besides, this show of force gave them another fine opportunity. There was that Galilean Rabbi who, with His vaunted independence of the great teachers of the Law and His increasing authority over the people, deserved a good formal, public lesson, precisely on a question of Law. This particular woman's case seemed made on purpose to give Him that lesson. Before delivering the culprit to the Sanhedrin, they must propose it to Him, as though asking His opinion as to whether she should be stoned or not. If He should answer no, He would stand self-confessed an enemy of the public welfare and a destroyer of the Mosaic Law. If He answered that they should execute the stoning, He would lose His hold on the people whom He had won particularly with His precepts of mercy and kindness. This was a fine chance; and the Pharisees made the most of it.

Jesus accepted their challenge. He listened to their explanation of the case but remained serenely seated. When the woman's accusers had finished, He did not answer a word, but like one with nothing in particular to do except to pass the time, He stooped over and began to trace signs or letters with His finger on the pavement. His manner said in substance that He had no answer to give and that He was idling the time until the matter should be ended. The accusers waited a little, and Jesus kept on tracing flourishes on the ground. They stated their question again. Only after another little while did Jesus slowly sit up and glance from the accusers to the crowd and the woman; and then He said simply: "Let him who is without sin among you be the first to cast a stone at her." Then He bent over again, as if it were the most natural thing in the world to do, and began to trace more flourishes. It was all over; in fact, it should never have begun. If He had answered them, it was only to stop their insistence. Let them look to it, but let them also conform to the principle He had given them.

And that principle touched them to the quick. It was not a question of passing judgment on some elegant law case to determine how many blows were to be administered to someone else's back, or how high the gibbet must be on which someone else's body was to hang. It was a question of judging their inner selves before the invisible tribunal of the conscience where accuser and judge are one and the same. It would have been a simple matter to answer that Rabbi with "I have not sinned so I will throw the first stone!" But it was much wiser not to fool with Him. He had shown Himself the reader of souls, and He was quite capable of repeating the apostrophe of the ancient Daniel to the old men who accused Susanna and of answering there before the whole crowd: "Are you without sin when you have behaved thus and so with this particular married woman; and when another day you did thus and so with this other?" No; it was too dangerous to prod such a hornet's nest. And so "hearing this, they went away, one by one, beginning with the eldest. And Jesus remained alone, with the woman standing in the midst. And Jesus, raising himself, said to her: 'Woman, where are they? Has no one condemned thee?' She said: 'No one, Lord.' Then Jesus said: 'Neither will I condemn thee! Go thy way, and from now on sin no more'" (John 8:9–11).

He who had come not to destroy the Law of Moses but to complete it had not violated that Law; He had penetrated to its essential spirit. The essential of every honest law can only be to divert from evil and direct toward good. Justice had been sublimated by mercy.

The Man Born Blind

After the discourse on the spiritual light, which ended in the attempt of some of Jesus' adversaries to stone Him, John narrates the cure of the man born blind. The event must have occurred a little later, when excited spirits had had a chance to calm down.

One Sabbath, Jesus passed by a blind man who was begging alms, perhaps near the Temple. Reflecting on the man's misfortune, the disciples accompanying Jesus asked: "Rabbi, who has sinned, this man or his parents, that he should be born blind?" We see in this question the old Hebrew notion that every physical ill was a consequence of wrongdoing. Jesus rejected the idea, saying that neither the man nor his parents had sinned, and that this case had been permitted that the works of God might be made manifest: "As long as I am in the world I am the light of the world" (John 9:5). When He said this, Jesus spat on the ground and with His spittle made a little clay, which He spread over the blind man's eyes. Then He said to Him: "Go wash yourself in the pool of Siloe." And the man went and washed, and when he returned, he could see.

The inevitable discussions follow the cure, because the man is a professional beggar and very well-known throughout the entire city as one blind from birth. Now, of course, he can see. So some said: "It is the same man!" Others said: "No, it is someone who looks like the blind man." But when the man himself was questioned, he replied: "No, I am truly he, the beggar who was born blind." Then they asked him: "Well then, how have your eyes been opened?" And he answered simply: "The man who is called Jesus made a bit of clay, put it on my eyes, and said to me: 'Go wash yourself in Siloe.' I went, and washed, and I see.

The Pool of Siloe

That is all!" To carry the inquiry further it was necessary to question Jesus. "Where has He gone?" they asked the cured man. He did not know. The matter was serious both of itself and because it had taken place on the Sabbath. So the man was brought before the Pharisees, who asked the same questions and received the same answers. There was no doubt about it: this man standing before them was the beggar born blind, and now he could see very well.

But there was still that matter of the Sabbath. Hence, some of the Pharisees declared: "This man is not of God because He does not observe the Sabbath!" Yet there were others, a little less Pharisee, who observed: "But if He were a sinner, how could He perform miracles like that?" And the two sides began to argue. It was certain the blind man had been cured; but it was even more certain that whoever made a fingerful of clay on the Sabbath day was a sinner and therefore could not work miracles. There was no escape from the dilemma. In this impasse they turned to the cured man himself for help and asked his opinion: "What do you think of the man who opened your eyes?" And he answered promptly: "For me, He is a prophet!"

This was bad, very bad indeed. They were obliged to go back a step and revive their doubts concerning the man's identity. So they sent for his parents. Is this really your son? Was he actually born blind? Then how is it that he can see now? The two old people, frightened by that gathering of illustrious doctors, took refuge behind the facts themselves and declined to accept any responsibility for what had happened: That this is our son is certain, and it is also certain that he was born blind. But how it happens that he can now see or who has opened his eyes — we know nothing at all about that. Ask him! He is of age. Let him speak for himself. Thus nothing more definite could be dragged out of the old couple. The inquisitors then returned to the son.

They assumed a confidential tone with him. Perhaps the man would be touched and "open up." "Come! Give glory to God! We know very well that this man is a sinner. Tell us the truth of the matter." And he answered: "Whether He is a sinner I do not know; I know only that before I was blind and that now I see!" And they said: "But what did He do to you? How did He open your eyes?" The man, using his eyes for the first time in his life to contemplate those inquisitors, preferred perhaps to be out admiring more pleasant sights, and he began to lose patience: "But I have already told you all that! Why do you want to hear it again? Do you too perchance want to become disciples of Jesus?"

Heaven forbid! A deluge of curses and insults fall on the impertinent beggar who had dared ask that sarcastic question, and the opprobrious insinuation is hurled right back at him: "You are that fellow's disciple; we are the disciples of Moses. We know that God spoke to Moses; but as for this man, we do not know where He is from!" But the man stands his ground and replies undaunted: "Well, this is exactly what is so strange, that you do not know where He is from when He has opened my eyes. It is very certain that God listens, not to sinners, but to just and pious men; since the beginning of the world no one has opened the eyes of a man born blind. Now, if this man were not from God, He could not have done it!" What irreverence! Was this insolent rogue, begotten in sin as his blindness proved, presuming to teach the most outstanding representatives of Hebrew "tradition" and learning! They answered indignantly: "You were wholly born in sin, and you want to teach us? Out of here!" And they threw him out.

Shortly afterward the man met Jesus, who said to him: "Dost thou believe in the Son of Man?" And he answered: "Who is he, Lord, that I may believe in him?" Jesus replied: "Thou hast both seen him [referring to the cure], and he it is who speaks with thee." Then the man exclaimed: "I believe, Lord!" and falling down before Jesus, worshiped Him. Jesus added: "For judgment have

I come into this world, that they who do not see may see, and they who see may become blind." Some Pharisees had approached meanwhile and over-hearing these last words, they took them as an allusion to themselves. So they asked Jesus: "Are we also blind?" Jesus answered: "If you were [only] blind, you would not have sin. But now that you say 'We see,' your sin remains." In other words, blindness is a general condition, but it can be cured only if one recognizes that he is afflicted with it; anyone who deludes himself that he can see will never be cured.

The Good Shepherd

The cure of the man born blind and the discussions concerning it had their aftermath. It was probably a few days later, but still in Jerusalem, that Jesus had recourse to a parable, which is part allegory based on everyday customs in Palestine. He compares His work to that of a shepherd, and the society He has founded to a sheepfold. The sheepfold in modern Palestine (and it was more or less the same twenty centuries ago) is simply an enclosure within a low stone wall where the sheep of one or more flocks pasturing in the vicinity are gathered in the evening. The animals go in and out one by one through a low, narrow door in the wall, which makes it easy to count them. At night one shepherd stands guard to protect the fold against thieves and wild beasts; and toward dawn, it is he who opens the little door to the shepherds coming to claim their flocks. Each shepherd gives his own particular call, and his sheep come crowding to the door and trot out one by one to follow him all day long over the heath. Thus, flock by flock, the sheep go out by the little gate in obedience to the cries of the shepherds, who sometimes even call their favorite sheep by name. That little door, then, is the mainspring of the fold, and it alone inspires confidence. Whoever does not pass through it but climbs over the wall proclaims himself an enemy — a thief or a wild beast.

That is why Jesus said:

Amen, amen I say to you, he who enters not by the door into the sheep-fold, but climbs up another way, is a thief and a robber. But he who enters by the door is shepherd of the sheep. To this man the gatekeeper opens, and the sheep hear his voice, and he calls his own sheep by name and leads them forth. And when he has let out his own sheep, he goes before them; and the sheep follow him because they know his voice. But a stranger they will not follow, but will flee from him, because they do not know the voice of strangers. (John 10:1–5)

Arab shepherds and their flocks

But His listeners did not understand the allusion and so Jesus continued: "Amen, amen I say to you, I am the door of the sheepfold. All whoever have come [before me] are thieves and robbers; but the sheep have not heard them. I am the door. If anyone enter by me he shall be safe, and shall go in and out, and shall find pastures. The thief comes only to steal, and slay, and destroy. I came that they may have life, and have it more abundantly." Who the "thieves and robbers" were Jesus did not explain, but historical circumstances were sufficient to make them recognizable. As the ancient prophets had found the greatest obstacle to their mission in the hostile activity of pseudo-prophets prophesying "lies ... and the delusions of their own heart," so Jesus, who speaks here as the Messiah, is alluding to the activity of the pseudo-messianic preachers who mushroomed in Palestine both before and after Him. When He declares that the "sheep have not heard them," He is speaking of the good, sound portion of the people, who were still the majority in His time, though later they diminished in number.

Still using the similitude of the sheepfold, Jesus continues:

I am the good shepherd. The good shepherd lays down his life for his sheep. But the hireling, who is not a shepherd, whose own the sheep are not, sees the wolf coming and leaves the sheep and flees. And the wolf snatches and scatters the sheep; but the hireling flees because he is a hireling, and has no concern for the sheep. I am the good shepherd, and I know mine and mine know me, even as the Father knows me and I know the Father; and I lay down my life for my sheep. And other sheep I have that are not of this fold. Them also I must bring, and they shall hear my voice, and there shall be one fold and one shepherd. (John 10:11–16)

Jesus, therefore, like the true shepherd and not the hireling, is ready to lose His life for His followers. Besides, He is the shepherd not only "of this fold" of the chosen people of Israel, but also of "other sheep" who will one day hear His voice. Then there will be "one fold" of His followers, come from Israel and other nations without distinction, and the one shepherd of the whole new flock will be Jesus the Messiah. The ancient prophets, too, when they spoke of the times of the future Messiah, had contemplated this expansion of the limited fold of Israel:

> And in the last days, the mountain of the house of the Lord
> shall be prepared on the top of mountains ...
> and all nations shall flow unto it,
> and many shall go, and say:
> Come and let us go up to the mountain of the Lord,
> and to the house of the God of Jacob. (Isa. 2:2–4)

And Jesus concluded: "For this reason the Father loves me, because I lay down my life that I may take it up again. No one takes it from me, but I lay it down of myself. I have the power to lay it down, but I have the power to take it up again. Such is the command I have received from my Father."

These words, too, caused dissension among the Jews. Perhaps the majority commented on them scornfully, concluding: "He has a devil and is mad. Why do you listen to him?" But there were others who replied: Ah, no! "These are not the words of one who has a devil. Can a devil open the eyes of the blind?" (John 10:19–21).

Expansion of the Kingdom of God in Judea

Now that the last discussions during the feast of Tabernacles were at an end, Jesus departed from Jerusalem. Judea was the field of activity Jesus chose when He abandoned Galilee. Of His varied activity in this period to spread the Kingdom of God in Judea, we have only isolated incidents and discourses, but not a complete or organized report.

Incidentally to the narrative, three different men are presented to us as desiring to follow Jesus (Luke 9:57–62). Matthew mentions only two of them

(8:19–22), and it is very likely that the three came to Jesus at different times and in different places although they are all grouped together in the editing of the material.

One of these men — a "scribe" according to Matthew — overtook Jesus along the road and said to Him: "Master, I will follow thee wherever thou goest." The good man was perhaps thinking that a prophet as powerful as Jesus would have a suitable home as headquarters for His activity. Jesus disenchants him frankly. "The foxes have dens, and the birds of the air have nests; but the Son of Man has nowhere to lay his head." In other words, the first to follow the rule of complete faith in Providence laid down in the Sermon on the Mount was the preacher of the Sermon Himself.

To another, who, according to Matthew, was one "of the disciples," Jesus said: "Follow me!" The man was well-disposed, but he first asked permission to "go and bury" his father. Jesus answered him: "Follow me, and leave the dead to bury their own dead," to which Luke adds: "but do thou go and proclaim the kingdom of God!"

There has been much discussion about this brief dialogue. Some have thought that the disciple's father was not actually dead, otherwise his son, according to Jewish custom, should have been with his body and not with Jesus. Hence, he was really asking permission to stay and help his aged father through his declining days. In all likelihood the father was actually dead. Jesus wants to emphasize the imperiousness of the summons to the Kingdom of God, which could in certain cases brush aside even the most legitimate customs. The Mosaic Law forbade the high priest and the "Nazirite" to bury their own parents personally; surely the Messiah, Jesus, had much greater reason to demand of the heralds of God's kingdom at least the same freedom from social ties and a complete dedication to their office. Those living outside the Kingdom of God were spiritually dead, and to turn back even for a short time among those dead might be dangerous for this particular disciple.

The exhortation addressed to the third postulant is substantially the same. He says to Jesus: "Lord, I want to follow thee; but first let me go and say farewell to those at home." Jesus answers: "No one, having put his hand to the plow and looking back, is fit for the kingdom of God!" Just as the plowman cannot make a straight furrow if he keeps turning to look behind him, so one who is bound for the Kingdom of God must not turn back to look at the things of the world that he has left behind.

Now in Judea, Jesus again dispatched His collaborators on a special mission as he had done in Galilee. They had grown in number, and so this time seventy-two were sent out. It is probable that among the new messengers were all or some of the Twelve who had gone out the first time. The norms and the goal of the new mission were substantially those of the previous one. The zone of action must have been Judea and perhaps also the Transjordan, though we have no information in this regard. Nor can we say how long this new evangelizing journey lasted, but it seems to have been more than a fortnight.

On their return the messengers of the kingdom were jubilant. Gathering about Jesus, they told Him how even the devils had been subjected to them at the mention of His name. Jesus rejoiced with them, telling them that He had seen Satan fall as lightning from Heaven; then He confirmed for them their dominion over the powers of the enemy in the future. But at the same time He warned them that their true joy should spring not from their power over the spirits of evil but from the fact that their names had been written in Heaven.

The success achieved by the disciples in the propagation of the Kingdom of God occasions in Jesus a joy that is greater and more sublime. He lifts His thought to His heavenly Father, contemplates His designs for the salvation of humanity, and notes that the means used for their accomplishment are, humanly speaking, the least expedient, men who were least prized or conspicuous. And there bursts from His heart a joyous thanksgiving to the heavenly Father. "In that very hour he rejoiced in the Holy Spirit and said: I praise thee, Father, Lord of heaven and earth, that thou didst hide these things from the wise and prudent and didst reveal them to little ones. Yes, Father, for such was thy good pleasure. All things have been delivered to me by my Father, and no one knows who the Son is except the Father, and who the Father is except the Son, and him to whom the Son chooses to reveal him." Then turning to the disciples, He proclaimed them blessed because they saw and heard things that the ancient prophets in vain desired to see and hear.

The Good Samaritan

During this period of travel about Judea, probably shortly after the return of the seventy-two disciples, Jesus was approached by a doctor of the Law who wanted a clearer idea of Jesus' views on certain fundamental points. There was so much being said about the Galilean Rabbi that the doctor was anxious to learn the truth and put Him to the test. Hence, he asked Him simply: "Master, what must I do to gain eternal life?" Jesus was glad of the question, and He replied with other pointed queries to lead the man gently to his own answer.

The "Spring of the Apostles" on the road to Jericho

Therefore He asked: "What is written in the Law? How dost thou read?" And the man answered that it is written we must love God with all our strength and our neighbor as ourselves. Jesus heartily approved the answer: "Thou hast answered rightly; do this and thou shalt live!"

But there was no passage in the Law that linked the two precepts of love of God and love of neighbor, and in any case, there was still the uncertain meaning of the term *neighbor*. Did it refer only to relatives and friends or also to all one's countrymen and coreligionists, or was it, by some stretch of the imagination, also to be extended to one's enemies, the foreigners, the uncircumcised and idolaters? Among all these people, who was the Israelite's true neighbor? The doctor here showed that his question had been well considered; what he was after was precisely the answer to this problem. Hence, "wishing to justify himself, he said to Jesus: 'And who is my neighbor?'" Jesus answered him with a parable.

"A certain man was going down from Jerusalem to Jericho, and he fell in with robbers, who after both stripping him and beating him went their way, leaving him half-dead."

The distance from Jerusalem to Jericho by the modern road is twenty-five miles, but in ancient times it was somewhat shorter. The man "was going down" because the road is almost a continuous descent, the difference in altitude between the two cities being about three thousand feet. From about the fifth mile beyond Jerusalem almost to the gates of Jericho, the road travels through regions that are uninhabited, mountainous, and often impassable. Hence in every age it has been infested by robbers, since it is practically impossible to drive them out of the various hidden dens and shelters that line the roadside and it is very easy for them to disappear after a holdup.

Dangerous as it was, the road was well traveled, for it was the only one connecting Jerusalem and the greater part of Judea with the fertile and populous plain of Jericho and with Transjordan beyond.

Our traveler, then, is lying in the middle of the road, beaten and stunned, unable to help himself and forced to await the merciful assistance of some other wayfarer. Now, "as it happened, a certain priest was going down the same way; and when he saw him he passed by. And likewise a Levite also, when he was near the place and saw him, passed by." Evidently both the priest and the Levite have just finished their turn of service in the Temple and are returning home to Jericho or its vicinity. Then a third traveler comes along: "But a certain Samaritan as he journeyed came upon him, and seeing him, was moved with compassion. And he went up to him and bound up his wounds, pouring in oil and wine. And setting him on his own beast, he brought him

The Inn of the Good Samaritan

to an inn and took care of him. And the next day he took out two denarii and gave them to the innkeeper and said: Take care of him; and whatever more thou spendest, I, on my way back, will repay thee."

The Samaritan may have been a merchant on his way to buy stock in the district of Jericho and so would be returning in a short while. He was also well-off because he was traveling on his own beast. The pity he immediately felt for the unfortunate man prompted him to give him the best care he could in that lonely place. He applied to his wounds the usual medicines of the time, oil to soothe and wine to disinfect, and he improvised bandages to bind them up. He then placed the unconscious victim on his own beast, and holding him on as best he could, he took him to the inn.

The latter was certainly the caravan stopover on that particular route. It was perhaps situated on the site of the modern *Khan Hathrur*, which even today is commonly known as the "Inn of the Good Samaritan." The two silver denarii, or about fifty cents, were sufficient to provide care for the wounded man for several days. In any case, if the sum fell short, the Samaritan promised to reimburse the innkeeper.

The parable was finished. The doctor of the Law had asked who his neighbor was, and Jesus closes the parable by making him answer his own question: "Which of these three, in thy opinion, proved himself neighbor to him who fell among the robbers?" The doctor naturally answered: "He who took pity on him." And Jesus said to him, "Go and do thou also in like manner."

Note the apparent discrepancy between the doctor's question ("Who is my neighbor?") and Jesus' answer ("Do thou also in like manner!"). It is a discrepancy in form only. The doctor is still within the realm of pure ideas; Jesus comes down to the realm of fact, because the most beautiful ideas in the world are nothing but words if they are not realized in actual life. That is why when the doctor wants to know who his neighbor *is*, Jesus pictures for him one who *acts* like a neighbor and admonishes him to follow that example.

In the parable, the official "neighbors" of the wounded man were certainly the priest and the Levite, but the fine ideal failed to materialize. Of the three, only the Samaritan behaves as a neighbor; hence any man, of any race or creed whatever, can *be* a neighbor because he can *act* as a neighbor.

Martha and Mary; the Parable of Prayer

In the course of His journeyings, Jesus reached the immediate vicinity of Jerusalem and entered a village Luke does not name, where two sisters, Mary and Martha, received him into their home. Since they are the sisters of Lazarus,

General view of Bethany

whom John also mentions (11:1ff.), the unnamed village must be Bethany. This coincides with the setting of the whole account because Bethany is on the treacherous highway from Jerusalem to Jericho, and therefore, if the parable of the Good Samaritan was recited shortly before the arrival at Bethany, it was inspired by the very places through which Jesus was traveling.

Martha seems to be the manager of the hospitable home, which Jesus had undoubtedly visited before. She is not called Martha (in Aramaic *lady*) for nothing, for she sees to everything that can make a worthy welcome for their revered guest and friend. Their brother Lazarus does not figure in this episode at all; was he perhaps already ill of the malady that a few months later led to his four-day sojourn in the tomb? We do not know. As for Mary, she takes advantage of her sister's busyness to sit quietly at the feet of Jesus. Since Martha is taking care of everything, the younger sister is free to listen to those words that change men's hearts. Martha is bustling about the room, and she, too, is trying to hear Jesus' words, but she can catch only a few crumbs because she has so much to do. Hence, at a certain point, a touch of affectionate envy — or better, emulation — toward her sister as well as their familiarity with Jesus, who is a friend of the family, embolden her to speak her mind. And she came up and said: "Lord is it no concern of thine that my sister has left me to serve alone? Tell her therefore to help me!" Martha, the good housewife and the devoted admirer of Jesus, merely points out that the two of them together could perform these domestic tasks much more quickly and then both could enjoy the Master's words. Jesus, with the same frankness but with reference to a much loftier idea, replies: "Martha, Martha, thou art anxious and troubled about many things, while there is need of only a few, or of only one. Mary has chosen the good part, which shall not be taken away from her."

The material "things" about which the good Martha was concerned were indeed "many" but they could be reduced to only a "few," given the frugality of Jesus and the disciples, and even these few things were negligible compared with the "one," which was spiritual. Had He not admonished them in the Sermon on the Mount that the Kingdom of God was to be sought first, with the certainty that everything else would be added? That was the "good part" that Mary had chosen.

Immediately after the episode of Bethany, Luke records the teaching of the Lord's Prayer, which Matthew included instead in the Sermon on the Mount. Luke's arrangement seems the more probable historically because it includes the reason why Jesus gave the prayer. "And it came to pass as he was praying in a certain place, that when he ceased, one of his disciples said to him: "Lord, teach us to pray, even as John [the Baptist] also taught his disciples." And he said to them: "When you pray, say: Father,..." But was this really the first time Jesus taught His disciples how to pray? If it was, then we must explain why Jesus, who had given them so many principles for the perfection of their

A section of Bethany today

spiritual lives, should have postponed to the last months of His life such an important matter as this. Or was He returning here to a subject He had already treated, explaining and confirming what He had said before? That seems more likely, and then Luke and Matthew would both be right.

Having taught them the formula, Jesus went on to illustrate particularly the most important qualities of prayer: persistence and confidence. Prayer, according to Jesus, must be so insistent and tenacious as to seem almost petulant. And a little parable He gives in illustration is a lovely example of Palestinian petulance.

In a certain village there live two friends, one of whom is unexpectedly visited late at night by an acquaintance on a journey who wants to stay with him. It is easy enough to prepare a place to sleep for him; but the traveler is hungry, too, and all the bread in the house was eaten up at supper. There is nothing to do but go and borrow some, but where? It is late and everyone is asleep. There is nothing to do but go and bother a friend; it is already midnight, but he will not mind, so the man goes to his friend's house and begins to knock loudly on the door: "Wake up! Wake up! Lend me three loaves, for a friend of mine has just come to me from a journey, and I have nothing to set before him!" The other man, so rudely awakened, considers this a fine imposition: "Don't bother me! The door is already locked and my children and I are in bed! I can't get up!" But if the man outside refuses to be discouraged by that first rebuke and keeps up his knocking and shouting, then his friend will finally give in, if not out of friendship, then certainly to stop the nuisance. And Jesus concludes: "And I say to you, ask, and it shall be given to you; seek, and you shall find; knock, and it shall be opened to you."

So much for the persistence of prayer. But what moral principle is to nourish that persistence? What is the source of the confidence that we shall be heard? Jesus illustrates this point, too, with a few practical examples: "But if one of you asks his father for a loaf, will he hand him a stone? or for a fish, will he for a fish hand him a serpent? or if he asks for an egg, will he hand him a scorpion? Therefore if you, evil as you are, know how to give good gifts to your children, how much more will your father in heaven give good things to those who ask him?" (Matt. 7:11).

The Cure of the Demoniac; the Blasphemy of the Pharisees; the Praise of Mary; the Sign of Jonas

In Luke's narrative the instruction on prayer is followed by the cure of a dumb man possessed of a devil (Luke 11:14ff.). Matthew records the same incident

(12:22ff.), but in his account the demoniac is blind as well as dumb. Luke's order, which records both cure and discussion during this sojourn in Judea, seems preferable to that in the other two Synoptics, which set it earlier.

Jesus, then, publicly cured a dumb (and blind) demoniac who had been brought to Him. Among those present were several scribes from Jerusalem and some Pharisees. They did not deny the cure but explained it by declaring that Jesus' power over devils was due to the fact that He Himself was on such good terms with the prince of devils, Beelzebub. In ancient times this name had been *Ba'al zebub,* "Baal [god] of the flies," a Philistine divinity. Later it indicated an object of idolatrous worship in general and was altered slightly to *Ba'al zebul,* "Baal of dung," the highly disparaging epithet for all idols and their worship. Jesus, now, is supposed to be on friendly terms with this Beelzebul.

Jesus answered the insult in a way the scribes and Pharisees relished least, that is, He invited them to a little objective reasoning. Appealing to contemporary Jewish angelology, He observed that the kingdom of Satan was compact and hierarchically constituted, and that if it were divided within itself, it would fall.

How then can you, scribes and Pharisees, say that I drive out Satan in the name of Satan? In that case, his kingdom would be divided against itself and would fall. After all, you scribes and Pharisees also have your exorcists; ask them if it is possible to drive out Satan in the name of Satan. If, then, I cast out devils in the name of God, and cast them out personally with so much ease, and if I also empower my disciples to cast them out, all this shows that something quite extraordinary is taking place among you, namely, that the "kingdom of God has come upon you." But you do not see this because you do not want to see. This is a direct sin against the Holy Spirit, who is the source of light; you are blocking the roads of salvation that God has laid out for you and you are vitiating His plans. Take heed, therefore, because "every kind of sin and blasphemy shall be forgiven to men; but the blasphemy against the spirit will not be forgiven. And whoever speaks a word against the Son of Man, it shall be forgiven him; but whoever speaks against the Holy Spirit it will not be forgiven him, either in this world or in the world to come." Whoever does not wish to open the eyes of his soul to the light of the Spirit remains in darkness for eternity. Nor is it enough to open them for a moment; it is necessary to keep them open always, because Satan, driven out once, returns to assault, and take renewed possession of his former domain.

Among those present at this discussion were a number of people friendly to Jesus, and from among them rises a woman's cry: "Blessed is the womb that bore thee, and the breasts that nursed thee!" Jesus accepted her blessing but at the same time raised it to a higher plane: "Rather, blessed are they who hear the word of God and keep it." This was substantially the same answer that He had given those who told Him His mother and brethren were waiting to speak with Him.

And the discussion, after the woman's cry, began anew. Some of the scribes and Pharisees declared, almost condescendingly, that they were disposed to recognize Jesus' mission, but naturally they wanted proofs, "signs"; the miracles Jesus had thus far wrought would not quite do. Some "sign" with the rabbinic stamp of approval was necessary: some event to take place as if at the touch of a magic wand; and it would be all the better, of course, if some meteor could be arranged to come flashing down the heavens. Substantially the same request had been made of Jesus a short time before by other Pharisees.

This time, too, Jesus refused to satisfy them, and He added a number of other statements besides: "An evil and adulterous generation demands a sign, and no sign shall be given it but the sign of Jonas the prophet. For even as Jonas was in the belly of the fish three days and three nights, so will the Son of Man be three days and three nights in the heart of the earth" (Matt. 12:38–41). The expression "day and night" in rabbinic usage meant the full cycle of twenty-four hours, *or any part of such a cycle*. So Jesus here announces that the Son of Man will be in the heart of the earth during three complete or partial periods of twenty-four hours, and that then He will come forth again like Jonas from the fish. This "sign," which largely fulfills their requisites, will take place at a preestablished time, namely, at the time of the death of the Son of Man. Though He will not descend from the opened heavens where the angels of power have their dwelling, He will instead rise from the closed abyss where dwell the helpless dead. Finally, the sign will not represent a prideful manifestation of personal power because the Son of Man will then have ended His present controversies and will be in the heart of the earth, but instead it will represent the triumph of an idea, as the adventure of Jonas represented the triumph of "repentance" among the inhabitants of Nineveh. The Queen of Sheba will also condemn them on that day, for she came from the ends of the earth to wonder at the wisdom of Solomon, "and behold a greater than Solomon is here."

The Pharisees understood the allusion to the triple "day and night" to be spent in the heart of the earth. As soon as Jesus dies, they run to Pilate and request him to take the proper measures in time, for they remember "how that deceiver [Jesus] said while he was yet alive: After three days I will rise again" (Matt. 27:63). Hence they reject the sign of Jonas that fulfilled so well the conditions they required.

Jesus at Dinner at the Home of a Pharisee; Denunciations and Warnings

Evidently the conflict between the Pharisees and Jesus was growing deeper and more serious. The former could not forgive Him for that independence from their legal formalism that He claimed and proved with His miracles. And Jesus, on His part, never ceased to address the sternest rebukes to the spiritual emptiness clothed in Pharisaic formalism, to the obstinacy and arrogance of those men of the Law. Besides, He showed He had deeply felt their insult in calling Him the friend and minister of Beelzebub.

Nevertheless, shortly after the controversy just described, a Pharisee invited Jesus to dinner. We do not know whether he did this out of some sympathy for the much-discussed Rabbi or from a desire to entangle Him in treacherous questions; in any case, there was no one more skillful than a Pharisee in saving appearances and distinguishing theory from practice. Jesus accepted the invitation, and having entered the banquet chamber, He went straight to His divan until the dinner should be served. Such conduct was extremely reprehensible to the Pharisees' way of thinking. Jesus had just come in from the street and from contact with the crowd; how could He presume to take food without having first performed the prescribed ablutions? His host was disgusted. In his heart he was thinking that his guest, far from being an authoritative Rabbi, was but a "rustic." The Pharisee's thoughts were legible in his face, and Jesus read them. And a tense dispute followed:

> Now you Pharisees clean the outside of the cup and the dish, but within you are full of robbery and wickedness. Foolish ones! did not he who made the outside make the inside too? Nevertheless give that which remains as alms and behold, all things are clean to you! But woe to you Pharisees! because you pay tithes on mint and rue and every herb, and disregard justice and the love of God. But these things you ought to have done, while not leaving the others undone. Woe to you, Pharisees! because you love the front seats in the synagogues and greetings in the market place! Woe to you! because you are like hidden tombs, over which men walk unaware. (Luke 11:39–44)

It is reasonable to suppose that at this everyone stopped eating. The host and his "colleagues" probably answered as best they could, but certain teachers of the Law were also present at the dinner, and they felt that they too were being rebuked; and so one of them said with resentment: "Master, in saying these things, thou insultest us also!" But he and his fellows also came in for their share, because the indomitable Rabbi continued: "Woe to you lawyers also! because you load men with oppressive burdens and you yourselves with one of your fingers do not touch the burdens. Woe to you! for you build the tombs of the prophets, whereas your fathers killed them. So then you are witnesses and approve the deeds of your fathers, for they indeed killed them and you build their tombs.... Woe to you lawyers because you have taken away the key of knowledge; you have not entered yourselves and those who were entering you have hindered!" (Luke 11:46–52).

These invectives are aimed at the prevailing practice, not at the theory. Besides not all the scribes and Pharisees, collectively or individually, merited these invectives; there is no question about that. But Jesus is aiming not at individuals but at the generality, and this did deserve them without any doubt. When Jesus rebukes them for building tombs for the prophets, it is not to censure a work in itself pious. His rebuke is aimed rather at the fact that their piety stops with the material act, while from the spiritual point of view the conduct of those building tombs for the prophets was a continuation of the work of their fathers, who had killed them. The lawyers and scribes in particular had arrogated to themselves the monopoly of the Mosaic Law, and they claimed that they alone had the key to this ivory tower. But it was a broken and rusty key and could barely admit them to the outer court, called "the dead letter," while it could not open at all, either for its possessors or others, the inner courts of the tower, which were called "living charity."

The result of that banquet was exactly what should have been expected. When Jesus had left, the "Pharisees and the lawyers began to press him hard and provoke him to speak on many things, setting traps for him and plotting to seize upon something out of his mouth, that they might accuse him." The conflict, then, was becoming more and more intense, and it was clear that the end must be in sight.

Jesus took occasion from what had happened further to admonish His followers. The crowd at this particular time had grown so great that some were in danger of being trampled (12:1). Luke here has Jesus pronounce a discourse, almost all the elements of which are to be found in Matthew but not all in the same context. Let His disciples beware of the leaven of the Pharisees, which is hypocrisy. No disciple is greater than his teacher; if Jesus has been called Beelzebub, His disciples cannot expect any better treatment

(Matt. 10:25). Let them speak openly and frankly nevertheless; there is nothing secret that must not be revealed, and what they have heard in secret they
must preach from the housetops. They are not to fear those who can kill the
body only but not the soul; let them fear instead whoever can kill both body
and soul in Gehenna. They are not to worry for their own lives, but trust to
the providence of the heavenly Father, who watches over all things. The field
sparrows are worth practically nothing, for they may be purchased for two
as (less than a cent), and yet not one of these little creatures is forgotten by
God. The disciples are to be calm and serene, therefore, for their worth is far
greater than that of a multitude of sparrows, and all the hairs of their heads are
numbered. Whoever shall confess the Son of Man before men, him shall the
Son of Man confess before the heavenly Father and His angels; but if anyone
denies Him, the Son of Man shall deny him in turn. The disciples are not to
worry about defending themselves when they shall be summoned to trial in
the synagogues and various courts, because the Holy Spirit will teach them
in that moment what they must say in their own defense.

A Warning against Avarice; the Ultimate Expectation

One day during this traveling, a certain man came to Jesus and besought Him
to use His authority in a question of money: "Master, tell my brother to divide
the inheritance with me" (Luke 12:13). This was a very imprudent request
to make of one who in the Sermon on the Mount had clearly distinguished
between God and mammon; the adequate answer could only be an invitation
to abandon the mammon and give himself entirely to God. But Jesus did not
give the adequate answer; He did not even enter into the question at all: "Man,
who has appointed me a judge over you?" It might almost be said that money in
itself disgusted Jesus, that He shrank from soiling His hands with it even though
handling it in the service of others. He will have nothing to do with the case.

The little incident is followed by various considerations on the fallacy of
material goods, which Jesus illustrates with a parable. There was a rich man
whose harvest every year was very abundant, and he concentrated all his mind
on that harvest, seeking ways to store and preserve it. And he began to say:
"I shall throw down my granaries and build larger ones, and there I will store
all this great harvest." Beaming with satisfaction over his plans, he gloated
within himself: "Be merry, for you have an abundance of good things assured
to you for many years! Take your ease, eat, drink, and be merry!" But lo, God
Himself unexpectedly enters upon the scene and says to the blissful rich
man: "Fool, this night you must die, and then whose shall be all these goods

of yours?" Such is the lot, concludes Jesus, of the man "who lays up treasure for himself, and is not rich as regards God." And He continued, recalling the concept of the Sermon on the Mount: "Sell what you have and give alms. Make for yourselves purses that do not grow old, a treasure unfailing in heaven ..." (Luke 12:32–33).

Now does all this mean communism? It is much more than communism, because it is the altruism of charity. It is that complete and absolute altruism that, by virtue of a supernatural principle, provides for the material needs of others to the point of neglecting self: Sell what you have and give alms. Modern communism, on the other hand, fails of its very essence to reflect even the least shadow of Jesus' doctrine, because it does not recognize at all the "purses that do not grow old" and the "treasure unfailing in heaven." It lacks the supreme expectation.

Shortly afterward, Jesus returns to this expectation, as to the essential basis of all His teachings. Why are we to renounce riches? Why must we place our trust only in the treasure of Heaven? Why is the present world but a fleeting shadow? For answer we have Jesus' admonitions:

"Let your loins be girt about and your lamps burning [such was the garb of alert servants] at night, and you yourselves like men waiting for the master's return from the wedding; so that when he comes and knocks, they may straightway open to him." The master has told his servants that he was off to a wedding feast, and so he will be very late in returning home. But they are extremely thoughtful and do not want him to be kept waiting even an instant at the door; hence with loins girt and lamps lit, they keep their vigil through the nighttime, listening for the sound of his arrival. "Blessed are those servants whom the master, on his return, shall find watching!" Touched by their solicitude, good as he is, he will gird his own loins and make them recline at table and serve them himself. He indeed has dined at the wedding, but these matchless servants have not taken the time to prepare themselves any food.

Similarly, a prudent householder has his house watched because he does not know at what hour the thief may come and break into it. And Jesus concludes: "You must also be ready, because at that hour that you do not expect, the Son of Man is coming."

What is this "coming" of the Son of Man? It is the coming that will make manifest the eternal and unchanging consequence of Jesus' teaching. He had spoken of renouncing riches, of choosing instead one's treasure in Heaven. Riches must be renounced, the present world be viewed as something fleeting precisely because of the "coming" of the Son of Man, which shall dispel the shadow and reveal the abiding substance, melt away the accumulated riches of earth and distribute the invisible treasure of Heaven, fill the expectations of those who have hoped in that "coming" and establish in eternity their lot of blessedness. "Blessed are those servants whom the master, on his return, shall find watching!"

Peter asked Jesus for an explanation: "Lord, art thou speaking this parable for us or for all alike?" He had been impressed with the statement that the master of the zealous servants would himself serve them as a reward, and he wanted to know if this was to be true of all or of only a few privileged souls. By way of answer, Jesus presents for consideration the servants who prove negligent and unreliable, and He establishes a hierarchy of duties and responsibilities for servants in general. The principle is that much will be required of him to whom much has been given; more will be demanded of him to whom more has been entrusted (Luke 12:35–48).

Hence, at the "coming" of the Son of Man, the lot of everyone will be fixed and unchanging, but that lot itself will be subject to differences and degrees. Above all, no one knows the exact time of Christ's "coming."

The Sign of Contradiction; the Necessity of Repentance

Teachings of this kind upset every human scale of values. These were not the overlabored arguments of Pharisaic casuists regarding eggs laid on the Sabbath or the washing of hands and dishes before meals. This was a fire sweeping wreckage and confusion through the world of Jewish thought, and it was to flame through other worlds as well. Jesus recognized this, for He immediately continued: "I have come to cast fire upon the earth, and what will I but that it be kindled?" It is the trial of fire through which the disciples of Jesus must pass, and He Himself will lead the way: "But I have a baptism to be baptized with; and how distressed I am until it is accomplished!" With Jesus' figurative baptism the fire will be manifest; both are a trial, the first for Jesus personally, the second for all the earth.

Nor will the trial bring peace and harmony on earth, but war and discord. Jesus Himself describes the consequences of His teaching: there will be strife and division in a family of five, and there will be three against two and two against three. The father will be divided against his son, the mother against her daughter, the mother-in-law against her daughter-in-law, and vice versa. All has been agreement and concord among them, but once the message of Jesus penetrates their hearts, it brings discord in its wake, for some will bless and some will curse Him (Luke 12:49–53). More than thirty years before, the aged Simeon in the Temple had contemplated the infant Jesus as "the sign that will be contradicted": the person and the teaching of Jesus will be the sign of contradiction for all mankind. Anyone today with even a slight knowledge of history can easily ascertain whether these predictions of twenty centuries ago have been verified in that time and in the centuries since.

Meanwhile Pharisees and Sadducees, mingling with the populace, continued to dog Jesus' steps, still trying to pick up charges against Him, and He took occasion to address certain words of exhortation to them along with the people. The days are passing and events are plunging to a climax, while they, instead of giving thought to their supreme interests, are straining every nerve and fiber to hinder the Kingdom of God. But do they not see what is happening around them? Do they not recognize the signs of the new times? The signs of the physical world they indeed recognize very easily: when in the evening they see a cloud rising in the west, they immediately remark that rain is coming; and when the south wind blows, they say it is going to be hot weather; and so it is. But from the spiritual signs made manifest since the time of John the Baptist, can they not see that the time has come for spiritual regeneration and a "change of mind"? The old useless matter is to be cut away. Let them open their eyes and judge for themselves what they must do while there yet is time (Luke 12:54–57).

Two events that occurred shortly afterward furnished the occasion for reemphasizing these things. Since Jesus was a Galilean, people were quick to tell Him of Pilate's massacre of certain Galileans while they were offering sacrifices in the Temple. Whereupon Jesus, alluding to the ancient Hebrew notion that physical calamity was invariably a punishment for moral evil, answered: Do you perhaps think that because these murdered Galileans have suffered these things they were worse sinners than all the other men of Galilee? Quite the contrary; indeed I say to you that "unless you repent, you will all perish in the same manner." And He spoke also of another disaster that had occurred shortly before and also in Jerusalem. In the Siloe quarter, that is, on the edge of the residential district, a tower that formed part of the city's fortifications suddenly gave way and came crashing down, killing eighteen people. Well — proceeded Jesus — do you think that those eighteen people were more guilty than all the other dwellers in Jerusalem? Not at all; indeed I say to you that "unless you repent, you will all perish in the same manner."

What is the end that threatens the impenitent? We note that both examples refer to violent death, for Pilate's victims died by the sword and the others were crushed beneath the tower, two common forms of death in the wars and sieges of the time, together with death from starvation. Hence the threat is of death mid the violence common to wars, while in the previous parables of the servants awaiting their master's coming, there has been no hint whatever of such things. The parables, in fact, spoke of an event that was unavoidable though the time of its occurrence was not specified, namely, the time of the "coming" of the Son of Man, who will determine the eternal destiny of each individual. Here, on the other hand, the violent end can be avoided; it is enough to repent. Jesus' words clearly outline a dilemma: Either you will not repent and then you will all perish as those who have died in these two disasters, or you will repent and thereby save yourselves from violent death.

This is clearly confirmed in the brief parable with which Jesus continues. A man had in his vineyard a fig tree that never bore any fruit. So he said to his vinedresser: "For three years now I have come looking for fruit on this fig tree, and I do not find any. Cut it down, therefore, because it bears no fruit and makes the ground around it sterile besides!" But the vinedresser interposed: "Master, let it stay this year too. I will dig around the roots and manure it and then we shall see. If it gives fruit, well and good; otherwise, after this last test, you will cut it down and throw it away" (Luke 13:6–8).

The figure is self-evident. As we have remarked before, the tree's three years of barrenness seen an allusion to the length of Jesus' public life, for He was now in His third year of preaching. In any case, it is clear that the tree represents Judaism, the master of the vineyard God, and the vinedresser Jesus Himself. And so here is the same threat again; in this last delay, the tree either will bear, or it will be cut down.

The Stooped Woman; the Man with Dropsy; the Parable of the Banquets

Did these threats produce any effect? Did the fire that Jesus came to cast on the earth begin to burn?

Luke does not give us a direct answer to these questions, but there seems to be one implicit in the next anecdote wherein we see how rabbinic formalism weighed on the spirit like a leaden mantle and was not even scratched by Jesus' threatening words. It is the episode of the stooped woman, cured on the Sabbath (Luke 13:10–17), and the evangelist, who takes delight in coupling incidents, records shortly afterward the other similar scene of the man with dropsy, also cured on the Sabbath (14:1–6). It is evident, however, if we compare Luke with the other evangelists on this point, that the two events do not belong together in time; the woman was cured in Judea a little before the feast of the Dedication, and the man shortly after it, probably in Transjordan.

In Judea, therefore, Jesus went one Sabbath to a certain synagogue and began to preach. Present was a woman who had been ill for eighteen years — perhaps from arthritis or some form of paralysis — and she was so bent that she could not even lift her head to look up. When He saw her, Jesus called her to Him and said: "Woman, thou art delivered from thy infirmity." And He laid His hands upon her. On the instant she straightened and began to thank and glorify God. The ruler of the synagogue presiding at the services was extremely angry at this performance on the Sabbath, but since he did not dare to tackle Jesus directly, he vented his feelings on the crowd, scolding them angrily: "There are six days in which one ought to work; on these therefore come and be cured, and not on the Sabbath!" The miraculous cure meant nothing at all to this zealous worthy, but the Sabbath — which, after all, had not actually been violated — meant everything. Jesus, therefore, answered him and all others of like mentality: "Hypocrites! does not each one of you on the Sabbath loose his ox or ass from the manger, and lead it forth to water?" Tying and untying a knot in a rope were included in the thirty-nine categories of prohibitions for the Sabbath, but in actual practice, provision was made in one way or another for taking care of domestic animals. This much having been granted, Jesus argues: "And this woman, daughter of Abraham as she is, whom Satan has bound, lo, for eighteen years, ought not she to have been loosed from this bond on the Sabbath?" Satan was commonly held responsible for ills of every sort. What day could possibly be more suitable than the Sabbath, the day consecrated to God, to demonstrate the triumph of God over Satan, of good over evil? Hence, Jesus more than any of them, understood the true spirit of the Sabbath, having wrought on precisely that day a victory of God over Satan.

The parallel incident takes place not in a synagogue but in the home of a prominent Pharisee who has invited Jesus to dine with him. It is again the Sabbath, and the Pharisees are on the alert as usual. At this point a man suffering from dropsy presents himself to Jesus, hoping to be cured. Jesus turns to the lawyers and the Pharisees present and asks: "It is lawful [or no] to cure on the Sabbath?" They gave Him no answer though many aspects of the question had been considered and decided by the doctors of the Law. As the silence continued, Jesus drew the man to Him, cured him, and let him go. Then He said to his hushed audience: "Which of you shall have an ass or an ox fall into a pit, and will not immediately draw him up on the Sabbath?" But, according to Luke, he did not receive any answer this time either.

At first reading, the two episodes seem very similar, except that in the latter Jesus' adversaries confine themselves to keeping silent. Hence, we are tempted to conclude that the lawyers and Pharisees of the Transjordan, farther away from Jerusalem, were a little less fanatic and bigoted than those of Judea, who were under the direct influence of the capital.

This seems further evidenced by the fact that the banquet lasted a long time and that in the course of it many questions were treated without rancor or resentment, beginning with the matter of the first seats.

These good Pharisees would not have been Pharisees had there not been some question among them as to who should have the places of honor next to the host: "That is my divan!" "No, it is mine, for I am more worthy!" "You more worthy! What do you think you are?" "I am older and more learned than you!" And so on. Jesus commented on the arguing, and to confound all parties concerned He showed them how not even their vanity was shrewd enough to assure them a real social triumph:

> When thou art invited to a wedding feast, do not recline in the first place, lest perhaps one more distinguished than thou have been invited by him, and he who invited thee and him come and say to thee: "Make room for this man." And then thou begin with shame to take the last place. But when thou art invited, go and recline in the last place; that when he who invited thee comes in, he may say to thee: "Friend, go up higher!" Then thou wilt be honored in the presence of all who are at table with thee. For everyone who exalts himself shall be humbled, and he who humbles himself shall be exalted.

The guests' vanity having been shamed by the spectacle of their very ama-teurishness, there remained the question of the host's attitude and that of hosts in general, too often motivated by vainglory and material advantage. Besides, both would profit from the lesson in a much higher sphere by being made to think of the norms and advantages governing a spiritual banquet. And so, turning to the host, Jesus continued: "When thou givest a dinner or a supper, do not invite thy friends, or thy brethren, or thy relatives, or thy rich neigh-bors, lest perhaps they also invite thee in return, and a recompense be made to thee. But when thou givest a feast, invite the poor, the crippled, the lame, the blind, and blessed shalt thou be, because they have nothing to repay thee with; for thou shalt be repaid at the resurrection of the just." Intimately akin to this principle is the saying, not in the four Gospels, that St. Paul attributes to Jesus: "It is a more blessed thing to give than to receive." The common basis for all these norms is, as always, the fundamental principle of the Sermon on the Mount, the principle of a supernatural, not an earthy, sanction. Here it is called the "resurrection of the just," elsewhere the "kingdom of heaven" or the "coming" of the Son of Man, but it is substantially the same foundation stone, without which the structure of Jesus' teaching would crumble.

The mention of the supernatural reward had lifted the guests — as Jesus intended — to the thought of a spiritual banquet. And one of them exclaimed: "Blessed is he who shall feast in the kingdom of God!" Jesus took the opportunity to describe the Kingdom of God as a banquet, in a parable that is recorded for us by both Luke (14:16–24) and Matthew (22:2–14). Luke's account is as follows.

A certain man gave a great supper and invited many guests. As the time drew near, he sent his servant to bid them come because everything was ready, but they all began to find excuses. One said: "I have bought some land and must go out and have a look at it. Please excuse me!" Another said: "I have bought five yoke of oxen and I must go try them. Do excuse me!" A third gave him short shrift: "I have married a wife and I cannot even think about it!" The servant reported these answers to his master, who became very angry and ordered him to go through the streets and marketplaces of the city and bring back to the supper the poor, the lame, the halt, and the blind! The servant obeyed and then reported: "All those unfortunates have come, but there is still room." So the master sent him out into the country to bring in all whom he found in the byways and hedges, for he was determined that his house should be filled with these poor people and that not one of the invited guests should taste his supper.

It is clear that the banquet symbolizes the Kingdom of God, the reluctant guests are the Jews, and the poor who take their places are the Gentiles. This is even clearer in Matthew's version.[141]

---

[14] The chief differences in Matthew's account are as follows. The host is a king who has prepared a wedding feast for his son. The king sends several servants to his invited guests a first and a second time with no results; the second time, in fact, some of those invited lay hands on the servants, maltreat them, and kill them. Then the king sends out his armies to destroy the murderers and burn their city. Finally, he sends other servants through the highways to invite people of every kind, and these new guests fill the banquet chamber. In this version, the historical allusions are even more clear and emphatic. The king is the God of Israel; the servants are the prophets who have been killed; the armies that kill and burn are the Roman legions, which in 70 burn and destroy Jerusalem; the wretched who fill the banquet chamber in place of the original guests are the Gentiles who enter the kingdom of the Messiah in the place of the unwilling Jews.

Luke's account ends here, but Matthew adds another scene. When the banquet chamber is filled, the host enters to see his guests. Suddenly he notices one of them who has not put on the prescribed wedding garment. And the king says to him: "Friend, why have you entered here without your wedding garment?" But the man is silent with shame. Then the king commands his servants: "Bind him hand and foot and throw him into the darkness outside, where there shall be weeping and gnashing of teeth!" And Jesus concludes: "For many are called, but few are chosen."

The end of this unique passage ceases to be figurative and refers directly to the true moral of the parable ("weeping and gnashing of teeth"). It adds, besides, a new element to the parable, and that is that not all the new guests are worthy of the banquet. Not all the Gentiles, then, who have taken the seats of the Jews in the kingdom of the Messiah are worthy of the kingdom, but only those who have the proper spiritual dispositions. Jesus had, in fact, warned Nicodemus that "unless a man be born again of water and the Spirit, he cannot enter into the kingdom of God." This rebirth of the soul is essential for being admitted legitimately to the messianic banquet.

The exclamations of Jesus' fellow guest — "Blessed is he who shall feast in the kingdom of God" — had also been a question that sought somehow to know just who was to enjoy that blessedness. Jesus answered the implied question by showing who would refuse and who would accept the messianic invitation, and who, among those who accepted, would prove worthy and who unworthy.

Chapter 14

∞

From the Last Feast of Dedication to
the Last Journey through Judea

The Feast of the Dedication

About two months and a half were consumed by the events we have just described. At the end of December of the year 29, Jesus went to the capital, there
to continue His ministry throughout the patriotic "festival of lights."

His presence in the city was immediately noticed. The recent discussions
in His journey throughout the surrounding district of Judea had made the
Galilean Rabbi the object of special vigilance to the supreme authorities of
Judaism. One day while Jesus lingered in the Temple, teaching and walking
in Solomon's Porch, perhaps because of the rain — the precise John says particularly that "it was winter" — His usual adversaries, the "Jews," confronted
Him and said: "How long dost thou keep us in suspense? If thou art the Christ
[Messiah] tell us openly!" The question appears to be not only a friendly one;
it is almost an entreaty and a prayer. One might think that all they were waiting for was Jesus' frank declaration that He was the expected Messiah before
they gave themselves to Him body and soul. Actually the question was a trap:
Jesus' adversaries were waiting for that open declaration only that they might
twist it into an accusation against Him and bring Him to His ruin.

Jesus Himself reveals the treacherous nature of the query, for His reply
is substantially the statement they were expecting but not in the form they
desired. He declares who He is but without springing the trap:

> I tell you and you do not believe. The works that I do in the name of
> my Father, these bear witness concerning me. But you do not believe
> because you are not of my sheep. My sheep hear my voice, and I know
> them and they follow me. And I give them everlasting life; and they
> shall never perish, neither shall anyone snatch them out of my hand.

What my Father has given me is greater than all: and no one is able to snatch anything out of the hand of my Father. I and the Father are one.

His questioners had hoped Jesus would say explicitly, "I am the Messiah." Instead, He has said: You determine whether I am the Messiah from the works that I do — thereby avoiding a clear, precise affirmation as He had done before during the feast of Tabernacles. The reason for this indirect answer is still the same. Anyone contemplating calmly and objectively the miracles performed by Jesus could conclude that the Kingdom of God was "at hand" and that He was the Messiah. At the same time this appeal to the miracles afforded no pretext for denouncing Him to the political authorities.

As soon as they heard His last words, "the Jews took up stones [again] to stone him." With the adverb "again" the evangelist recalls the similar attempt made against Jesus during the feast of Tabernacles a few months before, when He had declared that He was before Abraham and had described Himself as the good shepherd of a faithful flock. Here He goes further. He declares first of all that His adversaries do not believe in Him because they are not of His sheep, and that these cannot be snatched out of His hand nor the hand of His Father; and the reason for this is that He "and the Father are one." Does Jesus, then, though not explicitly declaring Himself the Messiah, proclaim Himself God?

That is the way the Jews interpret His words, and they say so openly. Seeing them pick up the stones, Jesus asks them: "Many good works have I shown you from my Father. For which of these works do you stone me?" The Jews answered him, "Not for a good work do we stone thee, but for blasphemy, and because thou, being a man, makest thyself God!" The rush to stone Him was momentarily checked. In the Orient, in the shops and marketplaces, people suddenly blaze with anger over nothing; they shout and gesticulate but without any tragic consequences. And so it happened this time, and the menacing crowd stopped to listen to Jesus' explanation: And yet it is written in your Law, "I said you are gods." If God Himself addresses men as gods and does so in the Holy Scriptures, the testimony of which is inviolable, why do you accuse me of blasphemy because I have said that I am the Son of God when the Father Himself has sanctified me and sent me into the world? In any case, observe my works; if I do not perform the works of my Father, do not believe me, but if I do perform them, then let yourselves be convinced by them and you will recognize that "the Father is in me and I in the Father" (John 10:34–48).

In the passage in Scripture cited as proof, the term *gods* is used loosely to mean human judges who represent the authority of God in the courts. Nevertheless, it was an effective argument to silence Jesus' adversaries with their own respect for the Scriptures. Jesus did not come down to particulars, which would only have added fuel to the fire; but the incriminating phrase, "I and the Father are one," He defined by asserting "the Father is in me and I in the Father." Far from explaining or qualifying, this was a confirmation of His previous words.

This time, too, the Jews understood Him perfectly, and their fury burst into flame again: "They sought therefore [again] to seize him; and he went forth out of their hands."

These Jews were very intelligent; they understood immediately and perfectly that Jesus was declaring Himself equal in all things with the Father.

Jesus in Transjordan

Shortly after the feast of the Dedication, or at the very beginning of the year 30, Jesus went into Transjordan (Perea) to the district where John the Baptist had baptized, and He stayed there for some time (John 10:40; cf. Matt. 19:1; Mark 10:1; Luke 13:31ff.). From there He must have made various short journeys through the northern districts of Judea, finally crossing Samaria and going as far as Galilee, since Luke (17:11) has Him come from the latter direction on His last journey to Jerusalem.

One day a certain man asks Jesus: "Lord, are only a few to be saved?" Christ's reply repeats the concepts of the Sermon on the Mount. Strive to enter by the narrow gate, for many will seek in vain to enter when the master, seeing that all the invited guests have arrived, will rise and go to shut the door. Then it will be too late, and in answer to their knocking they will hear: I do not know where you are from!

The question reflected the prevailing Jewish opinion that the chosen were to be much fewer in number than the damned. Jesus neither rejects nor approves the notion; He simply invites men to strive to enter the banquet chamber because the entrance is not easy. That one is a Jew, a member of the chosen people, is no help whatever in gaining admission. In fact, Jesus continues: When you see yourselves shut out, you will persist, saying: "How does this happen? We have eaten and drunk with you, and you have taught in our marketplaces!" And yet the answer still will be: "I do not know where you are from; depart from me you workers of iniquity." And you will remain without where there is weeping and gnashing of teeth. Nor will your places at that banquet remain empty, for other guests, not Jews, will come from the east and the west, and the north and the south, and sit down to feast in the Kingdom of God!

Certain Pharisees then approached Jesus and said to Him in a confidential tone: "Depart and be on thy way, for Herod wants to kill thee" (Luke 13:31). This was Herod Antipas, the murderer of John the Baptist, and Jesus was in His territory.

Did Antipas really intend to put Jesus to death? Probably not, for he could have done so easily and in secret. But he was beginning to be annoyed with this Galilean Rabbi who had reappeared in his territory to excite the populace and whose character reminded him so much of John the Baptist whom he had killed. Let Him leave the territory of His own will, without forcing him to use violence. But how was He to be persuaded to do this? There were the Pharisees, quite ready to render a service, because once Jesus was in the district of Jerusalem, they could do what they wanted with Him. It was indeed the fine cunning of the "fox."

And Jesus, knowing very well what was going on, said to these solicitous Pharisees: "Go and say to that fox: Behold, I cast out devils and perform cures today and tomorrow, and the third day I am to end my course. Nevertheless, I must go my way today and tomorrow and the next day, for it cannot be that a prophet perish outside Jerusalem." In other words, they were to tell Antipas, the "fox," not to worry: Jesus was going to continue His miraculous activity in the tetrarch's territory and elsewhere for two more days and on the third His course would be consummated. It was to end not in Antipas's territory, however, but in Jerusalem, out of respect for that city's tragic privilege of murdering prophets.

Once more, then, Jesus clearly appeals to His miracles as proofs of His mission. He declares besides that this mission is to last a day and another day and part of a third. Is this only a general and indefinite expression of time or is it specific? The first is certainly possible, but the second seems more probable. If Jesus spoke these words in January of the year 30, His death was about two and a half months away, represented by the two and a half days here mentioned.

The Following of Christ

After the Pharisees' warning St. Luke records the dinner at the home of the Pharisee and the discussions that followed it. Next comes a list of requisites for following Jesus, which He enumerated one day when great crowds had gathered about Him. Some of these requisites Matthew records in other places. They may be grouped under three principal headings: love for Jesus must prevail over love of kin no matter what the degree of kinship; it must prevail over one's love for oneself and one's own life; it must prevail over one's love for material goods.

> If anyone comes to me and does not hate his father and mother, and wife and children, and brothers and sisters, yes, and even his own life, he cannot be my disciple.
>
> And he who does not carry his cross and follow me, cannot be my disciple.
>
> Every one of you who does not renounce all that he possesses, cannot be my disciple.

The Semitic phrase for liking one person less than another was to "hate" one and not the other. That is what Jesus means when He says His disciple must "hate" his own blood relatives. Luke reports a double parable that illustrates all three of the essential conditions for becoming a disciple of Jesus. Let everyone ponder and calculate well before setting out, therefore, whether or not he is disposed to fulfill them; otherwise he had better not set out at all.

Who, indeed, wishing to build a tower, does not first estimate the expense to see if he has the means to finish it? Otherwise, having laid the foundations, he may find he has no money left to complete it and the half-finished structure will become a byword throughout the countryside, and everyone will make fun of the presumptuous builder.

Or what king setting out with ten thousand soldiers to wage war with another king who has twenty thousand does not first determine whether or not his strategy or the bravery of his army or other circumstances will be likely to compensate his numerical inferiority? If not, he does not engage in battle but begins to negotiate for peace.

Similarly, one who wishes to follow Jesus must love Him first and foremost above all other things. It may well be that other loves will not conflict with this supreme love for Him, but when they do, they must give way before Him who is to be the absolute master of the field. Otherwise, one cannot be a follower of Jesus in the true sense of the term.

Jesus stated these conditions with almost brusque frankness to the "great crowds" that were with Him. Their historical significance is clear. Among those so eagerly thronging after Him were many, in fact very many, who were attracted by the magnetism of His spiritual superiority, by His miracles, by vague hopes of triumph and glory, by the expectation of sharing somehow in His messianic kingdom, but these, at the first difficulties, would beat the hastiest retreat. Jesus, anticipating this, pricks each bubble with the harsh requisites for all who would follow Him. These things are not to be taken lightly. At any moment a disciple of Jesus may be asked to become a giant of heroism. Anyone who does not feel he has the strength for it, renouncing all "human arguments," may become the disciple of some prominent Pharisaic teacher but not of Jesus.

The Lost Sheep and the Lost Coin

Here Luke sets a row of parables, which are sheer gems. The first of them may be called the pearls of divine mercy and confirm for the jeweler the title Dante decreed for him of "the scribe of the mercy of Christ."

A few words of introduction furnish the thread on which they are strung: "Now the publicans and sinners were drawing near to him to listen to him. And the Pharisees and the Scribes murmured, saying: This man welcomes sinners and eats with them." Jesus had answered this kind of grumbling before. Now He had recourse to His favorite device, the parable, which had a message both for the grumblers and for the people they condemned.

The first is drawn from pastoral life. A shepherd has a hundred sheep, and in the morning he leads them from the sheepfold out to pasture over the heath. But sometime during the day he notices that one sheep is missing. Look as he will, he cannot find it. It has been lost along the way. Perhaps it wandered from the fold into some little hollow where the grass seemed greener and more abundant while the rest of the flock went munching on its way leaving it there alone, deceived by this moment of plenty and exposed to the wolves that prowl by night. He must find it quickly before the swift shadows of the Palestinian evening descend over the valley.

The anxious shepherd entrusts his other ninety-nine sheep to the hirelings and hastens in search of the one that was lost. Down through the hollows, up over mound and hill he goes, stopping now and then to gaze searchingly over the open stretches with worry in his heart. He watches the hawks, he calls, he listens; and finally, to his joy, comes the answering bleat. It is the lost sheep! He runs to it, and with never a word of reproach, he lifts it and sets it on his shoulders; he gives it the privilege of the little nursling lambs that cannot manage their legs. When it discovered it was lost, the poor sheep must have suffered no less than its shepherd; it has earned the privilege! Nor is it heavy on its shepherd's shoulders; his joy makes the burden light. Then, in the evening, when he comes home, he does not bother about the ninety-nine sheep he knows are safe, but he calls his friends and companions about him because he has to share his relief and joy: "Rejoice with me, because I have found my sheep that was lost!" And Jesus concludes: "I say to you that, even so, there will be joy in heaven over one sinner who repents, more than over ninety-nine just who have no need of repentance."

The second parable has a domestic setting, but its moral is the same. A certain good, thrifty woman has scraped a few savings together from her industry and small economies. They amount to ten drachmas, ten shiny coins worth a little over two gold dollars. She keeps them carefully tied in a kerchief, hidden in a niche in her house, where she goes to look at them now and then to make sure they are all right and to gladden her eyes with their glimmer. But one day she opens the kerchief to find not ten drachmas but only nine.

What a bitter surprise! Where in the world could the other coin be? When did it disappear? Greatly upset, the woman thinks of the last time she looked at her little hoard; perhaps the missing drachma dropped and rolled off somewhere that time she paid for something in such a hurry, or even the other day when she turned the house upside down in her cleaning. Armed with lamp and broom she searches every nook and cranny in her house, sweeps out every crack in the floor, pries into every hole and chink, until finally she spies the missing coin stuck fast between two boards. Then she fairly explodes with joy, gathering all her friends and cronies about her to tell them all her happiness, just as the shepherd has done. And Jesus concluded: "Even so, I say to you, there will be joy among the angels of God over one sinner who repents."

The Prodigal Son

The two preceding parables illustrate God's attitude toward the sinner who repents and returns to Him; but what must be the attitude of the nonsinner toward the repentant one? The answer to this is in the parable of the prodigal son, which also confirms once more the attitude of God.

From the purely literary point of view this parable is itself a miracle. No writer in the world has ever condensed so deep a power to move within a tale so brief, so true, so free from all literary artifice. It is extremely simple; yet its effect is far greater than other narratives justly famous for their skillful structure and limpid style. To retell the parable in other words unquestionably clouds its beauty; but to clarify its historical setting, we are forced to mar it in this fashion.

"A certain man had two sons," and they all lived together in the country very comfortably, taking care of his vast possessions and managing the numerous servants and hired men. The older of the two boys was a gem, a serious, quiet young man who had no interest but the farm and wasted no time in merry-making with his few sensible friends. The younger son was different; his head was full of restless notions, and he felt stifled by that methodical way of life. Work in the fields bored him, the smell of flock and herd irritated him, and the whole estate seemed a prison where the hired hands were so many jailers spying on what he did. The scatterbrained friends he had in the neighborhood had told him wonderful things about distant cities where there were gay dining, dancing, music, and festivals, where at every step he might meet perfumed women and pleasant friends instead of his father's smelly shepherdesses and dirty farmhands. That was living! So he thought gloomily through the summer evenings when, after a lazy day, he lay stretched on the grass, resigned to the shrill singing of the grasshoppers and reflecting that the months and the years were relentlessly flying by while his youth was evaporating in sheer empty boredom.

One day he decided he could stand it no longer. And without further ado he went to his father and said to him: "Father, give me the share of the property that falls to me." His request was not irregular. According to Hebrew Law, the firstborn had a right to a double portion; since there were two sons in this case, the younger could expect one third of the estate. The father must have looked long and searchingly into his son's eyes, but he said nothing, nor did the young man have the courage to add a single word to his request. They parted in mutual silence, which lasted some days. During this time the settlement was arranged and the property due the boy was converted into cash, "and not many days later, the younger son gathered up all his wealth, and took his journey into a far country."

Life, at last, was about to begin for him! His new world was very far from home and entertained none of the Hebrew prejudices about morality. The young man entered it furnished with an abundance of money, and he could do whatever he pleased. Long thirsty for pleasure, he plunged headlong into all that came his way. The text says that he began to live "dissolutely" or "extravagantly," "as a wastrel."

The days passed swiftly and pleasantly, but the consequences had one day to be faced. After a while, he found that his money, the sole source of his pleasures, had fled with the time; his purse, however full, was not without a bottom. The life of bliss was over for him, and another, quite different, was beginning.

"And after he had spent all, there came a grievous famine over that country, and he began himself to suffer want." Yesterday's playboy is assailed from within and without at the same time; not only is his purse empty, but a famine has spread over the region, such as pinches even those who ordinarily never feel want; and it is hardly necessary to say that the flattering friends of the day before all left our young man when his money did and were now busy looking out for themselves. Reduced to these straits and in a strange land besides, he did not have to think very hard to realize where his choice lay: it was a question of either starving to death or doing any kind of work at all, even the most humiliating and disgusting. "And he went and joined one of the citizens of that country, who sent him to his farm to feed swine." This was not Jewish country, otherwise there would have been no such occupation.

And so the playboy became a swineherd; but if he thereby escaped death, he did not escape hunger. There was want everywhere. The pigs, rooting all day through the fields as he watched them, found little or nothing, but at least when they returned to the pen at night, they received their ration of carob pods. But he received nothing — not even a pod. The swineherd was worth much less than the swine. And he a Jew! "And he longed to fill his belly with the pods that the swine were eating, but no one offered to give them to him."

He spent some time in these frightful circumstances. When in the intense heat of the day the famished and exhausted swine stretched out in the shade, their emaciated herdsman dropped down beside them in the dirt; but his thoughts kept traveling back to those summer nights when he lay on the grass before his father's house listening to the song of the grasshoppers and dreaming with desire his gay dreams of the future. Those rosy dreams had now all come true; he could feel them about him in the grunting pigs, in the stinking rags that covered him, in the hunger stabbing through his belly.

"But when he came to himself, he said: How many hired men in my father's house have bread in abundance, while I am perishing here with hunger!" What should he do? Return to his father? But how could he have the courage to do that after all that had happened? Yet he could go back to him, not as a father but as an employer; to earn his living as the least hireling on his father's estate would still be an immense gain over the life he was now leading. Certainly it would take great goodness and condescension on his father's part to forgive the injury he had done him and take him back into his household — not as a son, of course, only as a simple hired hand. But he was such a good man, perhaps he would relent! "I will get up and go to my father, and will say to him: Father I have sinned against heaven [God] and before thee! I am no longer worthy to be called thy son! Make me as one of thy hired men!"

Sustained by this hope, he gathered up his last energies and set out for his father's lands. Along the roads he dragged himself as best he could, and finally he came home. It was a bright afternoon. His father was in the fields superintending the work, but his quick eyes, as he glanced from plow to plow, were not so clear and bright as they once had been. They were dimmed with a suffering that was old but not spent; and every now and then he fixed his gaze on the far horizon and stood motionless, contemplating who knows what ghosts. "But while he was yet a long way off, his father saw him and was moved with compassion, and ran and fell upon his neck and kissed him."

Certainly the father recognized his son even in that state; then why did he kiss him? Why did he not command his farmhands to drive him away? Was he not the son who denied his father? Perhaps the old man should be reminded of these things. "And the son said to him: Father, I have sinned against heaven and before thee. I am no longer worthy to be called thy son." It was the speech he had been practicing, but he could not add the final entreaty he had intended: "Make me as one of thy hired men." Had he lost the heart to ask for a job in the face of his father's exuberant goodness, or was his request cut short by other kisses?

Anyway, what good would it do to speak his petition? His words would be utterly useless; his father did not even hear him. In great excitement the old man turned to the farmhands who had come running and exclaimed: "Fetch quickly the best robe and put it on him, and give him a ring for his finger and sandals for his feet!" And why not? Was this not the young master come home again? When he had been cleaned up and dressed, they must all celebrate together. No more plowing and hoeing today; there was a great dinner to be prepared: "And bring out the fattened calf and kill it, and let us eat and make merry; because this my son was dead, and has come to life again; he was lost, and is found!"

And not long afterward, in the servant's dining room, the feasting and the music and the dancing began.

The older brother was not present at these things. That jewel of a boy was working as usual, attending that afternoon to some urgent matters on the farthest corner of the estate. So he returned home when the merrymaking was well advanced and plentiful libations had reinforced the singing and the dancing. When he heard all that commotion, our sober young man came tumbling out of the clouds, and "calling one of the servants, he inquired what this meant. And he said to him: 'Thy brother has come, and thy father has killed the fattened calf, because he has got him back safe.'" Naturally the servant did not stop there but went on to tell him all the rest, how his brother came home in such a state that by comparison the mangiest dog on the place looked like the high priest in Jerusalem.

The older boy was hurt. Was his father celebrating like that over the young rakehell who had been the family shame and liability? Had his father gone crazy? Well, if the old man had lost his mind, his one good son, who had always been extremely sensible, had no intention of imitating him.

> But he was angered and would not go in. His father, therefore, came out and began to entreat him. But he answered and said to his father: "Behold, these many years I have been serving thee, and have never transgressed one of thy commands; and yet thou hast never given me a kid that I might make merry with my friends. But when this thy son comes home, who has devoured his means with harlots, thou hast killed for him the fattened calf." But he said to him: "Son, thou art always with me, and all that is mine is thine, but we were bound to make merry and rejoice, for this thy brother was dead, and has come to life; he was lost, and is found."

Note that the older son speaks of his brother as "this thy son"; but the father answers him with "this thy brother." The older boy is almost afraid of soiling his lips by calling that libertine his "brother," and he would like to disown him. But the father reminds him that the libertine is his "brother" and he must therefore treat him as such, just as he has treated him as his son. This is the whole lesson in this second part of the parable: as the father is always a father, so the brother must be always a brother.

Indeed, the whole parable moves toward the lesson illustrated in the second part. The first half underlines the mercy bestowed on the penitent sinner by God who is his father, but this is not a new thought, for it has already been set forth in the parables of the lost sheep and the lost coin. The second part teaches that mercy must be bestowed on the penitent sinner also by man, who is his brother; this obligation follows from and is intimately associated with the pardon accorded him by God. Hence, this second part is the real roof of the edifice, and its crown.

The Unjust Steward and Dives

Besides being the scribe of mercy, Luke is also the evangelist of poverty; and among the parables we are now examining, the pearls of divine mercy are followed by others of human poverty that have been saved for us by Luke alone.

That Jesus' disciple shows foresight and shrewdness in renouncing riches is demonstrated in the parable that follows.

A certain rich man had a steward, who was accused of squandering his master's possessions. So the master summoned him and said abruptly: "I have heard ugly things about you; bring your accounts immediately!" The steward began to cast about for a way out of his difficulty; unless he found some means to live through his old age, he was lost. If the stewardship is taken from me — he reasoned — how can I support myself? I am no longer able to work in the fields and I am ashamed to beg. After some thought, he fell upon a cunning trick to make the master himself bear the burden of his support in the years to come. He would alter in their favor the records of the debts his master's tenants owed him so that the latter, fraudulently benefited thereby, would be grateful and show it in some form of compensation. Calling one tenant to him, therefore, he asked: "How much do you owe the master?" And he answered: "A hundred jars of oil." And the steward said: "No, take the receipt and write fifty instead." So the first debtor had half his debt forgiven him. Then calling another he asked him the same question, and he replied: "A hundred measures of wheat." And the steward said: "No; here, take your receipt and write eighty!" Naturally he treated the other tenants the same way, and they obligingly showed their gratitude at the time and afterward as well. In that way the discharged steward provided for his old age.

This was really a theft; there is no doubt. But it was a clever theft, and it showed the foresight and shrewdness of the steward. Now, the whole parable — apart from the dishonesty involved, which does not enter into consideration at all here — emphasizes just that shrewdness and foresight. In fact, it goes on to relate that the master, commenting on the fraud of which he was the victim, praised his trickster steward "in that he had acted prudently." He had something of a sense of humor, this master, and he could take displeasures in life with a lordly spirit, appreciating their interesting aspects. The parable closes with the admonition that "the children of this world are in relation to their own generation [their own kind] more prudent than the children of the light."

But to explain just how this "prudence" works, Jesus adds: "And I say to you, make friends for yourselves with the mammon of wickedness, so that [when it shall fail] they may receive you into everlasting dwellings." The functioning of this "prudence" is clear, and the parable, transferred to a higher plane, is given a specific application. Earthly riches are to be spent not to acquire earthly goods, which are just as ephemeral and deceptive, but goods that are everlasting and reliable instead. How? By their use in helping the poor. This yields an imperishable profit because those benefited become the "friends" of the benefactor, and at the end of "this world" they will repay him by receiving him into "everlasting dwellings." Here again the thing most in evidence is the supernatural sanction at the basis of all Jesus' teachings: to give away one's own wealth in view of the future life. In that view, poverty is the height of prudence.

The Pharisees, who did not share the final expectation, found the whole business very silly. "Now the Pharisees, who were fond of money, were listening to all these things, and they began to sneer at him." What kind of talk was this? This was not merely an idiot's raving; it was blasphemy! The Hebrew Law was clear on this point. Material prosperity is a blessing from God and a reward for those who observe His laws.

Jesus' answer was addressed to the real motive behind the Pharisees' defense of money: "You are they who declare yourselves just in the sight of men [in that you boast you are just because you are rich], but God knows your heart; for that which is exalted in the sight of men is an abomination before God." As for the Law and tradition, this was one of the points where the Old Law needed to be completed and perfected. In fact, "until John [the Baptist] came, there were the Law and the Prophets; since then the kingdom of God is being preached, and everyone is forcing his way into it" (Luke 16:15–16). The Law lured its disciples with the promise of riches, but since the time of John the Baptist, the Law has been supplanted by the Kingdom of God, which holds out no promise of material goods and, moreover, demands a detachment from those goods that is a violence against our feelings. After all, the true spirit of the Old Law itself did not intend that one should become attached to riches but rather that he should rise above them, for it contemplated them as a means, not an end.

This is illustrated in another parable, which is so faithful to various Judaic concepts that it seems, in that sense, the most Jewish of Jesus' parables.

There were two Jews, one very rich and the other very poor. The rich man wore garments of Tyrian purple and Egyptian linen, and the banqueting in his hall had no end. The poor man, who bore the ordinary name of Lazarus, lay covered with sores in the street outside the rich man's atrium. There the sound of the banquet merriment reached his ears, and his happiest dream was to satisfy his hunger with what fell from those laden tables; but no one paid any attention to him. Moreover, black as his poverty was, he seems to have been of some use to Dives, for dogs (perhaps the latter's) would stop to lick the matter from the festering sores that covered him. But in God's good time, both men died and then their positions were reversed. Lazarus died first, and the angels came and bore him away to the place of everlasting bliss, where they set him in the bosom of Abraham, in the arms of the privileged "friend of God" and founder of the Hebrew race. Then Dives died and he was buried with great splendor, which proved to be his last, for from his gorgeous tomb he went hurtling down to Sheol where he was plunged into unspeakable torments.

The once rich man now raised his eyes, and on high, he saw Abraham gently holding Lazarus, the onetime beggar. And then he raised his voice as well, crying aloud: " 'Father Abraham, have pity on me, and send Lazarus to dip the tip of his finger in water and cool my tongue, for I am tormented in this flame.' But Abraham said to him: 'Son, remember that thou in thy lifetime hast received good things, and Lazarus in like manner evil things; but now here he is comforted whereas thou art tormented.' " The just Abraham points out the justice of their lot: since Dives has been declared "just in the sight of men" (Luke 16:15) because of his riches, and since his religion has resided entirely in them, he has been sufficiently rewarded; but since, on the other hand, "that which is exalted in the sight of men is an abomination before God," the same wealth becomes before God the cause of his suffering. The exact contrary befalls Lazarus for the reverse reason. After all, the destinies of the two men are immutable, and Abraham can do nothing even for one of his race who is not in Heaven with him: "And besides all that, between us and you a great gulf is fixed, so that they who wish to pass over from this side to you cannot, and they cannot cross from your side to us." Here, too, the inversion is complete and perfect: just as in life Dives would do nothing for Lazarus, now Lazarus can do nothing for him.

Yet even immersed in Sheol, Dives thinks of his relatives and desires that they may escape his destiny. And so he beseeches Abraham anew: "Then, Father, I beseech thee to send him [Lazarus] to my father's house, for I have five brothers, that he may testify to them, lest they too come into this place of torments." Abraham did not grant this request either but answered drily: "They have Moses and the Prophets, let them hearken to them!" That is, let them conduct themselves according to the canons of Moses and the Prophets preserved for them in the Holy Scriptures, and that will be enough to save them from the place of torment. "No, Father Abraham, but if someone from the dead goes to them, they will repent [change their minds]." Abraham rejects the reason and ends the discussion: "If they do not hearken to Moses and the Prophets, they will not believe even if someone rises from the dead."

In conclusion, the Hebrew Law not only is not abrogated; it is declared more efficacious than personal revelation from a dead man risen again. Besides, the spirit of the Law would use wealth as a ladder to ascend to God, but one is not to stop on the ladder itself. The Kingdom of God throws the ladder away altogether.

Chapter 15

∞

From the Last Journey through Judea to Passion Week

The Ten Lepers and the Coming of the Kingdom of God

Jesus had now come back into Judea from Transjordan and must have gone as far as Galilee when He came down for His last journey to Jerusalem.

At the beginning of this journey, at the entrance to a little village on the border between Samaria and Galilee, ten lepers came toward Him. Keeping a certain distance away as the Law commanded, they began to cry out to Him to have pity on them. Jesus, as on similar occasions, answered by telling them to go and present themselves to the priest. This was a promise of cure, and that is the way the lepers interpreted it. They set off obediently, and on their way they found that they were completely healed. Their joy made them forget the obligation of gratitude, and they promptly went about their own business — except one, a Samaritan, who, glorifying God, returned to thank Jesus. Jesus was pleased with his homage, observed that he alone had felt any gratitude, and declared it was his faith that had saved him.

Here Luke introduces the Pharisees again and records a discussion between them and Jesus, followed by a conversation between Jesus and His disciples. The conversation is elicited by a question of one of the Pharisees: "When is the kingdom of God coming?" (Luke 17:20). Was the query ironical, or did it allude seriously to the spectacular coming of the nationalistic-messianic kingdom? Jesus' answer would incline us to the second thought. He answered the questioner summarily, as one does with persons who are not disposed to be convinced: "The kingdom of God comes unawares. Neither will they say: 'Behold, here it is,' or 'Behold, there it is.' For behold the kingdom of God is within you." The last phrase meant "in the midst of you all" and not "within each one of you," for Jesus is pointing out that the Kingdom of God does not grow in any showy manner as the Pharisees expected, but "unawares"; in fact, it has already come among them. And Jesus said nothing further to His ill-disposed interlocutors.

It was an important subject, however, and He returned to it when He was alone with His disciples, to whom He said: "The days will come when you will long to see one day of the Son of Man, and will not see it." The days predicted here are days of calamity and want; then Jesus' disciples will desire "one day" of those when the Son of Man shall come "in power." Yet there will not be that longed-for day of manifest renewal and clear mastery over disaster. Instead there will be false rumors, against which Jesus warns them: "And they will say to you: 'Behold, here he is; behold, there he is'" — the Son of Man you yearn for, returning victorious; but do not believe them, "do not go, nor follow after" such directions. "For as the lightning when it lightens flashes from one end of the sky to the other, so will the Son of Man be in his day." Hence the Son of Man will surely come in triumph to complete the consummation of the messianic kingdom, but "his day" will be sudden and unexpected like the bolts of Heaven and no one will be able to foresee it. Besides, His triumph is to be preceded by His suffering: "But first he must suffer many things and be rejected by this generation" (Luke 17:25).

Since the coming of the Son of Man is certain but the time unknown, His disciples must be always ready and never yield to negligence: "And as it came to pass in the days of Noe, even so it will be in the days of the Son of Man. They were eating and drinking, they were marrying and giving in marriage, until the day when Noe entered the ark, and the flood came and destroyed them all. Or as it came to pass in the days of Lot.... In the same wise will it be on the day that the Son of Man is revealed." Hence on the day of the Son of Man many will be thinking of everything except Him and His triumph. These will be stubbornly attached to the world that now envelops them, and they will not notice that the new world is at hand. "On that day, he who is on the housetop, having his goods in the house, let him not descend to take them away; and let him likewise who is in the field not turn back. Remember Lot's wife! Whoever attempts to save his life shall lose it, and whoever loses shall save it alive." Hence the glorious advent of the Son of Man demands detachment from everything, even one's own life, that one may immediately follow the victor when He suddenly appears. This detachment is to be the criterion of selection among those who shall follow Him: "I say to you, on that night there will be two on one bed; one will be taken, and the other will be left. Two women will be grinding together; one will be taken, and the other will be left."

But where will those taken go? Evidently to the victorious Son of Man. The disciples ask Jesus: "Where, Lord?" Jesus does not answer this; He simply points out that the chosen will gather naturally about the Victor from all the corners of the world, with the same swiftness with which the eagles gather over a body: "Wherever the body is, there will the eagles be gathered together."

To sum up the dialogue, Jesus spoke of the Kingdom of God both to the Pharisees and to His disciples. To the Pharisees He declared that the kingdom is a fact, neither clamorous nor dazzling, but a reality nevertheless and already present among them. To His disciples Jesus spoke of a new coming of the Son of Man, which would bring about His triumph and the end of the messianic kingdom; it is to be sudden and unforeseen, and since it will determine the lot of the elect and the damned, all must keep themselves ready by absolute detachment from every present good.

The Godless Judge; the Pharisee and the Publican

The preceding dialogue had certain echoes. Its words, as regarded earthly prospects, were of darksome hue through which one glimpsed, beyond the final suffering and the rejection of the Master, those days of calamity when the disciples would yearn in vain to see just one of the days of triumph of the Son of Man. But if the disciples prayed in those days of trial, would they not be heard? Would the trial not be shortened? Would God not render justice to His elect, anticipating a little the final victory of the Son of Man?

Yes, certainly; Jesus expressed this in a parable very similar to that of the persistent friend and given us only by Luke (18:1–8). "And he also told them a parable — that they must always pray and not lose heart."

There was in a certain city a judge who had no fear of God or respect for anyone. In the same city lived a poor widow who constantly suffered abuse from a certain individual. Every now and then she went to the judge and besought him: "Do me justice against my adversary!" For some time the judge ignored her, but finally, irritated by her insistence, he reasoned thus with himself: "Although I do not fear God, nor even respect man, yet because this widow bothers me, I will do her justice, lest by her continual coming she finally wear me out." And Jesus concluded: "Hear what the unjust judge says, and will not even God avenge his elect, who cry to him day and night? And will he be slow to act in their case? I tell you that he will avenge them quickly. Yet when the Son of Man comes, will he find, do you think, faith on the earth?"

This last sentence seems to refer to the times in which the disciples will long in vain to see one day of the Son of Man. Those times will be so difficult that the confidence of many will be shaken (cf. Matt. 24:12; Mark 13:22) so that it may well be asked if the "Son of Man will find ... faith on the earth."

The parable of the widow led to another on the nature and spiritual disposition of prayer. This parable, too, is recorded only by Luke (18:9–14), and its characters are a Pharisee and a publican, the two extremes of the Jewish scale of moral values. Jesus addressed the parable to "some who trusted in themselves as being just and despised others."

A Pharisee and a publican go up to the Temple at the same hour to pray. The Pharisee acts and thinks in the full confidence that he is a just man. He proceeds as close as he can to the "sanctuary" where dwells the God of his nation and of his sect. That God is a powerful being, but He has a particular fondness for him, just man and scrupulous Pharisee that he is, and so he can treat Him with some familiarity. He can speak to Him as his king, but in the manner of a subject come to enumerate a series of handsome things that he has done in His service. In fact, standing there (the Hebrews generally prayed standing), he began his catalogue of virtues: "O God, I thank thee that I am not like the rest of men, robbers, dishonest, adulterers, or even like this publican. I fast twice a week, I pay tithes of all I possess." The parable does not continue the list, but it may well have gone on to include any number of other choice virtues, like the washing of hands and dishes before meals and knowing by heart the 613 precepts of the Torah. In short, the man's prayer has been nothing more than an account of the benefits he has bestowed on God.

The publican, meanwhile, conscious of the scorn decreed him by all good Jews and certain that God shared the same feeling, has stopped just within the entrance of the "court of the Israelites," like a barely tolerated beggar. There, afar off, without even daring to lift his eyes toward the "sanctuary," he stands and strikes his breast, imploring: "O God, be merciful to me the sinner!" This is the whole prayer of the man the rabbis defined as a "boor," because he knows that he cannot give God anything like what the Pharisee is giving Him. Hence, he trusts in God's mercy, confessing himself a sinner with deep humility.

The contrast between these two men directly belied the judgment each had passed upon himself. For Jesus concluded: "I tell you this man [the publican] went back to his home justified rather than the other; for everyone who exalts himself shall be humbled, and he who humbles himself shall be exalted."

The Question of Divorce; Jesus Blesses the Little Children

The Pharisees meanwhile approached Jesus and posed the following question: "Is it lawful for a man to put away his wife for any cause?" (Matt. 19:3). The evangelist warns us that they came to test Him. In the Mosaic Law divorce was permitted only to the husband as follows: "If a man take a wife, and have her, and she find not favor in his eyes for some uncleanness, he shall write a bill of divorce, and shall give it in her hand, and send her out of his house" (Deut. 24:1). The wife so divorced could marry again, but if this second marriage came to an end — either through the death of her new husband or another divorce — the first husband could not take her back again (Deut. 24:2–4). The rabbis were proud of this faculty of divorce and considered it a special prerogative granted by God only to the people of Israel. But differences arose when they tried to determine sufficient cause for divorce, described in the Law only as "some uncleanness" that the husband discovered in the wife. One school took "some uncleanness" in a moral sense to mean adultery; another school referred it to anything annoying in family or social life, for example, allowing a husband's dinner to burn.

It is hard to say whether the Pharisees who proposed the question to Jesus were of one school or the other. Their words, "Is it lawful ... *for any cause?*" suggest the laxer teaching, but are they an invitation to accept this doctrine or a warning to reject it?

As on other occasions, Christ goes back to the very origin of the question. "But he answered and said to them: Have you not read that the Creator, from the beginning, made them male and female, and said, 'For this cause a man shall leave his father and mother, and cleave to his wife, and the two shall become one flesh?' Therefore now they are no longer two, but one flesh. What therefore God has joined together, let no man put asunder" (Matt. 19:4–7). The answer, and especially its conclusion, studies the institution of marriage at its very source, which antedates even the Law of Moses; the double quotation from Genesis calls God Himself, the author of matrimony, to witness, and the conclusion is simply "what God has joined together let no man put asunder."

The Pharisees' reply was easy to foresee: "Why then did Moses command to give a written notice of dismissal, and to put her away?" Was divorce not a privilege of the Israelites? Had it not been regulated by the very Law of Moses? If Jesus' norm, "let no man put asunder," was valid, it meant the renunciation of the privilege of divorce, and this, for the Pharisees, was absurd.

Jesus answers the legal difficulty by correcting their views. This was not a privilege but a concession forced by the dispositions of those to whom it was granted for fear they might do worse. "He said to them: 'Because Moses, by reason of the hardness of your heart, permitted you to put away your wives; but it was not so from the beginning.'" Again the question is brought back to its source. This passage in Matthew is followed by another substantially parallel to one in his report of the Sermon on the Mount.

(Matt. 19:9)	(Sermon on the Mount, Matt. 5:32)
And I say to you that whoever puts away his wife, except for immorality,	But I say to you that everyone who puts away his wife, save on account of immorality, causes her to commit adultery;
except for immorality,	and he who marries a woman who has been put away
commits adultery.	commits adultery.

The same judgment occurs in the other two Synoptics, where, however, the restrictive phrase, "except for immorality," "save on account of immorality," is wanting:

(Mark 10:11–12)	(Luke 16:18)
Whoever puts away his wife and marries another, commits adultery against her;	Everyone who puts away his wife and marries another, commits adultery;
and if the wife puts away her husband and marries another, she commits adultery.	and he who marries a woman who has been put away from her husband commits adultery.

To these two Synoptics we must add the testimony of St. Paul, which is even earlier than the primitive Christian catechesis. He writes: "To the married, however, I command — indeed not I, but the Lord — that the wife shall not separate from her husband (but even if she does separate let her remain unmarried, or else be reconciled to her husband) and that the husband shall not divorce his wife" (1 Cor. 7:10–11). Here St. Paul clearly distinguishes between separation and divorce; he admits the possibility of the first, provided the wife does not contract a second marriage, but he simply denies the lawfulness of the second.

We have, therefore, two groups of testimonies representing the earliest catechesis: one is that of Matthew, whose testimony is repeated twice (5:32; 19:9), and the other that of Mark, Luke, and Paul. The first group contains the restrictive phrase "except for immorality," and the second does not. Is there any contradiction between the two? Matthew's text, with its special difficulty, seems to have more faithfully preserved Jesus' words. But what is the real meaning of the phrase in question?

We must remember that the Pharisees have asked Jesus if it is "lawful for a man to put away his wife for any cause" referring, unquestionably, to the Hebrew divorce. In answer, Jesus states that she may be put away only in the case of "immorality" (adultery). This represents a twofold departure from Hebrew legislation: in the first place, in Hebrew Law the adulteress was threatened with death, not with divorce; in the second, He does not permit the man who has put away his wife because of adultery to marry anyone else, in complete accord with the principle He has just enunciated that "what God has joined together let no man put asunder." Hence, even if His questioners did have in mind the actual Hebrew divorce, Jesus has not granted its possibility even in the case of adultery, because the husband cannot remarry and so is not divorced. Jesus has not granted "divorce" but separation. Could the Jews make this distinction?

Whatever may have been their purely legal concepts in this regard, it is certain that in practice married couples did "separate" while still remaining husband and wife. The passage cited from St. Paul proves this. But stronger than these considerations is the fact, first, that Mark and Luke omit the restrictive phrase altogether precisely because the early catechesis considered it did not at all affect the indissolubility of marriage or favor the Hebrew divorce; and, second, Jesus' disciples, of pure Hebrew mentality, fully appreciated the inflexibility of the canon He set forth.

In fact, after the discussion with the Pharisees, the disciples returned to the painful subject (some of them, like Peter, were married) (Mark 10:10), and a spontaneous exclamation burst from their hearts: "If the case of a man with his wife is so, it is not expedient to marry!" They had thoroughly understood the uncompromising nature of Jesus' ruling. Now, according to His words, a man must consider himself irrevocably bound to his wife even though she had committed adultery against him. Their Jewish minds were disturbed; Jesus was certainly right, but in that case they thought it better not to marry at all.

Far from tempering His previous words, Jesus deemed the exclamation of the disconcerted disciples too general a statement; it could be applied to some but not to everyone. Some will be able to repeat the exclamation with free full conscious acceptance, and these are the privileged ones; others repeat it through some necessity imposed on them by nature or human society, hence out of compulsion; others do not repeat it at all, and these marry. Jesus is not concerned with the latter, for He wishes to show the disciples the merits of celibacy freely chosen for a religious motive. "Not all can accept this teaching; but those to whom it has been given. For there are eunuchs who were born so from their mother's womb; and there are eunuchs who were made so by men; and there are eunuchs who have made themselves so for the kingdom of heaven's sake. Let him accept it who can!" Hence this is not a law binding on all. It is a suggestion with certain advantages in the pursuit of the "kingdom of heaven"; it is offered only to those who "can" accept it and it can be accepted only by those "to whom it has been given [to accept it]." The rest are to act freely and marry if they wish, always on condition, however, that what God has joined together no man may put asunder.

In short, Jesus has in no sense condemned marriage, but He has brought it back to its original purpose and norm, though subordinating it to virginity freely chosen for the Kingdom of God. A proof of this is the fact that immediately after the discussion on matrimony, Matthew and Mark narrate the welcome Jesus gave the little children who are the fruit of that very institution of marriage that He has just pruned of deadwood and parasitic growths. He receives them with delighted warmth, showing a particular love for these little innocents.

"And they were bringing little children to him that he might touch them; but the disciples rebuked those who brought them. But when Jesus saw them, he was indignant, and said to them: 'Let the little children come to me, and do not hinder them, for of such is the kingdom of God. Amen I say to you, whoever does not accept the kingdom of God as a little child will not enter into it.' And he put his arms about them, and laying his hands upon them, he began to bless them" (Mark 10:13–16).

Among these "little children" there were undoubtedly both boys and girls, and Jesus put His arms around them all with equal affection. About thirty years before this incident, in the year 1 BC, an Egyptian peasant working away from home wrote his wife, with child when he left her, a letter preserved for us among recently discovered papyri. It closes with this admonition to the mother-to-be: "When you have brought forth the child, if it is a male, raise it; if it is a female, kill it." Nor was that peasant any different from so many other fathers in Egypt and elsewhere.

The Rich Young Man; the Danger of Riches

As Jesus started to leave the place where the little children had been brought to Him, a young man came hurrying up and, falling to his knees before Him, asked: " 'Good Master, what shall I do to gain eternal life?' But Jesus said to him:

'Why dost thou call me good? No one is good but God only'" (Mark 10:17–18). These words, confirmed by Luke, are recorded somewhat differently in Matthew 19:16, 17; for it was feared that the statement as reported in Mark and Luke would cause scandal since it might be interpreted as a denial of Jesus' goodness and divinity. But precisely because it is more difficult, it is more probable that the text as given in Mark and Luke is the oldest and most exact.

If we consider for a moment the circumstances in which the words were spoken, they are easily explained. The epithet "Good Master" was never used in addressing rabbis, not even the most prominent of them, for it seemed an exaggerated piece of flattery. But the young man, who had seen Jesus put His arms around the children and fondle them, calls Him "good" in the human sense rather than the academic or philosophic one, and Jesus takes occasion to offer him the means to deepen his acquaintance with the Master he is now addressing. Coming down to the young man's own level, as He had done with the Samaritan woman (John 4:22), He says in substance: You call me "master" as you would any doctor of the Law, and in addition you call me "good." "Why do you give me this title? Do you not know that it is commonly reserved for God?" The young man could have answered: "But You are the Son of God!" Instead he did not answer at all.

Since the young man made no reply, Jesus went on to satisfy his question: "But if thou wilt enter into life, keep the commandments." And the young man asked: "Which?" And Jesus, confirming again the Hebrew Law, recited for him the Ten Commandments: "Thou shalt not kill; thou shalt not commit adultery ..." In wonder, the young man answered: "But I have observed all these since I was a boy. I should like to know if something is still lacking to me." At this confident and eager response, according to Mark (10:21), "Jesus, looking upon him, loved him," and then He said to him: "You lack one thing. If you wish to be perfect, go, sell all your goods and distribute the proceeds to the poor, for thus you will have treasure in Heaven; and then follow me!" With this invitation, the whole picture changes. The young man suddenly went cold and was "much grieved" (Luke 18:23), because he was very rich. And gloomily he went away.

The bitter proposal that he give up his goods had been sweetened by the promise of treasure in Heaven, but the young man could not taste the sweet and the bitter seemed very, very strong. He was unquestionably a good young man, but his was an ordinary and down-to-earth kind of goodness, whereas Jesus had warned His followers that at any moment they might have to become giants of heroism. He would have made an excellent official for the Roman

Empire, but he failed his first examination for high office in the Kingdom of Heaven.

When the young man had gone off, Jesus commented on his reaction for the disciples:

> "With what difficulty will they who have riches enter the kingdom of God!" He exclaimed. But the disciples were amazed at his word. But Jesus addressed them, saying: "Children, with what difficulty will they who trust in riches enter the kingdom of God! It is easier for a camel to pass through the eye of a needle, than for a rich man to enter the kingdom of God." But they were astonished the more, saying among themselves: "Who then can be saved?" And looking upon them, Jesus said: "With men it is impossible, but not with God; for all things are possible with God." (Mark 10:23–27)

The simile of the camel is typically Oriental. The interpretations that would have it that the Greek word for "camel" was mistakenly substituted for the similar word for a thick rope or that "the eye of a needle" referred to some narrow and pointed gate in the walls of Jerusalem are unfounded. Jesus is speaking of a real camel and the eye of a real needle. Jesus used the simile to suggest not a great difficulty but an impossibility. The rich man cannot enter into the Kingdom of God simply because a man cannot serve both God and mammon.

Can no rich man, then, ever enter the Kingdom of God? Yes; he may enter it provided that he becomes poor, either in fact or "in spirit." But this change is *humanly* impossible, because men will always prefer the tangible gold of earth to the intangible treasure of Heaven. However, "with men it is impossible, but not with God," and God will accomplish the miracle whereby a rich man may prefer the far-off treasure to the gold at hand.

These ideas were not new, for Jesus had already set them forth both in the Sermon on the Mount and in His recent discussion on wealth with the Pharisees. The new element is the statement that the abandonment of wealth for admission into the Kingdom of God will be the fruit not of human effort but of God's power.

The apostles applied these words to themselves and found they had the advantage over all other men. It is Peter, as usual, who interprets their feelings and says to Jesus: "Behold, we have left all and followed thee." They had willingly and gladly become poor for Jesus and the Kingdom of Heaven, thereby fulfilling the conditions He had just laid down. Then there follows a question recorded for us by one Synoptic only: "What then shall we have?" (Matt.

19:27). Jesus' answer was directed both to the apostles who were His particular followers and collaborators and to all His other followers present and future.

The part that applies to the apostles is recorded here only by Matthew (19:28); Mark omits it and Luke (22:28–30) sets it among the discussions at the Last Supper. The part addressed to Jesus' other followers is reported by all three Synoptics, but in Mark and Luke a distinction is made in the time for the fulfillment of its separate parts.

To the apostles Jesus said: "Amen I say to you that you who have followed me, in the regeneration, when the Son of Man shall sit on the throne of his glory, shall also sit on twelve thrones, judging the twelve tribes of Israel." This will happen at the "regeneration" or the new birth, which will renew the present "world." Then, the Son of Man will sit upon the "throne of glory," which the rabbis reserved for God, with the twelve apostles on lesser thrones beside Him; and with them He will judge the "twelve tribes" of Israel to whom He had directed His personal ministry. This solemn assembly of judgment will close the present "world" and inaugurate the "world to come."

Jesus' promise to His other followers reads as follows in Mark (10:29–31): "Amen I say to you, there is no one who has left house, or brothers, or sisters, or mother, or father, or children, or land, for my sake and for the gospel's sake, who shall not receive now in the present time a hundredfold as much, houses, and brothers, and sisters, and mothers, and children, and lands — along with persecutions, and in the age to come life everlasting." Here the reward is not associated with the solemn judgment of the twelve tribes, but it is clearly divided into two parts. The second will be had in the "world to come" and will consist of "everlasting life"; the first is to be had "now in the present time." In other words, Jesus' followers are promised in the present world a hundredfold as much as what they have left for Him. This "hundredfold" certainly refers primarily to spiritual goods; but from the viewpoint of history, we will find that even in material goods the early Christians received ample compensation for those they had foresworn. From the Acts and various epistles we learn that the Christians of widely separated communities felt bound together by ties of charity so strong that they felt fully repaid, even in the matter of affection, for the bonds they had broken to follow Christ.

The Laborers in the Vineyard

What is to be the basis for the distribution of these promised rewards to Jesus' followers? He Himself gave the answer in a new parable, this, too, based on the farm life of Palestine.

At the first signs of spring there is a great deal to be done in the vineyards, pruning, weeding, and so forth, before the vines begin to bud. Hence there are several weeks of intense labor when all the husbandmen are looking for help. Now, the Kingdom of Heaven is like the owner of a vineyard, who at this season went out early in the morning in search of workers. He found some in the marketplace, and having agreed to pay them a silver denarius (a little more than twenty cents) for the day, he sent them into his vineyard. Around the third hour, or about nine o'clock in the morning, he again went to the marketplace where he saw other laborers standing idle. So he said to them: You also go into my vineyard, and I shall pay you what is just. Then he went out about the sixth and ninth hours (toward noon and three in the afternoon), and finding some idle laborers still there, he sent them also into his vineyard promising them a just wage. At the eleventh hour, or an hour before sunset, he went out once more, and still finding men standing there idle, he said to them: "But why have you stood here all the day idle?" And they answered: "Because no one has hired us." Then the owner said: "Well, do you go also into my vineyard." At sunset, he said to his steward: "Call the laborers and pay them, beginning with the last to arrive and proceeding backwards to the first." So the steward called all those hired last and gave each of them a silver denarius. When the other laborers, who were eying the paymaster, saw that the last to come were paid so generously, they began to hope they would be paid off with proportionate liberality. But as their turn came, those of the ninth and the sixth and the third hours all received the same amount; even those hired in the early morning got only one silver denarius. Disappointed, they began to grumble, saying: "How is this? The last to come have worked hardly an hour and that when it was cool, and you have treated them like us who have borne the whole burden of the day and the heat?" But the owner replied: "Friend, I do you no wrong. Did we not agree on one denarius a day? I have given it to you, so go your way. If I want to give the last worker who came as much as I have given you, can I then not do what I please with my money? Or am I not permitted to be generous with your colleagues just because you are envious of my generosity?" And Jesus closed the parable saying: "Even so the last shall be first, and the first last."

In general, the moral of this parable is that God showers His generosity on whom and in what manner He wills, and that the final reward of Jesus' followers will be essentially the same for all. The hired men do not strictly parallel the souls rewarded in the Kingdom of Heaven, for the latter certainly do not grumble, or accuse Him who has rewarded them of partiality, or feel envy toward others. But historically they do represent those followers of Jesus who considered themselves for any reason whatever more adorned with merits than the rest, and especially those Jews of pure intention but strictly Judaic mentality who still believed themselves more acceptable to God because they belonged to the chosen nation. He is teaching that all such priorities are to disappear and that in His generosity the King may send the last to the first places so that those who were first will become last.

The Resurrection of Lazarus

About two months had passed since the feast of the Dedication and it must have been now about the end of February or the beginning of March of the year 30. In His travels down from the borders of Galilee, Jesus must have neared the Jordan and followed for a stretch the road to Jerusalem that flanked the river. It seems that at a certain point He crossed the river into Transjordan and stayed there a while, perhaps in the same favorite spot to which He had withdrawn after the Dedication.

There sad news reached Him from Bethany, the village of Mary and Martha. Their brother Lazarus, who may have been ill at the time of Jesus' last visit, had grown much worse and lay in imminent danger of death. Though the two sisters remained at home caring for the sick man, they had kept more or less informed of Jesus' travels, and having learned that He was now only about a day's walk from Bethany, they sent Him word of their brother's condition. Confident in the affection He bore them, they hoped He would come immediately to their aid and by His very presence prevent their brother's death. John (11:3) relates the sisters' message and Jesus' reaction as follows: "The sisters therefore sent to him, saying: 'Lord, behold, he whom thou lovest is sick.' But when Jesus heard this, he said to them: 'This sickness is not unto death, but for the glory of God, that through it the Son of God may be glorified.' Now Jesus loved Martha and her sister Mary, and Lazarus."

We might expect that this love that the evangelist mentions especially would have sped Jesus on His way to the friends, but instead the account continues: "So when he heard that he was sick, he remained two more days in the same place. Then afterwards he said to his disciples: 'Let us go again into Judea.'"

From where Jesus was now staying, to go into Judea meant to go to Jerusalem or its environs, right into the lair of His enemies. The disciples thought immediately of the danger and reminded Him of it: "Rabbi, just now the Jews were seeking to stone thee; and dost thou go there again?" In Jesus' answer we find once more the themes that John sought out and recorded with particular care: "Jesus answered: are there not twelve hours in the day? If a man walks in the day, he does not stumble, because he sees the light of this world. But if he walks in the night, he stumbles, because the light is not in him." The twelve hours of Jesus' mortal day were not yet finished although the evening was drawing near. He, the light of this world, was to finish His walk to the last hour, nor could His enemies work Him any harm on the way, for their hour was not yet come; the hour of their mastery would be the hour of darkness.

Then Jesus continued: "Lazarus, our friend, sleeps. But I go that I may wake him from sleep." The disciples answered confidently: "Lord, if he sleeps, he will be safe." Medicine at that time, in fact, considered deep sleep a sign that the body was reacting against the sickness. Here was another reason, then, for not going into Judea to visit Lazarus now, in order not to disturb him. "So then Jesus said to them plainly: 'Lazarus is dead; and I rejoice on your account that I was not there, that you may believe. But let us go to him.'"

The disciples were thunderstruck by the news of Lazarus's death, nor did they even suspect Jesus' real intentions. Since the worst had befallen and there was nothing more to be done, why should they go into Judea, into that den of chief priests and Pharisees? The disciples did not relish the idea of the journey at all, and they hesitated between their fear of the Pharisees and their respect for Jesus. On the other hand, the Master seemed determined to go. Therefore, they had to go with Him even at the cost of losing their lives. The apostle Thomas was the one who spoke the words of persuasion though he made no secret of his own misgivings: "Let us also go, that we may die with him!" So they all set out for Bethany, arriving there at the end of the day. But here we must listen to John.

> Jesus therefore came and found him [Lazarus] already four days in the tomb. Now ... many of the Jews had come to Martha and Mary, to comfort them on account of their brother. When, therefore, Martha heard that Jesus was coming, she went to meet him: But Mary remained at home. Martha therefore said to Jesus: "Lord, if thou hadst been here my brother would not have died. But even now I know that whatever thou shalt ask of God, God will give it to thee."
>
> Jesus said to her: "Thy brother shall rise." Martha said to him: "I know that he will rise at the resurrection, on the last day." Jesus said to her: "I am the resurrection and the life; he who believes in me, even if he die, shall live; and whoever lives and believes in me, shall never die.

Dost thou believe this?" She said to him: "Yes, Lord, I believe that thou art the Christ, the Son of God [the one who comes] into the world."

And when she had said this, she went away and quietly called Mary her sister, saying: "The Master is here and calls thee." As soon as she heard this, she rose quickly and came to him....

When, therefore, the Jews who were with her in the house and were comforting her, saw Mary rise up quickly and go out, they followed her, saying: "She is going to the tomb to weep there."

When, therefore, Mary came where Jesus was, and saw him, she fell at his feet, and said to him: "Master, if thou hadst been here, my brother would not have died." When, therefore, Jesus saw her weeping, he groaned in spirit and was troubled.

We may well suspend the narrative here for a few considerations. By the ancient highway, Bethany was truly "close to Jerusalem," some three thousand yards (today the village stretches farther way, toward the east). Since it was so near Jerusalem, many Jews had come from the city to express their sympathy for the distinguished family of the dead man, as social convention required.

Among the Jews, a person was buried on the day he died. It was commonly thought that the soul of the deceased lingered around the body for three days hoping to be able to enter it again, but on the fourth, when decay began to set in, it departed from it forever.

The family of the deceased received visits of condolence for seven days, but these were more numerous during the first three. The visitors first expressed their grief with the usual Oriental noisiness — weeping, moaning, wailing, and tearing their garments; then they sat on the ground and stayed awhile in gloomy silence.

When Jesus arrived, Martha and Mary were surrounded by such visitors. John calls them "Jews," which is his usual term for Jesus' adversaries, and that is exactly what some of them proved to be.

Martha, whom we have already met as lady of the house, went to meet Jesus first, and then came Mary followed by the visitors. When He had exchanged a few words of greeting with the sisters and seen all those people crying, Jesus "groaned in spirit and was troubled," as true man, with a real heart in His breast, who deeply feels all human loves and sorrows.

Then He asked:

"Where have you laid him?" They said to him: "Lord, come and see." And Jesus wept. The Jews therefore said: "See how he loved him." But some of them said: "Could not he who opened the eyes of the blind, have caused that this man should not die?"

Jesus therefore, again groaning in himself, came to the tomb. Now it was a cave, and a stone was laid against it. Jesus said: "Take away the stone." Martha, the sister of him who was dead, said to him: "Lord, by this time he is already decayed for he is dead four days." Jesus said to her: "Have I not told thee that if thou believe thou shalt behold the glory of God?" They therefore removed the stone. And Jesus, raising his eyes, said: "Father, I give thee thanks that thou hast heard me. Yet I knew that thou always hearest me; but because of the people who stand around, I spoke, that they may believe that thou hast sent me." When he had said this, he cried out with a loud voice: "Lazarus, come forth!" And at once he who had been dead came forth, bound feet and hands with bandages, and his face was tied with a cloth. Jesus said to them: "Unbind him, and let him go."

In Palestine at the time of Jesus, tombs were situated either on the outskirts of inhabited places or not far from them. In the level places those of more prominent persons were usually dug into the rock like a grave; in hilly regions they were hollowed out of it like a cave. They consisted of a burial chamber with one or two niches for the bodies and often a little vestibule before the chamber itself. The narrow doorway between the two was always open, while the outside entrance to the vestibule was shut with a huge stone. After the body had been washed and anointed with spices, it was wound in bandages or wrapped in a sheet and laid in its niche in the burial chamber. Hence it was exposed to the air inside, and it is easy to imagine how after three or four days the interior of the tomb would be tainted with the odors of the decaying body, the spices notwithstanding.

Today, on the site of ancient Bethany, there is a tomb that a tradition, attested in the fourth century, identifies as that of Lazarus. It is certainly a typical Palestinian sepulcher, but it is difficult now to form a correct idea of its relation to the original terrain because of the modifications the whole place has undergone throughout the centuries.

Whether or not this is the tomb of Lazarus, John's narrative is strictly faithful both to Palestinian burial customs and to archaeological data from that region. Nor is the narrative any less faithful to the psychology of the Jews both during the incident and immediately afterward. During it, some of the Jews object that Jesus did not prevent Lazarus's death although He

Entrance to the tomb of Lazarus

had restored the sight of the blind man in Jerusalem. Afterward, there was a division of opinion among them, as our eyewitness relates: "Many therefore of the Jews who had come to Mary, and had seen what he did, believed in him. But some of them went away to the Pharisees, and told them the things that Jesus had done."

Jesus in Ephrem and Jericho

The prominent Jews of Jerusalem took the denunciation of Jesus' resuscitation of Lazarus very seriously. The Pharisees became anxious and turned to the chief priests for a decision. A council was called, to which no doubt came many members of the Sanhedrin. And the question was stated: "What are we doing? for this man is working many signs. If we let him alone all will believe in him, and the Romans will come and take away both our [holy] place and our nation." They did not discuss the reality of Jesus' miracles, nor did they discuss Jesus Himself at all. The Roman masters of Palestine were beginning to be annoyed by the interminable procession of subversive wonder-workers that had been cropping up for a long time, and perhaps this Galilean Jesus would be the one to provoke the extreme severity that would end the procession forever. It was easy to foresee what would happen. Jesus would continue to work His miracles; the people would flock to Him and proclaim Him king of Israel. The Roman cohorts stationed in Palestine and eventually the legions of Syria would fall upon the rebels; the result would be first a massacre of the Jews and then the destruction of the "[holy] place" and the entire "nation." The danger was grave. Some measure must be decided upon immediately.

Caiphas, then high priest, after listening a while to various remedies being proposed, expressed his opinion with all the imperiousness permitted by his office: "You know nothing at all; nor do you reflect that it is expedient for us that one man die for the people, instead of the whole nation perishing." Caiphas had not named anyone, but they all understood: the "one man" to die "for the nation" was Jesus. True, He was not inciting the populace nor had He ever paid any attention whatever to matters political; true, He was innocent, as some of those present had probably just pointed out. But what did that matter? If He died, the whole nation would escape ruin, and that was reason enough for Him to die. In saying this, Caiphas had spoken as a politician and for the interests of the Sadducean sacerdotal class, which here fully coincided with those of the Pharisees. But the evangelist sees in his words a much deeper meaning and he observes: "This, however, he said not of himself; but being high priest that year, he prophesied that Jesus was to die for the nation; and not only for the nation, but that he might gather into one the children of God who were scattered abroad."

The phrase, "being high priest that year," has been warrant for accusing the evangelist of not knowing that the office of high priest was not an annual one. This is by no means a rare piece of information, for any reader of the Old Testament knew very well the office was for life, although in Jesus' time — as we have seen— a high priest rarely lasted that long. Hence, John, mindful of the prevailing abuse, merely wants to specify that in the solemn year of Christ's death Caiphas was the lawful high priest and as such pronounced the words that bore a much deeper significance than he intended.

The council decided to act on Caiphas's suggestion: "So from that day forth their plan was to put him to death."

The apostles, or Jesus Himself, were probably told of the decision by some kindly person who learned of it. And Jesus withdrew with His disciples from the district of Jerusalem to "a town called Ephrem," about twenty miles north of Jerusalem on the edge of the desert.

It was Jesus' custom to withdraw to lonely places on the eve of important events in His mission.

He did not stay at Ephrem many days. The Pasch was drawing near, and the first companies of pilgrims were beginning to travel up toward the Holy

City, where His arrival, too, was awaited from moment to moment. In any case, to make sure the council's deliberation would not be confined to wishful thinking, "the chief priests and Pharisees had given orders that, if anyone knew where he was, he should report it, so that they might seize him" (John 11:57).

Despite these orders, Jesus left His retreat at Ephrem at the beginning of the month Nisan of the year 30 and set out for Jerusalem along the road that followed the Jordan and passed by way of Jericho. The disciples sensed tragedy, and they walked slowly and reluctantly, though ahead of them strode the Master, betraying no reluctance whatever: "They were now on their way, going up to Jerusalem; and Jesus was walking on in front of them, and they were in dismay, and those who followed were afraid" (Mark 10:32).

At a certain point Jesus beckoned the twelve apostles to Him and "began to tell them what would happen to him, saying: Behold, we are going up to Jerusalem, and the Son of Man will be betrayed to the chief priests and the Scribes; and they will condemn him to death, and will deliver him to the Gentiles; and they will mock him, and spit upon him, and scourge him, and put him to death; and on the third day he will rise again." The prediction was not new, but under the circumstances it was well to recall it to their minds. Since the time was drawing so close when Jesus would be made manifest to the world as the Messiah, it was an opportune moment to remind His followers of the correct concept of His messianism. But this time, too, the corrective bore little fruit. Luke (18:34) patiently tells us that the Twelve "understood none of these things and this saying was hidden from them, neither did they get to know the things that were being said."

How thick and heavy their incomprehension was is evidenced in a little scene that follows immediately.

Among those who "understood none" of His prediction were the brothers James and John, the sons of Zebedee. In the group following at a distance was their mother, who was perhaps one of the good housewives who provided for the material needs of Jesus' helpers. The two young men must have told their mother of Jesus' announcement, and all three commented on it in the rosiest and most mistaken fashion. They probably spoke of the Messiah as ruler of a throne and a court and courtiers, and of the other dreams dear to political messianism. And since the time was getting short, they considered it expedient to do something toward securing good places for themselves. That is why, in a little while, the mother, accompanied by her two sons, presented herself in all reverence before Jesus to ask Him a question. It is so important to them that they all talk at once and interrupt one another, so that while Matthew

(20:20ff.) attributes the question to the mother, Mark (10:35ff.) assigns it to the sons: Now that Jesus is about to found His kingdom, He must not overlook these two good young men. They have always loved Him very much, and for love of Him they have left their homes and their father's boats. Will Jesus please be grateful and in His messianic court assign them to the places on the right and on the left of His throne? The mother asks nothing for herself, but she hopes before she dies to have the consolation of seeing her two fine sons in positions of honor beside the glorious Messiah.

They have finished speaking. Jesus looks long at all three, and then with infinite patience, He says to the youths: "You do not know what you are asking for. Can you drink of the cup which I drink, or be baptized with the baptism with which I am to be baptized?" The glory of the Messiah will come, yes, but first He must drink a chalice and receive a "baptism" that fulfill the tragic prediction He has just given His apostles: before the life of glory there will be an ignominious death, and can they face it? The young men, with the fearlessness of the confident, answer, "We can!" Jesus unexpectedly agrees with them, but He refuses their request: Yes, yes, you will drink of my chalice and receive my baptism, but it is not in my power to give you the places on the right or the left; they will belong to those for whom they have been prepared by my heavenly Father.

The other apostles learned of the ambitious request and could not contain their jealous indignation against those who had made it, thereby betraying that they, too, shared the ambition. Jesus gathered them all about Him again to admonish them and once more turned their notions upside down: among the pagans the rulers lord it over the rest and make them feel the weight of their authority, but among the followers of Jesus whoever wishes to be greater than the rest must become less, and whoever wishes to be first must be the slave of all in imitation of Jesus, who "has not come to be served but to serve, and to give his life as a ransom [from slavery] for many" (Matt. 20:25–28). Jesus had pictured Himself as the good shepherd who serves His flock and gives His life for them; here He returns to the latter concept and declares He gives His life as a "ransom" from slavery for His many followers. This is the teaching that St. Paul later emphasizes so much.

Now Jesus arrived in Jericho. The aristocratic city of those times was a place of delight and diversion especially in the winter, for there Herod the Great had indulged his passion for building, and so, to a lesser extent, had his son Archelaus. But the site of this city was not that of the ancient Jericho of the Canaanites, the ruins of which lay almost two miles to the north near the

Vicinity of Jericho

fountain of Eliseus. However, the proximity of the precious fountain brought many people there and in time gave rise to a cluster of dwellings, which in Jesus' time formed a kind of suburb to the Jericho of His day.

Anyone coming from the north, as Jesus was, first had to pass through this suburb near the site of ancient Jericho, and after about a half hour's walk reached the Herodian city at the entrance to the narrow valley through which lay the road to Jerusalem. At this point an incident occurred that is related with interesting discrepancies by the three Synoptics (Matt. 20:29ff.; Mark 10:46ff., Luke 18:35ff.).

According to Matthew and Mark the episode took place when Jesus had left Jericho, and according to Luke, when He was approaching it. In Mark and Luke, it is one blind man who is cured, whom Mark calls "Bartimeus ... son of Timeus," while according to Matthew there were two. The problem is an old one and many solutions have been presented. The best seems to be one that remembers there were two Jerichos, the ancient city and the Herodian. Anyone crossing the short distance between the two could very well be described as "leaving" (ancient) Jericho or "drawing near" (Herodian) Jericho. As for the difference in the number cured, we have met it before in the incident of the Gerasene demoniac, who according to Matthew had a companion with him; here again it is only Matthew who records two unnamed blind men. But if we transport ourselves back to those times, the difference is not hard to understand. The blind often went about in pairs in Palestine, more or less to help each other, and the more enterprising of the two comes to personify them both. Here it is Bartimeus who speaks, but the careful Matthew notes that he is speaking for two.

Bartimeus, then, accompanied by his more timid companion, was begging alms beside the road. The sound of many footsteps told him a large group of people was passing by, and he asked who they were. The answer was that Jesus of Nazareth was going by, whose fame for miracles was certainly known to him. Whereupon both beggars began to cry out: "Lord, Son of David, have mercy on us!" Those in the crowd shouted at them to keep still, but the two kept crying out all the louder: "Lord, have mercy on us, Son of David!" Jesus stopped and bade that they be brought to Him. Then those nearest Bartimeus said to him hopefully: "Take courage. Get up, he is calling thee!" Up he jumped, throwing off his cloak, and approached Jesus followed by his lesser partner. Jesus asked them: "What will you have me do for you?" What was the only thing a blind man could want? Bartimeus answered: "Rabbi, that I may see!" And then both of them talking at once and saying over and over: "Lord, that our eyes be opened!" Jesus said: "Go thy way, thy faith has saved thee!" He touched their eyes; they were both cured instantly and immediately joined the crowd following Him.

Jesus then entered Jericho naturally amid great enthusiasm. People came running from all directions to see the famous Rabbi who had just cured the familiar pair of blind men, right there before you could draw a breath; and the excitement was fed by the men themselves who were showing their eyes to whoever wanted to examine them.

Among those who came running out was a certain Zaccheus, one of the chief publicans. Being a border city and an important commercial center, Jericho must have harbored many tax collectors, and one of those in charge was none other than this Zaccheus. He was a rich man, but in him, as in Matthew, wealth had not stifled all spiritual feeling; rather, a surfeit of material things at times nauseated him and sharpened his desire for riches far superior to gold and silver. This was Zaccheus's state of mind on that day when Jesus entered Jericho, and he yearned to get near Him and speak to Him, or at least to see Him. But when he got to the road, he realized this would be very difficult; Jesus was surrounded by a close-packed throng and to squirm one's way through was impossible. On the other hand, poor Zaccheus was a short man, and from where he was standing, he could not even glimpse the top of Jesus' head. Should he give up the idea? Not for the world! The resourceful

Zaccheus ran ahead of the crowd, which was progressing somewhat slowly, and catching sight of a handy sycamore tree, up he scrambled into it. It was one of those low trees, still to be seen in Jericho, with long hanging roots that look like ropes, and with their convenient help it was nothing at all to climb the tree. He presented a startling picture, however. Had he been some humble townsman, no one would have paid any attention to him; but that little man up there was a chief publican, one of the superintendents of those leeches who bled the very heart out of the people. Perhaps more than one of those passing by thought it would be a good idea to send him flying from his roost or at least to light a good fire under him; in any case, they were all pointing at him with an accompaniment of jibes and jeers.

At last Jesus approached the sycamore. Everyone was looking up into it, and so did He. The people of Jericho near Him explained that the ridiculous little man perched up there was a no-good, a "sinner," in fact a chief sinner and head leech who was named *Zakkai* ("pure") when there were any number of other names he might more appropriately be called. It would not be fitting for the Master to speak to him nor even to stop and look at him. But Jesus not only stopped and looked at him, He seemed entirely unimpressed by all the information He had just received. When His informants had stopped chattering, He turned to the little man in the tree and said to him of all things: "Zaccheus, make haste and come down; for I must stay in thy house today."

This was a general scandal. Joyfully Zaccheus tumbled out of his tree, and the Master started off with him, but "upon seeing it all began to murmur, saying: 'He has gone to be the guest of a man who is a sinner.'" Since Zaccheus's house was the home of a sinner, it was unclean, and so those faithful to Pharisaic norms stayed outside. Zaccheus, who had more than a few little things weighing on his conscience, chose to honor his guest by making ample amends for his past; and so he said to Jesus: "Behold, Lord, I give one half of my possessions to the poor, and if I have defrauded anyone of anything, I restore it fourfold." And his guest, entirely pleased, answered: "Today salvation has come to this house, since he, too, is a son of Abraham. For the Son of Man came to seek and to save what was lost." In like manner had Jesus defended another publican, Levi-Matthew, who became His disciple.

The miraculous cure of Bartimeus had excited the wonder and admiration of the crowds. The amends offered by Zaccheus probably excited the wonder and admiration of no one, and there were some, perhaps, whose remarks in this regard were not a little malicious. Yet, in Jesus' eyes, the conversion of Zaccheus was no less a miracle than the cure. If in the case of Bartimeus, a blind man was restored his sight, in the case of Zaccheus, a camel had passed through the eye of a needle, a thing that "with men ... is impossible, but not with God."

The Parable of the Gold Pieces

Perhaps Zaccheus's offer of retribution and Christ's answer were spoken during a dinner that the publican offered his guest. Besides the disciples, there probably were other admirers of Jesus present, and a tremulous anxiety must have quivered through the room as the guests spoke in hushed tones of the Kingdom of God and the glorious Messiah, of gleaming thrones and courtiers resplendent with beatific glory. But these things were mentioned with reserve in order not to displease the Master, for they all knew that for reasons of His own He did not approve such talk. Yet there was no doubt this was the eve of decisive events; everything indicated that from one day to the next the wonder-working power of the Master would be completely unfurled, and the Kingdom of God openly inaugurated.

But Jesus overheard part of these subdued conversations, and in any case He understood the state of mind of all those present; and so "he went on to speak a parable, because he was near Jerusalem, and because they thought that the kingdom of God was going to appear immediately" (Luke 19:11). And this was the parable.

A certain nobleman departed for a far-off country to be invested as king and then return to rule with full power. In order not to leave his wealth lying idle, he gave a mina — a little over twenty gold dollars — to each of ten of his servants, charging them to trade with it until he returned. But his citizens hated him, and they sent a delegation of their own after him to tell the one who was to invest him that they did not want him as their king. Nevertheless, the kingdom was granted him, and he returned as the lawful ruler.

This short preface to the parable was suggested by actual historical fact, as we have seen, for it corresponds exactly to the journey Archelaus had made to Rome some thirty years before to receive from Augustus the kingship over his own territories, and to the delegation of fifty Jews sent after him from Jerusalem. We must also remember that while Jesus was speaking, His listeners could have pointed without hesitation toward the nearby palace of the same Archelaus, which had been standing empty so long there in Jericho.

When the new king returned, he asked his servants for an account of the minas he had entrusted to them. First came the servant who had earned ten more gold pieces with the one given him; and the king praised him because he had been "faithful in a very little" and rewarded him by giving him authority over ten towns. Then came a second who had earned five gold pieces, and he was rewarded with authority over five towns. Then came a third who said: "Lord, here is your gold piece, which I have kept tied up in a handkerchief; I was afraid of you because you are a stern man and you withdraw what you have not deposited and reap where you have not sown!" Evidently the servant had not supported the hostile delegation sent after the pretender to the crown, but neither had he bestirred himself in his master's favor. Knowing him to be a very exacting man, he had kept the sum just as he had received it so that the future king would not be able to accuse him of unfaithfulness or theft. But the king answered: "Out of thy own mouth I judge thee, thou wicked servant. Thou knewest that I am a stern man, taking up what I did not lay down and reaping what I did not sow. Why, then, didst thou not put my money in a bank, so that I on my return might have gotten it with interest?" Then turning to the bystanders, he said: "Take away his gold piece and give it to the one who has ten!" But they observed: "Lord, he already has ten minas." The king, however, replied: "It makes no difference! To him who has shall be given, and from him who has not even that which he has shall be taken away. In addition, let all those enemies of mine who did not want me to rule over them be brought here and slain in my presence!"

The eager expectation of the messianic kingdom cherished by Jesus' listeners could hardly be satisfied with this parable. In the first place, it teaches that the triumph of the Kingdom of God will be either a reward or a punishment according to the previous behavior of the individual, and, in the second place, that this triumph will come about only after the departure and prolonged absence of the claimant to the throne, who will appear and act as king only on the occasion of his future coming. Hence, the claimant is Jesus Himself, who is already in full possession of His royal rights but has not yet gone away to be solemnly and publicly vested with kingship in His heavenly country, absenting Himself from His subjects, some of whom are openly hostile to Him and do not want Him to reign over them. His absence is not a brief one, for the claimant to the throne departs for a distant country and entrusts business to his servants, which requires a great deal of time. (Matthew 25:19, in fact, says that the master in the parable returned "after a long time.") When Jesus returns from His heavenly Father, then will His kingdom be openly and solemnly inaugurated with the distribution of rewards to His faithful subjects and punishments to the negligent or rebellious.

Hence the disciples are not to live in continual anxiety, expecting at any moment the solemn triumph of the Kingdom of God. Before that triumph will come to pass, Jesus must depart for a far-off country and remain absent from them until His second coming. During this indefinite absence, His enemies will scheme and plot that He may not reign; moreover, when they are invited to recognize His royalty as the Hebrew Messiah, they will promptly reply that they recognize no royalty except the pagan Caesar's (John 19:15). Hence His absence will be a period of bitter trials for the faithful subjects left alone, but in surmounting them they will earn the right to share in the final triumph.

Though the definitive triumph was reserved for the second coming, Jesus had already promised a great manifestation of the "power" of the Kingdom of God, which might well be considered a partial anticipation of its final victory; He had also promised particular assistance precisely during the times of difficulty and trial.

The parable of the gold pieces, characteristic of Luke, is also recounted by Matthew (25:14–30) but in other context and with some differences; yet the two parables are substantially parallel. Matthew's account may be a shortened version of Luke's, or it may be that the additional material in Luke (especially the punishment of the enemies) derives from a different parable.

The Banquet at Bethany

On His way up from Jericho to Jerusalem, Jesus had to pass through Bethany, which He had left only a few weeks before. He arrived there "six days before the Passover" (John 12:1), that is, on a Sabbath. Since the trip from Jericho to Bethany was too long to be permissible on the Sabbath itself, He probably made it on Friday, arriving in the town around sunset when the Sabbath officially began.

In going to Bethany, Jesus seemed to be deliberately exposing Himself to danger. His enemies, who had decided He must be killed and ordered His arrest, were only a short walk away. The danger was there undeniably, but it was less immediate than it seemed. In the first place, after the order had been given for His arrest, Jesus disappeared, and so the first intense animosity had somewhat abated — except that His reappearance would be sufficient to re-kindle it instantly. In addition, it was a time entirely devoted to preparations for the Pasch, and crowds of Jews were arriving hourly in Jerusalem; since countrymen and admirers of Jesus were certainly among them, it would not be wise to risk a riot by using violence against Him while the city was so jammed with people. In any case, the Sanhedrists and Pharisees, while not at all neglecting their decision, would proceed according to the dictates of prudence.

Meanwhile the ordinary Jews of the capital were curious to see the outcome of the conflict, to see whether the Sanhedrin or Jesus would win in the end.

At Bethany Jesus must have been given a triumphant welcome. On the evening of that Sabbath, a dinner was given in His honor in the house of a certain Simon the Leper, who was undoubtedly one of the wealthy men of the town and owed his nickname to the sickness from which he had been cured, perhaps by Jesus. Lazarus could not have failed to be among the guests, and, in fact, was there. His sister, the good housewife Martha, directed the serving, while his other sister Mary, less expert in domestic matters, contributed in her own way to the honor of their guest. The guests reclined on divans with their heads toward the table and their feet away from it, as we have already seen. At a certain moment Mary entered carrying one of those slender-necked alabaster vases in which the ancients used to keep valuable perfumes. Mary's vase contained a pound of "genuine nard of great value." The adjective "genuine," or "trusty" as the Greek said, was most appropriate, for nard ointment was easily adulterated by means of a "false-nard" herb that grew everywhere. Mary's nard was as valuable as it was genuine. Judas, who knew his prices, estimated it at "more than three hundred denarii," or more than eighty dollars.

When Mary reached Jesus' divan, instead of removing the seal from over the mouth of the vase, she broke off the neck of it, as a sign of greater homage, and poured the perfume abundantly on His head first, and then all that was left on His feet. Also as a sign of special homage, she wiped the Master's feet with her hair. "And the house was filled with the odor of the ointment."

Mary's act was not unusual. It was customary at banquets to offer exquisite perfumes to special guests after their hands and feet had been washed. This delicate attention was all the more natural in Mary since she was bestowing it on Him who had raised her brother from the dead. She did use an extraordinary amount of ointment, but this, after all, only reflected the exuberance of her feeling.

Her prodigality surprised some of the disciples, and especially their treasurer Judas Iscariot, who, as John explicitly mentions, protested bluntly on the pretext of charity: "To what purpose has this waste of ointment been made? for this ointment might have been sold for more than three hundred denarii, and given to the poor" (Mark 14:4–5). But the evangelist John, as realistic as he is spiritual, offers his own observation: "Now he said this, not that he cared for the poor, but because he was a thief, and holding the purse, used to take what was put in it" (John 12:6).

Thus, we learn that the little group of Jesus' constant followers lived together, undoubtedly with the Master, pooling their resources, which they deposited in a "purse" entrusted to Judas. He was their steward, then, and was undoubtedly helped on occasion by the pious women who, when they could, followed the group and provided for their needs. But Judas was a thief, and he took money from the purse. Now, it would have been difficult for the apostles to notice this continued stealing because they were occupied with the spiritual ministry and left all practical matters to Judas. But there was every possibility that the pious women would notice it since they often took care of the expenses, furnishing a good part of the money themselves. Hence, they could check approximately what went in and what came out of the "purse," and it would not escape them when Judas subtracted more than usual from the common fund. Perhaps they had told the other apostles or even Jesus Himself about these private forays of Judas, and from then on the unfaithful steward was perhaps watched with sorrowful pity; but nothing was said to him, and they let him keep his office hoping that he would change his ways. On this occasion, however, Judas betrays that he has become hopelessly calloused. The thief cannot help revealing his annoyance, using the poor as an excuse, when he sees that three hundred denarii (almost a year's pay for a laborer) evaporate into thin air.

Jesus answered Judas's protest: "Let her be — that she may keep it [it is as if she kept it] for the day of my burial. For the poor you have always with you, but you do not always have me" (John 12:7–8; cf. Matt. 26:10–13; Mark 14:6–9). For Jesus, therefore, this anointing merely anticipated His imminent burial. Even this new prediction, however, does not seem to have persuaded the apostles that Jesus' death was near at hand except perhaps for Judas, who, being a good earthly financier, foresaw the bankruptcy of the rest and from then on thought only of saving himself.

Chapter 16

Passion Week — Sunday and Monday

The Triumphal Entry into Jerusalem

Jesus' arrival in Bethany was known immediately in Jerusalem, either through pilgrims or through spies of the Sanhedrin. The news caused a stir in the city. Perhaps even before the Sabbath began and certainly as soon as it was over, any number of curious persons hurried from Jerusalem to Bethany to see Jesus and Lazarus together. And a great number yielded to the evidence of the miracle and believed in Jesus. This, too, was immediately known in Jerusalem, and then the chief priests, more determined than ever to put Jesus to death, "planned to put Lazarus to death also" (John 12:10) and thus dispatch once more to the next world the witness who had returned from it to the great scandal of Jewish orthodoxy.

Certainly this remedy was, or seemed, definitive. But the plan was difficult to carry out, not only because of the great influx of Paschal pilgrims but also because of the excitement that might explode in violence and lead to complications with the Roman authorities. From then on, therefore, the Temple authorities began a watchful waiting for opportunity to carry out their design without any noisy consequences. Jesus, for His part, continued to go His own way unafraid. In fact, Jesus Himself makes the next move, going straight to meet the danger by leaving Bethany for Jerusalem.

It was Sunday morning. Early that morning as well as the evening before, many enthusiasts had been gathering about Jesus, some of them His countrymen come from Galilee for the Pasch and others citizens of Jerusalem persuaded by the miracle of Lazarus. The crowd was aquiver with emotion, and it could not refrain from doing Jesus honor in some solemn manner. This was a good opportunity to do so because it was customary for the citizens of the Holy City to go out to meet the largest or most important groups of pilgrims and conduct them into it amid singing and other joyous manifestations.

Jerusalem: the north wall from the Bethany road

Hence, when the Master declared His intention to proceed to Jerusalem, it was no more than right to prepare a solemn entrance into the city for Him. Even if He should be as unwilling as He had in the past, some such solemn manifestation was absolutely necessary after what had happened in Bethany and Jerusalem, and the Master would have to yield to them.

But contrary to all expectations, Jesus was not reluctant. He announced His intention to go that very morning to Jerusalem and chose the shortest, most crowded road — about three thousand yards long — which went from Bethany up the Mount of Olives and then down its western slope, entering the city near the northeast corner of the Temple. The whole company was climbing joyously toward the top of the Mount of Olives and was already in sight of the ancient village of Bethphage when Jesus gave an order that filled them brimful of happiness. Calling two of His disciples to Him, He said: "Go into the village opposite you, and immediately on entering it you will find a colt tied, upon which no man has yet sat; loose it, and bring it. And if anyone say to you: 'What are you doing?' you shall say that the Lord has need of it, and immediately he will send it here." Matthew, careful as usual to show how the messianic prophesies came to pass, points out that here was fulfilled the prediction of the ancient prophet Zacharias (9:9) that the king of Sion was to come to her meek and seated upon an ass and upon a colt. That is why only Matthew records the fact that in Bethphage in the place Jesus had indicated there were an ass and a colt that were both led to Him, while the other evangelists mention only the colt, on which He actually rode.

Upon the arrival of the two animals, the crowd could contain itself no longer. Now they could make a truly triumphal entry into the city. The procession was quickly formed. Some threw their cloaks over the little donkey by way of a saddle and trappings, and Jesus was made to mount him. Others ran ahead and spread their coats across the road before Him like carpets, and as the procession neared the city many more came thronging along the way, strewing it with fresh branches and waving the festive palm leaves they broke from nearby trees, while all of them kept shouting and crying out: "Hosanna! Blessed is he who comes in the name of the Lord! Blessed is the kingdom of our father David that comes! Hosanna in the highest!" (Mark 11:9–10).

Through these shouts swelled all the fiery emotionalism of the Orient; but through them also swelled the feverish expectation that the cheering multitude had cherished and so long repressed, the expectation of the messianic kingdom. The terms they use are typical: "He who comes in the name of the Lord" is the Messiah, and the "kingdom" of David "that comes" is the messianic kingdom established by the Messiah, son of David. The tokens of its inauguration were certainly very modest — a little donkey and a few branches of palm; but those enthusiasts found no scandal in that, so sure were they that any day now troops of proud warhorses would take the place of the colt and that the palms would give way to a forest of lances.

Just this once do the messianism of the people and the messianism of Jesus meet, if only fleetingly and almost by chance. For the multitudes, the triumphal entry into Jerusalem was to be the first spark of a vast conflagration to come; for Jesus, it was the one and only official display of His messianic royalty. The royalty that He had concealed so carefully and confided with so many precautions and correctives only to His most intimate friends had to be made manifest officially at least once now that His days were growing short and there was so little probability that the mistaken political interpretation would have time to take root. Well, this was His solemn and official manifestation, and it was in perfect harmony besides with the ancient prophecy of Zacharias; but it would all end there, with that little colt and the cheering crowd of some few hundred people.

However humble, the triumph in Jerusalem was an enthusiastic one; John (12:16ff.) tells us that the enthusiasm was great even among the citizens of Jerusalem who had either witnessed the resurrection of Lazarus or heard it described. No doubt the fervor of Jesus' disciples was equally great, though still inspired by superficial motives and unaware of the profound significance of what was taking place, for according to the same evangelist, "these things his disciples did not at first understand. But when Jesus was glorified, then they remembered that these things were written about him, and that they had done these things to him."

But Jesus Himself defended the triumphal character of the procession. Since the Pharisees remained Pharisees even amid the general exuberance and fervor, and since they also understood that it would be dangerous to say anything to the excited mob, a few of them decided to protest to Jesus Himself. "Master, rebuke thy disciples," they said, just as if most of the responsibility for that display lay with His disciples and not with the Jews who had seen the resurrection of Lazarus. But Jesus answered: "I tell you that if these keep silence; the stones will cry out" (Luke 19:40).

The protest was repeated a little later when, after Jesus had entered the Temple, groups of children in the crowd began to shout: "Hosanna to the Son of David!" under the very noses of the chief priests and the scribes. These worthy persons, irritated by the cries of the urchins, objected to Jesus: "Dost thou hear what these are saying?" And this time Jesus answered: "Yes; have you never read: Out of the mouth of infants and sucklings thou hast perfected praise?" (Matt. 21:16). The quotation (from Ps. 8:3) was most appropriate, because in it the poet is contrasting the ingenuous praise lifted to God by babes and sucklings to the forced silence of His enemies. If these children in the Temple, therefore, were praising God, it was not hard to recognize in the priests and scribes the enemies of God reduced to silence.

Jesus' answers and His unquestioned triumph must have driven the Pharisees nearly mad. Balancing up what they had accomplished with all their plans to seize Jesus, to have spies reporting on Him, to put Him to death along with Lazarus, they had to admit complete failure. Jesus was moving freely about Jerusalem itself, His life and Lazarus's were protected by the ardent enthusiasm of the people, He kept winning more and more followers, and He even dared to make a triumphal entry into the Holy City. The Pharisees recognized their own defeat, and they said one to another: "You see that we avail nothing.[15] Behold, the entire world has gone after him!" (John 12:19). This confession did not mean surrender; rather it set the seal on their hatred, and they kept waiting the chance to move against Him.

[15] See alternate reading in Confraternity version.

At one point the triumphal procession crossed the top of the Mount of Olives to descend the western slope in the direction of the Temple. The entire city lay spread before them. At the foot of the mount, and just beyond the Cedron, rose the majestic structure of the Temple dazzling in its sun-white marble and sparkling gold. At its northern corner, like a roost of hawks brooding on their prey, stood the formidable square tower of the Antonia where the Roman troops were garrisoned. On the opposite side, toward the west, rose the palace of Herod, guarded on the north by three towers. Two walls protected the northern part of the city, and beyond the outer wall stretched the suburb of Bethsaida.

And as He gazed on this scene spreading before Him, Jesus wept.

His tears amid so much joy and before so impressive a panorama were indeed unexpected. The disciples may have wondered in their hearts if this was another of the messianic correctives the Master was used to applying. But He Himself explained why He wept, for turning toward the city He exclaimed: "If thou hadst known, in this thy day, even thou, the things that are [necessary] for thy peace! But now they are hidden from thy eyes. For days will come upon thee when thy enemies will throw up a rampart about thee, and surround thee and shut thee in on every side, and will dash thee to the ground and thy children within thee, and will not leave in thee one stone upon another, because thou hast not known the time of thy visitation" (Luke 19:42–44). His tears were not for the present, but for the more or less distant future.

We all know that Jesus' words refer to the terrible siege with which Titus surrounded Jerusalem in 70. The "rampart" is the wall of thirty-nine stadia (about seventy-eight hundred yards) that the Roman legions threw up in three days around the city to starve it out; some probable traces of it have recently been discovered. It is interesting to note that the part of the rampart east of the city followed the stream of the "Cedron toward the Mount of Olives," where Jesus was when He wept.

The Greeks Ask to Be Presented to Jesus

Finally, the procession reached the city and entered the Temple. There, in the outer court, the cheers and the tumult continued, and the children repeated the cries quoted above. The blind and the lame, who flocked there where the begging was so profitable, had themselves brought to the triumphing wonder-worker to implore a cure; and Jesus healed them all.

The Temple was already crowded with pilgrims, and among them were also many who were not Jews but were interested in Judaism. The Jews of the

Diaspora had worked hard to win followers for their faith, and the latter were divided into two groups: the lower was that of the "devout" or "fearing God," who were obliged to keep the Sabbath, recite certain prayers, give alms, and fulfill other minor precepts but were still outside the chosen nation of Israel; the upper class was that of the true "proselytes," who had been circumcised and were therefore equal in all things, or almost all, to the Israelites and were bound by the same obligations.

When the procession entered the Temple, some of these "devout," who were "Greeks," as John calls them, were there in the outer court, having come "to worship on the feast," although they could not take part in the actual Paschal rites since they were not equal to the Israelites. Struck by the spectacle of the procession and above all by what they saw and heard concerning Jesus' miraculous power, they wanted to be presented to Him. In order to be able to get to Him through the crowd, they appealed to the apostle Philip, saying: "Sir, we wish to see Jesus." Philip was somewhat surprised and took counsel with his fellow townsman, Andrew, and finally both carried the request to Jesus.

John relates what happened next in his usual fashion, highlighting the eternal principles rather than the fleeting details of the episodes themselves. In his account the Greeks are not mentioned again; instead, Jesus speaks of His mission as solemnly confirmed by divine testimony. We might almost say that in these Greeks seeking Jesus John sees all of humanity that will come seeking Him in fuller measure, and he slights the episode itself to linger over its everlasting consequence. Jesus said to His two disciples: "The hour has come for the Son of Man to be glorified. Amen, amen I say to you, unless the grain of wheat fall into the ground and die, it remains alone. But if it die, it brings forth much fruit." Here again is the concept of the glorification of the Messiah Jesus, to be preceded, however, by suffering and death; the Kingdom of God will be completely diffused in the manner destined for it in the present "world" only after its founder has been destroyed like the grain of wheat buried in the damp earth.

And the destiny of Jesus' followers is like His own: "He who loves his life, loses it; and he who hates his life in this world, keeps it unto life everlasting. If anyone serve me, let him follow me; and where I am there also shall my servant be. If anyone serve me, my Father will honor him." And then Jesus thinks of the supreme trial He must face before His glorification, and He says: "Now my soul is troubled. And what shall I say? Father, save me from this hour? No, this is why I came to this hour! Father, glorify thy name!" The possibility of hesitating in that supreme trial no sooner suggests itself than it is rejected; it comes back in a different way and with different consequences in Gethsemane.

The heavenly Father heard the invocation; and as at Jesus' baptism and Transfiguration, there came a voice from Heaven, saying: "I have both glorified it, and I will glorify it again." The object of this glorification is not expressed, but it is clearly the name of the Father that will be glorified by the mission of His Son Jesus and above all by the conclusion of that mission.

The crowd standing around heard the sound but did not understand the words; and so some thought there had been a clap of thunder, which the Hebrews often called the "voice of God," while others supposed that an angel had spoken with Jesus. And then the Master explained: "Not for me did this voice come, but for you. Now is the judgment of the world; now will the prince of the world be cast out. And I, if I be lifted up from the earth, will draw all things to myself." In other words, God was about to fulfill the judgment of damnation on the present world and Satan, its prince; the visible sign that the judgment was beginning was the voice they had just heard. The judgment would reach its climax when Jesus was "lifted up from the earth," for then He would draw all men to Him, delivering them from their subjection to Satan. No sooner has the "lifting up" been mentioned than the evangelist hastens to add: "Now he said this signifying by what death he was to die." We do not know for certain, however, just how Jesus' listeners interpreted His prediction; from their words it seems they were thinking of a kind of "assumption" similar to that of Henoch. "The crowd answered him: 'We have heard from the Law that the Christ [Messiah] abides forever. And how canst thou say: "The Son of Man must be lifted up"? Who is this Son of Man?'" According to the Holy Scriptures (the "Law") the kingdom of the Messiah was to be eternal; instead, Jesus had just said that He was to be "lifted up" or, as they interpreted it, "assumed" into Heaven. Hence His kingdom here on earth would not last forever. Besides, the title "Son of Man" was not clear to these listeners, who perhaps were not familiar with the book of Daniel.

This time, however, He gave no long explanations, or at least, none have been handed down to us. All we have is what seems a general, final exhortation: "Jesus therefore said to them: 'Yet a little while the light is among you. Walk while you have the light, that darkness may not overtake you. He who walks in the darkness does not know where he goes. While you have the light, believe in the light, that you may become sons of light.'" As Jesus was speaking, the first shadows of evening were falling, and Mark (11:11) tells us specifically that "it was already late." But while his words suggested the time of day, in reality they referred to the days of Jesus' life and to His spiritual light, which was near its setting.

When the last rays of that day of triumph had faded into the dusk, Jesus returned with His apostles to Bethany, where He spent the night.

The Cursed Fig Tree

The division of these last days of Jesus' life is clearer in Mark than in the other evangelists. He explicitly mentions the night between Sunday and Monday (11:11–12), the night between Monday and Tuesday (11:19–20), Wednesday (14:1), Thursday (14:12) and Thursday evening (14:17), and finally Friday morning (15:1) and afternoon (15:25, 33). The other evangelists are more indefinite regarding the first days of this week. Luke (21:37–38) adds the general information that "in the daytime he was teaching in the temple; but as for the nights, he would go out and pass them on the mountain called Olivet. And the people came to him early in the morning in the temple, to hear him."

We cannot with absolute certainty distribute the various events narrated by the four evangelists through these several days. But certainly His activity in these last days was very intense, and it is justifiable to suppose that only part of it has been recorded. The favor of the populace, which lasted two or three days after that Sunday of triumph, was still a protection against the hatred of the Jewish leaders and permitted Him to spend the day teaching and discussing openly in the Temple. But at night, when the people could do little to help Him, Jesus left the treacherous city and withdrew to the neighboring Mount of Olives, where lay the friendly town of Bethany.

On Monday morning Jesus left Bethany early for Jerusalem, accompanied by His apostles. He had not eaten before leaving, and so He felt hungry along the road. It is strange that He could have left the house governed by the careful Martha without taking any food. But this is not the only paradox in the episode.

To stay His hunger, then, Jesus approached a fig tree near the road and sought among its luxuriant foliage for a bit of fruit. But there could be no fruit for the simple reason, as Mark says (11:13), that "it was not the season for figs." It was, in fact, the first of April, and in the sunnier regions of Palestine the fig trees might have already budded, or have put forth the so-called "fig flowers," but these would not be edible at this date, ripening only toward the first of June. The second or autumn crop of fruit may hang on the tree until the beginning of winter but would never last until the following April. If we were to judge the tree as we would a responsible person, we should have to say it was "not guilty" for having no fruit in that season. Jesus was, in reality, seeking what was not to be found in the normal course of things. Nevertheless, He cursed the tree, saying: "May no one ever eat fruit of thee henceforward forever!"

All these considerations indicate that Jesus' act was intended to be symbolic, and the crux of the symbol lay in the contrast between the abundance of useless foliage and the lack of useful fruit. Those who — like the apostles present — knew the nature of Jesus' ministry, and had listened to His discussions with the Pharisees and His invectives against their hypocrisy, would have had no trouble understanding the reference. The true culprit was the chosen people of Israel, then luxuriant with Pharisaic foliage but for a long time now obstinately void of moral fruit and hence meriting the curse of eternal barrenness. And if at first there could have been any doubt in the apostles' minds as to the meaning of the symbol, it was soon dispelled by the parables of rebuke that Jesus spoke the next day and addressed specifically to the Israel of His time.

As for what happened after the curse, Matthew tells us briefly (21:19) that the tree withered immediately, and he records next Jesus' admonition to the apostles in this regard. Mark gives us a more precise sequence, recounting that on the next morning — Tuesday — when they were coming back the same way from Bethany to Jerusalem, the apostles noticed that the tree had withered, and he assigns Jesus' admonition to that day. As they passed the place, then, Peter was ingenuous enough to exclaim: "Rabbi, behold, the fig tree that thou didst curse is withered up!" (Mark 11:21). Jesus answered without making any reference to the symbolic meaning of His act, but merely admonished the apostles again to have faith and they would be able to move mountains.

Chapter 17

∞

Passion Week — Tuesday and Wednesday

The Authority of Jesus; the Parable of the Two Sons

That Tuesday morning Jesus went to the Temple where the people were awaiting Him, and He began to teach; but soon along came the chief priests, the scribes, and the ancients of the people, that is, the representatives of the various groups in the Sanhedrin, so that all the forces of opposition were represented. For the time being, the two opposing forces were poised in the balance, but once the obstacle between — the favor of the people — was removed, the balance would be broken and the clash precipitated.

The leaders that morning were seeking to remove that obstacle, and so in the presence of the crowd, they asked Jesus: "By what authority dost thou do these things?" and "Who gave thee this authority to do these things?" (Mark 11:28). Their tone was that of cross-examination, and they treated Jesus as if He had already been brought to trial before their court. At the same time the question was intended to discredit Him before the people. The leaders probably hoped that Jesus would speak disparagingly of Moses or his Law and irritate the popular sensibilities. But this time, too, Jesus accepted the challenge and on the enemy's own ground, choosing a stratagem very common with the doctors of the Law, namely, answering with a question as if to establish a point admitted by both sides: "But Jesus answered and said to them: 'I also will ask you one question, and answer me; then I will tell you by what authority I do these things. Was the baptism of John from heaven, or from men? Answer me.'" The question was most embarrassing, especially there in front of the multitude. The evangelist describes their embarrassment thus: "But they began to argue among themselves, saying: 'If we say "From heaven," he will say, "Why then did you not believe in him?" But if we say "From men ...?"' [But they do not say it because] they feared the people, for all regarded John as a prophet. And they answered and said: 'We do not know.' And Jesus answering said to them:

'Neither do I tell you by what authority I do these things.' " The duel was over, and it certainly had not been won by those who had chosen the weapons.

To substantiate His victory and clarify further the relationship between His mission and that of the Baptist, Jesus told a parable.

> A man had two sons, who worked for him in his vineyard. One day, he said to the first: "Son, go and work today in my vineyard." And the son answered: "Yes, I'll go." But he did not go at all. Later the father gave the same bidding to his second son, who answered: "I will not go." But then he repented his answer and went as he was bid.

And Jesus concluded: "Which of the two did the father's will?" And they answered: The second." And Jesus applied the parable to the present circumstances: "Amen I say to you, the publicans and harlots are entering the kingdom of God before you. For John came to you in the way of justice, and you did not believe him. But the publicans and harlots believed him; whereas you, seeing it, did not even repent afterwards, that you might believe him" (Matt. 21:31–32). Hence the son who obeyed with words and then rebelled in fact represented the irreproachable scribes and Pharisees. On the other hand, the discards of the chosen people — the publicans and the harlots — had unquestionably sinned but they had found their way back by accepting the mission of John, and so they had imitated the son who at first rebelled but then became obedient.

Of the two, the one who had done wrong but then "changed his mind" and did good is to be preferred to the one who never made up his mind to be good although constantly protesting his readiness to do so.

The Parable of the Vinedressers

This parable had been a rebuke for those who considered themselves the most illustrious representatives and guides of the chosen people; but Jesus adds another, also of rebuke, which sums up the whole history of Israel in its relation to God's plan of salvation. The veiled significance of this new parable is exactly what Jesus had symbolized a few hours before when He cursed the fig tree so that it withered. The similitude is the same used seven centuries before for the same purpose by the prophet Isaias.

In his famous canticle, Isaias (5:1ff.) described a vineyard on which the master had showered the most affectionate care. He had chosen fertile ground, picked out the stones, and planted the choicest vines; and then he fenced it in, built a tower within, and set a winepress in it. But despite his attention the vineyard brought forth hard, sour, little wild grapes instead of sweet and fragrant clusters. And the prophet explained that the ungrateful vine was the nation of Israel, and its owner was the Lord, who, exasperated by its sterility, would beat down the fence, abandon the vineyard to devastation, and let the briars grow up to choke it.

Jesus takes the same similitude, thus linking once more His mission to that of the ancient prophets; and He amplifies the figure with allusions to what had taken place in the seven centuries from Isaias's day to His.

> "There was a man, a householder, who planted a vineyard, and put a hedge about it, and dug a wine vat in it, and built a tower; then he let it out to vine-dressers, and went abroad. But when the fruit season drew near, he sent his servants to the vine-dressers to receive his fruits. And the vine-dressers seized his servants, and beat one, killed another, and stoned another. Again he sent another party of servants more numerous than the first; and they did the same to these. Finally he sent his son to them, saying: 'They will respect my son.'
>
> "But the vine-dressers, on seeing the son, said among themselves: 'This is the heir; come, let us kill him, and we shall have his inheritance.' So they seized him, cast him out of the vineyard, and killed him. When therefore, the owner of the vineyard comes, what will he do to those vine-dressers?" They said to him: "He will utterly destroy those evil men, and will let out the vineyard to other vine-dressers, who will render to him the fruits in their seasons."
>
> Jesus said to them: "Did you never read in the Scriptures,
>
> > 'The stone which the builders rejected,
> > has become the corner stone;
> > By the Lord this has been done,
> > and it is wonderful in our eyes'?
>
> "Therefore, I say to you, that the kingdom of God will be taken away from you and will be given to a people yielding its fruits." (Matt. 21:33–43)

It was hardly necessary to have the Pharisees' proficiency in the Holy Scriptures and their knowledge of the religious history of their nation to perceive that the vineyard was Israel, the owner was God, and the servants abused or killed were the prophets, whose violent deaths form a continuous obituary down through the pages of Scripture. But Jesus concludes with another allusion, this time to the future, saying that the very son of the householder, whom he had sent last into the vineyard, was beaten and killed. Clearly the son was the speaker Himself, and so He had in the parable implicitly proclaimed Himself the Son of God and accused in advance those guilty of the crime soon to be committed. It was too plain to leave room for any misunderstanding. And the result tallied perfectly with the respective dispositions of His listeners: "And when the chief priests and Pharisees had heard his parables, they knew that he was speaking about them. And though they sought to lay hands on him, they feared the people, because they regarded him as a prophet."

Tribute to Caesar

Once again, therefore, the favor of the people had been a protection for Jesus and a serious obstacle for the Jewish leaders. So the latter, simmering to end the conflict once and for all, decided to remove that exasperating obstacle by compromising Jesus in such a way that all the love of the people would not be able to help Him.

Having taken counsel on what they should do next (Matt. 22:15), they sent some of their disciples along with a few Herodians to Jesus to propose a special question to Him in public so that the crowd could not but hear. The presence of the Herodians suggested that it was to be a political question, a subject Jesus had always avoided. The messengers approached Him exuding ostentatious respect and said to Him unctuously: "Master, we know that thou art truthful, and that thou teachest the way of God in truth and that thou carest naught for any man; for thou dost not regard the person of men. Tell, us, therefore, what dost thou think: Is it lawful to give tribute to Caesar, or not?" (Matt. 22:16–17). The question, as the evangelist warns us, was a trap. If Jesus answered that it was lawful, He would draw upon His head the hatred of the people, for the Messiah and national hero could never declare it lawful to pay tribute to a foreign authority. If He answered that it was unlawful, that would be cause for denouncing Him to the Roman procurator as an instigator of revolt. The expert Pharisees considered the horns of dilemma inescapable. They probably expected that Jesus would declare the payment of the tribute unlawful and in that case His immediate denunciation by the Herodian witnesses would have greatly impressed the Roman procurator.

But their expectations were disappointed, for Jesus handed the dilemma right back to His questioners: "Why do you test me, you hypocrites? Show me the coin of the tribute." So they brought Him a Roman denarius of silver, worth a little more than twenty cents in our money. It was the coin commonly used in payment of taxes, and it was minted outside of Palestine because it was of precious metal and bore the image of a human being.

Jesus' request to see a coin of the tribute, as if He had never seen one before, was strange enough, but even stranger was His question when He held it in His hand: "Whose are this image and the inscription?" Surprised, they answered: "Caesar's." Jesus now had what He wanted, and He concluded: "Render, therefore, to Caesar the things that are Caesar's, and to God the things that are God's." The conclusion derived logically from the Pharisees' own answer. Was the coin Caesar's? Well then, let them render it to Caesar, for the simple fact that they accepted and used the coin showed that they also accepted the sovereignty of the one who had issued it. Hence the question was solved without Jesus' entering at all the political field He so carefully avoided.

Nevertheless, the question was not solved, according to Jesus, by defining only the obligation toward Caesar. The goal of His mission was the Kingdom of God; and when men had rendered to their respective Caesars what belonged to them, they had performed only part, and not the most important part, of their duty. Hence, Jesus adds the injunction to render also to God, not only to make His answer complete but also to emphasize the first injunction to render to Caesar. Jesus knows none of the Caesars of this world personally. He knows only that they are invested with authority that must be respected. Now, why are men subject to Caesar? Precisely because they are subject to God. Whoever belongs to the Kingdom of God must, by virtue of this membership, fulfill his duties toward his Caesar; but when he has done so, let him rise to higher planes and soar through the imperishable dominions of his heavenly Father.

The Sadducees and the Resurrection

The treacherous question on the tribute completely routed the ones who had asked it; "hearing this they marvelled, and leaving him went off" (Matt. 22:22).

Their rivals, the Sadducees, were gratified by this defeat and immediately decided to try a new engagement on their own account. This was to concern the question of the resurrection of the body, which they denied. So they came to Jesus and presented not the abstract question of the resurrection but a concrete case. First they quoted the law of the "levirate," in which Moses prescribed that if a Hebrew died without issue, his brother was to marry the widow in order to provide an heir for the deceased. Then they presented their "case." There were seven brothers, the first of whom died without leaving children, and so the second married his widow. But he also died without leaving children, and so the third brother married the widow. This continued until she had married the seventh and last, and after his death she died too.

Now — the Sadducees inquired — whose wife would that woman be when she had risen with all seven of them together? It was a typical academic case.

According to the Sadducees, their case proved the resurrection impossible, for if the woman rose again, she would have to be the wife of all seven resurrected husbands at once, and this was clearly absurd and indecent as well. If Jesus tried to defend the doctrine of resurrection, He would become entangled in a thicket of nonsense and lose all credit with the crowd.

Their reasoning presupposed a materialistic concept of the resurrection, which was the very reason why the Sadducees rejected it. The resurrection was pictured as an awakening from sleep, in which the risen one would be physically just as he was in life.

Jesus brushes aside these puerile imaginings and answers: "You err because you know neither the Scriptures nor the power of God. For at the resurrection they will neither marry nor be given in marriage, but are as angels of God in heaven." The risen will be the same men as before, but their condition will be changed; they will be as the angels in Heaven. And Jesus continued:

> But as to the resurrection of the dead, have you not read what was spoken to you by God, saying:
> > I am the God of Abraham,
> > and the God of Isaac,
> > and the God of Jacob? [Exod. 3:6]
> He is not the God of the dead, but of the living.

The passage quoted is part of the Torah, the only portion of the Holy Scriptures that the Sadducees accepted. This seems to be the reason why Jesus ignored other scriptural passages that are much clearer testimonies of the belief in the resurrection and based His argument on this, which the Sadducees could not reject as they could the others. In any case, He takes for granted the basic concept of Hebraism: the God of the Hebrew patriarchs is not the God of the dead but of the living; hence those patriarchs are still living after the death of their bodies, and therefore the resurrection is attested by the Holy Scriptures.

The Great Commandment; the Messiah, Son of David

The Pharisees and Sadducees continued to take turns throughout that day, which must have been a very busy one for Jesus. His answer to the Sadducees delighted a certain scribe present at the discussion, and so he came forward to propose a question to Jesus, which was quite in keeping with the rabbinic method: "Which is the first commandment of all?" (cf. Mark 12:28), or as Matthew records it (22:36): "Which is the greatest commandment in the Law?"

According to the rabbis the written Law, or Torah, contained 613 precepts, 248 of which were commandments while 365 were prohibitions. Both commands and prohibitions were divided into two groups, the "light" and the "heavy," according to their importance. Now, there must have been some kind of hierarchy among all these commandments. And that is what this particular scribe wanted to know.

Jesus' answer is the one He had given the doctor of the Law to whom He spoke the parable of the Good Samaritan. He recited the beginning of the *Shema.* "The first commandment of all is, 'Hear, O Israel! The Lord our God is one God; and thou shalt love the Lord thy God with thy whole heart, and with thy whole soul, and with thy whole mind, and with thy whole strength.' This is the first commandment. And the second is like it: 'Thou shalt love thy neighbor as thyself.' There is no other commandment greater than these." Really the scribe had asked for only one commandment, the greatest of them all. Jesus gave him the commandment of the love of God, but almost as if this were not complete by itself, He added the other to love one's neighbor. These two interwoven precepts are, for Jesus, the "greatest" commandment, and He had expressed the same idea in the Sermon on the Mount.

The scribe heartily approved the answer and added, for his part, that this twofold love of God and neighbor was worth more than all the holocausts and sacrifices in the Temple. In reward for his reply, Jesus said to him: "Thou art not far from the kingdom of God." All he lacked was belief in the mission of Jesus. Whether he ever found it we do not know.

When this discussion was ended, we are told that "no one after that ventured to ask him questions" (Mark 12:34).

It was Jesus Himself who resumed the battle. In the Temple He approached a group of Pharisees and set before them a question concerning the Messiah: From what blood was he to descend? Whose son was he to be?

In complete agreement with all Hebrew tradition, they answered him: David's.

Jesus then observed that in the Holy Scriptures David himself, whose name is in the inscription over the psalm (109 [110]), speaks thus:

> The Lord said to my Lord:
> Sit thou at my right hand,
> Until I make thy enemies
> as thy footstool.

From this passage Jesus argues: "If David, therefore, calls him 'Lord,' how is he his son?"

The strength of the argument lay in two points admitted also by the Pharisees: first, that it is David speaking in this psalm, and, second, that the psalm concerns the future Messiah, as we should gather from its wide use in this sense in the New Testament (where it is quoted more than fifteen times).

If the future Messiah was to be David's descendant, why does David call him "Lord"? According to Jesus, this proved the Messiah was more than merely the "son of David" and possessed qualities that made him "greater than Jonas and greater than Solomon" and greater also than David. But Jesus wanted the Pharisees' explanation of this apparent inconsistency. And they could not answer Him.

The "Èlenchos" against the Scribes and the Pharisees; the Widow's Mite

In ancient Greek terminology, the *èlenchos* was that part of a forensic oration that set forth the charges against one's opponent together with their respective proofs. It was, therefore, a rebuke that demonstrated another's dishonor, and in earlier times the term *èlenchos* had meant "rebuke" and "dishonor" both.

That stormy Tuesday, most of which Jesus spent battling with the scribes and Pharisees, could not fail to produce its *èlenchos*, which summed up all the charges He had previously expressed against His adversaries. All three Synoptics, in fact, assign such a list of reproaches to this particular day but with the usual differences: Mark (12:38–40) is very brief; so is Luke (20:46–47), who, however, recorded a long series of accusations on the occasion of the banquet offered Jesus by the Pharisees. On the other hand, Matthew's account (chapter 23) is very long, and it includes almost all of Luke's list with some additions besides.

Matthew's version follows:

> The Scribes and Pharisees have sat on the chair of Moses. All things, therefore, that they command you, observe and do. But do not act according to their works; for they talk but do nothing. And they bind together heavy and oppressive burdens, and lay them on men's shoulders; but not with one finger of their own do they choose to move them. In fact, all their works they do in order to be seen by men; for they widen their phylacteries, and enlarge their tassels, and love the first places at suppers and the front places in the synagogues, and greetings in the

market place, and to be called by men "Rabbi." But do not you be called "Rabbi"; for one is your Master, and all you are brothers. And call no one on earth your Father; for one is your Father, who is in heaven. Neither be called masters; for one only is your Master, the Christ. He who is greatest among you shall be your servant. And whoever exalts himself shall be humbled, and whoever humbles himself shall be exalted.

In this first part of the discourse, Jesus sketches the characteristic features of the Pharisees, and so it contains some echoes of His previous discussions with them. And since He is speaking here to the crowd gathered in the Temple, He exhorts them not to imitate them but to do exactly the opposite. The Pharisees' vanity found expression in the "phylacteries" among other things, little boxes containing rolled-up strips of parchment on which were written passages from the holy Books. While praying, the Israelite wore (and still wears) these strips bound around his forehead and his left arm. The more vainglorious provided themselves with broader and more showy strips to attract attention, just as they exaggerated the "tassels" on their cloaks, which also had a religious significance and were worn by Jesus too.

The second part of the discourse forms the true *èlenchos*:

But woe to you, Scribes and Pharisees, hypocrites! because you shut the kingdom of heaven against men. For you yourselves do not enter in, nor do you let those entering pass in.

Woe to you, Scribes and Pharisees, hypocrites! because you traverse sea and land to make one convert; and when he has become one, you make him twofold more a son of hell than yourselves.

Woe to you, blind guides, who say, "Whoever swears by the temple, it is nothing; but whoever swears by the gold of the temple, he is bound." You blind fools! for which is greater, the gold, or the temple which sanctifies the gold? [You say also] "And whoever swears by the altar, it is nothing; but whoever swears by the gift that is upon it, he is bound." Blind ones! for which is greater, the gift, or the altar which sanctifies the gift?...

Woe to you, Scribes and Pharisees, hypocrites! because you pay tithes on mint and anise and cummin, and have left undone the weightier matters of the Law, right judgment and mercy and faith.... Blind guides, who strain out the gnat but swallow the camel!

Woe to you, Scribes and Pharisees, hypocrites! because you clean the outside of the cup and the dish, but within they are full of robbery and uncleanness....

Woe to you, Scribes and Pharisees, hypocrites! because you are like whited sepulchres, which outwardly appear to men beautiful, but within are full of dead men's bones and of all uncleanness....

Woe to you, Scribes and Pharisees, hypocrites! you who build the sepulchres of the prophets, and adorn the tombs of the just, and say, "If we had lived in the days of our fathers, we would not have been their accomplices in the blood of the prophets." Thus you are witnesses against yourselves that you are the sons of those who killed the prophets. You also fill up the measure of your fathers.

Here are the charges, and the statement of them was in itself equivalent to proof because all Jesus' listeners knew from experience that the things He said were every one of them true.

The statement that the Pharisees have filled up "the measure" of their fathers is followed by a sorrowful description of the consequences, just as in a forensic oration the penalty followed the proof of the crime. It is the third part of the discourse:

Serpents, brood of vipers, how are you to escape the judgment of hell? Therefore, behold, I send you prophets, and wise men, and scribes; and some of them you will put to death, and crucify, and some you will scourge in your synagogues, and persecute from town to town; that upon you may come all the just blood that has been shed on the earth, from the blood of Abel the just unto the blood of Zacharias the son of Barachias, whom you killed between the temple and the altar. Amen I say to you, all these things will come upon this generation.

Jerusalem, Jerusalem! thou who killest the prophets, and stonest those who are sent to thee! How often would I have gathered thy children together, as a hen gathers her young under her wings, but thou wouldst not! Behold, your house is left to you desolate. For I say to you, you shall not see me henceforth until you shall say, "Blessed is he who comes in the name of the Lord!"

This last part is not so much a threat as a lament. Jesus deplores the fact that His repeated attempts to save the city and the nation have been frustrated, and that the whole structure gradually built up by God for the salvation of Israel is to be gradually demolished by the perversity of men. What happened in the days of the Law when the prophets of Yahweh were stoned will happen again in the time of the Messiah, whose messengers will meet a like fate. But in this way the whole weight of even the most ancient crimes will fall upon those who commit the last one, because they lay bare the deepest foundations of God's edifice and, filling up the measure, draw full vengeance down upon themselves. This is a salutary threat, therefore, one last anguished cry of warning that the blind guides of the chosen nation may stay their steps on the very brink of the abyss.

But all Jesus' attempts end with this last anguished and threatening appeal. When the citizens of the Holy City have repulsed Him the last time, when their last crime has been consummated, then their house will be left to them desolate, and He whom they rejected will withhold His help from them. Nor will they see Him again except in the far-distant future when the erring nation has repented its error and goes in search of the rejected with the words of acclaim addressed to Him in His brief triumph two days before: "Blessed is he who comes in the name of the Lord!"

After the èlenchos against the scribes and Pharisees, we are permitted to watch a humble but very noble little scene, which is in direct contrast to the spiritual world of the scribes and Pharisees. It is described by Luke (21:1–4) but is even more lively in Mark (12:41–44), while Matthew unexpectedly omits it altogether.

When Jesus had ended His sorrowful plaint against His adversaries, He walked through the inner parts of the Temple as far as the Women's Court, and there He sat down opposite the hall of the treasury. At the entrance to the latter stood thirteen chests for the offerings, called "trumpets" from the shape of the opening through which the money was dropped. The offerings were abundant during great feasts like this of the Pasch because many pilgrims took advantage of the occasion to pay the prescribed tribute to the Temple, and the faithful made spontaneous offerings besides. Hence several priests stood near the chests, checking the payment of the tribute and watching over things generally.

Seated opposite, Jesus watched the crowd. Many rich folk came and poured in handfuls of coins with great ostentation, confident that this won them great esteem not only among men but also with God. And in their midst, unnoticed and ignored, a poor little widow came dragging herself along to drop into one of the chests "two mites, which make a quadrans," or not even half a cent. Then Jesus "called his disciples together, and said to them: 'Amen I say to you, this poor widow has put in more than all those who have been putting money into the treasury. For they all have put in out of their abundance; but she out of her want has put in all that she had — all that she had to live on'"

(Mark 12:43–44). And with this observation the Master of the spirit again contradicted the masters of externals who were His adversaries.

The Discourse on the Last Things

It was drawing toward sunset as Jesus left the Temple to spend the night outside the city as He did all that week. Having crossed the Court of the Gentiles, He made His way beside the substructures of the Temple area that rose along the valley of the Cedron, presenting a truly powerful and magnificent spectacle. Looking at them the disciples were reminded of Jesus' last words to the scribes and Pharisees, which had rung so heavy with menace: "Behold, your house is left to you desolate." The first and best-loved house of every good Israelite was the house of Yahweh, the Temple of the Holy City. That Temple had necessarily to be eternal as their common faith required and the majesty of its buildings seemed to prove. What did Jesus mean, then, when He said that that house would be left desolate? Was this prediction associated with the other painful prophecies the Master had made?

One of the disciples decided to sound out Jesus' thought, and so he approached Him casually as the party wound along beside the revetments beneath the Temple and began to praise the vast edifice with great enthusiasm. But the disciples' exclamations did not dispel Jesus' thoughtfulness. Only after a while did He lift his head, and with a brief glance at the structures so praised, He said gravely: "Dost thou see all these great buildings? There will not be left one stone upon another that will not be thrown down." And He relapsed into silence.

The disciples were stunned. The Master's melancholy spread over them as the company continued its way without another word across the Cedron and up the slope of the Mount of Olives. When they reached the top, Jesus sat down facing the Temple (Mark 13:3) and contemplated it silently.

The dismayed disciples took advantage of the stop to ask the Master for an explanation of His dreadful prophesy. And Jesus' answer is commonly known as the "Eschatological Discourse" — the discourse on the last things.

The discourse treats of two great events, both to take place in a more or less distant future and somehow associated with each other. Since they belonged to the future, they were shrouded in mystery for anyone who heard the discourse from Jesus or from the apostles. A little later, but still within the first Christian generation, the first of these events actually took place and one part of the mystery was solved, but the rest of it was enveloped in still more distressing and even terrifying obscurity. If the first prediction had been so promptly fulfilled and it seemed so intimately connected with the second, then would not the latter come to pass soon also? On these questions the first Christians reflected with trepidation for many years.

Today we also recognize that the first of those events occurred in the first Christian generation, but we no longer have the same anxieties regarding the immediate fulfillment of the second. Twenty centuries of history have underlined the meaning of Jesus' words, which set between the two a measureless interval of time. Since the first prediction and the interval are now perfectly clear, the entire mystery today is concentrated on the second event, about which the modern reader is no less ignorant than the first Christians.

Taking as our guide Mark's account, though not unmindful of Matthew and Luke, we may sum up the discourse as follows.

The question the disciples asked Jesus on the top of the mountain had been expressed thus: "Tell us, when are these things to happen, and what will be the sign when all these things will begin to [be accomplished]?" (Mark 13:4). The expression "these things" in the first instance refers to the destruction of the Temple; but the second time it is certainly used in a broader sense to mean the universal catastrophe in which "all these things," namely, the present "age" or world, will come to an end. The parallel passage in Matthew (24:3) leaves no room for doubt on this point: "Tell us, when are these things to happen, and what will be the sign of thy coming and of the end of the world?" When the disciples heard Jesus prophesy the destruction of the Temple, therefore, they thought immediately of His promises that the "kingdom of God" would "come in power" and that "in the regeneration" the Son of Man would "sit on the throne of his glory," to say nothing of the several allusions in the parables; and they naturally associated all these things, thinking of the destruction of the Temple and of the end of the "world" as simultaneous or at least as following one right after the other. They wanted Jesus, however, to answer both questions, namely, when the Temple was to be destroyed and when the end of the world would take place, and also to describe the signs that were to precede each event.

He begins by warning His disciples against treachery and fraud, and so the first part of His answer describes the signs that will precede the destruction of the Temple (Mark 13:5–23). Many lying preachers will come forward and parade as the Messiah, drawing many after them into error, and there will be wars, seditions, earthquakes, and famine in various places, but all this is not yet the end — it is only the "beginning of sorrows." The great tribulation will fall directly on the disciples of Jesus, who will be denounced to Sanhedrins,

Ruins where Jesus foretold the destruction of Jerusalem

synagogues, and governors, will be beaten and imprisoned, betrayed by their closest relatives, and universally hated because of their faith. But despite all this and during this very period, "the gospel must first be preached to all the nations." Then the "great tribulation" will move toward its close: the abomination of desolation prophesied by Daniel will stand in the Temple and Jerusalem will be surrounded by armies. Then the disciples who have remained faithful to Jesus must flee for their lives. For these will be "days of vengeance, that all things that are written [in the Holy Scriptures] may be fulfilled" (Luke 21:22), and there "will be tribulations, such as have not been from the beginning of the creation which God created until now, or will be" (cf. Dan. 12:1), although those days will be shortened that the chosen may escape (Mark 13:19–20).

It is to be noted that up to this point, the discourse has made no mention of time but only of the signs of the "great tribulation." That this refers to the destruction of the Temple and Jerusalem is clearly indicated by the wording. Nor is there any difficulty in the statement that at the destruction of the Temple "the gospel must first be preached to all the nations." St. Paul spoke of this as an accomplished fact even before Jerusalem was destroyed. Now, the destruction of Jerusalem took place forty years after the discourse, or in a period that the Jews reckoned as a "generation." And Jesus, when He has described the signs, adds: "Amen I say to you, this generation will not pass away till all these things have been accomplished" (Mark 13:30).

To this point Jesus' answer has referred only to the first part of the disciples' question; it has described the signs that will precede the destruction of the Temple, and it comes to a clear and definite close with the admonition: "Be on your guard, therefore; behold, I have told you all things beforehand" (Mark 13:23). Now He must answer the second half of the question by describing the signs of the end of the world.

This second part (Mark 13:24ff.) begins with the words: "But in those days, after that tribulation, the sun will be darkened…" Here the expression, "in those days," is the usual formula, in both the Old and the New Testaments, for introducing a new subject but without reference to any specific time; it means, at the most, "in a certain time … in its time … in a given period." In this undetermined period, which will come after the "great tribulation," the end of the world and the second coming will take place together, and they are described here in terms derived for the most part from the Old Testament and common to apocalyptic literature as well: the sun and the moon will be darkened, the stars will fall, the powers of Heaven will be shaken, and then the Son of Man will appear coming on the clouds with power and glory, and He will send His angels to the four winds to gather His elect. This will be the end of the present "world" and the beginning of the future "world." In all three Synoptics the signs of the "great tribulation" are described at greater length than those of the end of the world.

The time when this second coming will occur is indicated right after the statement regarding the time of the "great tribulation." But while the latter indication is clear and specific — during this "generation" — the other is completely negative. "But of that day or hour no one knows, neither the angels in heaven, nor the Son, but the Father only" (Mark 13:32).

This last phrase is to be interpreted as meaning that Jesus simply was unwilling to be questioned on this point because the answer did not enter within the compass of His ministry. He had already answered the sons of Zebedee that it was not His duty but His Father's to assign the seats in His messianic kingdom. On the present occasion, St. Augustine says, "he said he did not know that day because it was not rightly within his mission that we should learn this through him, while it was within his mission to keep that time hidden; for as a teacher he knew both how to teach what was useful and how to avoid teaching what was disadvantageous."

Presented in this manner, the discourse is as clear as its subject matter permits. The first part of it deals with the signs of the "great tribulation," that is, with the events that preceded and accompanied the destruction of Jerusalem. The second part speaks of the signs of Christ's second coming and the end of the world. Then the time of the respective events is indicated: the great tribulation is assigned to the present "generation," while the other event is shrouded in a mysterious silence. It is still an impenetrable mystery.

The Parable of the Ten Virgins; the Last Judgment

Since the day of the coming is not known, those who await the final consummation of the Kingdom of God must be constantly ready, because at any time that day and hour may come. The uncertainty carries with it the danger of neglectfulness, against which we must labor with unceasing vigilance. This is the lesson of the parable of the ten virgins, recorded for us only by Matthew (25:1–13).

The parable is based on Jewish wedding customs. Ten maidens have been invited to the wedding of a friend and are to be in her procession; they have come from home, each bearing a terra-cotta lamp, not so much to light the way to the bride's house as to add to the gaiety of the feast when the groom arrives. It is expected, however, that since this is a fashionable wedding, they will have to wait quite a while for the groom, for he, too, must receive an interminable procession of callers. Hence, five of the maidens, being wise, take a small jar of oil to keep their little lamps well supplied. But the other five are careless and bring only their lamps, forgetting that they stay lit for a relatively short time.

Things turn out as the prudent virgins expected. The groom is a long time in coming. In the bride's house, meanwhile, the gay spirits of the assembled company gradually wilt.

> Then ... they all became drowsy and slept. And at midnight a cry arose: Behold, the bridegroom is coming, go forth to meet him! Then all those virgins arose and trimmed their lamps. And the foolish said to the wise: "Give us some of your oil, for our lamps are going out!" The wise answered, saying: "Lest there may not be enough for us and for you, go rather to those who sell, and buy [some] for yourselves."
>
> Now while they were away buying, the bridegroom came; and those who were ready went in with him to the marriage feast, and the door was shut. Finally there came also the other virgins, and said: "Sir, sir, open the door for us!" But he answered and said: "Amen I say to you, I do not know you."

Their repulse spontaneously suggests the moral: "Watch, therefore, for you know neither the day nor the hour!"

The purpose of the parable is twofold: to picture man's ignorance of the day and the hour, emphasized in the conclusion of the parable, and also the perils that beset the waiting and the danger of being unprepared. When the waiting is prolonged, it becomes treacherous, for the preparation so well begun is gradually neglected and the reality of the "coming" is forgotten. To have been prepared only at the first hour counts for nothing unless one is also prepared at the very last moment, at the moment of the "coming" itself.

It is Matthew again (25:31–46) who paints for us the great picture of the close of the present "world" and the inauguration of the future "world," the panorama of the Last Judgment. This theme had been treated by the ancient prophets but in another light and with a different purpose. The Last Judgment had been pictured in the past as the triumph of the Hebrew nation over pagan nations, or of a good and pious group over another that was wicked and impious; but here it assumes a moral character and touches every individual of the whole human race. This moral character is crystallized in charity, which is the distinctive feature of the Kingdom of God and the passport of admission to it; the Last Judgment is the triumph of charity.

> But when the Son of Man shall come in his majesty, and all the angels with him, then he will sit on the throne of his glory; and before him will be gathered all the nations, and he will separate them one from another, as the shepherd separates the sheep from the goats; and he will set the sheep on his right hand, but the goats on the left.
>
> Then the king will say to those on his right hand: "Come, blessed of my Father, take possession of the kingdom prepared for you from the foundation of the world; for I was hungry and you gave me to eat; I was thirsty and you gave me to drink; I was a stranger and you took me in; naked and you covered me; sick and you visited me; I was in prison and you came to me." Then the just will answer him, saying: "Lord, when did we see thee hungry, and feed thee; or thirsty, and give thee drink? And when did we see thee a stranger, and take thee in; or naked, and clothe thee? Or when did we see thee sick, or in prison, and come to thee?" And answering the king will say to them: "Amen I say to you, as long as you did it for one of these, the least of my brethren, you did it for me."
>
> Then he will say to those on his left hand: "Depart from me, accursed ones, into the everlasting fire which was prepared for the devil and his angels. For I was hungry, and you did not give me to eat; I was thirsty and you gave me no drink; I was a stranger and you did not take me in;

naked, and you did not clothe me; sick, and in prison, and you did not visit me." Then they also will answer and say: "Lord, when did we see thee hungry, or thirsty, or a stranger, or naked, or sick, or in prison, and did not minister to thee?" Then he will answer them, saying: "Amen I say to you, as long as you did not do it for one of these least ones, you did not do it for me." And these will go into everlasting punishment, but the just into everlasting life.

Wednesday — The Betrayal of Judas

Finally, Wednesday came, the next to the last day before the Pasch.

For the chief priests and the Pharisees the time was growing uncomfortably short; they must make up their minds what to do. Still protected by the love the populace bore Him, Jesus went about Jerusalem with impunity and even ventured to preach in the Temple. Was there no way to make Him disappear secretly, before the people realized what had happened? Certainly there was no time to lose; the matter must be settled once and for all before the Pasch to avoid consequences that might prove very serious. The Roman procurator looked upon feasts in general and the Pasch in particular about as he would upon an earthquake. On such occasions — as Josephus tells us — the Roman cohort garrisoned in Jerusalem was stationed along the Temple portico, "for during the feasts, they always keep armed watch so that the crowd may not provoke sedition." What could not happen, then, with that Galilean Rabbi loose in the city and the Temple, surrounded by groups of enthusiasts who believed Him the Messiah?

Another council was held that Wednesday to discuss the problem (Matt. 26:3–5). All agreed that Jesus must be killed, but a few of the more cautious pointed out the danger of arresting Him during the feast when so many pilgrims could rise up in His protection. On the other hand, it would not be expedient to postpone the arrest until after the Pasch because Jesus could leave the city with the departing pilgrims and thus escape. Hence they must act quickly, before the Pasch and with stealth. That was what these cautious counselors advised.

But this was precisely the difficulty. There were only two days left before the Pasch, and Jesus spent the whole day among the people; how could they take Him without the arrest being known until after it was over?

Help came from the most unexpected quarter of all. "Then one of the Twelve, called Judas Iscariot, went to the chief priests, and said to them: 'What are you willing to give me, and I will deliver him to you?' But they counted him out thirty pieces of silver. And from then on he [Judas] was watching for an opportunity to betray him." So says Matthew (26:14–16), and the other two Synoptics agree; the latter do not mention the specific sum of money, but they add the very understandable information that the chief priests were "glad" about Judas's proposal. With his collaboration it would now be easy to arrest Jesus quickly and secretly.

What could have been the reasons that impelled Judas to betray Jesus?

The Gospel has given us no other motive but the love of money. When the evangelists pictured Judas as a thief and the cheating steward of their common funds, they were preparing us for the little scene in which Judas goes to the chief priests and asks: "What are you willing to give me ...?" Yet even apart from the Gospels, when Peter speaks of the traitor, now a suicide, he mentions no other profit from the betrayal but a field purchased with "the price of his iniquity" (Acts 1:16–19). Hence we are certain about this one motive of money, but it does not exclude the possibility of other motives, and here the way lies open to reasonable conjecture.

Even apart from the flights of fancy made over this tragic field by romancing playwrights and historians, there still remains Judas's unexpected behavior only two days later. When Jesus had been condemned, the traitor suddenly repented of his deed; and having brought the money back to the chief priests, he went out and hanged himself. Now, this is not the behavior of an ordinary greedy man or miser. The typical miser, a man who loves nothing but money, would have been satisfied with his gain whatever the fate of Jesus, and he would never have thought of giving back the money, much less of hanging himself. Avaricious and greedy Judas certainly was, but he was something else besides. There exist in him at least two loves. One is the love of gold, which drives him to betray Jesus. But there is another love that is sometimes stronger, because it prevails after the betrayal and drives the traitor to return the money, to abjure the whole betrayal, to feel sorrow for his victim, and finally to kill himself in despair.

However much we think about it, we cannot find any other object for this second love but Jesus Himself. If Judas had not felt for Jesus a love so great that it sometimes prevailed over his greed, he would not have restored the money, nor would he have abjured his treachery. But if he loved Jesus, why did he betray Him? Undoubtedly because, though his love was great, it was not unequivocal; it was not the generous, trustful, radiant love of a Peter or a John. Its flame was still streaked with shadow. What this shadow was we do not know, and it remains for us the mystery of supreme iniquity.

Did Judas perhaps know that he had been denounced to Jesus as a thief and could he not stand being disgraced before Him? Peter, too, denied Jesus and felt himself disgraced in His eyes, yet he did not despair.

Or was his love of gold, perhaps, fortified by the anxiety to see Jesus soon at the head of His political kingdom; did he betray Him in the certainty of watching Him work prodigy upon prodigy against His adversaries and thus forcing Him to inaugurate at once that kingdom that was too long in coming? In that case, however, the traitor should not have killed himself before the death of Jesus but afterward, because he could not be sure just when the Messiah would resort to miracles, especially since at the time of the actual betrayal Judas saw the guards fall to the ground in terror in Gethsemane.

We could pile theory on theory but without shedding any definite light at all on the mystery of supreme iniquity.

This iniquity, besides, lay not only in selling Jesus but above all in despairing of His forgiveness. Judas had seen Jesus pardon usurers and prostitutes; he had heard from His lips the parables of mercy, including that of the Prodigal Son; he had heard Him command Peter to forgive seventy times seven times; and after all that he despaired of pardon for himself and hanged himself. Peter did not despair but burst into tears. This despair in itself shows that Judas felt a very great esteem for the Just whom he betrayed, which measured for him the atrocity of the crime he committed. But his esteem was incomplete and hence insulting, because faced with the responsibility for his betrayal, Judas stopped halfway and wrongfully considered Jesus incapable of pardoning his treachery. This was the supreme outrage against Jesus, the supreme iniquity of Judas.

The chief priests fixed the price of the betrayal at "thirty pieces of silver," but neither here nor later (27:3–10) does Matthew name the coins; all he says is "thirty pieces of silver." There is no doubt that the unnamed coin was the shekel or stater and twenty of them today would be worth about twenty-five and a half gold dollars, which was about the price of a slave.

Luke, who brought his account of the temptation of Jesus to a close with the statement that the "devil ... departed from him for a time," begins his story of the betrayal by saying that "Satan entered into Judas, surnamed Iscariot." For the disciple of Paul, then, the Passion of Jesus is the "time" and in some way represents a renewal of the temptations to which Satan subjected Jesus at the beginning of His public life.

Chapter 18

∞

Passion Week — Thursday

The Preparations for the Last Supper

Thursday dawned, the "first day of the Unleavened Bread [Azymes] when it was customary for them to sacrifice the passover" (Mark 14:12). The group with Jesus also had to prepare for the solemn ritual of the Pasch since Jesus would be obliged to remain that night in Jerusalem and forego His retreat of the previous nights in Bethany. So His disciples said to him: "Where wilt thou that we go and prepare for thee to eat the passover?" Jesus then sent Peter and John (Luke 22:8), saying: "Go into the city, and there will meet you a man carrying a pitcher of water; follow him. And wherever he enters, say to the master of the house: 'The Master says, "Where is my guest chamber, that I may eat the passover there with my disciples?" ' And he will show you a large upper room furnished; there make ready for us" (Mark 14:13–15).

The sign given the two apostles was unusual enough since it was the women who ordinarily drew and carried water. As they entered the city, undoubtedly through the gate opposite the Mount of Olives, they did meet the man with the pitcher, whom they followed to a house where the master placed at their disposal the room Jesus had mentioned. No doubt this master was a person who loved Jesus and had probably received Him into his home on other occasions. Who was this unnamed disciple? We think naturally of the father or some relative of Mark, whose house after Jesus' death became the habitual meeting place for the Christians of Jerusalem. In fact, as early as the sixth century, there was a tradition, old even then, that the house belonged to Mary, Mark's mother, and that Mark was the man with the pitcher.[161]

---

[16] The house where the Last Supper was held was undoubtedly demolished during the destruction of Jerusalem in 70 or 135. Contemporary Christians, however, must have carefully cherished the memory of the site, and as soon as possible they built there a "small church," which in the fourth century was

It is possible that the evangelists conceal the name of this disciple in order to shield him from the unwelcome attention of the enemies of Christ. For reasons of prudence also, Jesus sent Peter and John to prepare the supper and not Judas, the steward who would normally have performed that service. The traitor was busy contriving his betrayal, and this was not to be further facilitated by a premature announcement of the place where Jesus and the apostles were to gather for the last time.

The Chronological Problem

The preparations were completed during the day, and the supper took place that same evening. But here we run into the famous difficulty regarding the dates of the Last Supper and of the day after, on which Jesus died. The problem is to determine on what days of the month these two events occurred.

There is no doubt whatever about the days of the week, because all four evangelists set the Last Supper on Thursday and Jesus' death on the next day, Friday.

The difficulty lies in the fact that according to the Synoptics, the Thursday of the Last Supper was the fourteenth Nisan and consequently Jesus died on the fifteenth, while according to John it would seem this particular Thursday was the thirteenth Nisan and Friday the fourteenth. The Synoptics set the Last Supper on the day "when it was customary for them to sacrifice the passover" (Mark 14:12; cf. Luke 22:7), that is, on the afternoon of the fourteenth Nisan. He died on the next day, which would then be the fifteenth Nisan, the day of the Hebrew Pasch.

John, on the other hand, says that Jesus died on the "Preparation Day for the Passover" (19:14), the day before the Pasch, before the Jews sacrificed the lamb or ate the Passover meal. In fact, "they ... did not enter the praetorium, that they might not be defiled, but might eat the Passover" (John 18:28), and they were successful in having Jesus condemned and executed that same day. According to this, Jesus died on the fourteenth Nisan and the Last Supper, held on the preceding evening, was not the legal Passover meal.

But certain elusive references in the Synoptics themselves suggest further important considerations.

According to their sequence, Jesus was arrested during the night between the fourteenth and the fifteenth Nisan, and the various phases of His trial,

---

incorporated into a large basilica, the Sancta Sion, situated on the western hill of the city. It is now a mosque.

ending in His condemnation and execution, began early on the morning of the fifteenth Nisan and lasted until the afternoon of the same day. Now here we are confronted with a serious difficulty, namely, the supremely festive character of that particular night and day. That was the night on which the crowds that had flocked to Jerusalem ate the Paschal lamb with solemn ceremonial, and on this next day, which was the Pasch (the fifteenth Nisan), all manual labor was strictly forbidden. Hence it is inconceivable that Jesus' adversaries, however violent their hatred of Him, should neglect the Paschal supper on that night and violate the holy day rest on the next day to accomplish all that was necessary to bring Him to trial and condemn and execute Him. This would indicate that many of the Jews — if not all — did not observe that night and day as holy, that they had not eaten the Paschal lamb on Thursday evening as Jesus had, and that they did not celebrate the Pasch on Friday. This conclusion is all the more important because it derives from information given us only by the Synoptics.

In addition, Jesus dies on the afternoon of Friday, which according to the Synoptics seems to be the day of the Pasch (the fifteenth Nisan). As soon as He had died, Joseph of Arimathea hurries to bury Him the same afternoon, before sunset when the prescribed rest of the next day, the Sabbath, will begin (Mark 15:42ff.). Similarly, the pious women prepare the spices and ointments for the precious body that same afternoon, but when evening comes, "on the Sabbath they rested, in accordance with the commandment" (Luke 23:56). All this would be quite regular were only the weekly Sabbath rest concerned; but if that Friday on which Jesus died was also the day of the Pasch, then it was bound by the no less solemn obligation of holy day rest. Then why all that hurrying about on Friday afternoon despite the more rigid rest imposed by the Pasch? This together with the other information given us by the Synoptics suggests that Joseph of Arimathea and the pious women did not celebrate the Pasch on that Friday either, and therefore the Pasch for them was not the fifteenth Nisan.

There have been numerous attempts to compose the difference, many of them without the least foundation in reality. Such, for instance, is the theory that in that year the Jews postponed the Pasch a day — to the sixteenth Nisan — in order to have sufficient time to bring Jesus to trial and execute Him, whereas Jesus ate the Paschal lamb on the day prescribed. This hypothesis disregards the extreme tenacity of Jesus' adversaries regarding their traditions. They would not have budged an inch even in their hatred for Him — to say nothing of the absurdity of supposing that the Pasch, solely out of hatred for Jesus, could be postponed by decree within a few hours and the change

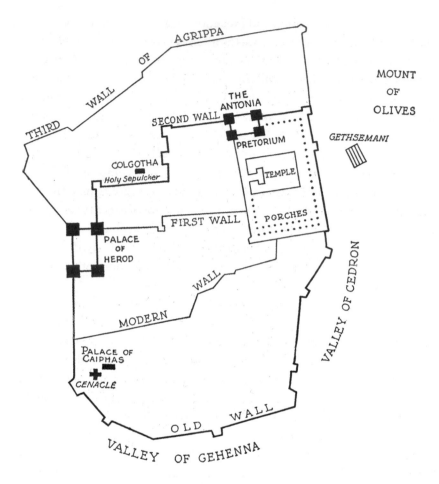

Principal places in the passion of Christ

imposed on huge crowds that did not even know Him by name as well as on people who loved Him, like Joseph of Arimathea and the pious women.

Recent studies of ancient documents have opened up a new, and perhaps the true, path through this highly intricate question. As we have noted before, the methods for fixing the calendar in Jesus' day were uncertain and the calendar itself was, from our point of view, incredibly elastic. Now the discrepancy between the Synoptics and John may have risen from just this elasticity. If the Friday on which Jesus died was both the fourteenth and the fifteenth — that is, if some Jews reckoned it the fourteenth and others the fifteenth — then the whole difficulty could be settled; that is, the Synoptics would be following the

Jews who considered that Friday the fifteenth, while John would be dating his account from the others, who considered it the fourteenth.

We find, in fact, that at the time of Jesus there was a serious controversy between Sadducees and Pharisees about the date of Pentecost and consequently of the Pasch as well, since the two feasts were interrelated. Some influential priests and Sadducees maintained that Pentecost should always be celebrated on a Sunday; and since the fifty days between the Pasch and Pentecost were counted from the day in the Paschal octave on which the first sheaves of barley were offered in the Temple, they also maintained that this offering must always be made on the Sunday of the said octave. The Pharisees, on the other hand, declared that Pentecost could be celebrated on any day of the week and therefore the wheat was always to be offered on the day after the Pasch — that is, the sixteenth *Nisan* — no matter what day of the week it was.

Because of this difference of opinion, the Sadducees used to rearrange their calendar, especially when the Pasch (fifteenth Nisan) fell on Friday or Sunday. If it fell on Friday, they pushed the calendar forward and made that Friday the day of the sacrifice of the lamb and the Paschal dinner (the fourteenth), celebrated the Pasch on Saturday, the Sabbath (the fifteenth), and made the offering of wheat on Sunday (the sixteenth). If the Pasch fell on Sunday, they pushed the calendar back a day so that the wheat offering would still be made on Sunday (the sixteenth), while they celebrated the Pasch on the day before, or Saturday (the fifteenth), and sacrificed the lamb on Friday (the fourteenth).

The Pharisees, however, did not consent to this arrangement of the Sadducees, and since it did not matter to them on what day of the week they celebrated Pentecost, they sacrificed the lamb, celebrated the Pasch, and offered the wheat on whatever days these rites naturally fell.

The majority of the people followed the Pharisees in celebrating the aforesaid rites, while the upper classes were more loyal to the Sadducees; and each group adhered to its own arrangement without paying any attention to the other. There must have been some in each faction, however, who for convenience's sake adopted the calendar arrangement of the other side, and still others who did not belong to either one, and so chose whichever of the two sets of dates suited them in any year.

This information tallies with what we know of Jesus' death, which occurred in a year when the Pasch fell on Friday. Hence the Sadducees, true to their principle, pushed the calendar back a day so that the offering of the wheat would fall on Sunday. The Pharisees, on the other hand, followed the regular calendar and made their wheat offering on that Sabbath. The people were divided between the two.

The first two columns in the following table show the differences between the Sadducees and Pharisees regarding the dates of the Paschal festivities, and the last two the respective positions of the evangelists:

The Month Nisan		Day of the Week	Synoptics	John
Sadducees	Pharisees			
12	13	Wednesday		
13	14 The Paschal Meal	Thursday	The 14 Nisan The Last Supper	The 13 Nisan The Last Supper
14 The Paschal Meal	15 The Pasch	Friday	The 15 Nisan The Pasch The Death of Jesus	The 14 Nisan The Paschal Meal of the "Jews" The Death of Jesus
15 The Pasch	16 Offering of the Sheaves	Saturday (Sabbath)		The 15 Nisan The Pasch of the "Jews"
16 Offering of the Sheaves		Sunday		

Note that John's sequence coincides with the Sadducean calendar, while that in the Synoptics agrees with the Pharisees' dates. The Last Supper was obviously the meal at which the Paschal lamb was eaten according to precept, and it was held on Thursday, the day on which the Pharisees and the great majority of the people ate the Passover; for them it was the fourteenth Nisan, and the next day, Friday, was the fifteenth and the Pasch. But the majority in the Sanhedrin, which condemned Jesus, were Sadducees, and they considered that Thursday the thirteenth Nisan; consequently, they postponed the eating of the Passover to Friday and the Pasch to Saturday. This would also explain why on the Friday of Jesus' death so many persons were not observing the holy day repose despite the fact that the Pasch fell on that day. It was the Pasch for the Pharisees, but not for many others who for one reason or another were following the Sadducean calendar. In conclusion, the Synoptics base their account on the calendar Jesus followed along with the Pharisees, although they contain clear evidence that others were not following it. John's narrative follows the calendar of the Sadducean Sanhedrists, the ones who officially condemned Jesus, but he takes it for granted that everyone knew the calendar Jesus followed was different.

Is this explanation of the problem absolutely certain? No, for there are still a number of obscure points to be cleared up. Nevertheless, it may be said to be the best founded, historically. The elasticity of the Jewish calendar of the time is a historical reality of prime importance; it entered not a little into the famous controversies that arose in the early days of Christianity regarding the celebration of the Christian Easter.

The Betrayer

That something extraordinary took place at the Last Supper is told us by John in the veiled manner peculiar to him, but easily comprehensible to his listeners who were used to it: "Jesus, knowing that his hour had come, to pass out of this world to the Father, having loved his own who were in the world, loved them [even] to the end." The Master, who has always loved His own, now shows that His love is "[even] to the end" — not only to the end of His life but to the furthest possible limits of love itself.

Luke, the disciple of Paul, also suggests this love when he tells how, at the beginning of the Supper, Jesus looked at His disciples and exclaimed: "I have greatly desired to eat this passover with you before I suffer; for I say to you that I will eat of it no more, until it has been fulfilled in the kingdom of God" (22:15–16). Here again is the concept that the Messiah must suffer before entering upon His glory, which will be the triumph of the Kingdom of God now symbolized by an eternal banquet.

The usual ceremony of the Paschal meal was undoubtedly observed at the Last Supper, with the four cups of ritual wine, the unleavened bread, the wild herbs, and the roast lamb, although not all of these are mentioned by the evangelists. Jesus acted as head of the family. Hence He blessed the first cup of wine, adding: "Take this and share it among you; for I say to you that I will not drink of the fruit of the vine, until the kingdom of God comes" (Luke 22:17–18).

The interior of the Cenacle, scene of the Last Supper

The meal was now begun, but the guests would not have been typical of their people and their time if several of them had not expressed dissatisfaction with their places at table and the desire to occupy a post of greater honor. These good men all had a fine opinion of themselves, and "there arose also a dispute among them, which of them was reputed to be the greatest" (Luke 22:24). The dispute was not new, but a hint in John (13:2–5) might imply that this time it was occasioned by the pretensions of Judas Iscariot.

Jesus must have treated the humiliating scene as He had treated similar discussions among the apostles in the past, but this time He chose to illustrate His words with action (John 13:4ff.). Seeing that despite all His exhortations to humility there was still no end to the grumbling of these poor blockheads, He rose from His divan, laid aside His garments, girded Himself with a towel, took a basin of water, and began to wash the feet of the disciples. The lowest slaves usually performed this office, and they could accomplish it easily since the guests reclined with their feet away from the table. When they saw the Master stoop to so menial a service, the apostles were struck dumb and passively accepted it as a humiliation; not even Judas dared to protest.

Only Peter, who was probably the first one approached, protested saying: "Lord, do you wash my feet?" And Jesus said to him: "You do not know now what I am doing, but afterward, you will know." But Peter did not give in: "You will never wash my feet!" And Jesus replied: "If I do not wash you, you shall have no part with me." At this, the impulsive Peter went to the other extreme and exclaimed: "Lord, wash not only my feet, but also my hands and my head!" Then Jesus concluded: "He who has bathed needs only to wash (his feet) and he is clean all over; and you are clean but not all of you."

Did Judas start at these words? Perhaps not; the traitor was probably satisfied that his crime was still hidden from his colleagues. But the matter did not end there.

When He had finished washing their feet, Jesus put on His garments again and resumed His place at table. Since the table was U-shaped and the divans were arranged around its outer edge, it is reasonable to suppose that Jesus, who had the place of honor, occupied the divan at the center of the curve. From what the evangelists say, it would also seem that the divans nearest Him were occupied by Peter, John, and Judas. Now if we picture each of the diners reclining with his head toward the table so that he leaned on his left elbow, Peter must have been behind Jesus (i.e., to the left of Him) and therefore in the second place of honor. In front of Jesus, or to His right, reclined John, who would thus be able to lay his head on Jesus' breast, and to John's right was Judas, so that Jesus could easily hand him a piece of bread. Their positions might be diagramed as follows.

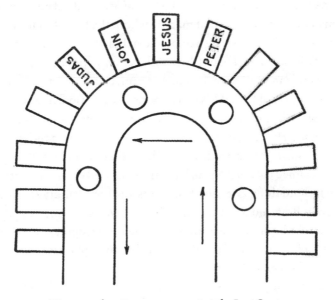

Diagram of seating arrangement at the Last Supper

The meal was resumed, but all was not yet serene; the apostles had been disturbed by Jesus' statement that they were not all clean, and they wanted to know what He meant. Jesus, too, wanted to speak of this again, not so much for the curiosity of those who were clean as for the purification of the one who was not. He must try once more to rescue that unhappy soul. So when they had begun to eat again, Jesus, still speaking in general, quoted a passage from the Psalms (40[41]:10): "He who eats bread with me has lifted up his heel against me." And after He had said this, "he was troubled in spirit" and added without naming anyone: "Amen, amen I say to you, one of you will betray me."

This produced a general consternation. How could a traitor be hidden among those twelve men who had dedicated themselves body and soul to the Master? And all of them began to ask at once: "Is it I, Lord?" Again, without mentioning any name, Jesus described the traitor: "It is one of the Twelve, who dips with me in the dish!" (Mark 14:20). All were, in fact, dipping their bread and the wild herbs in the Paschal sauce, and there was perhaps one such dish of sauce to every three persons; that in which Jesus dipped probably served John and Judas too. The apostles took this statement in a general sense, as if it meant the same as "one of the Twelve" and indicated in general whoever dipped in any one of the sauce dishes on the table. But there was one of them who did understand, and it was to him that Jesus addressed His next words, which were to be His last anguished cry of exhortation, His last warning of the abyss that stretched beneath him: "The Son of Man indeed goes his way, as it is written of him; but woe to that man by whom the Son of Man is betrayed! It were better for that man if he had not been born!"

Judas could no longer keep still; his silence amid the anxious trepidation of the rest would in itself have denounced him. Calm and measured, but not without a slight trembling of his voice, came his question, like all the others: "Is it I, Rabbi?" Most of those present probably did not notice Judas's words, and Jesus made His last effort to save him. The traitor was reclining not far from his victim and their heads especially were rather close. It may be that John, who reclined between them, had raised himself on his elbow to give his attention to something else, and Jesus took the opportunity to say to Judas softly: "Thou hast said it." It was the Hebrew way of saying yes. There was nothing more to be done. The traitor knew he was recognized and the choice was now his either to complete his betrayal or to implore forgiveness of the Master he still venerated.

Jesus' answer to Judas probably escaped the others with the possible exception of John. And they were still anxious to know something definite about the betrayal and the traitor, especially the warmhearted Peter. He did not question Jesus directly, perhaps for fear of a stern answer such as he had received on other occasions, so he enlisted John's assistance. Jesus was facing John and the latter could be said to be "reclining at Jesus' bosom"; where Peter was, at Jesus' back, the Master could not observe him directly. Taking advantage of his position, Peter made signs to John to ask Jesus who the traitor was. The young evangelist immediately understood what Peter wanted, and in his turn accomplished a little maneuver prompted by his confident love and familiarity with the Master. He twisted about so that he leaned on his right elbow, which brought him closer to Jesus' divan, and trustfully laid his head against the Master's breast, looking up at Him like a child expecting some favor from its father. Then he asked Him softly: "Lord, who is it?"

Jesus satisfied His youthful friend while offering at the same time another last courtesy to that other unhappy friend slipping toward the abyss. Among the ancient peoples of the Orient — as also among the modern — it was a gesture of courtesy to offer a fellow diner a fine morsel nicely prepared for him; for instance, one would break a piece of bread from the loaf, roll it up, dip it in the common sauce dish, and then offer it to the guest by holding it near his mouth. At John's request, therefore, Jesus announced: "It is he for whom I shall dip the bread, and give it to him." And breaking off a piece of bread, He dipped it and gave it to Judas.

The traitor had not yet been exposed, except in secret to the trusted John; this gesture of the Master was another opportunity to repent. But Judas ate the morsel without saying anything. He had made his final choice. "And after the morsel" — comments our witness, now aware of what was happening — "Satan entered into him."

But now Judas himself could stand no more, and he got up to leave. "And Jesus said to him: 'What thou dost, do quickly.' But none of those at the table understood why he said this to him. For some thought that because Judas held the purse, Jesus had said to him: 'Buy the things we need for the feast'; or that he should give something to the poor. When, therefore, he had received the morsel, he went out quickly. Now it was night."

And the traitor, going forth, plunged into his twofold night.[172]

---

[17] There has been a great deal of discussion as to whether or not Judas partook of the Holy Eucharist, and opinion has been divided from the time of the first Christian writers down to our own day. In reality, it is a question that can never be definitely solved because there are persuasive arguments on

The Institution of the Eucharist

The Paschal banquet must have been almost over by now; perhaps the second cup of ritual wine was almost finished, and the third was about to be poured.

Suddenly Jesus did an unusual thing, not mentioned in the precepts for the Paschal dinner. He took one of the flat, round loaves of unleavened bread, and having said the blessing over it, He broke it in pieces that He distributed to the apostles, saying: "Take and eat; this is my body, which is being given for you; do this in remembrance of me."

A little while later, probably when the third cup of ritual wine was poured, He took a chalice of wine mixed with water, and having given thanks, He made them all drink of it, saying: "All of you drink this. This cup is the new covenant in my blood, which is being shed for many. Do this as often as you drink it in remembrance of me."

The Synoptics do not tell us just what impression these two acts made on the apostles personally, but that does not really matter. Much more important is the permanent impression they left on all the first Christian society, which was, from every point of view, the most reliable interpreter of these two acts of Jesus and of the words that accompanied them. And here, for a check on the historicity of our data, we have two excellent vantage points some distance apart.

About twenty-five years after the Last Supper, Paul wrote to the Christians of Corinth the letter (1 Cor. 11:23–29) in which he described the Eucharist as a permanent rite, in which the faithful who partook of it ate the real Body and drank the real Blood of Jesus, and which derived directly from Jesus' twofold act of consecration at the Last Supper and His death for the redemption of men. There is no doubt that Paul had also given this teaching to the other communities he catechized just as he had to the faithful of Corinth, and that it agreed entirely with the catechesis of the other apostles.

Forty years after the epistle of Paul we find our second vantage point in the fourth Gospel, the only Gospel that does not narrate the institution of the

---

both sides. According to Matthew and Mark, Jesus first denounces the traitor and then institutes the Eucharist; in Luke's account, the institution of the Eucharist is recorded first and then there is a (very brief) mention of the traitor; we get no help whatever from John because he does not relate the institution of the Eucharist at all. Which sequence are we to follow, that of Matthew and Mark, or the one in Luke? The sequence in Matthew and Mark, both because it is given us by two of them and because it is more natural, seems preferable here, but we cannot be sure about it.

Eucharist. We have observed that this silence is in some ways more eloquent than the actual account would have been, but here we might consider still another aspect of the question. Even supposing (but not granted) that the author of the fourth Gospel were not the apostle John but an unknown mystic, he would very probably have known Paul's letter, and he would certainly have been acquainted with the Synoptics and the eucharistic liturgy, which was established by the end of the fifth century in every Christian community. Hence, he is a silent but no less effective witness of the faith of his times, for though he does not mention the institution of the Eucharist, he places special emphasis on its spiritual effects in the discourse on the Bread of Life. In short, the author of the fourth Gospel is in full agreement with the catecheses of Paul and of the Synoptics, which he confirms partly through his silent acceptance and partly by his careful emphasis.

As for the apostles' immediate reaction to Jesus' words, we must remember their impression would not be so new or so strange as we might think at first; rather, these words would in some way solve an old riddle that had long been tossing about in their minds.

Not only had they never forgotten the earlier discourse on the Bread of Life, but from time to time they must also have thought of that mysterious promise that was still unfulfilled: "Amen, amen I say to you, unless you eat the flesh of the Son of Man, and drink his blood, you shall not have life in you.... For my flesh is food indeed, and my blood is drink indeed. He who eats my flesh, and drinks my blood, abides in me and I in him.... He who eats me, he also shall live because of me. This is the bread that has come down from heaven ..." Jesus had made these statements a few months before at Capernaum, but until the Last Supper He had shown the disciples no way of obeying this commandment that was so essential to their "having life" in them. Many of Jesus' disciples had been scandalized by the "hardness" of His words and deserted Him, but the Twelve had remained faithful because the Master had "the words of everlasting life." Nevertheless, in the months that had passed, His words had not been verified, and the Twelve must have wondered how the Master would ever keep His promise.

And then that night, the Master distributes bread and wine, saying: "This is my body," "This is my blood." The old enigma was solved, the old promise fulfilled. The true meaning of Jesus' actions and words was wonderfully clear in the light of the discourse on the Bread of Life. The apparent bread and the apparent wine then being offered them were in reality the Body and Blood of the Master.

And in view of John's reflective and pithy style, it seems altogether possible that when he says Jesus had loved His own "[even] to the end," this very phrase is an allusion to the institution of the Eucharist that he has not recounted.

Peter's Denial Predicted

When the Supper had ended, the company still lingered a while in the supper room as was the custom. It was then, according to Luke (22:31ff.) and John (13:36ff.), that Jesus predicted the apostles would scatter and Peter would deny Him, although from Matthew and Mark we should conclude that He did so after they had left the room.

At a certain point, then, Jesus said to His apostles sadly: "You will all be scandalized this night because of me; for it is written, 'I will smite the shepherd, / and the sheep of the flock will be scattered' [cf. Zech. 13:7]. But after I have risen, I will go before you into Galilee." It was another of those forebodings that so disturbed the apostles. Their impatience was immediately written in their faces, and the impulsive Peter expressed his especially. But Jesus did not change his tone; in fact, turning to Peter he added: "Simon, Simon, behold, Satan has desired to have you, that he may sift you as wheat. But I have prayed for thee, that thy faith may not fail; and do thou, when once thou has turned again, strengthen thy brethren." Peter did not like these words at all; he loved Jesus with all his heart, and whatever Satan might attempt, he would never be guilty of any cowardly act against the Master from which he would have to "turn again."

Peter's reaction is colored with a little resentment too. The evangelists record detached phrases of his ensuing dialogue with Jesus, in which he said, among other things: "Even though all shall be scandalized because of thee, I will never be scandalized!" and "Lord, with thee I am ready to go both to prison and to death!" Certainly no one would have thought of questioning Peter's sincerity, and yet Jesus calmly and patiently gave him the following answer, recorded by Mark (14:30), who must have heard Peter repeat it hundreds of times in his preaching: "Amen I say to thee, today, this very night, before a cock crows twice, thou wilt deny me thrice." This was too much for Peter, and he burst into a torrent of protests. Mark, perhaps out of desire to use his spiritual father gently, says only that Peter "went on speaking more vehemently," repeating that though he should have to die with the Master, he would never deny Him. All the apostles were saying more or less the same thing.

But Jesus did not seem to have much confidence in the steadfastness of their promises. He continued to exhort them so that they would continue to trust Him, as they had in the past, through the bitter and difficult struggle that was about to begin (Luke 22:35–37). At this, the impetuosity of the apostles flared up the more. They would either conquer at the Master's side or they would fall weapon in hand! There were two swords in the room, perhaps by chance, and they showed them to Jesus, saying: "Lord, behold, here are two swords!" And with infinite patience, perhaps smiling sadly a little, Jesus answered: "Enough!"

How many things were spoken in that "Enough!" To the very last moment the apostles did not get over their slow-wittedness and Jesus' long-suffering and generous patience never once grew short.

Jesus' Last Discourses

John is the only one who records the discourses that follow, almost as if to compensate for his omission of the institution of the Eucharist.

Their style and concept make it impossible ever to summarize or classify them. They burst impetuously from a feeling that pours itself out as a volcano of love, to transform all that it covers into a flaming lake.

But though this last discourse is so sublime, it never loses sight of human reality; rather it closely follows it at certain points on purpose to transmute it into a supraterrestrial, supernatural reality.

The complete outpouring of love was checked for a moment by the presence of Judas, but when

> he had gone out, Jesus said: "Now is the Son of Man glorified, and God is glorified in him. If God is glorified in him, God will also glorify him in himself, and will glorify him at once.
>
> "Little children, yet a little while I am with you. You will seek me, and, as I said to the Jews, 'Where I go you cannot come,' so to you also I say it now. A new commandment I give you, that you love one another: that as I have loved you, you also love one another. By this will all men know that you are my disciples, if you have love for one another."

Thus does Jesus give His disciples their identification papers.

In both Jewish and Greco-Roman antiquity, the several religious, cultural, or other associations had some distinctive feature that marked their activity and served almost as a means of identification for their members. The distinctive mark of the disciples of Jesus must not be the knowledge of "tradition" as it was for the Pharisees, nor any knowledge or practice characteristic of other associations; it was to be the knowledge and the practice of love. Hence,

He called His precept a "new commandment," for in truth no founder of any society before Him had ever thought of giving it to his followers as their distinctive badge.

Rome had brought to the civilization of the time her creations of force and law, and in that same era the various Oriental religions were spreading their mystical influences through the Greco-Roman world; but no one had yet introduced love as a social force, because "love," in its broadest sense — which is charity — had not yet been "invented." From then on human society must reckon with this new force, invented and introduced by Jesus, and true progress will be measured according to the completeness with which the law of love or charity is really obeyed.

And after answering briefly questions of Peter, Thomas, and Philip, Jesus continued:

Amen, amen I say to you, he who believes in me, the works that I do he also shall do, and greater than these he shall do, because I am going to the Father. And whatever you ask in my name, that I will do, in order that the Father may be glorified in the Son. If you ask me anything in my name, I will do it.

If you love me, keep my commandments. And I will ask the Father and he will give you another Advocate to dwell with you forever, the Spirit of truth whom the world cannot receive, because it neither sees him nor knows him. But you shall know him, because he will dwell with you, and be in you.

I will not leave you orphans; I will come to you. Yet a little while and the world no longer sees me. But you see me, for I live and you shall live. In that day you will know that I am in my Father, and you in me, and I in you. He who has my commandments and keeps them, he it is who loves me. But he who loves me will be loved by my Father, and I will love him and manifest myself to him.

The poor apostles must have felt somewhat lost as they listened. Another question, this time from Jude (Thaddeus), deflects the discourse for a moment, and then Jesus resumes:

Peace I leave with you, my peace I give to you; not as the world gives [it] do I give [it] to you. Do not let your heart be troubled, or be afraid. You have heard me say to you, "I go away and I am coming to you." If you loved me, you would indeed rejoice that I am going to the Father, for the Father is greater than I. And now I have told you before it comes to pass, that when it has come to pass you may believe. I will no longer speak much with you, for the prince of the world is coming, and in me he has nothing. But he comes that the world may know that I love the Father, and that I do as the Father has commanded me. Arise, let us go from here.

It is likely that they did not immediately leave the Cenacle, for their departure from the city is recorded much later, only at the end of these discourses (John 18:1). Hence, this request was more like a general reminder that they must soon leave the warm intimacy of this room, where Jesus met with those He loved for the last time before His death. And as often happens at moments of parting, there followed another affectionate delay while Jesus continued to talk to them, perhaps in answer to questions from one or another of the apostles. Meanwhile, the beloved disciple gathered up each word and printed it deep in his vigilant memory; and later he retold them every one.

And so right after His suggestion that they leave, Jesus continues:

I am the true vine, and my Father is the vine-dresser.... I am the vine, you are the branches. He who abides in me, and I in him, he bears much fruit; for without me you can do nothing. If anyone does not abide in me, he shall be cast outside as the branch and wither; and they shall gather them up and cast them into the fire, and they shall burn. If you abide in me, and if my words abide in you, ask whatever you will and it shall be done to you. In this is my Father glorified, that you may bear very much fruit, and become my disciples.

As the Father has loved me, I also have loved you. Abide in my love. If you keep my commandments you will abide in my love, as I also have kept my Father's commandments, and abide in his love. These things I have spoken to you that my joy may be in you, and that your joy may be made full.

This is my commandment, that you love one another as I have loved you. Greater love than this no one has, that one lay down his life for his friends. You are my friends if you do the things I command you. No longer do I call you servants, because the servant does not know what his master does. But I have called you friends, because all things that I have heard from my Father I have made known to you....

These things I command you, that you may love one another. If the world hates you, know that it has hated me before you. If you were of the world, the world would love what is its own. But because you are not of the world, but I have chosen you out of the world, therefore the world hates you....

These things I have spoken to you that you may not be scandalized. They will expel you from the synagogues. Yes, the hour is coming for everyone who kills you to think that he is offering worship to God. And these things they will do because they have not known the Father nor me. But these things I have spoken to you, that when the time for them has come you may remember that I told you. These things, however, I did not tell you from the beginning, because I was with you. And now I am going to him who sent me.

Again the apostles ask questions, and then Jesus concludes His discourse, saying: "These things I have spoken to you that in me you may have peace. In the world you will have affliction. But take courage, I have overcome the world."

Here the spiritual evangelist immediately adds Jesus' own words to His heavenly Father, which scholars commonly describe as His "priestly prayer" (John 17:1–26). Jesus prays first for Himself, that the Father will glorify Him (17:1–5), then for the apostles, that they may be protected in their future mission (17:6–19), and finally for all those who shall believe in Him (17:20–26). It is the longest prayer spoken by Jesus that is recorded for us in the Gospels. John quite rightly considered it a kind of summary of all Jesus' activity on earth, almost like a last flower of flame leaping upward from the pinnacle of His life. Above its blazing radiance there is the Heaven of the Father alone.

These things Jesus spoke; and raising his eyes to heaven, he said: "Father, the hour has come! Glorify thy Son, that thy Son may glorify thee, even as thou hast given him power over all flesh, in order that to all thou hast given him he may give everlasting life. Now this is everlasting life, that they may know thee, the only true God, and him whom thou hast sent, Jesus Christ. I have glorified thee on earth; I have accomplished the work that thou hast given me to do. And now do thou, Father, glorify me with thyself, with the glory that I had with thee before the world existed.

"I have manifested thy name to the men whom thou hast given me out of the world. They were thine, and thou hast given them to me, and they have kept thy word. Now they have learnt that whatever thou hast given me is from thee; because the words that thou has given me I have given to them. And they have received them, and have known of a truth that I came forth from thee, and they have believed that thou didst send me.

"I pray for them; not for the world do I pray, but for those whom thou hast given me, because they are thine; and all things that are mine are thine, and thine are mine; and I am glorified in them. And I am no longer in the world — but these are in the world — and I am coming to thee. Holy Father, keep in thy name those whom thou hast given me, that they may be one even as we are. While I was with them, I kept them in thy name. Those whom thou hast given me I guarded; and not one of them perished except the son of perdition, in order that the Scripture might be fulfilled. But now I am coming to thee; and these things I speak in the world, in order that they may have my joy made full in themselves. I have given them thy word; and the world has hated them, because they are not of the world, even as I am not of the world. I do not pray that thou take them out of the world, but that thou keep them from evil. They are not of the world, even as I am not of the world. Sanctify them in the truth. The word is truth. Even as thou hast sent me into the world, so I also have sent them into the world. And for them I sanctify myself, that they also may be sanctified in truth.

"Yet not for these only do I pray, but for those also who through their word are to believe in me, that all may be one, even as thou, Father, in me and I in thee; that they also may be one in us, that the world may believe that thou hast sent me. And the glory that thou hast given me, I have given to them, that they may be one, even as we are one: I in them and thou in me, that they may be perfected in unity and that the world may know that thou hast sent me, and that thou hast loved them even as thou hast loved me.

"Father, I will that where I am, they also whom thou hast given me may be with me; in order that they may behold my glory, which thou hast given me, because thou hast loved me before the creation of the world. Just Father, the world has not known thee, but I have known thee, and these have known that thou hast sent me. And I have made known to them thy name, and will make it known, in order that the love with which thou hast loved me may be in them, and I in them."

Chapter 19

∞

Passion Week — Friday

Gethsemane

Right after the last words of Jesus' prayer, John says: "After saying these things, Jesus went forth with his disciples beyond the torrent of Cedron, where there was a garden into which he and his disciples entered. Now Judas, who betrayed him, also knew the place, since Jesus had often met there together with his disciples" (John 18:1–2). The Synoptics give us the name Gethsemane. The name, which means "oil press," suggests an olive grove containing a press and perhaps surrounded by a wall, all of which coincides with the name of the Mount of Olives.

It was just a comfortable walk from the Cenacle to Gethsemane. In the crisp spring night, clear and bright with the moon at the full, Jesus and the apostles left the city by the Fountain Gate. Then they began to climb in a northerly direction, crossed the Cedron, and reached Gethsemane. The garden probably belonged to some disciple or admirer of Jesus and that is why He used it so freely. Like other groves of its kind, Gethsemane must have had a little cabin near the gate that was used as a shelter for the gardener or as a storehouse, and further on there was probably a grotto in the side of the mountain in which was set the oil press that gave its name to the place.

On that night of the Pasch the region was deserted, since almost everyone stayed at home with his family. And the solitude matched the mood of the little company, for Jesus seemed sad along the way, and so the apostles were silent and thoughtful. When they reached the garden, Jesus bade His disciples make themselves as comfortable as they could for the night. For those of the Orient, this was easy, accustomed as they were to sleep outdoors wrapped in their cloaks. And as He left them, Jesus said: "Stay here, while I go yonder and pray. Pray that you may not enter into temptation!" Then He took with Him His favorite apostles, Peter, James, and John.

As they drew away from the rest, these witnesses of His former glory understood that they were now to watch a far different manifestation, for suddenly Jesus "began to be saddened and exceedingly troubled." And turning to the three, who perhaps tried in vain to comfort Him, He exclaimed: "My soul is sad, even unto death! Wait here and watch with me!"

Even their company gave Him no solace. In the anguish that overwhelmed Him, He yet sought to stay alone to pray.

His face livid, His knees trembling, and His arms stretched out for support, He made a supreme effort and "withdrew from them about a stone's throw," and at length exhausted He "fell on his face, and prayed." This was not the usual position for prayer, because the Jews prayed standing; this was the crumpling to earth of one who no longer has the strength to stand and prays prostrate in the dust.

Meanwhile, the three apostles, also in great distress, watched Him as He lay there, groaning. And He groaned: "Abba, Father, all things are possible to thee. Remove this cup from me; yet not what I will but what thou willest." The "cup" or "chalice" was a metaphor frequently used to indicate the lot that fell to a person; the lot that Jesus foresees here is the supreme trial that the Messiah must undergo to reach His triumph.

What a difference between the Sunday before and this night! Then, in the Temple, Jesus had promptly and resolutely rejected the mere thought of hesitation in the trial; now, as it is about to begin, He not only hesitates, He

The Mount of Olives and the Garden of Gethsemane

prays expressly to the heavenly Father that it be spared Him. Yet His prayer is subject to the supreme will of the Father; the will of man is subordinated to the will of God.

At no other moment in His life does Jesus seem so truly human. In place of the Roman Pontius Pilate, all of humanity might at that hour have presented Jesus on the balcony of the universe, proclaiming: Ecce homo! At that hour, more clearly perhaps than afterward, we can gauge the anguish that overwhelmed Jesus' spirit during His Passion.

He must have repeated the prayer to the Father over and over again with the tortured fervor of extreme need. "And there appeared to him an angel from heaven to strengthen him." Luke (22:43), who is not one of the three witnesses of the Passion but must have heard it from them, is the only one who records this information. And he is also the only one who, psychologist and physician that he is, gives us the details of what next took place: "And falling into an agony he prayed the more earnestly. And his sweat became as drops of blood running down upon the ground." He had resorted to prayer in all the most solemn moments of His life, and it becomes now His only refuge in this last hour. The marks of the struggle with death appear on His body: He sweats, and His sweat becomes "as drops of blood running down upon the ground."

In the clear moonlight and only "a stone's throw" away, our three witnesses could have noticed this effect easily enough, and in any case there was opportunity to confirm their impression when Jesus came to them, His face lined with crimson traces of the "drops of blood."

The agony lasted a long time; it must have been now past midnight. The three apostles, at first distressed by what they saw, sank gradually into numbness induced by sorrow and fatigue, and finally they slept.

At a certain point in His spiritual anguish, Jesus felt also the desolation of human loneliness, and He again sought the company of His three beloved friends. But He found them all asleep, including Peter who a little while before had poured forth torrents of words to protest his faithfulness. Then Jesus said to him: "Simon, dost thou sleep? Couldst thou not watch one hour? Watch and pray, that you may not enter into temptation. The spirit indeed is willing, but the flesh is weak." And this was all the comfort Jesus had from the three He loved best.

The spasm of suffering continued, and once more He turned from men to God. And again He made the same request to His heavenly Father: "My Father, if this cup cannot pass away unless I drink it, thy will be done!"

Time passed; the night was monotonously still, and after a little while the three apostles despite their efforts were again overcome by sleep. "And he

The Garden of Gethsmane today, looking toward the wall of Jerusalem

came again and found them sleeping, for their eyes were heavy. And they did not know what answer to make to him" (Mark 14:40). It is easy to recognize in this last phrase the confession of Mark's informant, Peter.

"And leaving them he went back again, and prayed a third time, saying the same words over" (Matt. 26:44). How long Jesus prayed this third time we do not know; perhaps not very long. Then He went back to the three sleeping men, and this time, in a different tone, He said to them: "Sleep on now, and take your rest! It is enough, the hour has come. Behold, the Son of Man is betrayed into the hands of sinners. Rise, let us go. Behold, he who will betray me is at hand." The first words, "sleep on now, and take your rest," are obviously not to be taken literally. It seems more reasonable to interpret them as a kind of affectionate irony, as if He said: Yes, yes, this is a good time to sleep! Do you not see that the traitor is here?

They could, in fact, hear the noise of the crowd coming up the road from Jerusalem, and in the distance the light of torches and lanterns came breaking through the nighttime.

Jesus led His three sleepy witnesses back to where the other eight apostles lay, undoubtedly in deepest slumber, and He waked them all. Then He waited, speaking meanwhile a few words of exhortation.

The Arrest

"And while he was yet speaking, behold Judas, one of the Twelve, came and with him a great crowd with swords and clubs, sent from the chief priests and elders of the people." Thus the Synoptics, while John adds a detail or two regarding the "great crowd." It was composed for the most part of Temple attendants (cf. Luke 22:52), but there was also a cohort with its tribune (John 18:3, 12). The soldiers were certainly there by order of the Roman procurator. What had happened?

It is not too hazardous to reconstruct the events immediately preceding the arrest in this way. When Judas left the Cenacle, he went straight to the leaders of the Jews, who had completed their preparations and mustered all their material and moral support: first they had told their attendants to be ready for a short but difficult assignment; and then they had gone to the procurator or the tribune, and having pictured that Galilean Jesus as a political agitator surrounded by other troublemakers, they had obtained an armed escort. This could not have been the whole cohort (about six hundred men) stationed in Jerusalem, but only a small detachment to which John gives the name of the whole. In any case, the presence of Roman soldiers was of great psychological value, especially since their tribune was with them.

All these people gathered right after nightfall, and there remained only to find Jesus and arrest Him. Where should they look for Him in order to take Him quietly and without risking a riot among the people? No one could help them better here than Judas. John tells us that Gethsemane was well known to the traitor "since Jesus had often met there together with his disciples," and he was also quite sure that after the Paschal dinner Jesus could not have gone all the way to Bethany. Hence He must be in Gethsemane or its vicinity.

In completing his arrangements with the chief priests, Judas fixed a sign by which they were to recognize Jesus: "Whomever I kiss, that is he! Lay hold of him!" In ancient times in the Orient it was customary for disciples to kiss the hands of their teachers as a mark of respect, while friends, as equals, kissed each other on the cheek. There was still some shred of decency in the sign Judas chose; he did not quite have the face to point his Master out to the guards shouting, "There he is," which is what anyone who really hated Jesus would have done, for the shout in itself would have given some vent to the hatred. The sign he chose was an attempt to save appearances. But here again we are faced with the strange riddle of Judas. He knew that the Master was already aware of his betrayal. Had he not heard the compassionate "Thou hast said it!" from Jesus' own lips a few hours before? If any such disconcerting thoughts did come to Judas's mind, he probably bolstered his courage by concentrating on the thirty shekels. This pretense of decency was also in a way a survival of his love for Jesus, which at that moment was completely stifled by his love for gold.

Everything went according to plan. Jesus was still speaking with His apostles when Judas entered the garden with the guards a short distance behind him. He walked toward the Twelve, peering through the darkness for Jesus. Then he went up to Him, laid a hand on His shoulder, and kissed His cheek, saying: "Hail, Rabbi!" Jesus looked steadily at him and said in a low voice: "Friend, for what purpose hast thou come?" And then, after a moment, "Judas, dost thou betray the Son of Man with a kiss?" But He received no answer; Judas had carried out his pact.

As soon as they saw the sign, the guards came forward pell-mell, and Jesus moved away from the apostles to go to meet them. "Whom do you seek?" He asked. They answered: "Jesus of Nazareth." And Jesus said: "I am he." At these words those closest Him drew back and fell flat on the ground. It may well be that the guards suddenly felt the full force of Jesus' personality and were utterly dismayed. Perhaps they thought of the tragic death that fell upon the soldiers sent to capture Elias. In any case it is obvious that John, the only one to relate this episode, intends to picture it as miraculous, thereby emphasizing the perfect freedom with which Jesus accepted His arrest. Then they stumbled to their feet again and repeated that they were seeking Jesus of Nazareth, and He answered once more: "I have told you that I am he. If, therefore, you seek me, let these go their way." Jesus refers tactfully to the apostles as "these," thus covering the fact that they were His special disciples in order to protect them from violence or abuse. This time, the guards "seized him and held him."

Those who executed the arrest must have been the Temple attendants since it was the servant of the high priest who was the first to suffer the consequences and since Jesus was taken immediately not to the procurator but to the high priest. The soldiers of the Roman cohort probably did no more than stand by ready to intervene if needed.

Jesus' concern to protect His apostles first, and then the sight of their beloved Master so humiliated and in the hands of such people, revived the pugnacious proposals they had made a few hours before.

So they pushed through the crowd to Jesus and said to Him: "Lord, shall we strike with the sword?" But Peter would not have been Peter if he had waited for an answer; without further ado, "having a sword, he drew it and struck the servant of the high priest and cut off his right ear. Now the servant's name was Malchus." John (18:10) is the only one who mentions Peter and Malchus by name; the Synoptics record the incident without naming either, probably through prudence prompted by the times in which they wrote.

Jesus intervened immediately and said to Peter: "Put back thy sword into its place, for all those who take the sword will perish by the sword. Or dost thou suppose that I cannot entreat my Father, and he will even now furnish me with more than twelve legions of angels? How then are the Scriptures to be fulfilled, that thus it may happen?" And having put Peter in his place, Jesus also healed the wounded man's ear with a simple touch of His hand. The cure is recorded only by the physician Luke (22:51). Then Jesus turned to the crowd, among whom were "chief priests and captains of the temple and elders," and He said to them: "As against a robber you have come out, with swords and clubs. When I was daily with you in the Temple, you did not stretch forth your hands against me. But this is your hour, and the power of darkness" (Luke 22:52–53).

The prisoner was bound, and they began to lead Him away. Between their first sleepiness and then their impulsive anger, the apostles had not yet fully grasped what was happening; now they began to understand. The Master was actually arrested; He was being led away like an ordinary criminal. Now they began to have some notion of what He meant by the bitter trial, the supreme suffering through which He had said so many times He must pass before entering upon His glory.

Between the heartbreaking sight before them and these grief-boding memories, the eleven weak little men were crushed. They completely forgot the distant future glory of the Messiah; they were aware only of the clink-ing of the chains, the glinting swords, the humiliation of their master. And in their overwhelming sense of loss and terror, they took to their heels and fled, every last one of them, and Jesus left Gethsemane accompanied only by His captors.

But one friend still lingered, although not very near. It is here we meet the episode of the young man clad only in a linen cloth. It is possible that this young man was the evangelist Mark. If he was the son or other relative of the owner of the Cenacle (and perhaps of the garden as well) as he may have been, we may suppose that when the Last Supper was over, he followed Jesus and His friends to Gethsemane and that he stayed there a while with the eight apostles, eventually falling asleep himself. The detail that he had only "a linen cloth wrapped about his naked body" is very important: the "sindon" was worn to bed only by wealthy persons, while ordinary people slept in their clothes. Probably, then, the youth was accustomed to spending the night in the little hut in Gethsemane, where he may have kept a pallet and the other comforts a well-to-do person would have when he went to bed.

If these suppositions are true, then the whole scene becomes clear. Suddenly awakened by the loud talking of the guards, the screams of the wounded servant, and the outcries of the apostles, the young man jumped from his pallet just as he was. He watched the last part of Jesus' arrest, and he saw the apostles all flee. Then either because he felt safe since he was still on his own property, or because youth is naturally more enterprising and he had besides a real affection for the prisoner, he began to follow the soldiery as they moved off. After a while the guards noticed the young man trailing them in that strange garb and seized him on suspicion. But they seized only his linen cloth, because he nimbly slipped out from under it and fled away naked.

And so Jesus was abandoned by this last friend, too, a lad without any clothes.

The Religious Trial before the Sanhedrin

It was probably now about two hours past midnight. The guards led their prisoner back over the same road He had come a few hours before and, having crossed the Cedron, climbed up the western hill of the city where stood the house of the high priest Annas. The prisoner and the guards of the Sanhedrin remained in the house, while the soldiers from the Roman cohort withdrew to their quarters.

It is likely that Annas and Caiphas, given their relationship, lived in separate apartments in the same house. If Jesus was led first to Annas, the reason probably was that the latter, no longer in office but still powerful, had suggested the way to take the prisoner. Hence, out of respect for this assistance and for his extraordinary influence, his son-in-law Caiphas had given orders that the prisoner be brought first to him.

At this point, then, the trial of Jesus begins. It has two phases, conducted in two different places on the basis of two separate sets of arguments. The first part of the trial is religious: Jesus is charged with a crime against religion and appears before the national-religious court of the Sanhedrin where He is pronounced guilty of death. But the Sanhedrin could carry out no death sentences without the explicit approval of the Roman authority. Therefore, the Sanhedrists appeal to the Roman procurator, and this opens the second, civil, phase of the trial. The judges in the first trial here act as accusers, and their charges are mostly political and only to a lesser degree religious.

The religious trial began with the questions Annas asked Jesus. This was not an official interrogation, however. Rather, it was an attempt to fix the charge, or it may reflect no more than the questioner's desire to satisfy his curiosity while waiting for the official judges and witnesses to appear at that late hour of the night.

Annas questioned Jesus about His disciples and His teaching, and Jesus answered: "I have spoken openly to the world; I have always taught in the synagogue and in the Temple, where all the Jews gather, and in secret I have said nothing. Why dost thou question me? Question those who have heard what I spoke to them; behold, these know what I have said" (John 18:20–21). The accused had answered according to His right; among all peoples, including the Hebrew, the accused could not testify in his own regard. The only valid testimony was that of other, trustworthy people, and Jesus' answer refers His questioner to just such witnesses. He has not taught any secret mysterious knowledge. He has spoken in public to all who came to Him. Hence these can all bear witness to His teaching.

At Jesus' unimpeachable answer, Annas must have made some gesture of annoyance, because he had certainly hoped the accused would say something that would furnish grounds for the official accusation to be made against Him. Annas's angry gesture was noticed by an overzealous servant, who thought it opportune to translate into action the unspoken impulse of the questioner. This servant was standing near Jesus, and he struck Him, exclaiming in a scandalized tone: " 'Is that the way thou dost answer the high priest?' Jesus answered him: 'If I have spoken ill, bear witness to the evil; but if well, why dost thou strike me?' " (John 19:22–23).

This blow concludes all we know of Annas's questioning, which probably did not last long. Since the accused was so completely controlled and since Annas perhaps did not want to become involved in the trial, he sent Jesus bound to the high priest then in office, his son-in-law Caiphas. The distance from one home to the other was very short, since, if our supposition is correct, it probably meant only crossing the courtyard into which the apartments of the house opened.

Various members of the Sanhedrin had in the meantime been gathering in the house of Caiphas, and when there were a sufficient number of them, they subjected Jesus to some sort of questioning, preliminary to the official procedure against Him. The Sanhedrin met in its real capacity as a court only later, however, toward morning, as if to complete and act upon the findings of their nocturnal investigation. Matthew and Mark seem to assign their accounts of the questioning to the night session; Luke, more accurate so far as time is concerned, records it at the morning meeting, and there is no doubt his order is the one to be preferred.

The morning session began "as soon as day broke" (Luke 22:66), that is, as soon as the sky began to lighten but before the full dawn. It must have been about five o'clock according to our time. Probably those who had been present at the night questioning were either Jesus' most bitter adversaries or the members who habitually frequented the high priest's house. At the morning session, however, members of all three groups of the Sanhedrin were present (Luke 22:66).

In observance of a sacred and ancient norm, they began by examining "many ... witnesses," who, however, were "false"; but because these witnesses had been primed too hastily and not specifically enough, or because in their reference to Jesus' former discourses and actions they confused very different particulars, "their evidence did not agree" (Mark 14:56). With such depositions, the trial did not progress, nor did they save even the appearance of legality. For though there did not exist at the time the later written rule that the witness had to specify the day, the hour, the place, and other minute circumstances of the alleged crime, nevertheless it was evidently required that the testimony should not contradict itself. And contradict itself this testimony certainly did.

Finally, however, two witnesses appeared who did seem to have the same story. Besides, they fulfilled the minimum legal requirement since there were two of them. They charged that Jesus had pronounced the following words: "I am able to destroy the temple of God, and to rebuild it after three days" (Matt. 26:61); or as Mark records it: "I will destroy this temple built by hands, and after three days I will build another, not built by hands." But upon further questioning, these two did not completely agree either; above all, their testimony was not true either to the spirit or to the letter of Jesus' words.

Their evidence obviously referred to what Jesus had said two years before when He drove the merchants from the Temple; but, as we have seen, His words on that occasion were figurative and referred to His own body, not to the Temple of Jerusalem. Besides, even if His statement were taken as a reference to the Temple, Jesus had not proposed to destroy it Himself but had challenged His adversaries to do so ("Destroy this temple ..."), and, therefore, He would be at the most the rebuilder of the Temple destroyed by the Jews. But to rebuild the Temple could carry with it titles of praise, not furnish the basis for denunciations. Even Herod the Great had gained some merit with the Jews by rebuilding the Temple a half century before. The witnesses and the judges certainly did not believe Jesus could do what Herod the Great had done; the most they could conclude, therefore, was that the accused was a conceited fool and a braggart. It would be difficult to convict Him of impiety and blasphemy on this evidence alone.

Realizing, in fact, that this last bit of evidence was about to evaporate into thin air, the high priest decided to take things into his own hands. Rising to his feet, Caiphas ostensibly tried to elicit from Jesus an answer to the charges made by these witnesses, but actually he was hoping to involve Him in discussion and force Him to some confession. So he said to Him: "Dost thou make no answer to the things that these men prefer against thee?" But the answer he wanted was not forthcoming; Jesus remained silent.

Then the high priest assumed an inspired and solemn tone and tried again: "I adjure thee by the living God that thou tell us whether thou art the Christ [Messiah], the Son of God." One would have thought that the high priest, consumed with desire for the truth, was awaiting just one word of assurance in order to throw himself reverently at the feet of Jesus and recognize Him as the Messiah of Israel.

It is to be carefully noted that Caiphas charged Jesus to declare if He was "the Christ, the Son of God." There are really two parts to the question. Jesus may affirm or deny that He is "the Christ," or Messiah, and He may affirm or deny that He is "the Son of God." Caiphas probably used the two terms more or less synonymously, but he himself and the other members of the Sanhedrin show later that they could make a distinction between them, and they give the term "the Son of God" a much more sublime significance than the title "Messiah."

The moment was in truth a solemn one. All Jesus' activity, His entire mission seemed to resolve into the answer He would give the high priest. His questioner wore the highest authority in Israel; the accused throughout His life had almost constantly hidden the fact that He was the Messiah for reasons of prudence, confiding it only recently to chosen persons.

But now the reasons for caution no longer existed. Dangerous as it was, the time had come to declare His identity to all of Israel, represented before Him by the high priest and the Sanhedrin.

But the answer Jesus had ready could not fail to scandalize those to whom He would speak it because of their particular dispositions. Besides, it would first be necessary to clarify certain principles on which they might equivocate. So He prudently warned them: "If I tell you, you will not believe me; and if I question you, you will not answer me" (Luke 22:67–68).

The warning momentarily disappointed the hopes of the entire assembly; and they all began to exhort the accused to speak, all repeating the high priest's question at once. Then Jesus turned to the high priest and answered: "Thou hast said it," which meant: "I am what you have said." After this brief declaration He turned to all those present and stated: "Nevertheless, I say to you, hereafter you shall see the Son of Man sitting at the right hand of the Power and coming upon the clouds of heaven." This was a quotation of two famous messianic texts (Dan. 7:9, 13; Ps. 109[110]:1), and it was intended to establish the meaning of His statement by linking it with the Hebrew Scriptures, while at the same time it appealed to the future proof of that declaration, namely, the glorious return of the Messiah "upon the clouds of heaven," as foretold by the Scriptures.

As soon as they heard Jesus' words, all the Sanhedrists rose toward Him in great excitement, vying with one another in demanding: "Art thou, then, the Son of God?" (Luke 22:70).

They already had Jesus' confession that He considered Himself the Messiah; but there could still be some doubt that He also considered Himself the "Son of God" in the essential meaning of that term. In reality, Jesus' reference to the two messianic texts made this point clear enough, too, but the Sanhedrists were anxious to have a complete declaration from the accused Himself, and so they asked him formally: "Are you then, besides the Messiah, also the Son of God?" A more exact and specific question could not be asked.

Neither was it possible for Jesus to give them a more exact and specific answer; across the throbbing silence of the tribunal it rang: "You yourselves say that I am," which meant: "I am what you have said — the Son of God."

Now that he had obtained this unmistakable declaration, the high priest shrieked in horror: "He has blasphemed! What further need have we of witnesses? Behold, now you have heard the blasphemy! What do you think?" And the one accord they shouted: "He is liable to death!"

To make his scandalized indignation the more impressive, the high priest had, with his exclamation, torn away the border of the upper part of his tunic as was customary at times of great mourning; but if the man had displayed his real feelings, his face would have shone with a deep and sincere joy. He really believed that he had succeeded in making Jesus blaspheme and so implicated Him that the death sentence was inevitable.

But the high priest's question constituted a completely illegal procedure. Since they had been unable to prove anything against Him with witnesses, they had tried to make the accused testify against Himself, and thereby surprise

Him in a supposed flagrant crime; hence, they now ignored all His alleged past crimes to concentrate entirely on the present one, and Jesus no longer figured as an accused answerable for former misdeeds but as an innocent man arrested in order that He might be provoked to blasphemy.

Besides, in declaring that He was the Messiah, Jesus had not blasphemed: in the first place because He had not used the name of God but had instead substituted for the personal or descriptive name of God the epithet "Power," as the rabbis used to do, and in the second place, to claim that oneself or another was the Messiah of Israel did not in itself constitute a blasphemy. Hence, even if Jesus' adversaries did not accept His claim that He was the Messiah, the most they could do was to condemn it as the empty boast of a fanatic or madman, but it could in no way be considered a blasphemy against the Divinity.

Why then did the president shriek and the court assent that Jesus had blasphemed? Evidently because of Jesus' affirmative answer to their second question: "Art thou then the Son of God?" Here the term "Son of God" obviously is not a synonym for Messiah; it represents a further step, and it carries a much higher significance. The questioners wanted to know if Jesus considered Himself, in the true and essential meaning of the word, "the Son of God." And when Jesus answered yes, He was adjudged a blasphemer.

So the religious trial was ended and the sentence passed. Jesus was pronounced guilty of death for blasphemy. The trial had exceeded the high priest's wildest hopes. The examiner had won in both fields: in the national-political one, because the accused had confessed that He was the Messiah of Israel, and in the strictly religious one, because the prisoner had confessed that He was the true Son of God. This second answer settled the case before the Sanhedrin; the first was brought before the Roman procurator and was equally decisive.

All this took place — as we have said — at the morning session of the Sanhedrin. But other things had taken place or were taking place in the meantime, which we shall here discuss by themselves.

The Insults Offered Jesus; Peter's Denials; the End of Judas Iscariot

When the night session was over and the fate of the accused practically decided, He was handed over to the custody of guards of the Sanhedrin until this council should meet in the morning.

The guards now had Him in their power, and He was to all intents and purposes outside the law. They were irritated because they had to stay up all night on His account, and they proceeded to compensate for their annoyance by subjecting Him to their ridicule and their brutal horseplay. For perhaps two hours — from about three to five in the morning — the accused was entirely at the mercy of these guards, who were probably joined by the most rabid members of the Sanhedrin come to cheer them on. Jesus was led across the court between the apartments of Annas and Caiphas and down into some dark underground room. There His guards struck Him, spat in His face, and showered outrage of every kind upon Him as one guilty of blasphemy.

Then they proceeded to more sober and better organized sport; they played a children's game, but in a cruel and atrocious way. They blindfolded the prisoner and then kept striking Him viciously across the face, asking Him to guess who had struck Him. The intended mockery is obvious, for Jesus, the prophet who had so often seen hidden things and read men's innermost thoughts, should have been able to name who had struck Him. At every blow, in fact, they asked: "Prophesy to us, O Christ [Messiah]! who is it that struck thee?" And others "caught him with blows," as Mark says. And the spitting and the curses and the jeers continued without interruption.

As the guards' inventiveness began to exhaust itself somewhat and their interest gradually succumbed to weariness, one by one they left Him sitting there, limp and crumbled as a rag, while they probably stretched out on the ground to sleep away the rest of their watch.

Shortly before this another incident had occurred in which the chief actors were not the enemies but the friends of Jesus.

We saw how the apostles all abandoned Him in Gethsemane except Judas. Where did they flee? Obviously they did not run very far but stopped when they saw there was no immediate danger. And with the sense of security came a natural reaction against their cowardice. Then some, if not all of them, must have returned cautiously to Jerusalem singly or by twos and threes.

Ahead of the rest went Peter with "another disciple" (John 18:15). Peter had probably remembered his promise of a few hours before to remain faithful to Jesus even at the cost of his life; deeply chagrined now to realize that he had taken to his heels instead, he had somewhat recovered his fighting spirit and was perhaps thinking up some way to find out what had happened to the prisoner. Carefully observing the movements of the guards from a distance, he noticed they had entered the house of the high priest, and with the "other disciple" he marched resolutely up to the door.

And here there is a curious incident. That other disciple was known to the servants of the high priest and so he had no difficulty entering the house, but Peter, who was not known, was left outside. But when the "other disciple" noticed Peter was no longer following him, he went back and spoke to the portress, and Peter was allowed to enter.

Who was this "other disciple," mentioned only in the fourth Gospel but without being named? It is reasonable to suppose, as so many scholars have done, that he is none other than John, who does not name himself here for the same reason that he constantly veils his identity throughout the rest of his Gospel. Nor is it surprising that he was known to the servants of the high priest. Whether there was some business relationship between the well-to-do family of John and the high priest, or whether there were other reasons that now escape us, a superficial acquaintance between the young man and the high priest's servants was nothing exceptional.

To form an accurate picture of what happened next, we must remember the arrangement of a wealthy home in Jerusalem. Entrance was from the street through a main door with its porter's lodge. A vestibule, resembling a long corridor, opened into a courtyard or atrium, shared by all the various apartments in the house.

What happened was this: When Peter entered at John's intervention, the portress eyed the strange visitor with a petulant curiosity not uncommon among lady doorkeepers and all the more natural on that night charged with suspicion. Struck perhaps by his unfamiliar face and embarrassed manner, she said to him, half in earnest and half with inquisitive sarcasm: "Art thou also one of this man's disciples?" (John 18:17). Taken by surprise, Peter managed to say promptly and evenly: "I am not." Then the leader of the apostles, almost as if to hurry away from his lie to some less dangerous place, plunged into the vestibule and made his way to the courtyard, where he found a group of guards gathered around the fire.

Assuming a casual air, Peter approached the fire and mingled with those about it. But the portress was still stalking her prey; more curious now than before, she followed Peter to the fire and repeated her suspicion in a loud voice so that all could hear it. Her question made some impression on them; they scrutinized the newcomer more intently there in the light of the fire and discovered that the portress's suspicion might have some basis. And they all began to repeat her question, some to each other and some to Peter.

Peter realized that he had put his head in the lion's mouth. His only thought was to save himself. He pretended not to hear some of the questioners and to others he answered vigorously that he did not know Jesus at all. But there, in the light of the fire and under the fixed gaze of so many people, his protestations were embarrassed and faltering. It would be better to go and stand somewhere else. Then Peter, his thoughts in confusion and his conscience far from easy, started back toward the door. At that moment, the shrill crowing of a cock pierced the dim morning stillness (Mark 14:68).

Meanwhile that pest of a woman had resumed her post beside the door and so there she was, under Peter's feet again. This odd fellow offered something of a pastime, and she continued her sarcastic sallies, communicating her suspicions to the servants passing by. Peter wandered vaguely back and forth between the door and the courtyard, but cornered once more, "again he denied with an oath: I do not know the man!" (Matt. 26:72).

Time passed, and the people seemed to have forgotten Peter. He, meanwhile, kept peering through the shadows and listening to see if he could find out anything of what was happening to Jesus. But at a certain point, "about an hour" (Luke 22:59) after Peter's entrance into that ill-omened house, the suspicions were revived. A little group approached him and challenged him with positive conviction: "Surely thou art also one of them; for thou art a Galilean. Thy speech betrays thee!" (Matt. 26:73; Mark 14:70). The Galileans spoke a dialect, and their accent betrayed them the minute they opened their mouths, like the drawl of a Georgia farmer in Boston.

This was a serious shock to Peter but worse was to come. For no sooner was he challenged on this score than another, who had been scanning his features, leaped forward and shouted in his face: "Did I not see thee in the garden with him?" (John 18:26). The person speaking with so much conviction was a relative of the man whose ear Peter had cut off a few hours before in Gethsemane.

In the face of such proof, Peter saw he was lost. Grasping instinctively for any means of escape whatever, he began to swear and curse that he had never known any Jesus of Nazareth and that as a matter of fact this was the very first time he had ever heard of such a person.

In the middle of this torrent of imprecations, the cock crowed a second time (Mark 14:72); at that very moment, Jesus, bound and surrounded by His jailers, crossed the courtyard where the fire was burning. The night meeting of the Sanhedrin had just ended, and He was being led to the underground cell to await the morning session.

This time the crowing of the cock struck Peter like a hammer blow; suddenly forgetting his annoyers, he lifted his gaze beyond them and saw Jesus passing through the court. And Jesus turned toward him one of those glances that always left Peter shriveled in his inmost being. The disciple remembered then what the Master had predicted a few hours before, that on that very night before the cock had crowed twice, he would have denied Him three times.

And the poor but generous-souled Peter abandoned the place of his defeat and "went out and wept bitterly."

When the morning meeting of the Sanhedrin was over, the news quickly spread that Jesus had been condemned to death. Perhaps the first person outside to learn of it was the man who had a supreme interest in the sentence, Judas Iscariot. The Master, whom in his own fashion he did love, had been condemned to death. Would He be able to free Himself? Would He use His miraculous power to break the net His enemies had woven about Him? The traitor doubted that He would.

Perhaps he realized then for the first time that the results of his treachery were far different from those he had foreseen. Certainly he realized for the first time the abysmal injustice he had committed. The love for Jesus at that moment overcame every other love within him, even his powerful craving for money. But it was a love incapable of rising to the hope of forgiveness. The thirty shekels he had received and that his greed had expected to satisfy his spirit, now became like thirty hot coals. He could not keep them on his person any longer, for they seemed to rivet his betrayal to him. So he ran to the chief priests and shouted: "I have sinned in betraying innocent blood." And he held out the purse full of shekels to them. The members of the Sanhedrin looked at him coldly. "What is that to us? See to it thyself!" The answer of these men who had hired his treachery rang in his ears like a cruel jest; he saw that no one was more caught in the meshes of his perfidy than himself. He alone was his own real victim. As for the Sanhedrists, since they had dutifully paid the thirty shekels agreed upon, they wanted to hear no more about the affair.

The traitor was seized with a mad fury. Every door was shut to him; the weight of the shekels was crushing him. He ran to the Temple nearby, and going as close as he could to the inner sanctuary, he began to throw shekels wildly toward the "holy place" as if he were tearing his heart free of the vipers knotted around it. The coins clinked mockingly across the pavement, scattering in front of the holy place, and then lay there as if waiting for something.

But even when their derisive jingle had stopped, the traitor felt no relief. Though his greed had been completely routed, his love for Jesus could see rising before it in tragic compensation only an insurmountable rock between him and the Master whom he had always loved. The abyss yawned on every side of him, and darkness seized upon his mind; fleeing from the Temple he went immediately and hanged himself.

We have two accounts of Judas's death with interesting differences, which have a value of their own as confirmation that both narratives relate the same occurrence. Matthew mentions only the hanging. Luke, quoting a discourse of Peter in the Acts (1:16–19) has preserved the tradition that Judas, "falling headlong," burst in the middle and all his bowels gushed forth. The two accounts apparently refer to different moments in the same event. First Judas hanged himself, and then the rope or the branch from which he hung broke, perhaps at the convulsive jerking of his body, and he plunged headlong. It is not unreasonable to suppose that the tree was on the edge of some ravine, so that the fall produced the consequences described by Luke.

Meanwhile the shekels were still lying in the Temple where the traitor had thrown them. The punctilious Sanhedrists consulted together to see what could be done with the money. According to the Law the income from any malodorous transaction such as prostitution, murder, or the like, could not be accepted as an offering to the Temple. So having gathered up the shekels, they observed: "It is not lawful to put them into the treasury seeing that it is the price of blood." On the other hand, those thirty shekels represented a sum it would be very foolish to waste. And so, good casuists that they were, they managed to find a compromise. Great crowds of pilgrims poured into Jerusalem from the various regions during the great Hebrew feasts, and it often happened that some died while they were there and the local authorities had to provide for their burial. Up to this time there had been no special cemetery for them, so the Sanhedrists decided that the thirty shekels might well buy a place commonly known as the "potter's field" — perhaps because the ground was clay and there was a pottery workshop there — which could be set aside as a cemetery for these pilgrims. When the purchase was made, the "potter's field" became commonly known as the "Field of Blood," in memory either of the original use of the money that purchased it or the suicide that had made the purchase possible. And Matthew records that the name, "Field of Blood," in Aramaic "Haceldama" (Acts 1:19), has stuck to it "even to this day."

Jesus' Civil Trial before Pilate and Herod

Since the sentence pronounced by the Sanhedrin could not be carried out without the approval of the Roman procurator, the Sanhedrists now had somehow to surmount this obstacle.

This could be done in two ways: either by inviting the Roman magistrate to accept the judgment of the supreme tribunal of the Jews, or by referring the accused to the procurator's court as if to open a new trial.

This second was the method chosen by the Sanhedrists, and shrewdly so. For if they asked Pilate to approve a death sentence pronounced on purely religious grounds, he certainly would investigate to see whether the charges were true and the procedure legal, or whether the religious pretexts merely served to hide personal rivalries and grudges. Such an examination might bring to light many things that were better kept hidden. No, the surest way to reopen the trial was to do so on different grounds. And if they were going to refer the prisoner to the tribunal of the procurator, then they must present the Galilean Rabbi as a political agitator who was stirring up rebellion against Roman authority. Once started on that road, there was not the least doubt that Pilate's disposition and the prevailing political conditions would bring about exactly what the Sanhedrists desired. So, with this in mind, as soon as the morning session was over, the Sanhedrin moved in a body to the praetorium of Pilate, taking Jesus with them.

The evangelist who witnessed these things points out specifically that it was early morning (John 18:28), probably about six o'clock by our time. The Romans were, at this time, early risers; they transacted their business from dawn until noon, reserving the afternoon and evening for personal affairs and entertainment. Jesus' accusers stopped, however, on the threshold of the praetorium, because it was a pagan dwelling and they could not enter it without being defiled, whereas they were anxious to remain ritually clean in order to celebrate the Pasch, which, according to their reckoning, began on the evening of that day. But where was the praetorium of Pilate?

For the Romans the *praetorium* was the place when the *praetor* discharged the duties of his office, and it might be a soldier's tent today, or a fortress tomorrow. The function of the praetorium had originally been of a military nature, and it never lost its military simplicity. It had two principal accessories, the "tribunal" and the curule chair. The "tribunal" was a kind of semicircular platform, quite high and wide but easily transported and set up wherever necessary. The curule chair was the old conventional chair of the Roman magistrates; it was set in the center of the platform, and from it the praetor officially administered justice. The defendants and plaintiffs, the witnesses and advocates presented themselves before the "tribunal," and the praetor, when he had heard the whole case and consulted his advisers or assistants, seated on either side of him, pronounced sentence sitting in the curule chair. In Caesarea, where the procurator of Palestine ordinarily resided, the praetorium was the palace of Herod the Great because that was his usual residence. In Jerusalem he usually stayed at Herod's palace there, too, but that does not mean that he always made it his praetorium. He might for special reasons stay elsewhere — in the Antonia, for example — in order to keep an eye on the crowds packing the nearby Temple for the great Hebrew feasts. Now where was Pilate's praetorium during the Pasch of Jesus' trial?

A precious hint is furnished by our eyewitness, John, when he says that in order to pronounce the final sentence Pilate "sat down on the judgment-seat, at a place called Lithostrotos, but in Hebrew, Gabbatha" (John 19:13). Hence, that day Pilate set up his praetorium in a place in Jerusalem that was commonly known by two different names: *Lithostrotos*, a Greek name, means "layer of stones," or "pavement"; *Gabbatha* is an Aramaic word, meaning a "high place," a "height." Hence the two names did not translate each other, but both designated the same place. To justify the use of both names recorded by the evangelist we must find a site in the ancient part of Jerusalem that was a "height," and on which there was a "pavement" of sufficient importance to give its name to the place.

To fulfill these requirements, we must conclude that Pilate's praetorium that day was in the Antonia. Besides being a better headquarters for the vigilance required by the festival day, it was truly situated on a "height," that of Bethsaida, which Josephus calls the "highest of all" the hills of Jerusalem. Hence it was natural to give it the term *height*.

But when the massive Antonia Fortress was built, the eminence of the hill seemed to be swallowed up within its huge structure, and so the new term, *pavement*, inspired by the new edifice, came to take the place of the old term,

Lithostrotos

height, although in the beginning both names were used indiscriminately, the old one being favored perhaps by the more conservative and the new foreign term by the more "modern."

It remains to be seen whether in the Antonia there did really exist this *Lithostrotos*, this "pavement" so important as to extend its name to the whole place. We can answer this only on the basis of ancient documents and recent discoveries. From the description of the Antonia in Josephus we gather that it was a four-sided enclosure fortified by a strong tower at each corner, but not a solid mass of buildings. In the center was a huge courtyard open to the sky and surrounded by porticoes, barracks, and the heavy walls of the fortress. There the soldiers of the garrison probably did some drilling, mustered for inspection, or spent their leisure time throwing dice, and so forth. It is obvious, therefore, that the courtyard had to be provided with a substantial "pavement" to protect the ground. Now this "pavement" has been discovered and clearly recognized by the archaeological research conducted there during the past few years. The "pavement" is of Roman construction such as was used by Herod the Great, who built the Antonia. The slabs of stone, broad and solid, are sometimes as much as six feet long by four and a half feet wide and a foot and a half thick. Among the many traces they bear of the intensive use made of them through the centuries, the most interesting are the various diagrams or squares for Roman games obviously cut in them by the soldiers to while away their leisure hours.[18]

It can be considered practically certain, therefore, that this recently discovered pavement is the *Lithostrotos* of the evangelist and that Pilate made this place, also called *Gabbatha*, his praetorium on that day.

Advised that the members of the Sanhedrin and a great crowd of people were outside the praetorium asking to speak to him about a certain Jesus of Nazareth, Pilate went out and, having glanced around at them, asked by way of a start: "What accusation do you bring against this man?" They answered: "If he were not a criminal we should not have handed him over to thee."

This answer was no accusation at all. It was merely intended to capture Pilate's good will, implicitly inviting him to trust the accusers and accept the judgment pronounced by the Sanhedrin. It as much as told the governor not to worry; they had the very same views he did regarding justice and equity,

---

[18] The whole courtyard extended beneath the modern convent of the Sisters of Sion, the Franciscan monastery of the Flagellation, and the so-called "Arch of the Ecce Homo."

and they referred this man to his court only because he was a real criminal deserving of death.

Pilate interpreted their words for what they were worth. The seasoned Roman understood immediately that this was another of the many questions that hinged on the Jews' religious beliefs and in which he had no desire to become involved. Hence, he took refuge in the existing norms and answered: "Take him yourselves, and judge him according to your law." This was merely a suggestion that they apply the laws of their nation, exclusive, of course, of capital punishment. But this was the very crux of the matter, and the accusers indirectly called it to Pilate's attention: "It is not lawful for us to put anyone to death."

This answer revealed their true purpose and also indicated what had taken place that night. If the Sanhedrin appealed to Rome's representative, it was not for permission to impose a fine or a sentence of excommunication or the thirty-nine legal stripes, all of which they could lawfully inflict without the procurator's approval. The accusers wanted permission to carry out the death sentence that the Sanhedrin had passed that night but was powerless to execute. Pilate, therefore, understood that the accusers wanted the prisoner put to death.

Thus Jesus' case was presented before the civil authority. But proofs were necessary to convince the new judge, who almost certainly had never heard of Jesus of Nazareth, and the accusers chose those calculated to make the most telling impression on him. The Jews, then, said to him: "We have found this man perverting our nation, and forbidding the payment of taxes to Caesar, and saying that he is Christ [Messiah] a king" (Luke 23:2). This was a strictly political charge and took the place of the religious charges brought against Jesus before the Sanhedrin. Here before the Roman magistrate, Jesus is represented as a political revolutionary, and more specifically as attempting to prevent the payment of tribute to Caesar as well as in posing as a political messianic king. The last part of the charge implied political royalty.

But Pilate was not so naïve as to accept the glitter for the gold; he sensed something quite different at the bottom of these charges. In any case, the accusers had chosen what was very delicate ground for him. To him, as Rome's representative, they had brought a man charged with conspiring against Rome, and although he immediately perceived that the charge was unfounded, he was forced to discuss it. If he did not, there was real danger that the disappointed plaintiffs would denounce him to Rome as being lax and negligent toward political movements against the authority that he represented. Hence, as a man of law, he was determined to expose the duplicity of the accusers, but as Roman magistrate, he must figure as the guardian of the imperial authority. There was nothing to do but question the prisoner himself.

Pilate reentered the praetorium, where the prisoner had been led, while the accusers remained scrupulously outside, and he began his inquiry with the most critical question of all: "Art thou the king of the Jews?" The question in substance repeated the last charge brought against Jesus, but as Pilate used it, the term "king of the Jews" was deliberately ambiguous. In reality it meant more or less: Are you the king of the Jews in any one of the supramundane and deiform meanings used so frequently in the writings of your nation; or are you king of the Jews in the sense in which Herod the son of Antipater was king here in Palestine a half century ago? Are you king of an ideal and invisible world, or are you king of this material and visible world? Jesus answered Pilate: "Dost thou say this of thyself, or have others told [it] thee of me?"

Pilate saw that this answer was intended to remove the ambiguity in his question. He was annoyed, and he replied somewhat scornfully: "Am I a Jew? Thy own people and the chief priests have delivered thee to me. What hast thou done?" Jesus' answer again distinguished between the two meanings in Pilate's original question: "My kingdom is not of this world. If my kingdom were of this world, my followers would have fought that I might not be delivered to the Jews. But, as it is, my kingdom is not from here." Somewhat surprised by this answer, Pilate determined to clarify one point at least and replied: "Thou art then a king?" undoubtedly expecting Jesus to deny it.

But Jesus did not deny it, for He answered: "Thou sayest it, I am a king," which meant: I am truly a king as you say. Nevertheless, he added an explanation that said what Pilate had perhaps expected: "This is why I was born, and why I have come into the world, to bear witness to the truth. Everyone who is of the truth hears my voice."

Annoyed, Pilate interrupted roughly: "What is truth?"

This was not so much a question as an exclamation, especially since Pilate immediately rose to go out and parley with the Jews. These words merely indicated that the discussion was going into abstract ideas that did not interest the magistrate at all. In Rome, Pilate had listened hundreds of times perhaps to the philosophical debates held in homes and marketplaces, and he had been woefully bored by the disquisitions on truth and error. And so on that morning he had not the remotest desire to hear another from this obscure Jew.

In any event, even this brief conversation with Jesus had convinced Pilate more than ever that he was innocent and that the whole denunciation had been prompted by hatred over some religious squabble. And here two distinct elements in Pilate's character met and intensified each other: one was the sense of law or justice that, as a Roman magistrate, he certainly possessed and that required him to demand respect for the law; the other was his scorn for the leaders of Judaism, which was being offered excellent opportunity in the name of the law to block their wishes. Both these sentiments clamored for acquittal.

Meanwhile, the mutterings of the crowd could be heard, and now and again a unanimous outcry seemed to fling one or another of the accusations into the building. Before going out to them, Pilate tried, as it were, to get some help or suggestion from the prisoner Himself in His own defense; and so he came back to Him again and asked: "Hast thou no answer to make? Behold how many things they accuse thee of" (Mark 15:4). But the prisoner who had just proclaimed Himself the witness of the truth made no answer.

Pilate was not a little surprised, but he still proposed to protect the defendant even without His help, and going out he declared: "I find no guilt in this man." This should have ended the trial then and there.

The Sanhedrists, more than the mob, were indignant. They protested violently, all shouting at once the various charges against Jesus, emphasizing particularly the political one: "He is stirring up the people, teaching throughout all Judea, and beginning from Galilee even to this place" (Luke 23:5). These last words especially caught Pilate's attention because they seemed to offer a solution to the problem. He asked if Jesus was a Galilean, and when they told him He belonged to the jurisdiction of the tetrarch Herod Antipas, he saw a way to use the fact to his own advantage.

Pilate was sure Jesus would appear just as innocent upon examination by Herod as He had in the questioning He had undergone in the praetorium. That would give Him another argument with which to silence the accusers and humiliate them besides with complete legality. In addition, this case afforded him a fine opportunity to better his relations with the tetrarch, which had been quite unfriendly of late, probably because Herod spied on the Roman magistrates in the Orient for the Emperor Tiberius. Hence he decided to send the tetrarch's subject to him for judgment ostensibly as a mark of deference. Actually, since Jesus had been accused before the tribunal of the representative of Rome, that was where He should have been judged; but Pilate, for these practical reasons, was quite willing to forego jurisdiction in this case.

Herod Antipas was in Jerusalem for the Pasch. When he learned the procurator was sending him the Galilean prisoner "he was exceedingly glad; for he had been a long time desirous to see him, because he had heard so much about him, and he was hoping to see some miracle done by him." We know, in fact, that Herod Antipas half believed Jesus to be John the Baptist risen again, and the innate superstition of the man who had murdered the precursor was heightened by memory of his victim.

Herod asked Jesus many questions, but without receiving one single answer from Him. If the accused refused to speak, however, His accusers, who had zealously followed Him, were generously articulate. Before the Jewish king, they probably emphasized the more typically Jewish charges, such as Jesus' alleged blasphemies, His violation of the Sabbath, His supposed threats against the Temple, and His declaration that He was equal with God. The prisoner's silence was a great disappointment to Herod; nevertheless, his legal judgment was sounder than that of the plaintiffs, and he did not fail to see that all their charges were inspired by hatred and that the accused was innocent. He should have proclaimed Him such immediately and set Him free; but the tetrarch's arrogance had to have its little revenge for the frustration it had suffered.

Herod ordered the guards to array the uncommunicative prisoner in a "bright" robe, one of those ornate garments worn by persons of distinction in the Orient on solemn occasions. Perhaps the tetrarch had one of his own robes, now worn a little and so not used anymore, brought out to mock the prisoner, who was thus dressed as the king He declared Himself to be. The very jest with which he chose to close his inquiry showed he considered the prisoner a stupid and ridiculous man, but certainly not a dangerous one, and it implicitly rejected the charge that Jesus was subversive and guilty of sacrilege. Otherwise He would have been punished with extreme severity, not made a laughingstock for the court.

Dressed in this fashion and accompanied by the sarcastic shouts of His accusers, who conscientiously trailed after Him everywhere, Jesus was sent back to Pilate. Luke, the only one to record this episode, says that "Herod and Pilate were made friends that same day; for before they were enemies one to another" (Luke 23:12).

When Jesus came back to him, Pilate saw that Herod did not want to get mixed up in the affair, and he began to be worried, for he realized it was much more serious and complicated than it had at first seemed. He still held firmly to the prisoner's innocence, but he decided to make some concession to the accusers in the hope of settling the matter. The man of law was retreating before the politician.

So he turned to the accusers and argued with them: "You have brought before me this man, as one who perverts the people; and behold, I upon examining him in your presence have found no guilt in this man as touching those things of which you accuse him. Neither has Herod; for he sent him back to us. And behold, nothing deserving of death has been committed by him." Up to this point, Pilate had spoken as a man of law inspired by his sense of justice. But the politician in him comes forward with this utterly unexpected conclusion: "I will therefore chastise him and release him." The "therefore" is a serious mistake in logic; if both Pilate and Herod had found "no guilt" — "nothing deserving of death" — in Him, how could this "therefore" be justified? How could the promised chastisement be considered legal, especially when it was the terrible Roman flagellation?

For the procurator, however, what was not permitted by the law was demanded by politics.

And Pilate immediately proceeded to offer the accusers another palliative. During the Pasch it was the custom for the procurator to release some prisoner at the request of the multitude. Hence it seemed to Pilate that it would be right and convenient this time to grant Jesus the favor, for justice would thus be saved (at least in part) and the accusers would be satisfied as well.

Now, there was in prison at the time a notorious malefactor called Barabbas. During a riot, which he probably started himself, Barabbas had killed a man, and he was besides a professional thief. He was now in prison awaiting the procurator's sentence. Pilate thought that, given the choice between Jesus and Barabbas, the accusers would certainly ask for Jesus. So he went to the threshold of the praetorium and said: "Whom do you wish that I release to you? Barabbas, or Jesus who is called Christ?" and by way of being still more specific, he added, "the king of the Jews?"

Pilate here betrayed his defective knowledge, not so much of the nation he governed but of its spiritual leaders. As a matter of fact, his proposal did make some impression on the mob. Jesus was certainly repugnant to that hireling rabble because he was repugnant to their masters, but at the same time they considered Barabbas such an out-and-out criminal as to deserve the most severe sentence. Hence, there was a short, perplexed pause while the hirelings hesitated between the choice prompted by whatever honesty remained in their consciences and that demanded by their unrelenting masters.

Here a curious incident occurred. Pilate, confident that he had at last found a way out, unexpectedly received a private warning from his wife in these words: "Have nothing to do with that just man, for I have suffered many things in a dream today because of him." This information is recorded by Matthew, the evangelist who is always careful to report divine messages communicated in dreams.

His wife's message must have made a deep impression on Pilate. However cynical he might be regarding philosophical theories about truth and error, he was certainly susceptible to the mysterious signs that enjoyed so much credence among the Romans of his day. All Rome was sure that Julius Caesar would have escaped the dagger thrusts on the fatal Ides of March if he had listened to his wife Calpurnia, who begged him not to go to the Senate that day because the night before in a dream she had seen him pierced by many wounds. So his wife's warning certainly was another reason for doing all he could to release "that just man," his prisoner.

Meanwhile, the rabble had gotten over its perplexity under the coaching of its masters: "The chief priests and the elders persuaded the crowds to ask for Barabbas and to destroy Jesus" (Matt. 27:20).

And the conflict began again, because both sides had received reinforcements: the procurator from his wife, the mob from the Sanhedrists. Pilate again asked the accusers: "Which of the two do you wish that I release to you?" And they answered unanimously: "Barabbas!"

Taken aback by the choice, Pilate asked instinctively: "What then shall I do with Jesus who is called Christ?" And with the proper coaching the crowded shouted: "Let him be crucified!"

"Why, what evil has he done?" the procurator insisted. Obviously, his legalist mind demanded some justification for the extreme penalty they wanted; and the justification he got was the same shout repeated over and over again: "Let him be crucified!" (Matt. 27:22–23).

Pilate was not exactly grieved by this reasoning, but he was baffled and sickened. He was getting nowhere trying to reason with that bawling rabble; it was also difficult to make himself heard above their continued shouting. Still, he was anxious to let them know he in no way shared their bloodthirsty wishes, and so he resorted to an act that they could see even if they would not stop to listen. He had a basin of water brought to him, and he washed his hands before the crowd while they continued to clamor for the death of the prisoner. The act was a conventional symbol not only among the Hebrews but also among other ancient peoples. In this instance it showed that the procurator refused to accept any responsibility for the request being made of him, whatever the outcome of the affair. Then at a moment when the din had somewhat subsided, he shouted: "I am innocent of the blood of this just man; look you to it!" Several of them heard his words, and their answer came back with promptness and confidence: "His blood be upon us and upon our children!"

This wish or prayer suggests a brief reflection that is, after all, not irrelevant to the trial of Jesus. It was expressed unanimously both by the spiritual leaders of Judaism and a large representation of the people of Jerusalem; it was therefore a truly representative "voice of the people," a strictly official prayer expressing the will of both the head and the members. It was not addressed to the Roman procurator but to a much higher Judge, to the Judge who was invoked so often in the Sacred Scriptures of Israel and who was the only one who could make that disputed blood fall upon the heads of Israel's future children. Only that supreme Judge could make the "voice of the people" a "voice of God," by making the wish come true. Today, anyone who can read can decide for himself whether or not it has come true merely by contemplating the evidence of history.

We mention this also because in our day the question has been taken up again by those very "children" mentioned in the prayer. These "children" in 1933 set up in Jerusalem a special tribunal composed of five outstanding Israelites in order to reexamine the sentence. Their verdict, passed with a four-to-one vote, was that the ancient sentence of the Sanhedrin should be revoked; they affirmed that "the innocence of the accused was proved, his condemnation was one of the most terrible errors ever committed by men, and the Hebrew race would be honored in making reparation for it."[192]

At this point Pilate found his own thoughts and feelings in no little conflict. His wife's message had strengthened his personal conviction of Jesus' innocence. Besides, the governor's cantankerous temperament saw a fine opportunity here to do the people he governed one of those mean turns he so delighted in, this time with the support of law and justice. On the other hand, the persistence of the accusers, instead of abating, had increased, and if completely opposed, it might easily lead to one of those tumults that were the principal worry of every Roman governor of Judea. The mere thought of such a possibility, to say nothing of his fear of the reports that might be given of him in Rome, made Pilate more than cautious about his decision, and as they beclouded the austere vision of justice in his eyes, the seductive features of political expediency gradually took its place.

Hence he tried one thing after another almost as if to beguile the accusers with minor concessions. In the first place, he granted the mob's request for

[19]   From the report in the Parisian review *Jérusalem*, 1933, May–June, 464.

the release of Barabbas; in addition, still hoping to make the accusers more pliable, he had Jesus scourged as he had promised.

Among the Romans the flagellation ordinarily preceded crucifixion, but sometimes it was a penalty in itself, and it could be inflicted in place of capital punishment. It was carried out by the soldiers. The prisoner was stripped and made to bend over a post to which his wrists were bound. The blows were administered not with rods but with a special instrument, the *flagellum*, a stout leather whip with several tails weighted with little metal balls or even with sharp points. Among the Jews the legal scourging was limited to a certain number of stripes, but among the Romans its extent was left to the caprice of the floggers or the prisoner's endurance. Especially if he was going to be executed, he was an empty image with which the law was no longer concerned, a body that could be beaten with merciless freedom. And usually one who underwent the Roman scourging was reduced to a sickening and terrifying monstrosity. At the first blows, the neck, back, hips, arms, and legs grew livid, and then became streaked with bluish welts and swollen bruises; then the skin and muscles were gradually lacerated, the blood vessels burst, and blood spurted everywhere, till finally the prisoner, every one of his features disfigured, was a bleeding mass of flesh. Very often he fainted under the blows, and sometimes he died.

It was to this torture that Pilate subjected Jesus, although his intention was to save Him, by this concession, from execution.

When the scourging was over, Jesus was left for a time at the mercy of the soldiers who had administered it and who gave Him the same treatment they usually gave those condemned to death. Any sport whatever, any brutal jest or inhuman mockery was permissible. So when the scourgers had finished flogging Jesus and set about clothing Him again, they called their companions to join in the hilarious performance that was to follow. Then they dressed Jesus in a red mantle, the kind worn by generals in a triumph; they plaited a crown of thorns and put it on His head; and then in His hands, still bound at the wrists, they set a reed for a scepter.

Had He not declared Himself the king of the Jews? Well, let Him present Himself as a king to the soldiers, complete with scepter, diadem, and cloak. These soldiers must have put all the more gusto into their jeers and jibes because they were not legionaries but cohort auxiliaries recruited for the most part probably from among neighboring peoples hostile to the Jews, especially the Syrians and the Samaritans. Hence it was a particularly diverting pastime to shower their scorn and ridicule on a king of those Jewish scoundrels they hated so much.

Then just as special homage was paid a general in his triumph, these brutal clowns began to file past Jesus, each one stopping to kneel in front of Him and repeat obsequiously: "Hail, king of the Jews!" and immediately rising again to spit in Jesus' face, and taking the reed from His hands, they would slam it down on the crown of thorns.

Meanwhile, from Jesus' first appearance before Pilate at dawn, no less than four hours must have gone by. It must now have been between ten and eleven o'clock in the morning. Pilate was still thinking how he might next try to save Jesus, and the mob was still waiting outside the praetorium, noisily persistent.

Pilate attached no importance whatever to the painful insults inflicted on the prisoner after the scourging since he had neither ordered nor prohibited them; but he did place some hope in the legal and psychological effect of the scourging. When Jesus, disfigured by the torture He had undergone and clad in His trumpery garments, was once more brought before him, he decided to base his last appeal to the mob on the impression he hoped such a bleeding rag of humanity would have upon them. Hence he ordered Jesus to be led out after him, while he announced to the crowd: "Behold, I bring him out to you, that you may know that I find no guilt in him."

Jesus, who by now could barely stand, was pushed across the threshold of the praetorium and appeared, as our eyewitness tells us (John 19:5), "wearing the crown of thorns and the purple cloak." Pointing to Him, Pilate exclaimed to His screaming accusers: "Behold the man!"

In Greek the exclamation meant something like our "Here's the fellow now," and it certainly carried with it no overtone of pity; but it did implicitly invite the accusers to reflect whether there was any point in using further violence against a man reduced to that condition.

The scene that followed can be described only in the witness's own words: "When, therefore, the chief priests and the attendants saw him, they cried out, saying: 'Crucify him! Crucify him!' Pilate said to them: 'Take him yourselves and crucify him, for I find no guilt in him.' The Jews answered him: 'We have a Law, and according to that Law he must die, because he has made himself Son of God'" (John 19:6–7). Pilate's words were not a permission to crucify the prisoner; they were a second invitation to reflect that he could not in conscience pronounce the sentence they demanded, and hence the prisoner could not be put to death because they did not have the power to execute Him. The accusers were quick enough to grasp the procurator's meaning, and their answer, which appealed to the Hebrew Law, drew the magistrate out of his own field to that of religion, in which the Romans had always shown the utmost respect for the beliefs of the conquered Jews. Substantially, they suggested to Pilate the possible threat that if he did not pass the death sentence, they would regard him as the protector of the impious and sacrilegious.

Here again, nothing can take the place of the evangelist's account: "Now when Pilate heard this statement, he feared the more. And he again went back into the praetorium, and said to Jesus: 'Where art thou from?'" Probably the uneasy procurator hoped that Jesus' answer would furnish him some new answer to give His accusers. But Jesus did not answer him at all. "Pilate therefore said to him: 'Dost thou not know that I have power to crucify thee, and that I have power to release thee?' Jesus answered: 'Thou wouldst have no power at all over me were it not given thee from above. Therefore he who betrayed me to thee has the greater sin.'"

At this answer, Pilate found himself alone in his opposition to the mob. The procurator's resistance was fortified only by his conviction that the prisoner was innocent and by his desire not to give the Jews what they wanted, but the first made no impression whatever on the accusers and the second he could not, in all prudence, make known to them. Hesitating and still uncertain, he could see no way out of the difficulty. His state of mind is described by the evangelist: "And from then on Pilate was looking for a way to release him" (John 19:12).

The accusers sensed the danger, and to obviate it they resorted to an argument that could not fail to have a telling effect on the procurator. They began to shout: "If thou release this man, thou art no friend of Caesar; for everyone who makes himself king sets himself against Caesar!"

At that shout, Pilate could not hesitate much longer, for he was a very ordinary mortal after all, a Roman official concerned only about his reputation in Rome and his own political career. But he was not yet disposed to give in.

Completely annoyed by the fact that his hated subjects, shrieking and chattering like monkeys, blocked him at every turn, he was still hoping for something unforeseen to save the situation, and he decided to face the conclusion of the trial in direct argument with the accusers.

Shortly before, they had threatened to consider him the protector of the impious and the sacrilegious if he freed Jesus. But had not the accused proclaimed Himself the spiritual king of the accusers themselves? As a political administrator, Pilate did not enter into religious questions; but for this very reason he could not take action against one who claimed for Himself a preeminence that was purely religious with nothing political about it. How did he know but what the prisoner had a whole crowd of disciples disposed to accept His religious royalty? Could he kill the leader of a strictly religious society and then persecute all its members too? Obviously not; as a layman and an impartial magistrate, he was obliged to respect the religious royalty of the accused and command respect for it. Pilate thought this reasoning might save Jesus, and he resorted to it as his last hope.

It was "about the sixth hour" (John 19:14) or a little before noon. With the intention of ending the trial and pronouncing his final judgment, Pilate had his "tribunal" with its curule chair set up outside on the *Lithostrotos* in the presence of the accusers. Then he came out, the prisoner being led after him, sat down in the curule chair, and reopened the discussion. Pointing to Jesus, he said: "Behold your king!" What did the accusers think of the prisoner's royalty? It was clearly not a political royalty, as the magistrate, who knew a thing or two on that score, could easily see. Was His a royalty in the religious sense of the term? Pilate knew nothing about such matters and did not want to have anything to do with them. Let the accusers answer therefore.

The procurator's words sounded like bitter sarcasm to the mob, and they shouted loudly: "Away with him! Away with him! Crucify him!" But Pilate persisted: "Shall I crucify your king?" The answer this time, as the evangelist expressly states, came from the "chief priests," who shouted: "We have no king but Caesar!"

Pilate saw his last loophole blocked. The royalty of the accused could not be taken seriously either by the magistrate or by the accusers. The latter, and precisely the most prominent among them, recognized no royalty in Jesus and proclaimed that their one and only king was the Roman Caesar. Obviously Caesar's representative could not express any different opinion on this point just as he was forced to crucify the false king in order not to offend the religious sensibilities of the accusers.

That must have been Pilate's reasoning more or less: and "then," concludes the evangelist, "he delivered him to them to be crucified."

The Crucifixion and Death of Jesus

The sentence had now been passed and nothing remained but to execute it.

The representative of Rome had condemned the prisoner to a Roman penalty at the request of the accusers; for when the Jews had shouted to Pilate: "Crucify him! Crucify him!" they had asked for a punishment not Jewish originally but Roman. The ordinary Jewish penalty for blasphemy, with which Jesus had been charged before the Sanhedrin, was stoning. At the time of Jesus, however, crucifixion had been in use for many years among the

Jews of Palestine; it had been introduced among them when they first came in contact with the Romans, especially in the year 63 BC when Pompey the Great captured Jerusalem.

The Romans always had a real terror of crucifixion; that is the very least we can say. It was, in fact, the penalty reserved for slaves and inflicted only for very serious crimes. Actually, however, it seems that Roman citizens were crucified on occasion, and even that the law permitted this form of death to be inflicted on freedmen and some provincials though they were Roman citizens.

Ignoring its most ancient forms, the cross in the time of Jesus might have any one of the three following forms:

The first at the left was called *immissa* or *capitata*, with reference to its shortest arm or headpiece. The middle one was called *commissa* and was the only one with three arms and no headpiece. The third, which was not used very much, was the *decussata* or "slantwise," commonly known as "St. Andrew's cross." The *immissa* was most probably the type used for Jesus.

This had two parts: the vertical beam, which was planted in the ground; and the crosspiece, fastened at a point in the crucifixion to the vertical piece. The latter, however, was not entirely smooth or flat. About halfway up there was a thick short block called in Latin *sedile*, "seat"; the person crucified straddled it, and it served to support his weight. Some such support was absolutely necessary; it would have been impossible for a body to be held on the cross by four nails alone, for the weight would have soon torn the hands away. This is so evident that the earliest Christian artists pictured Jesus' Cross with a support to which His feet are nailed. This foot support is an archaeological error, for it would not have supported the weight of the body either, but even the error proves the necessity of having the *sedile*.

When the sentence was passed, the place of execution was prepared — if it was not ready beforehand. The vertical beam, without the crosspiece, was set up in the ground. It was not ordinarily very high; the feet of the condemned man were at about the height of a man's head, and so the whole post could not have been more than twelve or fifteen feet tall.

A conspicuous and greatly frequented place was always chosen for the execution because the sight was to produce a salutary effect on slaves and other individuals who were liable to the same penalty. Hence, places where there was a great deal of traffic were generally preferred, outside the city but near one of the gates, and possibly among tombs.

Before being crucified the prisoner was scourged, sometimes on the way to the place of execution. The condemned man was entrusted to soldiers, usually four commanded by a centurion whose duty it was to certify his death. The horizontal beam of the cross was placed, sometimes tied, on the condemned man's shoulders. A servant of the court walked ahead of him bearing a tablet on which his crime was written in large clear letters, but sometimes this inscription was hung about the prisoner's neck. The procession always went through the busiest streets in order to make the execution as public as possible.

Even when he was not scourged along the way, the condemned man was the victim of every kind of brutal jest on the part of the curious and bloodthirsty rabble. He was no longer a man to them, but something beyond the law, a walking dunghill.

At the place of execution the condemned man was led to the vertical post, already set in the ground, and there stripped of his garments, unless he had been previously stripped for the scourging along the way. It was common among the Romans for a man to be nailed to the cross completely naked, but among peoples more sensitive it may be that he was covered with whatever rag happened to be handy.

Thus stripped, the prisoner was made to lie on his back on the ground so that his shoulders and outstretched arms lay on the crosspiece he had been carrying, and then his hands were nailed to it. Next, probably by means of a rope fastened about his chest and thrown over the top of the vertical beam, he was hoisted up the latter until he was able to straddle the *sedile*.

After the prisoner had been lifted up in this manner, the crosspiece was nailed or tied to the vertical beam, and then his feet were nailed. Naturally this required two nails and not one as Christian art has so often imagined, for since the prisoner was straddling the *sedile* his feet hung almost at the sides of the vertical beam and could not be crossed.

In this state, the crucified awaited death. Hour after hour he could see all kinds of people pass beneath him: patricians who refused him even a glance; busy merchants who might pause for just a moment as they passed; the riffraff and the slaves who amused themselves watching the progress of his suffering. He might perhaps glimpse some sign of compassion — the only one — on the face of a relative or former associate lingering in the vicinity; but it was a barren pity at best, for the soldiers prevented anyone from approaching to give the sufferer any relief whatever. The only things that could possibly reach the shred of humanity nailed to the cross were the stones thrown from a distance by urchins or by some former rival anxious for a last bit of revenge.

Death might result from loss of blood, fever, the acute suffering caused by hunger and especially by thirst, or from other physiological causes. Usually it was not long in coming because of the weakness that resulted from the terrible scourging that preceded the crucifixion. More robust constitutions, however, sometimes remained alive on the cross whole days together, dying gradually in the most frightful agony. Sometimes the executioners deliberately hastened the end either by lighting a fire at the foot of the cross to produce a cloud of heavy smoke, or by piercing the body of the victim with a lance, or by breaking his thigh bones with a club.

In earliest times the corpse was left hanging on the cross until it decayed. Around Augustus's time, however, friends or relatives were ordinarily granted permission to bury the body if they requested it.

All this was the general procedure in all crucifixions, and it was followed in the Crucifixion of Jesus also.

When the procurator had pronounced the sentence and written his statement of the crime on the tablet, it assumed an official character; it was to be transcribed in the government archives and communicated to the emperor in Rome, and it was also to be executed immediately. After all, not much preparation was necessary to carry out the sentence of crucifixion. The vertical piece was standing ready in the place of execution, or if not, it could be set up in a few minutes; and it would not take more than a few strokes of an ax to prepare the crosspiece from any kind of beam; hence all that remained to be done was to summon the soldiers, hand over the condemned man to them, and proceed to the place designated.

The place where Jesus was crucified fulfilled all the conditions mentioned above. Just outside the walls at the northern end of the city there was a little rocky mound, a few yards higher than the surrounding terrain, the appearance of which had prompted its picturesque name, "the Skull," or in Latin, *Calvaria*, and in Aramaic, *Golgotha*. It was an ideal spot for crucifixion, for on it the condemned man would hang in full view, and since it was such a short distance from the city gate, many people were sure to pass that way. Besides this, there was a tomb nearby and perhaps more than one, and so the place fitted this last condition too.

This, then, is where Jesus was sent to be crucified. It would not have been a long walk from the Antonia, only a little over half a mile. Not only were the streets crowded that day because of the Pasch, however, but it is also probable that the soldiers chose the longest and most congested route to give the execution the required publicity. Those most concerned about the latter were the chief priests and the other Sanhedrists who followed the condemned man in triumph and who would certainly not have lost the opportunity to prolong their victory and His humiliation in the sight of the populace.

Yet from the beginning, a very bitter fly turned up in their ointment. The procession was composed of the soldiers, the chief prisoner, Jesus, and two common thieves also condemned to death. Each of them was accompanied, according to rule, by the tablet that announced his crime to the public. Jesus' tablet was inscribed in the three languages commonly used in the district — Hebrew (Aramaic), Greek, and Latin — and its text, dictated by Pilate, read substantially as follows: "Jesus of Nazareth, King of the Jews." The sharp-eyed Sanhedrists caught a glimpse of this along the way, and they were able to read it even more clearly when it was nailed up on Jesus' Cross. Precise jurists that they were, they discovered an enormous error in this statement: the man was being crucified not because He was the "king of the Jews," as the inscription indicated, but because He had said He was the "king of the Jews" and He really was not. Touched to the quick, they hurried to the procurator and pointed out the terrible mistake that had to be corrected in the interests even of the government. The people might be insulted upon reading in an official document that the king of the Jews had been crucified, especially since only an hour before, that same devoted people had publicly declared that they recognized the Roman Caesar as their only sovereign.

"The chief priests of the Jews said therefore to Pilate: 'Do not write, "King of the Jews," but "He said, I am the King of the Jews."'" Pilate answered: 'What I have written, I have written'" (John 19:21–22). Pilate had somewhat recovered himself; now that there was no longer any danger of being denounced

A street in Jerusalem

to Rome, he took his revenge for the defeat he had suffered and repaid the Sanhedrists' exhibitions of loyalty with spiteful perversity.

And this was the first drop of bitterness in their cup of triumph.

From the Antonia the procession wound slowly through the crowded streets. Many of those who had been shouting in front of the praetorium were probably gone home to prepare for the Paschal meal. Several of the elders followed the procession, however, to make sure that nothing went wrong and that the matter was ended once and for all. The jokes and jibes the rabble always had ready for the condemned were certainly not wanting along the way, but the most exquisitely cruel jests were directed at the man whom the elders pointed out to the especial attention of the mob's brutality: the Galilean Rabbi was a much more worthy object than the two thieves for their obscene derision.

Carrying His crosspiece, Jesus managed to walk only with great difficulty. It was now about noon, and from before midnight He had passed through a succession of physical and mental sufferings of incomparable violence. For there had been His painful and affectionate farewell to the apostles in the Cenacle; then had come Gethsemane and the arrest, the trial before the Sanhedrin, the cruel mockery in the house of Caiphas, and finally the horrible scourging. Now He had no reserve strength left. He tottered under the weight

The Via Dolorosa

of the beam and stumbled at every step, and there was real danger that He might fall at any moment not to get up again. The possibility worried the centurion in command because it would either keep him from carrying out his assignment or it would delay it enormously, and he would be reprimanded as a consequence. So he resorted to "requisition."

There happened to be passing by a certain Simon of Cyrene. Mark takes care to point him out to his Roman readers as the father of Alexander and Rufus. He was coming from the country, where he had been working and was now on his way home, but the centurion, since the need was pressing, "requisitioned" him, ordering him to carry the crosspiece that Jesus could not hold up any longer. There is no reason for believing that Simon knew Jesus or was His disciple, and so the centurion's order must have been anything but welcome. If, however, his son Rufus later became a leading figure in the Christian community in Rome and if Paul through respect called Simon's wife "mother," we may conclude that the service he reluctantly lent Jesus begot the very best of consequences in a way unknown to us.

But Simon was not the only one who helped Jesus. Another comfort, this time spontaneous, came to Him from the women, and Luke, the evangelist of feminine pity, is the only one to record it for us. Perhaps when the crossbeam was taken from His shoulders and He straightened a little in relief, Jesus noticed in the crowd following Him a group of women who were weeping and lamenting Him: they were "daughters of Jerusalem," hence citizens of the capital although there may have been with them some of the Galilean women who ordinarily followed Jesus. There was in Jerusalem a kind of society of mercy composed of noble ladies organized to help in some way those condemned to death. Perhaps these women who now approached Jesus belonged to some such association, and they must have performed their act of mercy all the more wholeheartedly if they knew Jesus at least by name.

Jesus returned their compassion in kind. Thinking again of the imminent destruction of Jerusalem, He saw the anguish women and mothers would have to endure in that catastrophe, and He felt with them in their maternal grief, forewarning them of its future victims; and so He said to them: "Daughters of Jerusalem, do not weep for me, but weep for yourselves and for your children. For behold, days are coming in which men will say: 'Blessed are the barren, and the wombs that never bore, and breasts that never nursed.' Then they will begin to say to the mountains: 'Fall upon us'; and to the hills: 'Cover us' (cf. Hos. 10:8). For if in the case of green wood they do these things, what is to happen in the case of the dry?" (Luke 23:28–31). If these things that the pious women deplored with tears that day were befalling the Innocent condemned to death, what would happen forty years later when the destruction of Jerusalem would overwhelm "a sinful nation, a people laden with iniquity, a wicked seed, children of perdition," as Isaias had expressed it (1:4)?

When the procession reached the place called the Skull, the Crucifixion was carried out immediately. Wine mixed with myrrh, believed to numb the senses, was offered to Jesus, and certainly to the two thieves also; but it no sooner touched His lips than He refused it, choosing to drink with full consciousness to the last drop the chalice given Him by His heavenly Father.

All three were stripped of their garments, though it is possible they were conceded some kind of loincloth. The garments of the crucified fell to the soldiers, who divided them into equal shares. This they did with Jesus' garments, too, and the evangelist who watched them tells us exactly what happened.

A Jew usually wore an outer garment or cloak and beneath it a tunic. The cloak was made of two pieces of cloth sewed together, but the tunic might be without seam, woven in one piece from the top.

"The soldiers, therefore, when they had crucified him, took his garments and made of them four parts, to each soldier a part, and also the tunic. Now the tunic was without seam, woven in one piece from the top. They therefore said to one another: 'Let us not tear it, but let us cast lots for it, to see whose it shall be'" (John 19:23–24). The cloak could be divided along the seams with no great loss; but since the tunic was in one piece it would have lost most of its value if it had been cut into four parts. So the soldiers agreed to give it to the one favored by the dice. But in their action, the evangelist sees the fulfillment of the messianic prophecy in Psalm 21:19 [22:18], which says, "They parted my garments amongst them; and upon my vesture they cast lots."

Stripped of His garments, Jesus was laid upon the ground. His arms were stretched along the crosspiece He had carried, and His hands were nailed to it. Next He was lifted to the vertical beam, already set in the ground, and set astride the support. Then His feet were nailed.

His Cross was in the middle; the two thieves were crucified one on each side of Him. On His Cross was fixed the tablet telling His crime.

The Crucifixion was finished not long after noontime.

On this last point there seems to be a contradiction between John's statement that Pilate pronounced sentence at the "sixth hour" or a little before noon, and Mark's information: "Now it was the third hour and they crucified him."

Various hypotheses have been proposed to reconcile these two statements. The most reasonable solution seems the one based on the customs of the country at that time. The period from dawn to sunset was divided into twelve hours that varied in length according to the season of the year, but this division was theoretical rather than practical. In countries like Judea, where mechanical devices for measuring time were extremely rare, the people usually determined the time of day from the sun and so had ended up by dividing the hours of daylight into four equal periods, two before noon and two after noon. Hence from dawn to what we should consider 9 a.m. was always "morning" or the period of the "first" hour; from 9 a.m. until noon was the period of the "third" hour; from noon until 3 p.m. was the period of the "sixth" hour; from 3 p.m. until sunset was the period of the "ninth" hour. The Synoptics rarely deviate from this terminology (Matt. 20:1–6), but it is more usual for John to name some of the intermediate hours (John 1:39; 4:6, 52; 11:9) instead of the longer periods because of his desire to be specific. In all likelihood, the discrepancy between Mark and John with regard to the hour in which Jesus was crucified is due entirely to this one point: that Mark is referring to the period of the "third" hour, which lasted until the "sixth" hour or noontime, while John means literally the "sixth" hour of the day, or high noon.

So far as we know Jesus did not speak throughout the whole process of crucifixion. There was scarcely any strength left in His torn body, and His thought was absorbed in contemplation of His heavenly Father, to whom He was offering the sacrifice of Himself. The first words from the Cross that are recorded for us, however, while addressed to the heavenly Father, concern those on earth around Him. Perhaps it was while they were nailing His hands or His feet that He exclaimed: "Father, forgive them, for they know not what they do!" (Luke 23:34). He asks pardon not so much for the unwitting soldiers hammering on the nails as for those others who had deliberately arranged that He would be crucified. Even to them Jesus grants His own forgiveness and implores the Father's pardon for them because they do not know now what they earlier refused to know: He generously uses the consequence of their earlier guilt to excuse the present crime.

From the Cross, Jesus watched with drooping but still penetrating eyes all that was going on about Him. Below Him lingered the chief priests and the other Sanhedrists; really it was time for them to be returning home like good Israelites to superintend the preparations for the Paschal meal, but they preferred to loiter a little, gloating happily.

They kept walking back and forth beneath the three crosses. Sometimes they glanced angrily at the Cross in the middle; and now and again they planted themselves before it with their hands behind their backs and addressed the Crucified directly: "Thou who destroyest the temple, and in three days buildest it up again, save thyself! If thou art the Son of God, come down from the cross!"

Other Sanhedrists preferred an argument ad hominem, which was at the same time an apologia for their own behavior: "He saved others, himself he cannot save! If he is the King of Israel, let him come down now from the cross, and we will believe him. He trusted in God; let him deliver him now, if he wants him (cf. Ps. 21:9 [22:8]); for he said: 'I am the Son of God.' " But no answer came from that Cross nor did the One they had crucified descend from it; neither would have done those interlocutors any good.

And there were insults and reproaches also from the two crucified thieves. Matthew and Mark say "the robbers also," meaning that the insults came from the thieves without specifying whether from one or both. Luke does make a distinction, however, and says that one insulted Jesus while the other prayed to him. One of them, perhaps to suck some bitter consolation from the ruin that had overtaken his own life, kept repeating to Jesus: "If thou art the Christ [Messiah], save thyself and us!" But the other robber did not share his feelings, and he rebuked him saying: "Dost thou not even fear God, seeing that thou art under the same sentence? And we indeed justly, for we are receiving what our deeds deserved; but this man has done nothing wrong." Probably the good thief knew Jesus of Nazareth by reputation. And obviously, despite his crimes, there was a residue of goodness left in him. In the face of death, it rises to the surface and covers all his past; the dying man clutches the last hope left to him, personified in the Just Man unjustly killed. Turning to Him, he says: "Lord, remember me when thou comest into thy kingdom" — when You come reigning gloriously in that kingdom that You have foretold. And Jesus answers: "Amen I say to thee, this day thou shalt be with me in paradise."

Among the persons Jesus could see from the Cross there was only one small group that was any source of comfort to Him. Or was it perhaps an added source of sorrow? The names of those in the little group nearest the Cross have been given us by the evangelist who was with them, although he omits his own name, referring to himself only as "the disciple whom [Jesus] loved." With him were standing "his [Jesus'] mother and his mother's sister, Mary of Cleophas [Alpheus] and Mary Magdalene" (John 19:25). After Jesus' death the Synoptics mention another larger group at a greater distance from the Cross, composed of women who were weeping and lamenting. They were the women who had helped Jesus in His ministry and had followed Him from Galilee to Jerusalem (Matt. 27:55–56; Mark 15:40–41). Among those in this second group we have the names of "Mary Magdalene" [as in the first group], "Mary the mother of James the Less and of Joseph" (this Mary also appears in the first group as "Mary of Cleophas"), and in addition a "Salome" and the "mother of the sons of Zebedee," both of whom are the same person. That at least two of the women are mentioned in both groups is not surprising because they are mentioned at different times — the first group before Jesus' death, and the second group, standing a certain distance away, after it.

In the group nearest the Cross, then, stood the Mother of Jesus with the beloved disciple. Was her presence a comfort to Him as He hung on the Cross? The soldiers prevented her from approaching Him, and the nails prevented Him from making any gesture whatever to her. Mary's voice was stilled with grief, and Jesus could not speak from weakness; they could communicate only with their eyes. As the Mother gazed on her Son, she perhaps thought to how frightful a state that body, formed in her womb in a manner unique in the world, was now reduced. And as the Son looked at His Mother, perhaps He reflected how she who had been proclaimed "blessed among women" was now become the object of extreme pity. But at a certain moment, gathering all His strength, He nodded to His Mother and said: "Woman, behold thy son." And then to the beloved disciple He said: "Behold thy mother," In this His last will and testament, the dying Jesus united forever His two greatest earthly loves, the humble woman of Bethlehem and the young man who had heard the beating of His heart at the Last Supper. And from that day John took Mary into his home.

Jesus was failing rapidly. Suddenly it began to grow dark: "From the sixth hour there was darkness over the whole land until the ninth hour" (Matt. 27:45), or from noon until about three o'clock. The expression "the whole land" here means Judea.

It is clear that the evangelists viewed this darkening of the earth at Jesus' death as miraculous, like the miraculous signs that accompanied His birth. But whether it was produced by a dense mass of clouds or in some other way it is impossible to determine.

In the darkness that hung over physical nature, Jesus' earthly existence ebbed slowly away through an agony that lasted about three hours, and which the evangelists have shrouded in a reverent silence. His life and strength were bleeding from Him through His torn hands and feet and the gaping welts left by the scourging. His head was riddled with the thorns; not a muscle in His body could relax in that position on the Cross. There was no rest from pain as torture piled on torture and grew more and more excruciating with every moment.

In that dark spasm of agony, only the pinnacle of His soul was serene, lifted in contemplation of the Father.

He hung in silence.

Suddenly, about the ninth hour, Jesus cried aloud, saying in Aramaic: *'Eli, 'Eli, lema shebaqtani*. Rather than an exclamation in themselves, these words were a quotation. They were the beginning of Psalm 21 [22] and mean, as Matthew and Mark add in Greek: "My God, my God, why hast thou forsaken me?" Since this is a quotation, its full meaning must be derived from the entire composition that it introduces. This psalm, in fact, predicts the final sufferings of the future Messiah, and in reciting its first line from the Cross, Jesus meant to apply it to Himself. Among other things, the ancient psalm had said:

> My God, my God, why hast thou forsaken me? ...
> O my God! I cry by day, and thou dost not answer,
>> and by night, neither is there any rest for me!
> And I am a worm, and no man,
>> the reproach of men and despised by the people.
> All they that see me laugh me to scorn,
>> they open wide their mouths and wag their heads
>> [exclaiming],
> "Let him turn to the Lord: let Him deliver him,
>> Let Him save him, seeing he delights in him!"

* * *

> They have pierced my hands and my feet;
>> I can number all my bones.
> They look and see me,
>> they part my garments among them
>> and for my vesture they cast lots.

Hence Jesus' exclamation affirms once again that He is the Messiah and as proof indicates the manifest fulfillment in Himself of the prophecy He is quoting.

But some did not understand the very first words of the exclamation, *'Eli, 'Eli*. The learned scribes present certainly recognized the quotation, but others, less well-informed, took them as an invocation to the prophet Elias, unless they purposely misunderstood them to have a fresh excuse for jeering at the suffering Christ. And with mingled curiosity and sarcasm, they exclaim: "Behold! This man is calling Elias!"

As He hung waiting on the Cross, Jesus spoke again: "I thirst." Given His loss of blood and extreme exhaustion, this was natural, but it is not the whole explanation. In fact, the psalm that Jesus has just quoted also said:

> My mouth has become dry as a potsherd,
> and my tongue sticks to my jaws!

Thirst, then, was also a part of the prophetic vision of the suffering Messiah; hence John (19:28) calls attention to the fact that Jesus, "that the Scriptures might be fulfilled, said: 'I thirst !' "

This time Jesus' request — His last — met a compassionate response from one of the guards. For want of something better, the Roman soldiers used to quench their thirst with a mixture of water and vinegar, still commonly used by harvesters in Italian country districts. Foreseeing that they would have to spend quite a long time on guard below the crosses, the soldiers had brought a jar of it with them. At Jesus' cry, one of them soaked a sponge in it, set the sponge on a rod, and held it up to His lips. Those who had been shouting about Elias did not like the soldier's action at all, and they tried to dissuade him, exclaiming: "Wait, let us see whether Elias is coming to save him!" (Matt. 27:49). In their opinion, if Elias were going to save Jesus, he would also manage somehow to cure His thirst. It seems that the soldier answered them with the same exclamation (Mark 15:36: "Wait, let us see," etc.) as if to say that it might be better to comfort the crucified a little while they were waiting for Elias to come.

Jesus, who a few hours before had refused the wine and myrrh, now sucked the liquid from the sponge. The evangelists call it "vinegar" for a definite reason, to echo the passage in Psalm 68:22 [69:21], which says: "In my thirst they gave me vinegar to drink." When He had taken the mixture, Jesus murmured, "It is consummated!"

Shortly afterward, a shudder seemed to pass over His wracked body, and He again cried out in a loud voice, saying: "Father, into thy hands I commend my spirit" (cf. Ps. 30:6 [31:5]). Then He bowed His head.

He was dead.

At that moment strange things took place in the darkened city. Two great embroidered curtains hung within the Temple: one between the vestibule and the "holy place," and one between the "holy place" and the "holy of holies," to remind the devout of the inaccessibility and invisibility of God, who dwelt in the "holy of holies." About the ninth hour, as Jesus was dying, one of the curtains (probably the inner one) split in two from top to bottom, almost as if to signify that it no longer had any function, for the invisible God was no longer inaccessible.

There were earthquake tremors also: "And the rocks were rent, and the tombs were opened, and many bodies of the saints who had fallen asleep arose; and coming forth out of the tombs after his resurrection, they came into the holy city, and appeared to many" (Matt. 27:51-53). The resurrection of the dead is probably anticipated in this passage, for it seems to have taken place after the resurrection of Jesus, with which it is here connected.

When the centurion and the soldiers on guard saw the strange phenomena that accompanied Jesus' death and reflected on the calm and unusually rapid manner in which it had come, they recalled His whole attitude during the trial, and putting two and two together, were convinced that such a prisoner was not only innocent but a very extraordinary being. They began to exclaim: "Truly this was a just man" (Luke 23:47); and with reference to the disputed accusation against Him: "Truly this man was the Son of God" (Mark 15:39).

Then the attitude of the mob changed. As soon as Jesus was dead, the Sanhedrists had nothing more to fear from Him for the moment, and so they went home to prepare for the Paschal meal. Hence there was no one left to bully the crowd and prompt the jibes against the crucified, and so, they could show their true feelings. They, too, were impressed by the darkened day and the heaving earth, and remembering what had taken place at the trial, they began to walk away from the Cross, "beating their breasts" (Luke 23:48).

On their way home, the Sanhedrists suddenly remembered a precept of the Law. They kept reminding themselves that they had done a very holy deed in having Jesus crucified, but its holiness would be imperfect if His body were left hanging that night. No; it must be buried that same afternoon before sunset as the Law commanded, especially since sunset marked the beginning of the most solemn feast of the Pasch. So they went to the procurator and requested him to observe this precept, suggesting at the same time the simplest way to do so. It would be enough to break the legs of the three who had been crucified and in a few moments they would all be ready for burial.

Not many moments before, another Sanhedrist had gone to the procurator with a request to bury Jesus. Christ's death had somewhat revived the courage of His disheartened disciples. There was among them a certain Joseph, a native of Arimathea (northwest of Lydda), a wealthy man of great prestige, a member of the Sanhedrin and also "a disciple of Jesus, although for fear of the Jews a secret one" (John 19:38). Spiritually, then, he somewhat resembled Nicodemus, who was also a member of the Sanhedrin, although Joseph had had the courage to disagree with his fellow Sanhedrists when they condemned Jesus to death (Luke 23:51). Now he dared even more. Perhaps at the request of Jesus' relatives and friends, he went to Pilate and requested the body of Jesus for burial as Roman law allowed. Pilate heard his request willingly but was surprised that Jesus had died so soon; so he called the centurion who was in charge, and when he had confirmed Jesus' death, Pilate gave Joseph permission to take the body.

Almost at the same time the other Sanhedrists arrived, and Pilate, granting their request too, ordered other soldiers, not those still on guard at the crosses, to break the legs and then take the bodies down. The evangelist who witnessed their arrival says: "The soldiers therefore came and broke the legs of the first, and of the other, who had been crucified with him. But when they came to Jesus, and saw that he was already dead, they did not break his legs; but one of the soldiers opened his side with a lance, and immediately there came out blood and water" (John 19:32–34). Hence the two thieves had survived Jesus and were dispatched; Jesus' legs were not broken, because it was evident He was already dead. One of the soldiers struck with his lance in the direction of Jesus' heart, just to remove any possible doubts. The lance tore a wide wound in His side, as large as a man's hand (cf. John 20:25, 27), and from it flowed blood and water.

Learned English physiologists have tried to explain the water and blood by supposing that Jesus' heart was literally broken before being pierced by the lance. If the heart is ruptured, they claim, there is a hemorrhage within the pericardium and subsequently a decomposition of the blood. The red globules sink to the bottom and the watery serum remains on top. Hence when the pericardium is opened, the two come out separately. According to these physiologists, then, Jesus' rapid death is to be explained by a rupture of the heart produced by mental suffering. Jesus died literally of a broken heart caused by grief.

Whatever the merits of such an explanation, the evangelist who witnessed the incident sees much deeper and more mysterious meanings in it: "For these things came to pass that the Scripture might be fulfilled, 'Not a bone of him shall you break.' And again another Scripture says, 'They shall look upon him whom they have pierced.'" The first quotation is from Exodus 12:46 (Num. 9:12) and refers to the Paschal lamb. For the evangelist, Jesus was the true victim of redemption foreshadowed in the Paschal lamb. The second quotation is from Zacharias 12:10, who predicts that the Jewish nation will mourn for one whom they have pierced as one mourns for a firstborn.

The evangelist does not give us the name of the soldier who pierced Jesus' breast, but Christian legend has bestowed an unforgettable one on him, calling him "Lancer." In Greek, "lance" is *lonche*; and so the soldier was called Longinus.

The soldiers must have been performing their lugubrious work while Joseph of Arimathea stood waiting to use the permission granted him by Pilate. As soon as Jesus' body was taken down, Joseph set about giving it a fitting burial, which had, however, to be hasty because of the legal repose that began at sunset.

Joseph was assisted by others. His spiritual brother Nicodemus is mentioned by name, who "came … bringing a mixture of myrrh and aloes, in weight about a hundred pounds" (John 19:39). It is easy to imagine that the pious women who had been present at the Crucifixion also helped to prepare Christ for His burial, and first among them His Mother, who certainly would not have renounced the sorrowful joy of receiving His body in her arms as it was taken down from the Cross. Just as Nicodemus had brought the spices to anoint the body, Joseph had brought a "sindon," a shroud or winding sheet of fine linen.

Since there was not much time, the preparation of the body was quite brief: "They therefore took the body of Jesus and wrapped it in linen cloths with the spices, after the Jewish manner of preparing for burial" (John 19:40), in fact, in the manner Lazarus had been prepared. Then the body was wrapped in the shroud. Time also prevented their moving the body to a tomb any distance away, but this difficulty was easily overcome thanks to the generosity of Joseph, who offered his own tomb, which was right on the hill of the Skull: there was "a garden, and in the garden a new tomb in which no one had yet been laid" (John 19:41). The garden lay at the foot of the Skull and the tomb "had been hewn out of a rock" (Mark 15:46), which was a projection of the one that formed the little height of the Skull. Probably other wealthy citizens of Jerusalem also had their tombs built there. And this dovetails perfectly with the custom of carrying out a crucifixion near a burial ground.

The tomb Joseph gave up for Jesus' burial was arranged on the inside like all other Jewish tombs, with a vestibule and then a burial chamber with its niche for the body. The outer door was shut with a huge stone set against the opening. To enter, one had to push the stone — not without considerable effort — to the left or the right, and it moved along a little groove hewn out of the rock on either side of the door.

Since Jesus had died about three in the afternoon, all was over before six, when Joseph "rolled a great stone to the entrance of the tomb, and departed" (Matt. 27:60).

But the tomb was not left alone immediately: "Mary Magdalene and the other Mary [the mother of James and Joseph] were there, sitting opposite the sepulcher" (27:61). Other pious women also drew near to see where the revered body had been buried. Then returning to the city they took advantage of the last bit of daylight left and "prepared spices and ointments." Their devotion apparently was not satisfied with the abundant supply contributed by Nicodemus, and they planned to anoint the body of Jesus more carefully and hence to return to the sepulcher as soon as the Sabbath was over (Luke 23:55–56).

That night was a fine one indeed for the triumphant Sanhedrists. They celebrated the Paschal meal not only with the traditional air of gaiety but with a special inward satisfaction as well.

That Galilean Rabbi was actually gone; He was safely dead! There was no danger that they would ever have to listen to His invectives again and be humiliated in the eyes of the people. The few disciples He had managed to attract would unquestionably scatter now that their master was dead, and no one would speak of Him anymore. Theirs had been a splendid victory, and the thought of it must have added a special flavor to the Paschal supper.

And yet, as they thought of it, these worthies began to notice a little flaw in the shining crystal of their cup of triumph. A little thing certainly, but not to be neglected. They remembered that Jesus had predicted that three days after His death He would rise again. Now this was sheer boasting, there was no doubt about that; most of them were convinced Sadducees and so maintained that resurrection of the dead was impossible. But the boast might give rise to imposters, rumors, and other annoying consequences; hence it might be better to remedy the little flaw and forestall the trouble. So on the following day, although it was their Pasch, some of them took the short legitimate walk to Pilate's house to give him some very good advice: "Sir, we have remembered how that deceiver said, while he was yet alive: 'After three days I will rise again.' Give orders, therefore, that the sepulcher be guarded until the third day, or else his disciples may come and steal him away, and say to the people: 'He has risen from the dead'; and the last imposture will be worse than the first." Pilate answered them brusquely: "You have a guard [of your own]: go, guard it as well as you know."

The procurator's rudeness was apparent only; it merely served to cover the fact that he was giving in to them again. Actually, he had granted the request and again let the Sanhedrists use the detachment of guards, composed of Roman soldiers, that he was accustomed to put at their disposal (Matt. 28:14; cf. John 18:12). That was all they wanted, and on that same Sabbath they led the soldiers to the place.

But no one could surpass those Jewish leaders for wariness; they took precautions against a possibility that would hardly occur to anyone else. They foresaw that the soldiers, though they stayed on guard before the tomb, might be susceptible to the bribes of Jesus' disciples and let them into the tomb. So they affixed their seals between the stone rolled against the entrance and the rock from which the tomb was cut.

This was a wise precaution, since no one could possibly enter the tomb without breaking the seals, for which the soldiers were responsible, and the dead man would be sure not to rise again.

Chapter 20

෴

The Second Life

The same historical documents that have narrated the story of Jesus up to this point do not stop with His death, but with the same authority they relate His Resurrection and second life.

That is more than sufficient for those — ancients as well as moderns — who do not admit the possibility of the supernatural (cf. Acts 17:32) to promptly reject this whole second part of the Gospel narrative. These persons are logical, granted the principles from which they start. But it is significant that their conclusion is determined solely by those principles — not by any deficiencies or uncertainties in the documents.

In the account of Jesus' second life, the four evangelists follow the same procedure as before. They do not pretend to give a complete detailed, strictly chronological account of what happened. They choose the facts that seem most opportune to them, and they arrange their material in the order most convenient for their individual purposes. In relating the discovery of Jesus' empty tomb, Matthew and Mark are parallel enough. Luke does not give so many names, but he does not differ very much from Mark's account. Finally, John is more sketchy, because here again he wants to specify and fill out the familiar story of the Synoptics with a few points on his own authority as an eyewitness.

The Apparitions in Judea

No one saw Jesus in the act of rising from the dead. None of the evangelists says how He emerged from the sepulcher; one of them implies that He did so without disturbing the stone rolled against the entrance, although His Resurrection was accompanied by extraordinary signs: "And behold, there was a great earthquake; for an angel of the Lord came down from heaven, and drawing near rolled back the stone, and sat upon it. His countenance was like lightning, and his raiment like snow" (Matt. 28:2–3). Hence it was the angel who rolled away the stone, but the tomb was already empty, and the stone no longer served any purpose.

All four evangelists agree that the sepulcher was discovered to be empty very early Sunday morning. The soldiers sent by the Sanhedrists had been on guard there since the day before, and certainly at that early hour of the morning they were still stretched out asleep on the ground. The earthquake and the appearance of the angel and the wide-open tomb so terrified them that they fled for safety through the nearby city gate. Once surrounded by houses, and recovered somewhat from their panic, they remembered that their flight was formal desertion of their post and subject to heavy penalties according to Roman military discipline. They had to find some remedy and shrewdly perceived that their best hope lay with the Sanhedrists who had the greatest interest in the matter. So they went straight to them to make a bargain.

The sepulcher did not remain alone very long, for a group of pious women was already on its way from the city. They were the women who on Friday evening had prepared the spices in order to give the beloved body of Jesus a more fitting burial as soon as the legal repose of the Sabbath was over; from one or another of the evangelists we learn the names of Mary Magdalene, the other Mary mother of James, Salome, Joanna, and "the other women who were with them" (Luke 24:10). The time at which they arrived at the sepulcher is indicated in a very curious fashion by Mark (16:2): "And very early in the morning on the first day of the week [Sunday], they come to the tomb, the sun being now risen." At first glance it is difficult to reconcile "very early" with "the sun being now risen," since the former would mean the very first light of dawn or about four o'clock in the morning while the latter phrase would seem to refer to a time no earlier than six. It all becomes clear if we read between the lines: "Very early in the morning they come to the tomb [and reach it] the sun being now risen." Certainly they did not have to go a great distance to get to the tomb, but the reason why they took so long is given by Mark himself (16:1), who has just said, "when the Sabbath was past," that is, on that same morning, they "bought spices, that they might go and anoint him." Their devotion was not satisfied with the spices some of them had prepared two evenings before, and the rest wanted to make their own contribution of ointments, which it took some time to buy.

These feminine delays were too much for the most ardent and whole-souled among them, Mary of Magdala, the only one whom John mentions and the first one named by all three Synoptics. Sped by her great love, she left her companions and ran on alone to the tomb. She reached it, as John says in complete agreement with Mark, "early ... while it was still dark" (John 20:1). But what she saw as soon as she arrived struck her with dismay. She knew nothing about the soldiers placed there on the Sabbath, so she was not surprised by their absence; but she did see that the round stone had been rolled aside and the entrance stood open. A glance inside was enough to tell her that the tomb was empty.

What had happened? Who could tell her? She must go to the disciples; perhaps they knew, especially Peter and John. "She ran therefore and came to Simon Peter, and to the other disciple whom Jesus loved, and said to them: 'They have taken the Lord from the tomb, and we do not know where they have laid him'" (John 20:2). The plural "we" kept by John is an excellent link between his account and the Synoptics. They speak of several women at the sepulcher whereas he speaks only of Mary Magdalene, but he has her use the plural "we."

Mary's tardy companions meanwhile finished their purchases and were on their way to the tomb. But near the end of their walk they suddenly remembered a difficulty they had not thought of before: "And they were saying to one another: 'Who will roll the stone back from the doorway of the tomb for us?'" (Mark 16:3). We know that those round stones were very large and heavy, and the women certainly could not move the one in front of Jesus' sepulcher by themselves. As soon as they reached the sepulcher, however, and looked about them, "they saw that the stone had been rolled back, for it was very large" (Mark 16:4). No less startled than Mary Magdalene but less impulsive, they made their way in, and "on entering the tomb, they saw a young man sitting at the right side, clothed in a white robe, and they were amazed" (Mark 16:5). Luke says more accurately that there were "two men ... in dazzling raiment" (24:4).

The young man in Mark said to the women: "Do not be terrified. You are looking for Jesus of Nazareth, who was crucified. He has risen, he is not here. Behold the place where they laid him. But go, tell his disciples and Peter that he goes before you into Galilee; there you shall see him, as he told you" (Mark 16:6–7; cf. Matt. 28:5–7). The two apparitions in Luke say much the same thing, but they develop the last thought more fully and their words produce a different result. According to Mark, the women "fled from the tomb, for trembling and fear had entered into them; and they said nothing to anyone, for they were afraid." According to Luke, on the other hand, the women, "having returned from the tomb ... reported all these things to the Eleven, and to all the rest"; and this is what Matthew (28:8) says also.

Mark's account probably refers only to the women's first impression; they were in the beginning so stunned with fear and bewilderment that they said nothing. In any case, the news they were about to communicate was certainly not such as to win them a very cordial welcome, and that is perhaps another reason for the reluctance indicated by Mark. When they returned to the city, they "were telling these things to the apostles. But this tale seemed to them to be nonsense, and they did not believe the women" (Luke 24:11).

Meanwhile, Mary Magdalene's announcement had made a much greater impression on Peter and John. As soon as they heard her excited story, "Peter … went out, and the other disciple, and they went to the tomb. The two were running together, and the other disciple ran on before, faster than Peter, and came first to the tomb. And stooping down he saw the linen cloths lying there, and the handkerchief which had been about his head, not lying with the linen cloths, but folded in a place, by itself. Then the other disciple also went in, who had come first to the tomb. And he saw…. The disciples therefore went away again to their home" (John 20:3–10). What they saw was enough to convince them that the body had not been stolen, as Mary Magdalene supposed. If it had been, there would have been no purpose in unwinding the linen cloths or carefully folding up the handkerchief and setting it by itself. There was nothing more to be done there, however, and so the two hurried back to the city, anxious to consult with the other disciples.

Mary Magdalene, who had returned to the sepulcher either with them or shortly afterward, did not leave with them but "was standing outside weeping at the tomb" (John 20:11). After a little while, she stooped down to look once more at the niche in the burial chamber, for in her desolate love she still hoped against hope. But this time she saw two angels seated one at the head and one at the foot of the niche where the body had lain. And they said to her: "Woman, why art thou weeping?" She answered: "Because they have taken away my Lord, and I do not know where they have laid him!" And with this, she turned around, almost as if looking for Him still, and saw a man standing before her. But she hardly glanced at Him for, absorbed as she was in her own grief-filled thoughts, she mistook Him for the gardener. But the man said to her: "Woman, why art thou weeping? Whom dost thou seek?" She answered: "Sir, if thou hast removed him, tell me where thou hast laid him and I will take him away." But the man was Jesus.

"Jesus said to her: 'Mary!'

"Turning, she said to him: 'Rabboni' (that is to say, Master)!"

It was the first time that the risen Christ had been seen and recognized by any human being unless He had already appeared to His Mother, although the evangelists say nothing about this.

As soon as she recognized the Master, Mary threw herself at His feet to embrace them, but He said to her: "Do not touch me, for I have not yet ascended to my Father, but go to my brethren and say to them: 'I ascend to my Father and your Father, to my God and your God'" (John 20:17). It was urgent for His disciples, whom He calls His "brethren," to know that He was soon to ascend to His Father and God and theirs, and hence her natural expression of affection was not to delay the message.

She did immediately as she was bid: "Mary Magdalene came, and announced to the disciples: 'I have seen the Lord, and these things he said to me'" (John 20:18). But her announcement met a humiliating response: "And they, hearing that he was alive and had been seen by her, did not believe it" (Mark 16:11).

As a matter of fact, the immediate disciples of Jesus, as we shall see presently, were anything but ready to believe anyone — man or woman, and particularly woman — who said that he had seen Jesus alive again.

The Sanhedrists to whom the soldiers went after their flight from the sepulcher, on the other hand, seemed more ready to believe them. These Jewish leaders found nothing incredible in the story told them by the soldiers, still breathless from running and from fright. And they, like the soldiers, saw the need of some expedient to save themselves as well as the guards. So they began in their usual fashion to hang little screens up in front of the sun to blot out its unmistakable light. When the chief priests "had assembled with the elders, and had consulted together they gave much money to the soldiers, telling them: 'Say, "His disciples came by night and stole him while we were sleeping." And if the procurator hears of this, we will persuade him and keep you out of trouble.' And they took the money, and did as they were instructed; and this story has been spread abroad among the Jews even to the present day" (Matt. 28:12–15).

The coaching the runaway soldiers received from the Sanhedrists — "they stole him while we were sleeping" — was hardly a miracle of shrewdness; and St. Augustine's answer is still the final one, when he figuratively addresses the Sanhedrin to ask wittily: "How is this? Do you call on witnesses who were asleep?" But the lie took hold, and when Matthew was writing his Gospel, it had become the official Jewish explanation for the empty tomb.

But to return to the Gospel narrative, it was still the Sunday after Jesus' death, and two or three hours had passed while the various persons mentioned went back and forth to the tomb. Meanwhile, the news of the empty tomb had spread among the disciples of Jesus gathered in the city for the Pasch. The word that Mary Magdalene had seen Jesus and spoken with Him had not yet had time to circulate.

But all this was "nonsense" prattled by women, and it was not to be taken seriously. The Paschal solemnity did not require the pilgrims to remain in the Holy City for the entire octave, and on the day after the Pasch, the sixteenth Nisan, many of them were already setting out for home. And this was what two of Jesus' disciples did, one of whom was called Cleophas. Hopeless and dispirited over what had taken place, they set out together for Emmaus where they lived. It must have been about nine in the morning. Luke's account is written with such delicacy and psychological insight that it seems an idyll, and it would be impossible to tell it with any other words.

As they walked along, "they were talking to each other about all these things that had happened. And it came to pass, while they were conversing and arguing together, that Jesus himself also drew near and went along with them; but their eyes were held, that they should not recognize him. And he said to them: 'What words are these that you are exchanging as you walk [along]?'"

Who was this strange wayfarer who thus questioned them, putting His finger as it were on the wound in their hearts? Their surprise interrupted their journey for a moment. And they stood still, looking very sad.

But one of them, named Cleophas, answered and said to him: "Art thou the only stranger in Jerusalem who does not know the things that have happened in these days?" And he said to them: "What things?"

And they said to him: "Concerning Jesus of Nazareth, who was a prophet, mighty in work and word before God and all the people; and how our chief priests and rulers delivered him up to be sentenced to death, and crucified him. But we were hoping that it was he who should redeem Israel."

What "redemption" is Cleophas thinking of? It is difficult to exclude the nationalist-messianic meaning, namely, that Jesus would deliver the holy people from all foreign domination. But at Jesus' death, the hope had vanished, and so Cleophas continues: "Yes, and besides all this, today is the third day since these things came to pass. And moreover, certain women of our company, who were at the tomb before it was light, astounded us, and not finding his body, they came, saying that they had also seen a vision of angels, who said that he is alive. So some of our company went to the tomb, and found it even as the women had said, but him they did not see."

These last words show that the two left Jerusalem before Mary Magdalene's announcement that she had seen Jesus, otherwise they would have mentioned this, too, if only to cast doubt on it. But when Cleophas had finished, the unknown traveler's manner suddenly changed; rather than ignorant of all these things, He now seemed extraordinarily well informed.

"But he said to them: 'O foolish ones and slow of heart to believe in all that the prophets have spoken! Did not the Christ have to suffer these things before entering into his glory?' And beginning then with Moses and with all the Prophets" — or with the first two parts of the Hebrew Bible — "he interpreted to them in all the Scriptures the things referring to himself." Hence, the care taken by all the evangelists, but especially by Matthew and John, to demonstrate the fulfillment of the ancient biblical prophecies in the things pertaining to Jesus is but a continuation of what Jesus Himself did in this lesson.

The lesson lasted to the end of the journey, but to the disciples both seemed much too short. The narrative continues: "And they drew near to the village to which they were going, and he acted as though he were going on. And they urged him, saying: 'Stay with us, for it is getting towards evening, and the day is now far spent.' And he went in [to stay] with them." It is not necessary to suppose that it was already nightfall. The expression "toward evening" could apply any time from noontime on, and so if the two disciples had left Jerusalem about nine o'clock in the morning and traveled approximately twenty miles, it must have been now toward two or three in the afternoon. "And it came to pass that when he reclined at table with them, that he took the bread and blessed and broke and began handing it to them. And their eyes were opened, and they recognized him; and he vanished from their sight. And they said to each other: 'Was not our heart burning within us while he was speaking on the road and explaining to us the Scriptures?'" The fact that the two disciples recognized Jesus at the breaking of the bread has often been linked with the phrase "to break bread," which in the early Church designated the Eucharist. But the conclusion is not justified, historically speaking, for we do not know whether these disciples knew that Jesus had instituted the Eucharist three days before, or whether Jesus spoke to them of it along the way, or whether He would be likely to perform the rite for anyone who had no idea of it. If we restrict ourselves to the letter of the narrative, we may conclude only that the disciples recognized Jesus while He was breaking the bread, that is, before eating.

Their emotion and wonder were so great that they immediately set out again: "And rising up that very hour, they returned to Jerusalem, where they found the Eleven gathered together and those who were with them, saying: 'The Lord has risen indeed, and has appeared to Simon.' And they themselves began to relate what had happened on the journey, and how they recognized him in the breaking of the bread" (Luke 24:14–35). If they had left Emmaus again between two and three in the afternoon and taken the shortest route, perhaps on horseback, they could have been in Jerusalem by eight or nine in the evening.

But even when they reached the city, it was not easy to find the apostles, because no one knew where they were. They finally discovered them in a safe hiding place, with all the doors barred "for fear of the Jews" (John 20:19). But notwithstanding their outward caution, they were all much moved and excited. As soon as the two dust-covered travelers entered the room, certain that they were bearing astonishing news, they were greeted with an outburst that prevented them from saying a word. All the apostles crowded around them to announce: "The Lord has risen indeed, and has appeared to Simon!" Hence on that same day, after the two disciples had left Jerusalem and after He had appeared to Mary Magdalene, Jesus appeared also to Simon Peter, and the latter hastened to tell the apostles and other disciples, winning from them the belief that Mary Magdalene had not.

None of the evangelists relates any detail of Jesus' appearing to Simon Peter on this day, but it is unquestionably the same appearance that Paul sets first in his list of the resurrected Christ's appearances. Luke, the disciple of Paul, learned of it from his master, who in turn had learned of it from Peter himself, when, still new to the faith, he had gone "to Jerusalem to see Peter" (Gal. 1:18). The Rock of the Church had been singled out by virtue of his office; he who had denied Jesus had been abundantly forgiven because of his abundant tears of repentance, such as Judas had not shed.

When the two travelers finally got the opportunity to speak of their experience, their words were received with unexpected coldness. Whether it was a certain diffidence the apostles felt toward the two from Emmaus, or a subconscious resentment that these obscure disciples had received the same privilege just granted to Peter but still denied to them, it is certain that, if not all, at least several of those present "even then … did not believe" (Mark 16:12). And it is easy to imagine the discussions that arose between the two insisting they had seen the Master and those refusing to believe they had.

But that day was to end with certainty, not with discussions and disbelief.

Now whilst they were speaking these things [Jesus] himself stood in their midst, and saith to them: "Peace be to you." But they were terrified and stricken with fear and thought that they beheld a spirit.

And he said to them: "Why are ye troubled, and wherefore do doubts arise in your hearts? See my hands and feet, that it is my very self. Feel me and see; for a spirit hath not flesh and bones, as ye see me to have." And saying this, he showed them his hands and his feet. But as they still disbelieved for very joy and marvelled, he said to them: "Have ye aught here to eat?"

They handed him part of a broiled fish; and he took and ate ⌊it⌋ before them. (Luke 24:36–43)

We must remember that this scene is described for us by a physician and psychologist; the same episode related by John (20:19–23) does not contain the practical observations that show the scientific mind or the subtle notice that the apostles "disbelieved for very joy," that is, for fear of deceiving themselves since it is so easy to believe what one is anxious to believe. Their doubts were dispelled by physical reality. In His second life Jesus has the same body as before; He can eat as He did before. He is not a misty shade; His physical body has come to life again and rejoined His soul.

Having assured them of this fact Jesus tells them of the future, and that is what John records for us especially: "'As the Father has sent me, I also send you.' When he had said this, he breathed upon them and said to them: 'Receive the Holy Spirit; whose sins you shall forgive, they are forgiven them; and whose sins you shall retain, they are retained'" (John 20:21–23). The old promise made the apostles regarding the future government of the Church was here fulfilled.

Not present that evening in the apostles' retreat was the skeptical Thomas. Was his absence perhaps another manifestation of his character? Did he refuse even to discuss the assertions of Mary Magdalene and Peter and therefore avoid the company of the other apostles? Certain it is that when a little later he was with the apostles and they assured him: "We have seen the Lord," he shook his head, almost as if scandalized, and vehemently declared: "Unless I see in his hands the print of the nails, and put my finger into the place of the nails, and put my hand into his side, I will not believe!"

After all, they must be reasonable! How could a man rise again when He had been crucified, reduced to a mass of torn and wounded flesh, with His hands and feet pierced and a gaping hole in His side? Mary Magdalene had seen Him? Now what reason could there possibly be for believing a hysterical woman? The other apostles had seen Him, and had especially noticed His hands and feet? Well, those apostles were all fine men, but they were a little on the volatile side and too easily imagined they saw what they wanted to see! He, Thomas, was the calm, deliberate man among them, just the right man to have around in certain cases; and in cases like this, it was not enough to see — one must touch and feel, and put in one's fingers; only on this condition would he believe!

The prince of hypercritics remained unshaken in his conviction for eight days, and no argument the apostle might propose could budge him. But "after eight days, his disciples were again inside, and Thomas with them. Jesus came, the doors being closed, and stood in their midst, and said: 'Peace be to you!' Then he said to Thomas: 'Bring here thy finger, and see my hands; and bring here thy hand, and put it into my side; and be not unbelieving, but believing.' Thomas answered and said to him: 'My Lord and my God!' Jesus said to him: 'Because thou hast seen me, thou hast believed. Blessed are they who have not seen, and yet have believed.'" Did Thomas stick to his intention to feel the body of the resurrected Christ? We have every reason to believe he did not. His positivism collapsed, as it always does, not so much as the result of intellectual discussion as of a change in spiritual disposition.

The Apparitions in Galilee

All of the appearances of Jesus so far mentioned took place in Jerusalem or its environs, that is, in Judea. There were still others, also narrated by the evangelists, shortly afterward in Galilee; of those recorded by Paul some undoubtedly took place in Judea and some in Galilee.

The difference in place has an importance of its own. The angels at the sepulcher had charged the women to bid the disciples and Peter to go into Galilee where they would see the risen Christ.

When the festivities of the Pasch were ended, the apostles returned into Galilee, in obedience to Jesus' command (Matt. 26:32) and prompted besides by the fact that in Galilee they would be safe from the direct surveillance of the Sanhedrin. Jesus' promise had mentioned the place, but not the time, and so there was nothing to do but wait. Some days later, we find once more on the shores of Lake Tiberias Simon Peter, Thomas, Nathanael (Bartholomew), James and John, and two other unnamed apostles, who were perhaps Andrew and Philip.

The little group probably still supported themselves from their common earnings, just as they had when Jesus was with them. It may be that, after Judas's disappearance with all their resources and their expenses in Jerusalem and for the journey, they had little or nothing left. In any case, fishermen that they were, they could not remain idle with the lake rippling before them, and though awaiting from one day to the next the return of the risen Christ, they resumed their old occupations. One evening Simon Peter said to the others: "I am going fishing." And they answered: "We also are going with thee." For night fishing it was better to have a number of helpers because then they could use the long dragnets. So they got into the boat and cast their nets, but it was a bad night, and at dawn they had not yet caught anything. So they pulled toward shore again to disembark.

When they were about two hundred cubits (about a hundred yards) from land, they glimpsed a figure through the mist; they could not see it clearly, but it seemed to be a man waiting for them. Perhaps He wanted to buy their catch. When they were within calling distance, He asked: "Young men, have you any fish?" After that long night of wasted toil and effort the question sounded more than a little ironic and from the boat came a brusque "No!" which would normally discourage any further discussion. But the man shouted again through the morning mist: "Cast the net to the right of the boat and you will find them."

Who was this unknown giving them such confident advice? Did He know what He was talking about? In either case, one more attempt would not cost them too much after all they had done in vain. The net was cast where the man had said, "and now they were unable to draw it up for the great number of fishes."

At this, old memories rose in the minds of those fishermen. An instant of tremulous uncertainty and then the disciple whom Jesus loved leaped to Peter's side and, pointing to the man on the shore, shouted: "It is the Lord!" Then everything was perfectly clear and natural.

"When Simon Peter therefore heard that it was the Lord, he girt his coat about him — for he was naked — and cast himself into the sea. But the other disciples came with the boat, dragging the net full of fish; for they were not far from land, but about a hundred yards off." The impetuous Peter naturally could not wait; he had to get to shore as quickly as possible. To swim more easily he tied up his coat about him, which he wore over his bare skin while working. A few strokes carried him to shore, and he was soon at the feet of his risen Master, but the others stayed in the boat, which came in slowly because it was dragging the great weight of the fish.

When they disembarked, they saw a little fire already lit, with a fish laid upon it and the bread prepared for them. "Jesus said to them: 'Bring here some of the fishes that you caught just now.'" Peter went back in the boat, and with the other apostles hauled the net to land: it contained 153 large fish. "And though there were so many, the net was not torn. Jesus said to them: 'Come and breakfast.' And none [of the disciples] dared ask him: 'Who art thou?' knowing that it was the Lord." The apostles felt a certain reverent fear that prevented them from asking their risen Master anything about Himself. That He was Himself there was no doubt; but oh, how they would have liked to ask Him: How did you rise from the dead? Where have you been all these days? How did you come here? Where are you when you are not with us?

But they could not speak for reverence, and "none ... dared ask him."

Their reverence did not affect their appetites, however, and they ate joyously the bread and the fish that Jesus divided among them. And when their bodies had been refreshed, Jesus spoke to their souls.

> When, therefore, they had breakfasted, Jesus said to Simon Peter: "Simon, son of John, dost thou love me more than these do?" He [Peter] said to him: "Yes, Lord, thou knowest that I love thee." He [Jesus] said to him: "Feed my lambs." He said to him a second time: "Simon, son of John, dost thou love me?" He said to him: "Yes, Lord thou knowest that I love thee." He said to him: "Feed my lambs." A third time he said to him: "Simon, son of John, dost thou love me?" Peter was grieved because he said to him for the third time: "Dost thou love me?" And he said to him: "Lord, thou knowest all things, thou knowest that I love thee." He said to him: "Feed my sheep."

Jesus' threefold question, in tactful charity, made no explicit reference to the past, but in its threefold repetition it was nevertheless linked with a painful past. Three times had Peter denied the Master in the hour of darkness, and now, in the hour of light, he three times professes his love for Him.

But the question was linked with the past in still another way. On the day of Caesarea Philippi, Jesus had proclaimed the same Simon Peter the Rock that was the foundation of the Church and had charged him to govern it as a shepherd rules his flock. Now Simon Peter must remember that this office is to be a labor of love, a consequence of the love he has professed for Jesus. The supreme Shepherd will depart from His flock, but He will not leave it unprotected. In His stead, He places over it a shepherd who is His vicar and who must rule it with the same love and for the same love that has animated the supreme Shepherd.

The Shepherd has been killed for that love; hence it is possible that the same fate awaits His vicar. Jesus predicts this as a certainty for Peter personally, for He continues: " 'Amen, amen I say to thee, when thou wast young thou didst gird thyself,' " as Peter had actually done but a little while before, " 'and walk where thou wouldst. But when thou art old thou wilt stretch forth thy hands, and another will gird thee, and lead thee where thou wouldst not.' Now this he said to signify by what manner of death he [Peter] should glorify God." When John wrote this statement, Peter had already been killed, several years before, for his faith in Jesus and his love for the office entrusted to him. Others had in truth girt him with chains and led him to his execution, so that the vicar followed the Shepherd even in his death. That was why Jesus closed His message to Peter saying, by way of exhortation and of comfort both: "Follow me!"

But this and Jesus' other appearances in Galilee obviously did not have the solemnity of the occasion mentioned by Matthew (28:16ff.). This incident occurred on a mountain that, we are told incidentally, Jesus had already named to the apostles as the place where He would meet them. It is impossible to determine which mountain it was: it is possible that at the beginning or the end of this appearance, which must have been a long one, there were other disciples besides the apostles present; but it is not at all certain that Paul is referring specifically to this occasion when he mentions that the risen Jesus "was seen by more than five hundred brethren at one time, many of whom are with us still."

This time no details of the episode are recorded for us. Hence we do not know to what circumstances or persons the phrase "but some doubted" refers. Perhaps these doubters were not the apostles, and if they were the apostles, their "doubt" had nothing to do with the reality of the Resurrection but perhaps questioned some circumstance that was to establish the identity of the risen Master. When the apostles were certain it was He, Jesus said to them: "All power in heaven and on earth has been given to me. Go, therefore, and make disciples of all nations, baptizing them in the name of the Father, and of the Son, and of the Holy Spirit, teaching them to observe all that I have commanded you. And behold, I am with you all days, even unto the consummation of the world."

The Church founded by Jesus was now entering a new period in its history, a period that is to last until the end of the world. The vicar is to take the place of its Shepherd; the flock must be composed of all peoples of every race and region and not of the chosen nation of Israel alone; all the newcomers to the flock will be "disciples" of Jesus, just as those who had known Him personally had been His immediate disciples. They must enter into the flock through baptism and through faith "in the name of the Father, and of the Son, and of the Holy Spirit." The duty of the new disciples will be to observe what Jesus had commanded His first disciples to observe. Above all, the Shepherd Himself will help and protect His flock; in an invisible but no less effective manner, He will be among His future disciples "even unto the consummation of the world."

Here, therefore, the story of Jesus ends and that of the Church begins: the life of Christ "according to the flesh" comes to a close and that of the mystical Christ begins (Eph. 5:23; Col. 1:18).

The Ascension

Entirely absorbed in this idea, that the story of Christ according to the flesh is but the first chapter in the history of the Church, the evangelists have given little emphasis to His physical departure from the earth, namely, His Ascension. The loss of His visible and tangible presence did not matter so much now that they were convinced of His invisible presence and His continued assistance from Heaven. So we find that Matthew does not relate the Ascension at all; it is briefly mentioned in the appendix in Mark (16:19); John (20:17) barely suggests it and then in the form of a prediction; the only evangelist who describes it at any length is Luke (24:50ff.), but this is because when he brings to a close his Gospel, which is the story of Christ according to the flesh, he is already planning to follow it immediately with the story of the mystical Christ as well. His Acts of the Apostles are an episodic history of the Church, and at the beginning of this new work (Acts 1:1–11) he repeats the story of the Ascension with which he had ended his Gospel.

The Ascension occurred on the Mount of Olives near Bethany, forty days after the Resurrection. Since the apostles had left Jerusalem for Galilee no less than eight days after the Resurrection and were again in Jerusalem some time before the Ascension, they must have stayed in Galilee less than a month. It is to this period that we must assign the other many appearances indicated in a general way by Paul and also by Luke when he says that the risen Jesus appeared to the apostles, showing Himself alive "by many proofs," speaking to them of the Kingdom of God and meeting habitually with them (Acts 1:3–4). Undoubtedly, they had gone up to Jerusalem again at Jesus' bidding, and there they met for the last time. The risen Master gave them His last instructions, among them that they were not to leave the city but were to wait there "for the promise of the Father, 'of which you have heard ... by my mouth; for John indeed baptized with water, but you shall be baptized with the Holy Spirit not many days hence'" (Acts 1:4–5).

The promise referred to what took place shortly afterward on the day of the Jewish Pentecost when the Holy Spirit descended upon them. But even at this last meeting with the risen Master, the apostles felt vaguely that something extraordinary was about to happen. And in their minds rose again the old messianic ideas, so deeply rooted in their Jewish souls that they had survived in part even the realities of Jesus' death and Resurrection.

Hence they approached Jesus, full of hope and with an affectionate smile of expectancy as if to invite the confidence they had so long hoped for, and they asked Him: "Lord, wilt thou at this time restore the kingdom of Israel?" Poor Israel had, in fact, been shorn for many years now of all political power; this would indeed be the opportune time to create a fine kingdom for it with Jesus Himself as king and the apostles as His ministers. Jesus, who had raised Himself from the dead, could raise dead Israel to a new life of political glory.

But the risen Messiah's answer this time was just what it had been on this subject so many times before His death: "It is not for you to know the times or dates which the Father has fixed by his own authority; but you shall receive power when the Holy Spirit comes upon you, and you shall be witnesses for me in Jerusalem and in all Judea and Samaria and even to the very ends of the earth" (Acts 1:7–8). It is not for the apostles to worry about the manifest triumph of the Kingdom of God. Instead of thinking of political conquests, the apostles must propose to conquer the whole world, Hebrew and non-Hebrew, to the teaching of Jesus, and they will achieve this conquest not by military or political strategy but solely by virtue of that "power" that they will receive when the Holy Spirit descends upon them.

This was Jesus' farewell to the friends He loved best. When He had finished speaking, He left Jerusalem with them and led them along the dear familiar road to Bethany. Toward the top of the Mount of Olives, He gathered them about Him and raised His hands to bless them; "And it came to pass as he blessed them, that he parted from them and was carried up into heaven" (Luke 24:51). "He was lifted up before their eyes, and a cloud took him out of their sight" (Acts 1:9).

Jesus' four official biographers do not go beyond the earth; their narratives end with the Ascension or just before it. Only the appendix of Mark's Gospel (16:19) casts a fleeting glance heavenward and states that Jesus "was taken up into heaven, and sits at the right hand of God." These last words, which proclaim that the man Jesus was associated in glory and power with the heavenly Father, are especially dictated by the "mind of the Church"; but this "mind," which has given us the four accounts of Jesus' earthly life, shrank from even a single narrative of His heavenly life, and has recorded only what would be its fundamental theme: "He sits at the right hand of God."

About the Author

Giuseppe Ricciotti (1890–1964) was an Italian priest and a member of the Canons Regular of the Lateran religious order. He was a biblical scholar, a teacher, and an archaeologist. When, as a World War I chaplain, he lay in a field hospital, hovering between life and death, he promised God that if he lived, he would write a life of Christ. Later, as a procurator of his congregation's motherhouse, Fr. Ricciotti provided a safe haven for many refugees during World War II. He served as a consultant to the Vatican Congregation for the Clergy and authored several other books, including *History of Israel, Paul the Apostle*, and works on Scripture and Church history.

Sophia Institute

Sophia Institute is a nonprofit institution that seeks to nurture the spiritual, moral, and cultural life of souls and to spread the Gospel of Christ in conformity with the authentic teachings of the Roman Catholic Church.

Sophia Institute Press fulfills this mission by offering translations, reprints, and new publications that afford readers a rich source of the enduring wisdom of mankind.

Sophia Institute also operates the popular online resource Catholic-Exchange.com. *Catholic Exchange* provides world news from a Catholic perspective as well as daily devotionals and articles that will help readers to grow in holiness and live a life consistent with the teachings of the Church.

In 2013, Sophia Institute launched Sophia Institute for Teachers to renew and rebuild Catholic culture through service to Catholic education. With the goal of nurturing the spiritual, moral, and cultural life of souls, and an abiding respect for the role and work of teachers, we strive to provide materials and programs that are at once enlightening to the mind and ennobling to the heart; faithful and complete, as well as useful and practical.

Sophia Institute gratefully recognizes the Solidarity Association for preserving and encouraging the growth of our apostolate over the course of many years. Without their generous and timely support, this book would not be in your hands.

www.SophiaInstitute.com
www.CatholicExchange.com
www.SophiaInstituteforTeachers.org

Sophia Institute Press° is a registered trademark of Sophia Institute.
Sophia Institute is a tax exempt institution as defined by the
Internal Revenue Code, Section 501(c)(3). Tax ID 22-2548708.